HEADQUARTERS

To: Abraham + Ushi
March 22. 1985.
From: Joe + Guy

A HISTORY OF NEWMARKET AND ITS RACING
HEADQUARTERS
RICHARD ONSLOW

Our Very Best Wishes
Happy Memories
from
All at
Bedford Lodge Hotel.

GREAT OUSE PRESS

© Richard Onslow

All rights reserved. No part of this publication may be reproduced or transmitted, in any form or by any means, without permission.

Previously published by Arthur Baker in 1971 as The Heath and The Turf

Published in 1983 by
GREAT OUSE PRESS

Great Ouse Press
82 Castle Street, Cambridge CB3 0AJ
Telephone: Cambridge (0223) 521030

British Library Cataloguing in Publication Data
Onslow, Richard
    Headquarters: a history of Newmarket and its racing.
    1. Newmarket (Suffolk) — History
    i Title
    2. 942.6'43   DA690.N'

    ISBN 0-907351-10-7 (hardback)
    ISBN 0-907351-20-4 (paperback)

This book is sold subject to the condition that it shall not, by way of trade or otherwise, be lent, resold, hired out, or otherwise circulated without the publisher's prior consent in any form of binding or cover other than that in which it is published and without a similar condition including this condition being imposed on the subsequent purchaser.

Book design by Geoff Hayes Design Associates.

Printed in Great Britain

Contents

Acknowledgements		v
Foreword		vii
1	Newmarket in the Early Days	1
2	Newmarket under the Stuarts	4
3	Georgian Newmarket	15
4	The Great Races of the Heath	46
5	The Jockey Boys, Newmarket's Crew— Sam Chifney to Nat Flatman	67
6	James Godding, Macaroni and Palace House	81
7	Joe Dawson, Prince Charlie and Bedford Lodge	84
8	Tom Jennings, Phantom House and Lagrange	90
9	More about Palace House, the Rothschilds and their Trainers, the Hayhoes	96
10	A Pair of Gamblers—Captain Machell and Jack Hammond	99
11	Mathew Dawson	113
12	Sir John Astley	123
13	The Death of Fred Archer	133
14	Sir George Chetwynd versus the Earl of Durham —A Case of Libel	140
15	Robert Peck, Barcaldine and Beverly House	148
16	More Scottish Trainers—John Dawson, Jimmy Waugh and Jimmy Ryan	152
17	Caroline, Duchess of Montrose	158
18	Two Big Spenders—George Alexander Baird and Colonel Harry McCalmont	161
19	The American Influence	179
20	More about Victorian Newmarket	185
21	The Newmarket of King Edward VII	192
22	Newmarket in the Reign of George V	221
23	Newmarket in the Reign of George VI	229
24	Frank Butters, Marcus Marsh and the Aga Khan at Fitzroy House	233
25	Newmarket in the Early Years of the Present Reign	244
26	Modern Newmarket	270
Bibliography		297
List of Illustrations		301
General Index		302
Index of Horses		308

Acknowledgements

The original version of this book was published under the title of *The Heath and The Turf* in 1971.

As well as including an account of the most important events that have occurred on the Newmarket racing scene in the twelve years that have elapsed since then, this new edition contains much other material that did not appear in its predecessor. In as much as I thought an unknown lady examining a copy of the latter at the Newbury bookstall spoke for many other critics when deploring the scant treatment of Newmarket in the seventeenth and eighteenth centuries, the first three chapters have been considerably enlarged to give fuller treatment to the days when Newmarket Heath was an open-air leisure complex for the upper classes, under royal patronage for much of the time, with the hawk and the hound as much part of its sport as the horse.

Only perfunctory references are made to jockeys in those early chapters in order to justify a new one entitled 'The Jockey Boys, Newmarket's Crew', a quotation from a lampoon on the reported death of the fourth Duke of Queensberry. This chapter attempts to describe the careers and character of the early jockeys, from the Chifneys to Nat Flatman, who became first acknowledged champion in 1846, taking in along the way the likes of the Arnulls, the Edwardses and Frank Butler, as well as little Arthur Pavis and others not mentioned in the earlier version, mea culpa.

The other chapter that I hope helps atone for a deficiency in my first book is entitled 'The Great Races of the Heath'. In this will be found details of the origins of Newmarket's classics, The 2,000 Guineas and The 1,000 Guineas, and some of the other famous events run on the Rowley Mile and July Courses, together with notes on the most important, or most interesting, of the winners.

The chapter formerly devoted to Geroge Alexander Baird in its entirety now includes an account of the racing career of a man his equal in extravagance, though not in waywardness, Colonel Harry McCalmont, and is entitled 'Two Big Spenders'. Similarly Captain James Machell and his one-time employee Jack Hammond are bracketed together as 'A Pair of Gamblers'.

In collecting material for this book I have become heavily indebted to a number of Newmarket trainers, both past and present, as well as to members of their families, all of whom have been more than generous with their time, and commendably patient in answering my questions. In particular I am grateful to the late Sir Jack Jarvis and his sister-in-law the late Mrs Isobel Jarvis, widow of the royal trainer, Mr William

Jarvis, and must also express my appreciation of help received from Mr Jack Waugh, Mr John Waugh, Mr Harry Wragg and Mr Jack Watts.

For knowledge of events that occurred in the Clarehaven stable during the time of its builder, Peter Purcell Gilpin, I have to thank Mr John Hislop, who was assistant trainer to Victor Gilpin in that yard for a number of seasons between the wars. For information about the background of Colonel Harry McCalmont I am grateful to Mr Hugh McCalmont, whose father the late Major Dermot McCalmont, was second cousin and heir of the Colonel.

I would also like to acknowledge the enormous amount of help it was my good fortune to receive from the late Mr Bob Rodrigo, the well-known Newmarket freelance journalist, and the late Mr Alf Bowman, who became the Press Association's work-watcher at Newmarket after being travelling head lad to Mr Geoffrey Barling.

I am extremely grateful to the Stewards and members of the Jockey Club for permission to reproduce some of the exquisite pictures in their possession. I must also thank Mr Robert Fellowes, the Jockey Club Agent, for his characteristically courteous co-operation and for information about changes and improvements effected on the working grounds during recent years.

I remain under as much obligation as ever to Mr Peter Willett for his kindness in reading the original draft of the first book, and giving invaluable advice on the arrangement of material.

I offer my thanks to all the people who pointed out errors in that first version. They included *The Sporting Life*'s critic Mr John Bliss, who drew attention to an unforgivable misquotation of John Dryden. All I can say is I wrote the lines down from memory, with the, alas unfulfilled, intention of checking them later.

I thank Mr Andrew Pates, of the Great Ouse Press, for the great care he has taken in the production of this book, Mr Geoffrey Hayes for all the work he undertook to secure the best possible illustrations and Mrs Lesley Crichton for the diligence with which she read and revised a most indifferent typescript and for compiling such a comprehensive index.

Finally I have to thank Barbara, my wife, for the many helpful suggestions she has made while enduring the tedium of proofreading.

Foreword

There are some people who think that racing is only about horses. Others who claim that Newmarket is solely about people. Then there's Dickie Onslow, the only man that you'll ever meet who can rattle off both his own and the Derby winners' ancestors back to the good old days when Charles II was putting Newmarket on the map.

We're not quite certain just how many oranges the Earls of Onslow may or may not have bought from the royal favourite Nell Gwyn, but what we can be sure of is that few men have looked back with more relish than their Lordships' highly professional descendant Richard Onslow. With Newmarket he has racing's richest river of history to ponder on and anyone who dips into this book will be grateful for the initiative of the suitably aquatic sounding Great Ouse Press in re-launching Dickie's Newmarket study which first appeared in 1971.

Unlike its author who insists that the same blue suit that won him the Naps (best tipster) table in 1972 can only, like wine, improve with age, this book is an altogether newer, flashier version of Onslow's earlier classic. Newmarket has always needed a volume for both the novice and know-all to pick up with confidence. With this racy, well-researched runner, England's 'Headquarters of The Turf' has got the high standard it deserved.

It scarcely needs adding that in Dickie Onslow, the visitor has a guide of classic standards. Racing has always been at its most appealing when it combines historical scholarship, a love of life and a sense of the absurd. Despite the minor snag of being struck by assorted physical disabilities, and the major one of being born about two centuries out of his time, that mix has long been Dickie's forte. Read on and see.

Brough Scott

"The rhythmic thud of horses in strong work"

1 Newmarket in the Early Days

Newmarket Heath has almost as many moods as the sea. In the early morning in spring it is one of the most beautiful places on earth. The dew sparkles in the sun and larks rise vertically from the ground on the approach of a string of thoroughbreds while the rhythmic thud of horses in strong work is about the only noise to disturb acre upon acre of bright green turf. At the other end of the day at the other end of the year the Heath takes on an almost threatening mood as dark clouds roll low over the Devil's Dyke so that it seems none too fanciful to think that ancient earthwork of unknown origin really does have the diabolical powers inferred by its name. Then in winter these 2,500 acres in East Anglia feel the coldest place in all England as the wind comes off the North Sea having blown straight from Siberia across the flat plain of northern Europe unchecked by any mountain.

Like the wings of some great butterfly, the Heath stretches out of either side of the town. On the east, Bury Side as it is called because the road leads to Bury St Edmunds, are the fine gallops on the Limekilns, Railway Land, Waterhall, Bury Hill, Warren Hill, Long Hill and Side Hill. To the west, Racecourse Side, the Heath is altogether flatter, unrelieved by belts of trees and copses and less fragmented, the only road bisecting it being the one to Cambridge that cuts through the Devil's Dyke after some two miles. On the left of the Cambridge Road as you leave the town are the Links, where the jumpers are schooled. On the right of the Cambridge Road is the largest unbroken expanse of the Heath, where both the Rowley Mile and the July Courses are to be found together with the magnificent gallop Across the Flat on which horses can gallop a straight two miles.

Centuries before the Heath's potential for sport made its appeal to the sophisticated and erudite King James I in 1605, a very different ruler had used the ground for a very different purpose. This was Boadicea, queen of the ancient British tribe of the Iceni, a race of superb horsemen. Her principal settlement was two miles north of Newmarket at what is now the village of Exning, the very name a derivative of Iceni. Her warriors would drive their chariots, with vicious scythe-like blades protruding from the hubs of the wheels, across the open Heathland as they trained for battle. Boadicea was the widow of Prasutagus, the last male of the royal line of the Iceni. He had reigned as a client king of the Roman Empire whose armies occupied England along with much of the rest of western Europe. On the death of Prasutagus in AD60 he bequeathed half his lands to the Roman Emperor, Nero, and the other half for division between his two daughters. Rather than respect the wishes of the British chieftain the Romans declared their Emperor owner of all the lands of the Iceni, and Boadicea led the tribe in revolt against the occupying power in an attempt to assert the rights of her daughters.

With their forces spearheaded by the fearsome charioteers, the Iceni enjoyed considerable initial success. They sacked Colchester and Verulamium (the modern St Albans), capital of Roman Britain, but then the Romans were reinforced by legions from the Welsh border under Suetonius Paulinus. The Iceni were defeated somewhere near Towcester, and with the collapse of the rebellion Queen Boadicea committed suicide.

The Devil's Dyke, (probably built by the Iceni) runs out northward across the Heath until coming to the village of Reach six miles away. Excavation on this massive, primitive fortification, first mentioned in the *Saxon Chronicle* in 905, has revealed a great many weapons and the skeletons of men obviously killed in battle.

After the death of Queen Boadicea, Exning and the surrounding district receded into a backwater as the mainstream of national life ran its course elsewhere. While the Angles poured across the North Sea to oust the British descendants of Boadicea's Iceni, and they in turn, were conquered by the Normans, life went on, if not peacefully, at least unimportantly.

The only person of any note to be born in the Newmarket area in the years preceding the Norman Conquest was Ethelreda, daughter of the King of the East Angles. A princess of great beauty and piety, she wed the Prince of the South Gervii for political reasons on the condition that the marriage should not be consumated. On being widowed she founded a religious house at Ely. In due course this was enlarged and transformed into the beautiful Ely Cathedral, which can be seen from Warren Hill on a clear day.

Coming out of cloisters, Ethelreda contracted a second marriage to Egrid, son of the King of Northumbria, on the same terms as the first.

The name of this pious Saxon princess is commemorated by Ethelreda House, situated on the Newmarket Road on the outskirts of Exning. Ironically this was once the private stable of Lily Langtry, whose ideas on chastity were fundamentally different from those of Queen Ethelreda. While the former jockey Fred Webb was her trainer there during the closing years of the last century Mrs Langtry won the Cesarewitch of 1897 with the Australian horse Merman.

Following the Norman Conquest almost all of England was parcelled out amongst adherents of the new ruling dynasty. By 1167 much of Exning was held by Robert de L'Isle, but as Canon Peter May has shown in his scholarly and brilliantly researched book *Newmarket Medieval and Tudor*, privately published in 1982, the present writer, and others of recent times, have been quite wrong to accept the tradition that plague obliged the people of Exning to leave their village to establish a New Market two miles to the south-west in 1227.

Newmarket became detached from Exning, and began to acquire its own identity, when given as the dowry of Cassandra de l'Isle on her marriage to Sir Richard d'Argentine in the reign of King Henry III

(1216-1272). In furtherance of his vested interests as Lord of the Manor, Sir Richard d'Argentine either obtained from the King the grant of the right to hold a market on it, or revived, and then increased the importance of, an existing market. Whichever was the case the New Market, with the advantage of being situated half-way along the road between Cambridge and Mildenhall, was soon flourishing, and a small town grew up around it.

In 1437 the heiress of John d'Argentine married William Alington to whom she brought the Manor of Newmarket. In due course the property was acquired by the Dukes of Somerset and then, by marriage again, by the Dukes of Rutland. A constant reminder of the long association between Newmarket and the Dukes of Rutland, who also owned the Cheveley Park estate, is to be found in the name of one of the town's principal hotels, the Rutland Arms.

Just as the people of Exning had spent their lives in obscurity during the centuries before the Conquest, the inhabitants of Newmarket were to earn their living from the land without making any impact outside their own community for many years. During the first four centuries of its existence only one person of the remotest consequence was born in the town. This was Thomas of Newmarket, who became Bishop of Carlisle. He was a staunch supporter of King Richard II. After the deposition of that sovereign by Henry IV in 1399 he fell into deep disfavour with the new King, was deprived of his see and fobbed off with a titular German Bishopric. Thomas of Newmarket died in about 1405.

2 Newmarket Under the Stuarts

James I of England

The process by which Newmarket was transformed from a small agricultural town into one of international importance in the world of sport was set in train in quite haphazard manner.

It was in February 1605 that King James I stopped to course hares at Fordham as he made his way to Thetford two years after he had inherited the throne of England from his mother's first cousin, Queen Elizabeth I. So impressed was the king by the strength of the hares and the suitability of the terrain for sport that he soon became a regular visitor to that part of East Anglia, where just about the only accommodation available to visitors was in a little inn called The Griffin at Newmarket, the nearest town to Fordham.

King James I, not inappositely dubbed 'the wisest fool in Christendom' was a man of extraordinary contrasts. In appearance he was slovenly, generally unwashed, and having a tongue too big for his mouth was constantly slobbering and dribbling so that it was hard to believe a man of such singularly unattractive exterior had a remarkably incisive mind. Similarly he was so weak physically and ill co-ordinated that he was a most indifferent horseman who sat badly in the saddle, but despite these disadvantages was absolutely devoted to every kind of field sport.

Finding the facilities offered by The Griffin too primitive to sustain him when indulging in his passion for the chase for any period of more than a few days, he had a house built at Newmarket for his greater comfort. That new edifice did not meet the requirements made of it for long as the foundations began to sink with the result that all the doors and windows suddenly flew open in the middle of one night in early 1613, so the King had to quit his bed to take refuge in Thetford.

Although he and his attendants brought their horses on their increasingly frequent visits to Newmarket the racing of them provided no significant part in the sport. Of more interest to King James was the coursing of hares across the Heath, the opportunities afforded for hawking and for the shooting of partridges.

Determined to improve the sport he enjoyed so much James ordered Sir Robert Vernon, his verderer, to loose 50 brace of partridges and the same number of hares on Newmarket Heath every year. That was in 1619 but not until three years later, in 1622 does the record of the first match on the Heath appear. This was for £100 on 8 March when an unnamed horse belonging to Lord Salisbury beat Prince, a sorrel belonging to the Marquess of Buckingham. Both owners were well known courtiers. The Earl of Salisbury had inherited the title and estates of his father, Queen Elizabeth's famous minister twelve years earlier, and was described by Lord Clarendon as 'a man of no words except in hunting and hawking'.

The 30-year-old Marquess of Buckingham, though higher in rank than Lord Salisbury, came from a very much less distinguished background. The son of an obscure Leicestershire knight, he was one of those handsome, elegant, effeminate youths who readily found favour with King James I, and after coming to court in 1614 rapidly obtained preferment. Beginning with the appointment as cup bearer to the King that year, he rose to acquire a dukedom the year after he had run his horse in that match at Newmarket. His love of power and money, even more than his indifferent conduct of foreign policy, made him extremely unpopular with the result that no sense of public outrage was aroused when he was assassinated by a discontented naval officer at Portsmouth in 1628.

The amount of time that King James spent at Newmarket in the company of the Marquess of Buckingham and his other favourites was taken as a considerable affront by a parliament that was not without its puritan element. In 1621 the House of Commons petitioned him to turn his gracious attention to affairs of state and deputed twelve of its members to go to Newmarket to place the remonstrance in the royal hands.

The Commons had little need for further misgivings about the distractions afforded their sovereign by Newmarket as far as King James I was concerned. It was against the advice of his physicians that he went to see some hawks fly there in 1624 and when he returned with Buckingham and a small suite, after being confined to his room all Christmas, in February 1625 he was a very sick man. Leaving, for the last time towards the end of that month, the town he had come to love so much he travelled to Royston and then on to his palace of Theobolds, where he died of an ague on 27 March 1625.

James was succeeded by his 25-year-old son, King Charles I. The new King was every bit as much devoted to Newmarket and its sport as his father had been, but was, unlike his father, an excellent horseman. Despite the troubles that beset his reign and culminated in civil war, King Charles was also a constant visitor to Newmarket and it was during his time that the first stand of any kind was erected on the Heath. While at Newmarket in 1630 he knighted the Flemish artist and diplomat Peter Paul Rubens, who was negotiating a peace treaty on behalf of King Philip IV of Spain, and gave him a number of sittings. Among the retinue that accompanied the King to Newmarket was his personal physician William Harvey, who, while in attendance there is reputed to have done a measure of the research that led to his discovery of the circulation of the blood.

In the course of a visit that King Charles paid to Newmarket in 1642 a committee of both Houses of Parliament arrived to demand he took steps to maintain the religion and welfare of the country. His peremptory dismissal of that delegation was not the least of the causes of the ensuing Civil War, and four years later he returned to Newmarket a prisoner of Parliament. Although guarded by two regiments of the rebels' cavalary the King was allowed a large measure of freedom until he was removed to London, being able to take exercise by riding across the Heath and driving in his carriage.

The execution of King Charles on 30 January 1649 marked the beginning of a bleak, joyless decade, during which the English people were denied almost any form of pleasure by their puritan rulers. In 1654 meetings at Newmarket were proscribed, and the Heath ploughed to prevent its use for hunting, while the house that King James had built, together with almost all the rest of the larger houses in the town stood empty and neglected.

When the grim and dismal years of puritan rule came to an end with the restoration of the monarchy and the belated accession of King Charles II in 1660 there was an immediate reaction to the miseries of the previous decade as pleasure became the fashion again in towns and villages all over the country. Nobody was better suited to lead England in her new mood than the King, who far preferred to use his quick intelligence in seeking amusement than on the discharge of the duty of government.

Thus it was no more than in the natural order of things that Charles should return to the favourite sporting ground of his father and grandfather as soon as possible. Within two months of his accession Sir Allen Apsley had already been appointed Keeper of His Majesty's Hawks for life, with a staff of four falconers. Three years later, in 1663, Colonel Robert Kerr was given £200 with which to bring hounds to Newmarket 'for the King's disport'. At the same time proclamation was made that no other hounds might be hunted within seven miles of the town, nor any but the King's greyhounds be coursed within ten miles of it.

King Charles had a favourite hack called Old Rowley, to whom he was devoted. In due course the courtiers came to dub the King himself Old Rowley, a name that is perpetuated by the designation of a course as the Rowley Mile.

Early every year, and then for a second time later on, Charles would come to Newmarket, thereby starting the tradition of the Spring and Autumn Meetings still maintained today. During these seasons the town was the capital of England in all but name. Unfortunately the dilapidated royal residence built for James I could do no more than provide primitive lodgings for the King, his body servants and members of his immediate entourage like Thomas Killigrew who combined the post of Groom of the Bedchamber with the more onerous one of Master of the Revels. In consequence, the Lord Chamberlain and other great officers of state, the gentlemen ushers and the commanders of the guards, were all obliged to camp at the foot of Warren Hill, yearning for the comfort of Whitehall.

To solve these acute problems of accommodation a new palace was built on what is approximately the site of the Rutland Arms, though reaching rather further down the High Street, the land having been acquired from Lord Thomond. Not everybody was impressed by the new edifice on its completion in 1671. John Evelyn, the diarist, could only praise the cellars. The remainder he found too small for his liking, and the situation wholly unsuitable. "The arches of the cellar are well turn'd by Mr Samuel, the architect," he wrote. "The rest meane enough and hardly fit for a hunting house. Many of the roomes have had the chimnies plac'd in the angles and corners, a mode now introduc'd by his Majesty, which I do at no hand approve of. It does onely well in very small and trifling roomes, but takes from the state of greater. Besides this house is plac'd in a dirty street, without any court or avenue... whereas it might, and ought, to have been built at either end of the towne, upon the very carpet where the sports are celebrated, but... his Majesty was persuaded to set it on that foundation, although the most improper imaginable for a house of sport and pleasure".

Stables for the King's carriage horses and hacks, and almost certainly his racehorses, were erected across the lane that ran down the back of the palace. These boxes that were built for the horses of King Charles II more than 300 years ago are still standing, and form the main yard of the Palace House stables, the oldest training establishment in the world.

Returning to Newmarket in October 1671 John Evelyn recorded finding "The jolly blades raceing and dauncing, feasting and revelling, more resembling a luxurious and abandon'd rout, than a Christian Court. The Duke of Buckingham was now in mighty favour, and had with him that impudent woman the Countess of Shrewsbury, with his band of fiddlers &".

George Villiers, second Duke of Buckingham, was the son of James I's favourite. As his father was assassinated a few months after his birth he had been brought up at the court of King Charles I as the boyhood friend of the future Charles II and his younger brother the Duke of York, who would succeed Charles as James II.

Fickle to the point of being faithless, the Duke of Buckingham was a man of great charm and considerable wit. He was quite incapable of behaving responsibly for long, though he regarded himself as both a statesman and a general. He also dabbled in chemistry, in his capacity as one of the original Fellows of the Royal Society, and wrote several plays, of which *The Rehearsal*, a satire on heroic drama, attained some reputation. In early manhood he exerted considerable influence on Charles II, who was two years his junior, and did much to undermine what little inclination the King had to take life seriously. It was of Buckingham that John Dryden wrote:

> A man so various that he seem'd to be
> Not one, but all mankind's epitome;
> Stiff in opinions, always in the wrong,
> Was everything by starts, and nothing long.
> But in the course of one revolving moon,
> Was chymist, fiddler, statesman, and buffoon.

Quite the worst of all the scandals in which Buckingham was involved was his affair with the Countess of Shrewsbury. This culminated in his killing the Earl of Shrewsbury in a duel, while the Countess, disguised as a pageboy, held his horse. He celebrated the successful outcome of that meeting on the field of honour by joining Lady Shrewsbury in bed without even discarding his bloodstained shirt.

Shortly afterwards Buckingham brought Lady Shrewsbury home. Upon his duchess protesting to him that she was being placed in a quite impossible position he replied quite blandly, "So I thought, madam, and have therefore ordered your coach to convey you to your father".

Another of the favourite companions of Charles II during his spring and autumn visits to Newmarket was John Wilmot, Earl of Rochester. That young man was a wit and scholar whose debauchery and drinking bouts had made him a legend long before his early death at the age of 34 in 1680. It was he who pinned upon the King's bedroom door a scrap of paper bearing the lines:

> Here lies our sovereign Lord and King,
> Whose word no man relies on;
> Who never said a foolish thing,
> And never did a wise one.

Like Buckingham, whom Charles came to mistrust, Rochester frequently fell out of favour with the King. During one spell of banishment from court the pair of them set up as landlords of The Green Man at Six Mile Bottom in order to be able to make free with travellers' daughters. There was in the vicinity of that village an extraordinarily pretty young woman married to a notorious miser, who would never leave her unless she were safe in the company of his sister, a sour spinster of advancing years. After the man had made endless excuses for his inability to bring his wife to share their hospitality and then availing himself of it freely, the noblemen changed their tactics. While Buckingham remained at the inn to ply the miser with drink even more liberally than usual, the Earl dressed up as a woman, concealing a bottle of doped drink beneath his skirts, and pretended to faint outside the house wherein the spinster guarded her pretty young sister-in-law. On seeing one of their own sex apparently in distress, both women helped the distraught party indoors, whereupon the doctored bottle was produced by Rochester on the pretext that it would help effect his recovery. Having affected to take a few sips he passed it to the spinster, whom he knew to be far from indifferent to such refreshment, as a gesture of gratitude. Taking full advantage of the absence of her brother by abandoning all restraint she polished off the bottle with indecent haste and immediately passed into deep unconsciousness, leaving Rochester to reveal himself to the younger woman, whom he was delighted to find extraordinarily compliant. Not only did she receive the advances of the Earl with enthusiasm but agreed to return to The Green Man with him, taking with her as many of the guineas of her parsimonious husband as she could find. Returning to find his sister doped, and his wife and much of his money gone, the disconsolate miser hanged himself. Before long Rochester had tired of the newly made widow and passed her on to Buckingham. In his turn Buckingham was also casting around for fresh conquests before long, and left her with the eminently practical observation that the best thing she could do was to seek a dubious living in London.

Among the other constant companions of Charles II at Newmarket were the Duke of Monmouth, the eldest of his many illegitimate sons, Henry Bennet, Earl of Arlington, keeper of the privy purse, and James Howard, third Earl of Suffolk, First Gentleman of the Bedchamber at a salary of £1,000 a year and Lord Lieutenant of the county of Suffolk. Lord Arlington lived in great state in his magnificent Euston Hall mansion a few miles from Newmarket. His only child Isabella married the first Duke of Grafton. In due course Euston Hall passed to the Dukes of Grafton and it was there that the third and fourth holders of the title bred some of the best horses to run at Newmarket during the first part of the nineteenth century.

It would, of course, have been quiet contrary to the nature of Charles II to have maintained a predominantly male court. A dark, strikingly good looking man, with large brown eyes, strong nose above a small moustache, and sensuous lips he would let his admiration for a beautiful woman turn to lust as lightly as ever his maternal grandfather Henry of Navarre had done. Among the ladies who rode highest in his favours at Newmarket were the pert little Frenchwoman Louise de Querouaille, Nell Gwyn, the sloe-eyed Barbara Villiers, and Frances Teresa Stuart, 'La Belle Stuart', a distant cousin of her sovereign.

Louise de Querouaille, whom Charles created Duchess of Portsmouth, was a spy in the pay of the French government. She was held in very much lower esteem by the people of England than she was by their King by reason of her being a Roman Catholic. While a closed coach was travelling through Oxford, word of its carrying the King's French mistress quickly went round, and the people of the University city began to hurl abuse at it until Nell Gwyn poked her head out of the window, saying, "Be silent, good people, I am the protestant whore".

Nell Gwyn, who came from a Glamorganshire family, had been born in 1650, the daughter of an improvised officer in the Royalist army. Having been brought up in a brothel she achieved a certain amount of success as an actress in plays like Dryden's *Secret Love* before embarking upon her long affair with Charles II in 1668. The least acquisitive of all his mistresses, and quite possibly the only one to have loved him, she was rewarded with no title and very little money, though Charles Beauclerk, the eldest of the sons she bore the King, was to become Duke of St Albans.

When in Newmarket Nell Gwyn lived in a house across the street that ran behind the palace. According to tradition a secret passage ran between the two buildings to facilitate the royal assignations. Her house is still known as 'Nell Gwyn's House' and stands a little way up Palace Street from the Palace House stables.

Whereas Nell Gwyn, who was to die at the early age of 37, was not at all materialistic, Barbara Villiers was the greediest of the unofficial Queens of Newmarket. Her passion for money led her to the gaming tables of Newmarket and London, and her gambling together with her many other extravagances could cost the King as much as £30,000 a year. When Miss Villiers was most urgently in need of a wedding ring a Mr Roger Palmer was prevailed upon to furnish her with one in exchange for the Earldom of Castlemaine. Soon afterwards a court chaplain proclaimed, in the course of his sermon, "A virtuous woman is a crown to her husband," thereby provoking the response, "The Countess of Castlemaine is at least a coronet to hers".

Subsequently Lord Castlemaine took refuge in a monastery and Barbara was raised still higher in the peerage to be Duchess of Cleveland. She was the mother of the first Duke of Grafton as well as other children by the King, whose pious wife Catherine of Braganza proved unable to give him an heir.

Frances Teresa Stuart, a maid of honour to Queen Catherine, was at Newmarket when John Roettiers made the sketch of her on which he based his design of Britannia, still to be seen on the coinage today. Unlike Louise de Querouaille and Barbara Villiers, 'La Belle Stuart' did not need the exercise of the royal prerogative to become a duchess. To the very great annoyance of the King, she eloped with Charles Stuart, sixth Duke of Lennox and third Duke of Richmond at the age of 20 in 1667. As was usually the case with the easy-going Charles, he was unable to sustain his anger for long. The Duke and his beautiful young Duchess were brought back to court, where Charles gratified earlier intentions, and, when extremely drunk at a party given by Lord Townsend, boasted to her husband of his success.

The Duke of Lennox and Richmond did not live long to be cuckolded by his sovereign, dying childless just five years after marriage at the age of 33 in 1672. Having been so much incensed by the Duke's marriage, Charles seems to have derived ironic amusement from reviving his honours in favour of his own illegitimate son by Louise de Querouaille and giving the child the name of Lennox as well. Thus in 1675 the three-year-old infant known as Charles Lennox was created Duke of Richmond.

'La Belle Stuart' survived her husband by 30 years, dying during the Newmarket October meeting of 1702. Long before her death her beauty had been ruined by smallpox, but almost to the end of her life she retained the superb figure immortalised by the Flemish medallist Roettiers.

In the days when he was dallying with Nell Gwyn and the Duchess of Richmond, Charles II was at the height of his powers as a rider. As a result of early tuition from the Duke of Newcastle, one of the greatest horse-masters of sixteenth century Europe, Charles was an even finer rider than his father, and being very much more of an extrovert, loved to demonstrate his prowess in the saddle by riding races against his courtiers. Had the King been endowed with less skill in the saddle or been of a more retiring disposition, racing would have taken longer to come into vogue at Newmarket, where hunting, shooting, coursing and cocking would have remained the mainstays of the sport.

As early as 1664 he had founded the Town Plate, declaring that it should be run on the second Thursday in October for ever, and seven years later he is recorded as having ridden his own horse Woodcock in a match with a Mr Elliot on Flatfoot, which the latter won. Two days later, on 14 October, the King rode the winner of The Plate in which the Duke of Monmouth, Mr Elliot and Thomas Thynne, a forebear of the Marquess of Bath, were amongst the other riders. In March 1674 the King won the race again, inspiring Sir Robert Carr to write to a correspondent in Whitehall "Yesterday His Majesty rode himself three heates and a course, and won the Plate, all fower were hard and near ridden, and I doe assure the King wonn by good horsemanshipp".

The course over which King Charles raced against his favourite son, the Duke of Monmouth, one of the most accomplished riders at the court, and his other friends, was a well mown grass track about four miles round, marked out by tall, white painted stakes with a flag flying from the winning post.

The exhilaration of riding his horses on the course was far from being the only aspect of racing that appealed to Charles II. As was to be expected of a King who was a patron of scientists and gave the Royal Society its charter, he had to satisfy his enquiring mind by learning how the horses were trained. He would sit for hours at the top of Warren Hill, watching the horses in work from his vantage point in the King's Chair, a small summer house, or kiosk, with seats running round it.

As well as being a successful owner-rider and student of the art of training in its primitive form, King Charles II was the natural arbiter of all disputes that arose at Newmarket, where the courtiers would have thousands of pounds dependent upon his judgement. Unfortunately records of these cases are no more plentiful than those of contemporary racing. One of the earliest disputes submitted to him concerned a match over a mile and a half between a horse belonging to Sir Robert Carr and a gelding owned by Sir Robert Geere. In those days when four miles was the usual distance, that was considered no more than a sprint and a level start essential. On that occasion though, the starter, a Mr Griffin, performed his office with singular incompetence. Having given the word to go, he recalled them, but one went away to complete the course while the other rider held his horse in check, thus while backers of the horse to finish claimed their money on the grounds that the race had begun as soon as the starter shouted 'Go', backers of the other runner maintained its rider was correct in obeying the starter's instructions and that the race should be run again to obtain a true result. The King's verdict in that case is not recorded and in another the royal ruling is known but not the grounds for the controversy. At the Spring Meeting of 1682 a Mr Bellingham ran his horse Traveller in a match with one belonging to a Mr Roe, and after hearing the evidence of both riders on oath, the King declared Traveller to have won by a foot and a half.

Seventeen years after the Great Fire of London in 1666, Newmarket was ravaged by the same perennial hazard. Having begun in Lord Sunderland's stable, the blaze was fanned by a high wind until half the town had been destroyed, the palace being one of the few important buildings to survive the conflagration.

Because of the disruption to sport caused by the fire the King left Newmarket earlier than intended thereby unwittingly foiling a plot for his assassination. A group of ultra-Protestant whigs led by Lord William Russell and the Earl of Essex, had intended to kill him as he passed the Rye House near Ware in Hertfordshire on the day on which he had originally decided to return to London from Newmarket, but having no knowledge of his premature departure were unable to put their plan into effect.

King Charles II paid his last visit to Newmarket in 1684. On 6 February the following year he died at the age of 54 having consolidated the reputation of Newmarket as the most fashionable centre of sport in the country while laying the foundation of its enduring fame by his enthusiastic participation in racing in its formative stages.

The brother and successor of Charles II, King James II had no time in which to return to Newmarket during the three troubled years of his reign. In 1688 he was driven from the throne by his nephew and son-in-law, William, Prince of Orange and Stadtholder of the United Provinces of the Netherlands. Dutch William went to Newmarket more to demonstrate an identity of interests with an important element amongst his new subjects rather than love of sport, though he was much addicted to gambling and accepted reversals in a manner that could make life for the Gentlemen in Waiting distinctly uncomfortable for quite a considerable time.

Escorted by the Life Guards, resplendent in plumes and gold lace, King William III paid the first of several visits to Newmarket in 1689 to pass the days in hunting, hawking and cockfighting as well as racing, before repairing to the gaming tables of an evening. Regrettably the outcome of the match the King made between one of his horses with one belonging to the Duke of Somerset for 1,000 guineas a side is not known, but it is on record that the King's Turk beat Lord Carlisle's Spot on a tight rein for £500 and that much later in the reign another of the King's horses, Stiff Dick beat the Marquess of Wharton's Careless for the same stake. William took particular pride in that success of Stiff Dick, even though his horse had carried just a feather (the lightest available weight) against the nine stone of Careless, as Careless was generally regarded as unbeatable and few owners would make a match against him.

The Marquess of Wharton had the finest stud in England and was the outstanding racing man during the closing years of the seventeenth century. His particular delight was in winning races from horses owned by Tories. Whenever he heard about a high church nobleman or squire being sanguine about success at some local meeting he would descend upon the scene with Careless to win the stake.

Following the death of William III as a result of his horse stumbling

Tregonwell Frampton (1641-1727)

on a molehill at Hampton Court in 1702 he was succeeded by his sister-in-law, Queen Anne, the younger daughter of James II. Although Queen Anne earned immortality by the foundation of Ascot in 1711 she was also a staunch patron of Newmarket. It was there that she maintained a racing stable under the management of that remarkable character Tregonwell Frampton, who bore the title of Keeper of the Running Horses.

William Tregonwell Frampton had been born near Dorchester in 1641, the fifth son of William Frampton of Moreton. He seems to have come to Newmarket in about 1671 and rapidly made a name for himself by his astute betting on cockfighting and racing.

It was not often that Frampton came off second best but in those days when there was such intense rivalry between north and south he lost out badly to the Yorkshiremen on one celebrated occasion. The Yorkshire baronet Sir William Strickland had sent Old Merlin to Newmarket in the care of his groom Heseltine to be trained for a match that had been made with one of Frampton's horses. With the loyalties of the sporting fraternity deeply divided along territorial lines, and thousands of pounds dependent upon the outcome, Tregonwell Frampton suggested that it would be in the interest of those most intimately concerned if the horses were tried privately over the course and distance of the match, prior to their formal meeting. Rather to his surprise Sir William Strickland instructed Heseltine to agree to this proposal for a secret trial, and Old Merlin won by a little more than a length. Frampton was well pleased by that result, content in the knowledge that he had taken the liberty of allowing his horse to carry 7 lb more than had been agreed. For his own part Sir William was also delighted by the outcome. Realising such a shrewd party as Frampton would not have suggested that the horses should be tried without his own interests being substantially served, the baronet had also put up 7 lb overweight. In consequence both camps went on betting as though there were no settling, and the match, to the intense discomfort of Frampton, proved to be no more than an encore of the secret trial that he had fondly thought to have been entirely misleading.

There was another story told of still more unscrupulous chicanery on the part of Mr Frampton. After his celebrated horse Dragon had beaten a mare in a match for 1,000 guineas, the owner of the mare declared he would race her against any other mare or any gelding in England for 2,000 guineas the following day. That evening Frampton qualified Dragon to accept the challenge and the poor animal beat the mare again while still bleeding from the operation, then dropped dead. The likelihood of there being any truth in this disgusting tale is remote in the extreme. It did not appear in print until 70 years after the matches were supposed to have taken place when Dr John Hawkesworth contributed a fantasy entitled *Dragon in the Elysium Fields* to No 37 of *The Adventurer,* beginning with the words "It is true, replied the steed, I was a favourite; but what avails it to be a favourite of caprice, avarice and barbarity?" This is the only known account of the episode. It would seem very wrong to condemn Tregonwell Frampton on the strength of the imagination of a literary man, whose more substantial works were of a very different nature, notably an account of a journey in the South Seas, published in 1773, the year of his death.

According to all reports Tregonwell Frampton was as eccentric as he was deviously resourceful. Throughout three reigns he never changed his manner of dressing and was rough and ready in his ways, almost to the point of being uncouth. His indifference to fashion was no more than a reflection of his misogyny though he was careful not to allow his hatred of women to extend to Queen Anne, who always referred to his as 'Governor' Frampton.

In 1703, the year after the accession of the Queen, he received £700 from the Cofferer and Keeper of the Great Wardrobe for the "expenses of the Race horses" over the period from 8 March 1701 until 30 September 1703. An analysis of that and other evidence suggests that he was paid about £100 a year for each of the Queen's horses that he kept in his stable. In all probability this was the establishment known as the Gogmagog Stable that stood at the foot of Warren Hill on the site of what was the Heath House stable, where Mat Dawson was to train St Simon 200 years after the time of Tregonwell Frampton. The Heath House stable was in its own turn demolished and replaced by the new hotel that is to be seen next to Sir Mark Prescott's yard on the Moulton Road.

In those days, long before racing had been formalised along its present lines, Frampton made all kinds of challenges on behalf of Queen Anne. One was to the Dukes of Devonshire, Rutland and Somerset to combine their stables to find any six horses, save Somerset's great racer Windham, to run against six belonging to the Queen, matches to take place for £100 every seven days until each of the six pairs had run. Characteristically Frampton stipulated that he would decide whether the distance should be six or four miles or the weights 8 st 7 lb or 10 st and then for good measure insisted that if any of the horses in his stable should go wrong he could run another of them twice. Whether or not the challenge was accepted is not known. Quite possibly ducal dignities were too badly affronted by Governor Frampton's demanding conditions so favourable to the royal stable.

As well as having the palace extensively refurbished in 1705 Queen Anne showed her interest in Newmarket in other respects. She gave a thousand pounds for the paving of the streets and endowed two schools, one for 20 boys and the other for the same number of girls, with annuities of £50 each. On her death on 1 August 1714 the town found itself without a patron it could ill afford to lose and facing a period in which it would enjoy hardly any more importance than it had prior to the arrival of King James I in 1605.

3 Georgian Newmarket

Flying Childers, the first great racehorse

Queen Anne was succeeded by her first cousin once removed, the Elector of Hanover, who came to the throne as King George I. As the new sovereign had little liking for anything pertaining to England, except revenues accruing to the crown, it is hardly surprising that he had no inclination to participate in her sport.

With the King totally indifferent to the charm of Newmarket the town soon went out of fashion. The palace was allowed to fall into disrepair, just as its predecessor had done during the Commonwealth, until leased to the Duke of Somerset at a rent of just £30 a year for 31 years in 1721.

Rather than have his position undermined by royal indifference to racing, Tregonwell Frampton acquired new prestige. Not only did he retain the office of Keeper of the Running Horses but he came to be looked upon as the King's viceroy at Newmarket and as such the supreme arbiter in all disputes that arose in a much curtailed programme of sport. By the time that he died in 1727 he was acclaimed as 'Father of the Turf'. He left most of his property and his horses to the Earl of Godolphin, who had been Lord Treasurer to Queen Anne, and was buried in the chancel of All Saints' Church.

The outstanding horse to race at Newmarket during the last years of Tregonwell Frampton was the Duke of Devonshire's Flying Childers, a bay or brown colt bred by Leonard Childers near Doncaster in 1715. Although Flying Childers, who was by the Darley Arabian, only ran twice, he was acclaimed 'the fleetest horse that ever ran at Newmarket', or, as generally believed, 'that was ever bred in the world'. On 26 April 1721 he beat the Duke of Bolton's Speedwell at level weights over four miles for £500 and the following year started at Six Mile Bottom and beat Lord Drogheda's Chanter for £1,000 over the six miles to Cambridge Hill, a piece of rising ground on the Newmarket side of the July Course. He also put up an amazing performance in a trial by beating Fox, winner of three King's Plates and other races, by more than a furlong and a half. Flying Childers did not found a flourishing male line but transmitted his excellence as a successful sire of broodmares. He died in 1741.

Following the death of Tregonwell Frampton, Newmarket went still further out of favour with the sporting fraternity. For a few years it was all but desolate, so much so that there was not even a butcher in the town by 1753. A few years before that date, however, signs that the town's fortunes were on the mend began to appear. For close on 100 years almost all the races on the Heath were confined to matches made as a result of one owner offering to bet on his challenge to another, the exception being the races for the King's Plate and the Town Plate, both run at the October meeting. A minor, but significant change in this pattern was made in 1744 when the tradesmen of Newmarket gave a fillip to the sport, in the hope of custom from the participants by providing two plates of £50 each to be run in four-mile heats.

Within a few years the traders and innkeepers were drawing dividends from that early form of sponsorship as the town came back into vogue amongst a group of wealthy, pleasure-loving young men such as the Duke of Hamilton, the Earl of March and the Earl of Eglinton. They rode against each other on the Heath and there, too, they settled outlandish bets struck in the London clubs.

Heaviest and most resourceful of those aristocratic gamblers who helped restore the popularity of Newmarket in the middle of the eighteenth century was William Douglas, Earl of March. He was still only 23 when he made his first appearance on the Heath in 1748. At this time he was in love with Miss Frances Pelham, whose uncle, the Duke of Newcastle, was soon to become Prime Minister. Although she reciprocated his feeling her parents forbade their marriage and thereafter the Earl of March, rejecting any further ideas of finding a wife, devoted himself to satisfying a near insatiable sexual appetite and a wonderful variety of forms of gambling. Such tastes constituted eminently suitable qualifications for his becoming a leading member of the Hell-Fire Club, which held its orgies at Medmenham Abbey, Sir Francis Dashwood's property near High Wycombe.

An early match at Newmarket

A fine judge of a horse, Lord March had a trim, athletic figure that enabled him to exercise his skill as a race rider until relatively late in life. Among his earliest successes in the saddle were those he gained on his own horses Whipper-in and Smoker shortly after his arrival at Newmarket in 1748.

Two years later he made his celebrated bet with Theobald Taafe that he would produce a four-wheeled vehicle that could carry a man and be drawn 19 miles by four horses ridden by postillions within an hour. In those days when stage coaches rolled along at just a few miles an hour and a gentleman's carriage drawn by fast horses was hard put to it to reach ten miles an hour this appeared impossible to achieve. Approaching the problem with the same thoroughness that he did every other piece of frivolity, Lord March decided that elimination of weight was the essence of the matter. Accordingly he commissioned Wright, the Long Acre coachmaker, to construct him a vehicle with a framework made with the bare minimum of thin wood bound by wire so that it was virtually no more than a seat slung between four wheels. To ensure that this elementary contraption could be drawn at the maximum speed four sets of harness were made from whalebone and silk and the same materials used for the traces. Eyebrows must have been raised when Lord March produced this conveyance at Newmarket on 29 August 1750, but no objection could be made as it met with the stipulations of the wager by having four wheels and the capacity to carry a man. Having started somewhere near Six Mile Bottom it approached Newmarket through the Running Gap in the Devil's Dyke, turned right to complete three four-mile circuits and then returned to the starting point, making a distance of 19 miles that had been covered in just 53 minutes 27 seconds.

Lord March used even more ingenuity to win his bet that he could send a letter 50 miles within an hour. Securing the services of 24 expert cricketers, he stood them in a large circle, put the letter inside a ball and had them throw it from hand to hand so fast that it travelled the 50 miles well within the hour.

Doubts as to whether Lord March was entirely scrupulous in the winning of his wagers were raised on at least one occasion. After one of his horses had won a match at Newmarket in 1750 the owner of the loser alleged that March's jockey had emptied his saddle bags before starting and an accomplice had returned the dead weight to him as he went back to the scales. Lord March called out his accuser, who had a reputation as an expert duellist. On arriving on the field of honour he was confronted by a coffin bearing a brass plate inscribed with the legend, 'William Douglas, Earl of March. Born November 5th 1725. Died June 10th 1750.' Becoming thoroughly unnerved by the prospect of these words being translated into reality Lord March declined to fight and apologised profusely. For the remainder of his long life he never again contemplated another duel, no matter how grossly he might have been insulted; not even when a giant Irishman picked him up by the ears in the course of a game of cards, saying, "You see, gentlemen, how I treat this despicable little cock-sparrow."

Lord March could, when it suited him, show the same aptitude for foiling sharp practice as for indulging in it. When his jockey Richard Goodisson reported that he had been offered a big bribe to stop a horse against which some of the 'legs' had laid heavily, March told him to accept the money. With the rider apparently squared these gentry continued to bet against the horse until just as Goodisson should have mounted, March threw off his greatcoat to reveal himself in a duplicate set of his racing livery saying, "Stop Dick! This is a nice handy nag, I'll get up myself, just for the fun of the thing". And vaulting into the saddle he brought the horse home in a canter.

One of the finest feats of riding by Lord March was seen at the Newmarket Spring Meeting of 1757. For 1,000 guineas a side he rode a match with the Duke of Hamilton Across the Flat and won by what was widely regarded as a wonderful display of horsemanship.

In 1750 at about the time that Lord March became involved in that unedifying affair that finished with his refusal to fight a duel he became one of the founder members of the Jockey Club. To be surprised that a man of such dubious integrity should have been an early member of that body is both to misunderstand the use of language at that time as well as to make false assumptions about the composition and function of the Jockey Club during the early years of its existence.

As Mr Roger Mortimer pointed out in his excellent book *The Jockey Club* published by Cassell in 1958, the word jockey in the middle of the eighteenth century still denoted an owner of horses as much as a rider, just as it had done when old Tregonwell Frampton had been acclaimed 'the cunningest jockey in England' some 50 years earlier. Professional jockeys like Dick Goodisson and Sam Chifney were still only beginning to appear on the scene as so many owners kept horses for the pleasure and exhilaration of riding them in races against each other.

Just as the people of the eighteenth century gave a different meaning to the word jockey from that which we do today they also understood something different by a club. Unlike the modern clubs, which invariably have their own premises, that proliferation of clubs of 200 years ago, devoted to sport, politics, art, science and all sorts of other spheres of activity, held their meetings in a variety of places without having any property for their own exclusive use. The wealthy racing men who formed themselves into the Jockey Club in about 1750 met at several different venues in London such as the Star and Garter in Pall Mall, The Thatched Tavern in St James's Street, and The Clarendon in Bond Street, as well as the room provided for them by Richard Tattersall next door to his horse repository at Hyde Park corner. It was in those places that the most fashionable men of pleasure in the country drank and revelled and made their bets on the matches that their horses were to run at Newmarket. In those early days there was no question on the club vesting in itself any of the authority that it was to exert at a later date. The first evidence of it having been formed came casually in an advertisement for 'A Contribution Free Plate to be run for at Newmarket in April... by horses the property of the noble-

Sir Charles Bunbury (1740-1821), had his home at Great Barton near Newmarket, and was the first of the three Great Dictators of The Turf

men and gentlemen of the Jockey Club at the Star and Garter in Pall Mall' that appeared in *The Sporting Kalendar* published by John Pond in 1752.

In the same year that that anouncement appeared, the Jockey Club made the decision to acquire a property at Newmarket. Land in the middle of the town was leased from a Mr Erratt but it was not until 1771 that a lease was taken on the Coffee Room, the site of which was probably the one on which the Jockey Club stands today. Prior to 1771 the Club held its meetings in the Red Lion, which is reputed to have stood somewhere along Old Station Road.

The first man to impose the strength of his character on the Club was Sir Charles Bunbury. Through his influence it was transformed from a set of ribald, rowdy, none too responsible sportsmen into the ruling body of a sport that was becoming increasingly well organised as it began to acquire national importance.

Sir Charles Bunbury, who was born in 1740, the son of a parson, lived on his Great Barton estate near the village of Mildenhall which is some 20 miles from Newmarket. He was elected Member of Parliament for Suffolk at the age of 21 and three years later inherited the baronetcy. Although he had a seat in the House of Commons for 43 years he made little impact as a parliamentarian and proved a singularly poor speaker. An ardent Whig, he was fiercely opposed to the slave trade and was a friend and ally of the celebrated radical Charles James Fox, who was to become a regular visitor to Newmarket.

Sir Charles Bunbury's devotion to racing and all other forms of rural sport brought about the breakdown of his marriage to Lady Sarah Lennox, daughter of the second Duke of Richmond and the lady that King George III had once set his heart upon marrying. Thoroughly bored by country life in East Anglia she took a number of lovers before going to live with Lord William Gordon, finally obtaining a divorce, marrying the Hon George Napier and becoming the mother of three famous generals. Sir Charles Bunbury married again but remained childless.

Throughout almost the whole of the first half of the eighteenth century racing was confined to horses of four years and upwards carrying ten stone or more in four-mile heats. Sir Charles Bunbury was to become instrumental in developing the speed of the thoroughbred and taking away the heavy emphasis on stamina by the introduction of races for younger horses carrying lighter weights over shorter distances. Inevitably there was a good deal of ill-natured talk about him being motivated by the horses from his stud lacking the constitutions to hold their own in the old-fashioned marathons. Justice would have been better served by recognising him as the first man to appreciate that the essence of racing is, to borrow the words of the late Aga Khan, "speed, more speed and yet more speed".

When he was 28 Bunbury became Steward of the Jockey Club, there being only one holder of that office at a time in those days. Soon afterwards he was recognised as its perpetual president, and is now regarded as the first of the three great Dictators of The Turf. As his authority grew and he imposed his own high standards of integrity on his fellow members, the Jockey Club emerged as the paramount power in racing, both as arbitrator and legislator. The rules and regulations operative at Newmarket were adopted by other courses and the writ of the Jockey Club gradually began to run well beyond its own domain.

An early fillip was given to the prestige of the Jockey Club by William, Duke of Cumberland becoming the first member of the royal family to accept election to it. The second son of George II and the uncle of George III, who succeeded him on the throne in 1760, the Duke was a soldier of some ability. While still only 24 he commanded the allied forces in the battle with the French at Fontenoy in Flanders in 1745 after being severely wounded at the battle of Dettingen two years previously. In 1746 he commanded the army that crushed the Jacobite cause by defeating Bonnie Prince Charlie's Highlanders at Culloden, becoming known to the Scottish as 'Butcher' Cumberland by reason of his merciless treatment of the rebels. His subsequent military career was marred by his defeat by Marshal Saxe at Lauffeld in 1747 and another at Hastenbeck that was followed by his capitulation to the French at Klosterzeven.

The £25,000 a year that Parliament voted to him following the triumph of his army at Culloden went a long way to underwrite his passion for gambling both at the card table and on the racecourse. He paid his first visit to Newmarket in 1753 and the following year won a Jockey Club plate there with Marske. To reach the town he would leave his London home early in the morning and travelling by way of Epping Forest and Bishops Stortford complete the 64 mile journey in seven hours.

With regard to this first visit to Newmarket by the Duke, Horace Walpole wrote "The Duke of Cumberland is at present making a campaign (there) with half the nobility and half the money in England — they really say that not less than £100,000 has been carried thither for the hazard of this single week. The Palace has been furnished for him".

The Duke of Cumberland (1721-1765)

Possibly on account of the wound he received in the leg at Dettingen preventing him from taking exercise, the Duke of Cumberland became extremely corpulent very early in life. He never married and was apt to be more than a little arrogant and insensitive, but Newmarket seemed to bring out the best in him. Having lost his pocket book containing a great deal of money on the Heath he said to the man who found it, "I am glad it has fallen into such good hands; keep it. Had it not been for this accident, it would have been by this time in the hands of the blacklegs and thieves of Newmarket". The Duke cannot have been a very optimistic punter though he was certainly a very heavy one.

In 1764 the Duke of Cumberland's Dumplin beat a solitary rival in the first race for the Whip, a trophy for which members of the Jockey Club could challenge in the spring and autumn of every year. Competition for the Whip was never particularly intense, nor much

Eclipse

increased when the right to challenge was extended to members of the Jockey Club Rooms. Not infrequently no challenge was made and even when one did materialise there was often no acceptance forthcoming. In the latter case the principal beneficiary was the jockey who was paid his fee for walking over, thus obtaining a point in the championship table as Lester Piggott did on 1 May 1981 when going through the formalities on Sacrilege, the last winner of the Whip under the old conditions. In 1982 the distance was reduced from two miles to seven furlongs and entry confined to maiden three-year-olds instead of being open to all horses of that age or upwards, entry being £50, half forfeit. There were four runners for the first race for the Whip run under the new conditions and the winner was Noirio trained at Lambourn by Paul Cole, who had spent a formative part of his career working on the Cheveley Park Stud on the outskirts of Newmarket.

When the Duke of Cumberland died in October 1765 his fame as a breeder of thoroughbreds hardly seemed likely to be as lasting as proved to be the case. Among the bloodstock in his possession at the time of his death was a large yearling chestnut colt by Marske out of Spiletta foaled at his stud in Windsor Great Park during the eclipse of the sun of 1764. Given the name of Eclipse this colt with a long sock on his off hind and a narrow blaze, became a truly brilliant racehorse and, arguably, the most influential ever to have stood at stud. Among the outstanding stallions of the present time to trace back to him in tail male line are Northern Dancer and his son Nijinsky, Mill Reef, Roberto, Grundy, Bustino and Vaguely Noble.

Eclipse was the unbeaten winner of 18 races. The only time that there looked to be any likelihood of his being extended was in his match with Mr Wentworth's Bucephalus over the Beacon Course at Newmarket, but once having taken the measure of that horse Eclipse went on to win easily.

Six years after the breeder of Eclipse had made the first successful challenge for the Whip with Dumplin, that trophy was won by a horse of very much greater consequence in Gimcrack, after whom the famous two-year-old race at York is named. A beautifully moulded little grey, who stood no more than 14 hands and a quarter of an inch, Gimcrack was a horse of immense courage. He won 26 of his 36 races as well as a match against time by covering $22\frac{1}{2}$ miles in an hour on a trip to France in 1766. His final triumph was achieved when he returned to Newmarket at the age of eleven in 1771. He retired to stud at Oxcroft Farm, Balsham, a few miles from Newmarket and became the sire of a number of good winners including Grey Robin.

During the latter part of his racing career and all the time that he was at stud, Gimcrack was owned by the first Earl Grosvenor, one of the most munificent supporters of racing during the second half of the eighteenth century. His huge investment in horses, and almost unbelievably heavy gambling on them, is reputed to have cost him £250,000, a sum that he could afford better than most as he owned

Gimcrack

much of the West End of London and a vast estate in Cheshire, where he founded the celebrated Eaton Stud. When he was raised to the peerage in 1761 Horace Walpole was moved to write, "Sir Robert Grosvenor is made a Lord Viscount, or baron — I do not know which, nor does he, for yesterday when he should have kissed hands he was gone to Newmarket to see the trial of a racehorse".

Despite his wealth Lord Grosvenor was sometimes short of funds. When in need of a 3,000 guinea stake with which to match his colt by Gimcrack against the Earl of Abindgon's Cardinal of York, Mr Elwes, a notorious miser, stepped out of character by putting up the money so that the betting could open. After watching the Gimcrack colt win, Mr Elwes risked his elderly limbs by scrambling over the Devil's Dyke in order to avoid paying a turnpike.

One of the most important of the very many horses that Lord Grosvenor raced on the Heath was the curiously named Pot-8-o's. When his breeder Lord Abingdon gave the colt the name of Potatoes and asked the lad to chalk it on the door of his box the lad carried out the commission with the inscription Potoooooooo. So much amused was Lord Abingdon that he adopted the abbreviated version of that rendering of his colt's name.

A chestnut son of Eclipse, Pot-8-o's obtained his first success at the Newmarket First Spring Meeting as a three-year-old in 1776. The following year he was bought by Lord Grosvenor for 1,500 guineas. By the end of his long career he had won 28 races, many of them over the Beacon Course. Like Gimcrack he retired to stud at Oxcroft Farm, where he stood until moved to Lower Hare Park, Newmarket, in 1796, dying four years later. Pot-8-o's founded the most successful of the lines of Eclipse, all the modern stallions just mentioned being amongst his descendants.

The first Earl Grosvenor survived to reach the age of 71 in 1802. During the closing years of his life he won The Derby with Rhadamanthus in 1790, John Bull in 1792 and Daedalus in 1794. He also owned five winners of The Oaks.

Although racing at Newmarket became increasingly better organised after the Jockey Club had been formed for entirely different purposes, the Heath remained more of a country leisure complex rather than ground entirely devoted to the racing and training of thoroughbred. Throughout the second half of the eighteenth century devotees of Newmarket continued to make their wagers on contests that made high demands on the speed and endurance of horses, hounds and men or the ingenuity of the latter.

In the April of 1754 Mr Daniel Croker's pony mare, who stood 13 hands three inches, was backed for 100 guineas to cover 300 miles within 72 hours. Ridden by a boy weighing 4 st 11 lb without saddle or bridle, she went forwards and back from Six Mile House to the end of the Beacon Course until she covered the distance in 64 hours 20 minutes.

A few years later Hugo Meynell matched a couple of the Quorn Hounds against a couple belonging to a Mr Barry, to set off from the rubbing house at the top of the town and finish at the starting post on the Beacon Course. The Meynell Hounds were hopelessly beaten and the pace set by Mr Barry's couple to cover the ground in little over eight minutes so strong that only a dozen of the 60 horses that set out to follow them were able to carry their riders through to the finish. Hugo Meynell, 'Hunting Jupiter' they called him, was Master of the Quorn from the time that he was 18 in 1753 until 1800. He was a great man over Leicestershire but usually luck seems to have been against him at Newmarket. In 1761 Captain Jenison Shafto bet him 1,000 guineas that a man could ride 2,900 miles in 29 days, going 100 miles a day on any horse he chose. The professional jockey John Woodcock won that bet for Captain Shafto. The course agreed upon was back and forth between Hare Park and the Devil's Dyke with a circuit of Racecourse Side. This was marked out by posts with lanterns on them as Woodcock did most of his riding by night in order to spare his mounts the heat of the day.

Meynell House, the stables on the Fordham Road, where Jimmy Waugh trained towards the end of the last century and his son Tom during the early years of the present one, was almost certainly named after Hugo Meynell, who died in 1808. George Colling changed the name to Hurworth House shortly after the end of the Second World War, thereby maintaining the association with foxhunting, as it was the Hurworth hounds that he had followed with such enthusiasm as a boy in Yorkshire. The stables are now occupied by H. Thomson Jones, another trainer not unknown for his dash in the hunting field.

The daughter of John Pond who made first mention of the Jockey Club in his *Racing Kalendar,* appears to achieved some remarkable feats in the saddle during the middle years of the century. She aroused the admiration of Samuel Johnson, though the doctor showed he knew a lot less about equestrianism than lexicography, when he claimed Miss Pond rode 1,000 miles in 1,000 hours on the same horse in 1758.

The following year Captain Shafto brought off one of the heaviest wagers of the era. Having backed himself for £16,000 to ride 50 miles on the Heath within an hour, this inveterate gamester used ten thoroughbreds to cover the distance in 49 minutes 17 seconds.

There died in 1778 the 80-year-old third Duke of Queensberry, a straightforward, unassuming Scottish nobleman. So far as is known he had never set foot on Newmarket or any other racecourse in contrast to his cousin and heir, that Earl of March who had made his name at Newmarket in early manhood by his horsemanship while helping to set the fashion for making outlandish bets.

While making the transition into middle age the man who now became fourth Duke of Queensberry had developed his lust for women to an almost unbelievable degree while retaining his love of tippling and gambling so that his name was becoming a national byword for depravity. In the year in which he inherited the Dukedom he ran ten horses, quite an appreciable number in those days. Hydaspes and Rocket both won him matches at the Newmarket First

Pot-8-o's

Spring Meeting and Rosalba another at the Second October Meeting, but the best of them was Slim, a six-year-old bay by Squirrel. As well as carrying twelve stone to beat four others for a King's Plate at the Craven Meeting at Newmarket, Slim won in straight heats at Huntingdon and Peterborough, and beat the Duke of Grafton's Blunderbuss two heats to one for the Town Plate at Thetford. That same year the Duke's bay colt by Dapper ran, unsuccessfully, in a Town Plate with an interesting form of sponsorship over the last mile and a distance of the Beacon Course at the July Meeting. Of the £50 prize money 20 guineas came in the form of a bequest from the will of Mr John Perram.

These race meetings at Newmarket in the second half of the eighteenth century were quite unsophisticated in spite of the great wealth of their patrons. The stand was no more than an elementary structure and there were no enclosures, or running rails, just chains slung along low posts on the approach to the winning post to restrain the horde of mounted spectators. Much of the sport consisted of privately made matches for sums varying from 50 guineas to 500 guineas, and sometimes as much as 1,000 guineas, while many of the other races were run in gruelling heats of four miles one furlong and 138 yards around the Beacon Course, the first horse to win two heats outright being the winner of the stakes. As the noblemen who had reinvigorated Newmarket in the middle of the century grew older the professional jockeys were increasingly more in evidence. They wore the black velvet caps that were the traditional headgear of huntsmen and adopted the hunting seat too, sitting well back in the saddle and riding the full length of their leg just as their successors would continue to do until the monkey-up-the-stick style came over from the United States in the closing years of the next century. Those early jockeys wore the liveries of their employers which tended to be uniformly plain in contrast to the clashing colours of many modern racing silks. The jacket of the Duke of Queensberry, for example, was brown, that of the Duke of Grafton crimson, and that of the Duke of Devonshire straw, the same colour as the silks of the present Duke, while Lord Bolingbroke opted for black, Lord Clermont scarlet and Mr Panton buff. Rather more elaborate liveries though, were worn by the jockeys employed by Sir Charles Bunbury, pink and white stripes, Sir Lawrence Dundas, white with scarlet spots, the famous Aske spots, still registered by his descendant, the Marquess of Zetland.

What distinguished the horses of 200 years ago from their descendants of the present time was that they were docked, so that their short, stubby tails lent them an altogether more severe appearance than their modern counterparts, and it is hard to believe their action gave the impression of the same graceful fluency that is to be had from a horse with tail flowing behind it at full gallop. The practice of docking, which often involved much cruelty in the amputation of the tail bone, went out of fashion between 1820 and 1830 while George IV reigned. Thus most of the horses painted by Ben Marshall, who had been acknowledged as the greatest contemporary equine artist long before his death in 1835, are of horses with docked tails, while almost all the horses painted by his successor John Frederick Herring senior (1795-1865) have full tails. Docking eventually became illegal with the passage of the Docking and Nicking Act of 1948.

The Duke of Queensberry was already 63 when he had the most successful season that he ever enjoyed at Newmarket. This was in 1789, the year that saw the outbreak of the French Revolution. The highlight of it came when he matched his six-year-old Mulberry with Lord Derby's celebrated horse Sir Peter Teazle, who had won The Derby two years earlier over the Beacon Course for 500 guineas on Monday 29 September, the opening day of the First October Meeting. Mulberry, who started slight odds on, carried a mere 6 st against the 8 st 7 lb of Sir Peter Teazle. The 35 lb difference in the weights proved the deciding factor and Mulberry won. In the spring the Duke had made a match for another of his horses, Dash, against Sir Peter Teazle over the Six Mile Course for 1,000 guineas, but Lord Derby elected to pay forfeit. Sad to say Sir Peter Teazle broke down in a five-horse race on the Beacon Course four days after his unavailing effort to give all that weight to Mulberry.

Following the triumphs of Mulberry, Dash, Burgundy and his other horses in 1789, the Duke of Queensberry withdrew from Newmarket, though continuing to race and breed horses until 1806, in order to devote his remaining years to the pleasures of the flesh at his villa at Richmond, Surrey, and his house in Piccadilly. Almost universally known as 'Old Q' in the latter part of his life, and generally regarded as the wickedest man in the kingdom, he bathed in milk and drank huge amounts of Tokay, that would sell for 100 guineas a dozen after his death, in the hope of preserving his virility. The dapper figure of his youth had contracted into that of a shrivelled little old man, whose nose was pronouncedly hooked, and he became one of the sights of London as he sat on his balcony in his little brown chip hat, holding up his quizzing glass to ogle anything in a petticoat that passed down Piccadilly.

To Newmarket and the country at large he may have been 'Old Q' but for Londoners he was 'The Star of Piccadilly'. A fortnight after Lord Nelson had destroyed the French and Spanish fleets at Trafalgar on 21 October 1805 he entered upon extreme old age with the celebration of his 80th birthday. Thereafter rumours of the death of the ageing voluptuary swept London periodically, and satirists broke into verse with their premature elegies, one of which ran in part:

> And What is all this grand to-do
> That runs each street and alley through?
> Tis the depature of "Old Q",
> The Star of Piccadilly.

> 'Thank Heaven! Thank Heaven!' exclaims Miss Prue
> My mother and grandmother too,
> Can now walk safe from that vile "Q",
> The Star of Piccadilly.

The jockey boys, Newmarket's crew,
Who know a little thing — or two,
Cry out 'He's done! We've done "Old Q",
The star of Piccadilly.

Poll, Peggy, Cath'rine, Patty, Sue,
Descendants of old dames he knew,
All mourn your tutor, Ancient "Q",
The Star of Piccadilly.

Old Nick he whisked his tail so blue,
And grinn'd, and leer'd, and look'd askew,
"Oh ho" says he, "I've got my "Q",
The Star of Piccadilly.

Finally he died on 23 December 1810. For all his outrageous self-indulgence the fourth and last Duke of Queensberry was not without his redeeming qualities. He could be both broad minded and generous. He gave one of his estates to a number of elderly Roman Catholics seeking refuge from the French Revolution and donated a huge sum of money to Lloyds for the relief of disabled seamen. Most of his fortune he bequeathed to his illegitimate daughter Lady Yarmouth. Among his many minor legacies was one of £2,000 to his scruffy old jockey Dick Goodisson, who had ridden him so many winners at Newmarket. Memorials of 'Old Q' are still to be seen at Newmarket. Soon after entering the town from the direction of Cambridge one comes to Queensberry House standing behind the red brick wall on the right, while on the other side of the High Street is the small white building with the disused stableyard behind it known as Queensberry Lodge. Before the vastly increased flow of traffic in the post-war years made maintenance of stables along the High Street almost an impracticality, 'Chubb' Leach turned out many winners from Queensberry Lodge, which is now a horse transport depot.

Whereas William, Duke of Cumberland had been a regular visitor when the Duke of Queensberry had first come to Newmarket, the town had acquired a still more important royal patron in George, Prince of Wales, the future King George IV, by the time that Queensberry took his leave of the Heath.

Like almost any other opportunity for extravagance, horse racing made an inevitable appeal to the Prince of Wales, who might have become a great man had his strength of character matched his social attainments, artistic taste and love of sport. Having come of age on 12 August 1783 the Prince had his first runner the following year when he matched his bay horse Hermit, ridden by Mr Thomas Panton, againt Sir Harry Featherstonhaugh's grey Surprise, ridden by his owner, for 50 guineas over the last mile of the Beacon Course on Saturday 8 May, the last day of the Second Spring Meeting. The Prince's horse started 6-4 on but Surprise was the winner. Later that day the two horses were matched again over the same course and distance, though with professional jockeys up, and Hermit gave the Prince of Wales his first success as a racehorse owner. In the light of subsequent events it was ironic that the Prince's racing career should have begun with a reversal of form.

When the Prince of Wales made his appearance on The Turf at the age of 21 he had an automatic mentor in his 39-year-old uncle Henry, Duke of Cumberland, in whose favour the peerage had been revived shortly after the death of the breeder of Eclipse. The Duke of Cumberland would have been a deplorable influence on any young man, and had a particularly deleterious effect on one with the responsibilities of the heir to the throne. As well as being a reckless gambler he was a notorious philanderer. His passionate affair with Countess Grosvenor hardly guaranteed him universal popularity at Newmarket and when the Earl sued for criminal conspiracy he was hard put to it to find the £13,000 required for the payment of costs and damages. Having given up the quest for Lady Grosvenor as hopeless, he dallied briefly with the wife of a timber merchant and then married Anne Horton, a pretty young widow of 24, thereby precipitating the passing of the Royal Marriages Act that was to cause the Prince of Wales and his brothers so much trouble in the years ahead.

Having run just four horses in 1784, the Prince of Wales had a very much larger string in training with Frank Neale at Newmarket in 1785, during which his colours were carried by 18 different horses. Away from the strictures of his highly moral father and the ever increasing pressure of his numerous creditors, he loved the life at Newmarket, where he could race his horses, bet and drink in the company of his brother the Duke of York and friends like Sir Harry Featherstonhaugh, Lord Clermont, Sir John Lade and the harebrained Irish peer, Richard, Earl of Barrymore, who managed to squander £300,000 in four years until killing himself accidentally at the age of 25 while loading a musket.

In many respects Lord Barrymore was an unlikely friend for the fastidious Prince of Wales, as his companionship often called for a strong stomach. He once won a bet that he could produce a man who would eat a live cat. To his intimates he was known as 'Cripplegate' and his brothers Henry and Augustus, who followed him in the title in quick succession, as 'Newgate' and 'Hellgate', the latter gentleman being a clerk in holy orders. Their sister was always known as 'Billingsgate' by reason of her vocabulary being a match for the proverbial fishwives of that vicinity.

Unlike Richard, Earl of Barrymore, Sir Harry Fetherstonhaugh of Uppark, Sussex, survived the rigours of revelling with the Prince of Wales at Newmarket for many years, dying at the age of 92 in 1846. In about 1810 he quarrelled irrevocably with the Prince, retired from society completely, and remained a bachelor until marrying his head dairy maid, Mary Ann Bullock when over 70 in 1825. Dying childless, he left Uppark, his beautiful house on the South Downs, to the former dairy maid.

Of all the friends with whom the Prince of Wales raced, gambled and drank at Newmarket, Charles James Fox was looked upon with greatest abhorrence by the King and his government, whose interests

Charles James Fox (1749-1806)

were not invariably the same. The second son of Lord Holland, the dark, swarthy Charles James Fox was regarded as the champion of individual liberty and freedom of the press. Neither cause recommended itself to George III and his ministers who were haunted by the prospect of Fox making a Whig of the impressionable Prince. As well as being one of the greatest parliamentarians of the era Fox was among its heaviest gamblers and in perpetual debt on account of his enormous losses in the card room at Brooks. Until experience proved him all too wrong he entertained the idea of making good his losses by profiting from an analytical study of the form of racehorses. In the middle of the 1780s he and the second Lord Foley were partners in a large number of horses trained by Richard Prince, an Irishman, who had a stable on Mill Hill, Newmarket. During the early days of their confederacy they met with success far in excess of their expectations, but reaction soon followed. Among the dozen horses that ran in Fox's name while things were still going well in 1787 was Balloon, who beat three others over the Round Course at the First Spring Meeting and soon afterwards won a match from the Duke of Queensberry's Inca on the Beacon Course. The following year Grey Diomed, by Diomed, first winner of The Derby, ran in Fox's name when carrying the confederacy's green and white stripes, to win the Town Plate in a field of eight over an extended mile at the July Meeting.

In the year or two before the outbreak of the French Revolution, so warmly welcomed at first by Charles James Fox, the Duke of Orleans was a most unwelcome intruder into the Prince's circle at Newmarket. He had four runners there in the course of the 1788 season and the popularity of the pompous and humourless French Prince can hardly have been enhanced when his colt L'Abbé started at 10-1 in a field of three at the July Meeting and beat the even money chance Pellegrine. The Prince of Wales came near to causing a diplomatic incident when he tipped Orleans into a fountain so that he could have a better look at "de beautiful fish of gold". A few years later the Duke of Orleans plumbed still greater depths by voting for the execution of his cousin, the King of France, and was himself subsequently guillotined by the revolutionaries.

Although the Prince of Wales became the first member of the royal family to own a Derby winner when Sir Thomas beat Lord Grosvenor's Aurelius in 1788 and his horses were continually successful at Newmarket and elsewhere, the high cost of his passion for racing made a sizeable contribution to the enormous debts that he accumulated in early manhood. By 1787 his finances were in such a deplorable state that Captain Plume was his solitary runner that year but as soon as parliament had been prevailed upon to pay off his debts and increase his income he was buying horses again as though money were of no consequence. By 1791 he had no fewer than 40 in training with Frank Neale at Newmarket with Sam Chifney, the outstanding jockey of the era, retained for 200 guineas a year, a fee far in excess of that paid to any other rider.

However earnestly the King and his ministers might have wished that the Prince would be rid of the expense of maintaining the largest racing stable in the country they can hardly have been pleased by the manner in which their desires were gratified. What had been a matter of serious concern to court and government was to develop into a national scandal in the autumn of 1791.

On Thursday 20 October the Prince's horse Escape started at 2-1 on in a field of four over two miles at Newmarket but finished last behind Mr Dawson's Coriander, Lord Grosvenor's Skylark and Lord Clermont's Pipator. Twenty-four hours later Escape, again ridden by Chifney, and Skylark met again in a field of six over four miles. Lord Barrymore's Chanticleer was favourite at 7-4 with Skylark second in the betting at 11-5 and Escape easy to back at 4-1 and 5-1. Reversing the form of the previous day completely, Escape won easily from Chanticleer with Skyscraper third. Almost before Chifney dismounted pandemonium had broken out amongst the noble race-goers on the Heath. Backers of Chanticleer indignantly protested that they had been robbed, pointing out their horse had beaten Skylark fairly and squarely and Skylark had finished well ahead of Escape in his previous race. Allegations that Chifney, whose integrity was more than a little suspect, had stopped Escape on the Thursday to get a long price on the Friday were freely voiced. Some people went as far as to say he

The Jockey Club, Newmarket about 1790, a contemporary cartoon by Rowlandson

had done so on the orders of the Prince. There were even scurrilous rumours about Escape having received a bucket of water from the royal hands before running on the Thursday.

To allay, or substantiate, the misgivings about the running and riding of Escape the Jockey Club instituted an enquiry. The influence of the Club having grown considerably over the past 20 years there were now three stewards deputed to conduct its routine business, Sir Charles Bunbury having been joined in that office by Thomas Panton and Ralph Dutton. Tommy Panton, who had been the unsuccessful rider of the first horse the Prince of Wales had ever run, was not without connections with the court as his sister, the Duchess of Ancaster, was Mistress of the Robes to Queen Charlotte. Their father had been amongst the successors to Tregonwell Frampton in the office of Keeper of the Running Horses at Newmarket. Ralph Dutton, a younger brother of Lord Sherborne, was a tolerant, sociable individual with little taste for controversy. Sir Charles Bunbury took the lead in prosecuting the enquiry and demanded from Chifney an explanation of the difference in the performances of Escape and a declaration of the bets he had made on both races. Chifney explained that Escape was a stuffy horse who was short of work when he ran on the Thursday and a great deal better suited by the four miles of the second race than he was by the two miles of the first. Consequently he had no bet on Escape or any other runner in the first race and 20 guineas on Escape for the second in the expectation that he would be better for running on the Thursday and more effective over the longer distance. Although these factors of fitness and distance would seem to have accounted for the discrepancy in the form of Escape, Sir Charles refused to believe that the horse had been run fairly. He therefore let it be known that "If Chifney were suffered to ride the Prince's horses, no gentleman would start against him".

In later life the Prince was to earn an unenviable reputation for the readiness with which he would desert ministers, mistresses and friends for the convenience of his own interests. In this instance he behaved with great dignity and commendable generosity. Rather than have a scapegoat made of his jockey, he forsook the sport that he loved best of all, sold his huge string of horses and never again set foot in Newmarket or upon the Heath during the remaining 39 years of his life.

He informed Chifney that it was unlikely that he would ever again be an owner of racehorses, adding "But if ever I do, Sam Chifney, you shall train and manage them. You shall have you 200 guineas a year all the same. I cannot give it to you for life, I can only give it for my own. You have been an honest and a good servant to me".

The Escape affair that forced the heir to the throne to retire from The Turf has as many elements of mystery as of drama about it. There is not a shred of evidence of the Prince of Wales being party to malpractice in the running of Escape or any other horse, and the explanation given by Chifney for the discrepancy in the running of Escape in those two races on consecutive days in October 1791 reads convincingly, the difference in the distances, an incontrovertible fact, being the keystone of the defence. Why then, did Bunbury, an honest man with the good name of The Turf very much at heart, make a dead set at the Prince?

Perhaps the likeliest explanation is that Bunbury was absolutely certain that Chifney was a dishonest rider as well as a pernicious influence on The Turf while the Prince of Wales, perhaps wrongly convinced of his jockey's innocence, was determined to defend him in the councils of the Jockey Club. If that had been the case a rift between the two men would have been inevitable. It has also been suggested that Bunbury at the instigation of other leading owners, acted out of jealousy of the success the Prince enjoyed with his horses, or that he was inspired by some long held grudge against the royal family arising from his first wife having once been courted by King George III. There is also a theory, and it is not untenable, that either the King or his ministers were prepared to weather a scandal providing the Prince of Wales was relieved of the cost of keeping horses and obliged to part company with Lord Barrymore, Sir Harry Fetherstonhaugh and the rest of his high betting, hard drinking Newmarket friends.

Whatever Sir Charles Bunbury's motives may have been in the Escape affair, his handling of it had the important effect of establishing the authority of the Jockey Club. By his ultimatum to the Prince of Wales he had made it clear that the Stewards of the Jockey Club were not prepared to tolerate what they considered questionable riding by any jockey no matter how exalted his employer might be.

As an owner Sir Charles Bunbury had three distinctions. Not only were his colours carried by Diomed, who won the first Derby in 1780, but he also owned Eleanor, who first completed the double in The Derby and The Oaks in 1801, and Smolensko, who became the first horse to follow up his success in The 2,000 Guineas by winning The Derby in 1813. Eleanor was a bay filly by Eclipse's grandson Whiskey out of Young Giantess by Diomed. Just before she won The Derby her trainer Cox fell mortally ill. Bending down to hear what he expected to be a last confession the clergyman attending him was surprised to hear the dying man say "Depend on it, that Eleanor is a hell of a mare".

Eleanor went on racing until she was a seven-year-old in 1805. Not a few of the 26 races that she won from 43 appearances in public were at small East Anglian courses like Chelmsford, Ipswich and Huntingdon.

Sir Charles Bunbury, first of the three great Dictators of The Turf, died in 1820.

Nine years before the death of Sir Charles Bunbury another scandal had broken out at Newmarket. In those days all the trainers had their own troughs spread around the Heath at which to water their horses after work, and kept locked beneath padlocked wooden lids when not in use. Richard Prince was warned of a plot to nobble some of his horses, which had already been backed for the Spring Meeting of 1811, by the introduction of poison into his trough.

For a few weeks Prince refrained from watering his horses at the usual place until one particularly sultry day he said to head lad John Kent, "This rumour about the trough being poisoned seems to me to be gammon, as I have heard nothing about if for a long time".

"Nevertheless, if I were you," replied Kent, "I should pull out the plugs at the bottom of the troughs and let the water run off, after which I should fill the troughs again with fresh water brought from the well".

"Oh, that will take too long," said the trainer, "there is no danger, so let the horses drink their fill and I will be responsible for all risks".

Their highly developed sense of smell gave most of the horses instinctive warning of something being the matter with the water so that they snorted in alarm and refused to touch it, but some half dozen did drink a little. The latter were immediately seized with a fit of violent griping and could hardly hobble back to the yard. Dr Bowles, who treated animals, as well as people, was summoned from Cambridge, and while he was awaited Kent administered a strong dose of castor oil to Coelebs and Reveller, who belonged to Sir Sitwell Sitwell. His prompt action saved their lives, but Spaniard, Pirouette and The Dandy all died in agony before the arrival of the doctor, and were buried in the gravel pit near The Severals.

The following day Mr Weatherby offered a reward of 500 guineas for any information leading to the conviction of the culprit. Suspicion fell on Daniel Dawson, an educated man who had been reduced to earning a living as a tout. He lodged at the Five Bells, the little inn across St Mary's Square from Mill Hill, and had been seen loitering around Prince's stables on a number of occasions. Eventually tangible evidence was furnished by his inquisitive landlady Mrs Tillbrook, who discovered a bottle marked poison amongst the effects he kept under his bed. Soon it was discovered that Dawson was in the pay of a couple of bookmakers called Bland, who had laid heavily against some of Prince's charges. He had no intention of killing any of the horses but had obtained enough arsenic rendered soluble in water from a disreputable old chemist called Cecil Bishop to incapacitate them temporarily. Not knowing that Richard Prince had ceased to use his trough after being warned of the plot he supposed that Bishop had underestimated the dose required for his purpose. He thereupon increased it without seeking further advice from Bishop with the result that he caused the poor horses immeasurably greater suffering then he had meant to do. With the renegade chemist Cecil Bishop turning King's Evidence, Dan Dawson was found guilty at Cambridge Assizes and hanged in front of a crowd of 10,000 despite the efforts of Lord Foley, still one of the leading patrons of Prince's stable, to secure a reprieve.

During the last of those many years in which Sir Charles Bunbury was the power in the land at Newmarket, the racing there was to a large extent dominated by two enormously wealthy dukes, and one perennially impoverished royal one.

Frederick, Duke of York, second and favourite son of King George III, proved a rather more competent Commander-in-Chief of the army than the deficiencies in his character have led his critics to suppose. Incorrigible gambling was as much the cause of his insolvency as the cost of keeping his avaricious mistress Mary Anne Clarke. Long after his elder brother the Prince of Wales had turned his back on Newmarket he continued to keep horses in William Cooper's stable there. In 1816 he had about a dozen in training, though, perhaps out of deference to his creditors, they all ran in the name of his racing manager Mr Warwick Lake, including Prince Leopold, who won The Derby. Prince Leopold became so savage that it became necessary to cut him as a four-year-old but he died during the operation. The Duke of York won a second Derby with Moses, who ran in his own name when beating Figaro by a head in 1822. A year or two later the financial situation of the Duke of York had become so desperate that he was obliged to sell his racehorses and on 7 January 1827 he died. In London he is commemorated by the Duke of York's column and in Newmarket by York Buildings, which were not completed until 1832. Now the premises of Messrs Goldings, the tailors, and other businesses, York Buildings are to be found on the right of the High Street as one faces the Clock Tower.

Whereas Sir Charles Bunbury established the authority of the Jockey Club, the fourth Duke of Portland established it as a landowner in the Newmarket area. As well as lending the club the money with which to purchase the freehold of the Coffee Rooms he added to that part of the Heath that he had inherited from his father in 1809 by the purchase of many more acres. In 1820 he began to employ the most modern methods available to improve the land in order to make it still more suitable a terrain on which to race and train thoroughbreds. Large areas were cleared of furze and sown with grass seed, sheep were penned and the intricate road system, that almost made a fretwork pattern across the working grounds, was rationalised. When ruts made by Roman chariots many centuries earlier were uncovered the wheel gauge was found to be precisely the same as that of the coaches being used in 1825. The Duke of Portland personally superintended the work, walking amongst the workmen for hours on end, followed by a groom leading his black cob. The Duke also established the right of the Jockey Club to warn offenders off the Heath. In 1827 he brought an action for trespass against a man called Hawkins at the Cambridge Assizes after the latter had spoken in an unseemly manner to Lord Wharncliffe on the Heath. The jury found that trespass had occurred as ownership of the Heath had been vested in the Jockey Club as tenants of the Dukes of Portland since 1753.

Unlike his maternal grandfather, the celebrated gamester General John Scott, the Duke of Portland had no interest in betting, and only concerned himself with the breeding and racing of the best possible horses, obtaining his most important success with Tiresias in The Derby of 1819. For very many years until advancing age and illness restricted his activities before his death at the age of 85 in 1854 the Duke never missed a meeting at Newmarket. Although he had the Portland Stand constructed at the end of the Beacon Course his favourite method of watching the racing was rumbling around the Heath in a heavy wagon, equipped with every kind of comfort so as to serve him as a mobile stand.

The Duke of Portland was survived by three sons none of whom married. His successor as fifth Duke was a recluse who led a subterranean existence in a large suite of rooms of palatial dimensions he caused to be constructed beneath Welbeck Abbey. The youngest son, Lord Henry Bentinck devoted himself to the hunting field rather than the racecourse, but the middle brother Lord George Bentinck became the second of the three great Dictators of the English Turf. On the death of the troglodyte Duke in 1879 he was succeeded by a young cousin, the sixth Duke of Portland, who earned racing immortality as the owner of St Simon.

As a result of the lease it held from the fourth Duke of Portland and acquisitions made on its own behalf in about 1808, the Jockey Club was in control of almost the entire Heath by 1819. As well as from the Crown, the Club purchased land from a Mr Alix of Swaffham, a Mr Salisbury Dunn and a Mr Pemberton, as well as effecting an exchange of property with Pembroke College, Cambridge. Thus Sir Charles Bunbury lived just long enough to see the institution that he had moulded so much upon his own personality acquire ownership of the land over which it raced.

The third of the Dukes with whom Sir Charles Bunbury raced during the closing years of his long life was Augustus Henry Fitzroy, Duke of Grafton, whose great-grandfather, the first Duke was the son of King Charles II and Barbara Villiers, Duchess of Cleveland. His rank and wealth rather than any political ability or dedication to the public service were responsible for the third Duke being Prime Minister from 1766 to 1770. As head of the government he proved almost entirely ineffective. While easily bored by details of policy making and administration he rarely concealed his preference of Newmarket to Westminster. When the cabinet was to assemble for dinner at Lord Shelburne's London house he sent a message to say that he could not be in town until late in the evening as he was matching a horse at Newmarket in the morning. He then sent a second message announcing that he would not be in London until the following evening, with the result that the cabinet wasted a whole day in which it was unable to transact any business because of the absence of the Prime Minister at Newmarket.

Harshest of all the critics of the Duke of Grafton was the anonymous political comentator Junius. "The character of the reputed ancestors of some men has made it possible for their descendants to be vicious in the extreme, without being degenerate", wrote Junius. "Those of Your Grace, for instance, left no distressing examples of virtue even to their legitimate posterity, and you may look back in pleasure to an illustrious pedigree in which heraldry has not left a single good quality upon record to insult or upbraid you."

The private life of the Duke was hardly any more edifying than his public. Even robust Georgian England was scandalised by his taking

Lord George Bentinck (1802-1848), the second of the three Great Dictators of the Turf

his lovely mistress Nancy Parsons to the races at Newmarket and to the theatre.

Very early in his association with Newmarket the Duke of Grafton made one of the most celebrated matches ever staged on the Heath. For £1,000 a side he ran his horse Antinous against the Duke of Cumberland's Herod over the Beacon Course in 1764. So heavy was the betting that something like £100,000 is reputed to have been dependent upon the outcome and after a desperate race the verdict of a short neck was awarded to Herod, whose male line is maintained by Blakeney and Julio Mariner.

The year before he matched Antinous against Herod, the Duke of Grafton founded the great stud at his Norfolk home, Euston Hall, by the purchase of the seven-year-old mare Julia, whose sire Blank was by the Darley Arabian. She was the dam of Promise, by Snap, whose daughter Prunella, by Highflyer, was to become one of the most influential broodmares of all time. As well as Pope, who won the Duke his second Derby in 1809, and Pelisse, who won The Oaks for him in 1804, she bred Penelope, by Trumpator, and eight other good winners. Among the offspring of Penelope was Whalebone, who became the Duke's third Derby winner in 1810, and Whisker, who was to provide the fourth Duke with his only success in the race in 1815. The first of the three Derbies won by the third Duke had been with Tyrant in 1802.

In order to be able to drive the 18 miles from Euston Hall to Newmarket over grass the third Duke of Grafton gave orders for the plantation of an avenue through which his carriage could pass. Unfortunately he forgot that he did not own the land over which the last six miles should have run, so that this arboreal ornament to the East Anglian countryside came to an abrupt end after twelve miles.

As if to atone for transgressions against the Church and disservice to the State in early life, the Duke took to writing religious tracts and embraced Unitarianism in late middle age. While thus engrossed in matters theological he left the management of his horses to his sons the Earl of Euston, his heir, and the Reverend Lord Henry Fitzroy. The third Duke of Grafton died at the age of 76 in 1811, two years after the institution of The 2,000 Guineas and three before The 1,000 Guineas was run for the first time.

The fourth Duke of Grafton had many more claims to being a gentleman than ever his father had done and just as many to being a sportsman. Before succumbing to illness somewhat early in life he rode to hounds as frequently and with the same enthusiasm as he attended race meetings. Having taken a heavy fall into a ditch while out hunting one day a curate jumped over him shouting, "Lie still, your grace, and I'll clear you". To onlookers horrified at the clergyman having failed to come to the assistance of so great a personage the Duke said, quite coolly, "That young man shall have the first good living that falls to my disposal. Had he stopped to take care of me, I would never have patronised him".

Having inherited the Euston Hall Stud that had been so assiduously built up over a period of nearly half a century, the Duke had far greater opportunities to exploit its produce in the classics than had his father, by reason of the inauguration of The 2,000 and The 1,000 Guineas at about the same time as he came into the title. For a number of years his horses enjoyed an unprecedented rate of success in the Newmarket classics. Between 1820 and 1827 they won The 2,000 Guineas five times and between 1819 and 1827 The 1,000 Guineas no fewer than eight times. As well as winning The Derby with Prunella's son Whisker he owned six winners of The Oaks.

Unlike the majority of owners, before or since, the Duke was never desperate to obtain the services of the fashionable jockeys. He used to say "Let us find the horse, then we'll talk about the jockey". Acting entirely on his own initiative he engaged the little known country jockey John Barham Day to ride Dervise in The 2,000 and Problem in The 1,000 Guineas in 1826 when his judgement was vindicated by Day bringing off the double.

No small part of the credit for the achievements of the third and fourth Dukes of Grafton as owners and breeders belongs to their trainer Robert Robson, who ran the most successful stable at Newmarket during the first quarter of the nineteenth century. Robson commenced his career as private trainer to Sir Ferdinand Poole at Lewes in Sussex and came to Newmarket soon after winning the Derby of 1793 with Waxy, whom the third Duke purchased to stand as a stallion at Euston Hall.

Robson was very much less hard on his horses than any other trainer of his time, and had serious doubts about the desirability of sweating horses in heavy rugs and hoods in gallops of two miles or more. Moreover he was careful never to ask too much of his potential classic horses during their first season in training.

As well as winning The Derby with Waxy, and four times for the Dukes of Grafton, he was successful with Azor in 1817 and for a seventh time with Emilius in 1823. None of those colts ran as a two-year-old and Emilius never did a sweat before going to Epsom.

Among the jockeys who served their apprenticeship with Robson was James Robinson, who won the first of his six Derbies on Azor. Right to the end of his long career Robinson rated Robson far superior to any trainer he had ever known. On the retirement of Robert Robson at the age of 63 in 1828 the members of the Jockey Club subscribed to a piece of plate that was presented to him as a testimonial to his integrity and professional ability. He was still living at Newmarket when he died ten years later.

William Chifney, son of the Prince Regent's jockey Sam Chifney the elder, shared none of Robert Robson's misgivings about subjecting horses to too much exercise at home. A heavy gambler and a brilliant judge of a horse, he would give his charges any number of sweats to remove the last ounce of surplus flesh and bring them to maximum fitness, and if the legs or the temper of a horse did not stand up to his almost Draconian routine he reckoned he was better off without the animal in his yard.

Jem Robinson (1793-1865)

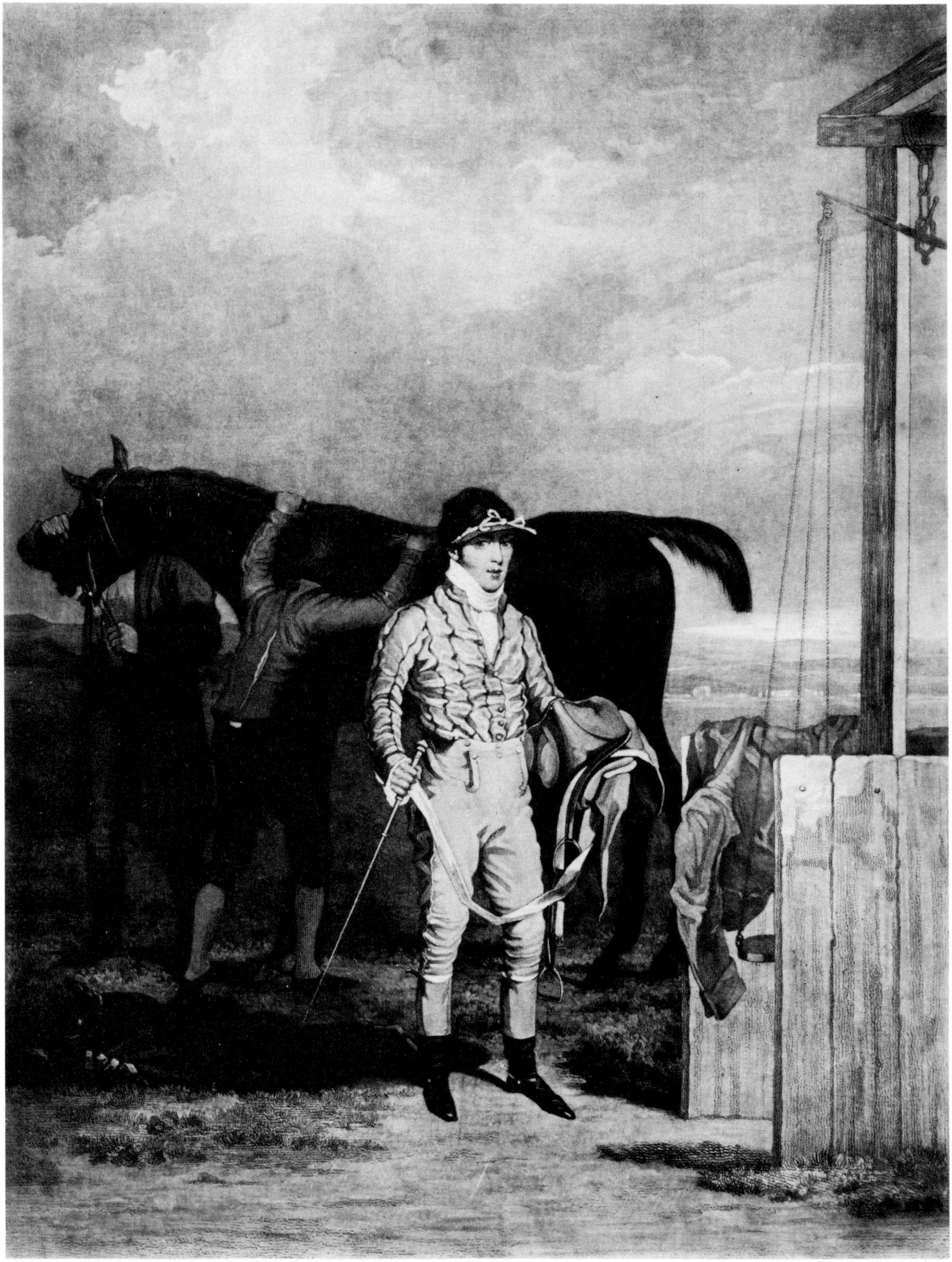

Sam Chifney the younger (1786-1854)

Whatever other failings the older Chifney may have had, he was a dutiful father, who gave his two sons as good a start in life as possible by teaching them all that he could about the riding and training of thoroughbreds. That devotion was reciprocated to the full. Thus although he was only seven years of age at the time of the Escape affair Bill Chifney vowed the day would come when he would thrash the Prince's racing manager Colonel Leigh for calling his father a cheat. Eleven years later he set upon the Colonel outside the Rooms at Newmarket with such violence that he must have killed the older man had he not been pulled off by onlookers. Subsequently charged with assault, Bill Chifney was sent to prison for six months. Considering himself such an expert at picking oakum, on his release he offered to make doormats against anyone in Newmarket for a pony (£25). In a nice gesture of reconciliation he shook hands with Colonel Leigh and they remained friends until the latter's death in 1850.

Being too tall to ride, Bill Chifney became a trainer with his brother Sam, two years his junior, as his stable jockey. Their first important success came when they won The Derby of 1818 with Sam, a chestnut colt by Scud, for Mr Thomas Thornhill, the corpulent, good-humoured squire of Riddlesworth in Norfolk. Two years later they won him a second Derby with Sailor, another chestnut son of Scud.

Season after season in the 1820s the Chifney brothers brought off a series of betting coups for Squire Thornhill, Lord Darlington, (later first Duke of Cleveland) and their other wealthy patrons. As a consequence of their enormously successful betting they could well afford to live in the grand style they affected, driving to the races in fine carriages and entertaining sumptuously. As Robert Robson came to the close of his long career it was Bill Chifney who was 'king' of Newmarket. Yet despite the splendour with which he surrounded himself, Bill Chifney always had the air of being a clergyman or a scholar, rather than a leading light of those high living days in which King George IV set the fashion. Tall, and solemn of expression, he was always soberly, if expensively dressed.

As a mark of their appreciation the Duke of Cleveland and other owners built Sam Chifney a fine neo-classical house, facing onto what is now Old Station Road. As a compliment to his principal employer Sam gave the name of Cleveland House to his impressive new residence, which was the Newmarket home of the late Lord Rosebery and is now that of his widow.

Beside herself with jealousy, Bill Chifney's wife Mary, the daughter of Vauxhall Clarke, a professional backer, demanded a house in which not a single old brick was used. To assuage her anger her husband built Warren House, complete with stable yard, next door to Cleveland House, on a site that has remained empty since its demolition some years ago.

Bill Chifney's judgement of the potentiality of a horse was rarely better exemplified than at the Epsom meeting of 1825. On the second day he claimed General Grosvenor's Wings after Frank Buckle junior had ridden her to win a selling race for Robson's stable. On the General asking if he could have her back as he wanted her to make the pace for his other filly The Brownie whom Sam Chifney was to ride in The Oaks two days later, Bill replied that he could on the condition that his brother took the mount on her and not The Brownie in The Oaks. The General agreed and Sam won the classic on a filly that had been claimed out of a seller 48 hours earlier.

The Chifney brothers reached the high water mark of their success when Priam, a beautifully moulded bay by Emilius, won The Derby in 1830. Priam was owned as well as trained by Bill, but as Sam could not ride because he was claimed for the Duke of Cleveland's runner, Sam Day was engaged. Both brothers backed Priam as though defeat were quite out of the question and were reckoned to have cleared something in the region £18,000 over the race.

Although racing was fast emerging as a highly organised sport by the time that Priam won The Derby for the Chifneys and their father's old patron King George IV died in 1830, the old-fashioned bets against time and on other feats of endurance were still settled on the Heath every now and again. It was at the Houghton Meeting of 1831 that the peppery little Yorkshire squire George Osbaldeston bet Colonel Charettie, who had charged with the Life Guards at Waterloo, £1,000 that he could ride 200 miles in less than ten hours using as many of his hacks and hunters, or any other horses as he liked. The wager was to be settled on the Round Course, plus the distance from the Devil's Dyke to the stand to make a lap of four miles, on 5 November. The previous evening the former prize fighter John Gully, one of the most fearless of the betting men, told Squire Osbaldeston that he had been offered 10-1 against the 200 miles being completed inside nine hours. On Osbaldeston telling him to take the odds Gully undertook to advance their mutual interest by lending him one or two of his racehorses.

Squire George Osbaldeston (1787-1866) – winner of the most famous of all the matches against time on Newmarket Heath

Starting his ride at 7 o'clock in the morning of a stormy, overcast day, the Squire won his bet by taking eight hours 42 minutes to cover the 200 miles on 29 horses. The fastest of his mounts was Gully's thoroughbred Tranby, who had run against Priam at the Craven Meeting. He was the only one of the 29 horses that the Squire rode four times that morning, completing the second of his laps in eight minutes flat. On the other hand Ikey Solomons took twelve minutes to do the four miles after nearly losing Osbaldeston the match. While going a great gallop he stumbled, shot his rider over his head and bolted. Fortunately the resourceful Osbaldeston had allowed for this contingency by stationing a couple of catchers in strategic positions with the result that he was able to remount after they had performed their offices.

Having won his bet Squire Osbaldeston rode back to the Rutland Arms in triumph, escorted by Bill and Sam Chifney and a host of other riders. On arrival at the inn he had a quick bath, was rubbed down with oils and within half an hour had joined Lord Portarlington, John Gully and seven or eight other friends for dinner.

Work on the construction of the Rutland Arms had commenced in

1815, the year of Waterloo. The builder was a native of Newmarket by the name of Kent, whose son was at one time head lad to Richard Prince as mentioned in connection with the Dan Dawson affair, and whose grandson John Kent won the Derby with Surplice and other important races during the many years he trained at Goodwood. The Rutland stands on the site of an earlier inn called the Ram, a name evocative of seventeenth century eccentricity. For reasons of his own it was the pleasure of Lord Orford to have his carriage drawn by stags instead of horses. One day he was driving to Newmarket when hounds picked up the scent of the stags, and the terrified coachman reached the safety of the nearest inn just in time for the ostlers to slam the courtyard doors on a pack in full cry. To commemorate the incident the name of the establishment was changed to The Ram, the word that has the meaning of a strong scent as well as that of a male sheep.

Lord Orford was the owner of Houghton Hall in Norfolk. It was there that he used to entertain some of the most influential members of the racing fraternity for the last of the season's Newmarket meetings, hence it becoming known as the Houghton Meeting.

When the Chifney brothers led that jubilant guard of honour that brought Squire Osbaldeston back to the Rutland Arms on the final day of the Houghton Meeting of 1831 Bill was 47 years of age and Sam 45. The money that they had won over Priam and their other horses was all but spent and funds were only infrequently being replenished. Maintaining their two fine houses on the road out to Ashley and meeting all their other expenses was becoming increasingly harder as the luck continued to run against them and coup after coup went amiss. In a desperate attempt to mend their fortunes they piled bets on the Duke of Cleveland's Shilelagh for The Derby of 1834. Wanting to get still more on the tall, leggy bay they sent out another colt of the same colour and conformation, with blistered legs and heavy bandages, to work with Shilelagh's regular companions two days before the race. Rumour of the Chifney Derby horse being completely wrong spread as fast as it was intended to do, the price went out and the money went on. Luck was still against them though. The considerable amount of ground that Shilelagh made up over the last furlong or so was not enough to enable him to get on terms with the favourite Plenipotentiary who beat him into second place by two lengths.

Two years later Newmarket had a visitation of unseasonably severe weather as autumn was drawing to its close. On the morning of 29 October 1836, the Saturday before the opening of the Houghton Meeting, there was a heavy fall of snow that lay over the week-end. Although the Criterion Course was cleared on Monday several of the races that should have been run that day had to be postponed, and early on Tuesday morning more than 100 men and a large number of stable lads began clearing a course of sufficient width to permit racing from the Ditch to the Turn of the Lands.

Not long after Bill Chifney had lost so heavily over Shilelagh over The Derby of 1834 he was obliged to close his stable and move to

Priam, winner of the Derby of 1830

London, where he lived in much reduced circumstances. Warren House, of which he and his wife had been so inordinately proud, he sold to John F. Clark, a young architect. Clark's father had been Jockey Club judge since 1806 and was also landlord of The Greyhound, the old coaching inn that stood on the site of the Cabaret Club in the High Street that used to be the Doric Cinema. In 1852 John Clark succeeded his father as judge of the racing at Newmarket and in his capacity of architect was responsible for the erection of Green Lodge as well as other buildings of importance in the town. When he retired in 1889 he lived at Fairstead House, which, like Green Lodge, faces The Severals. He was followed as judge by his son-in-law Charles Edward Robinson, who officiated until 1923. He in turn was succeeded by his nephew C. A. Robinson, who held the post for five years. Thus members of the same family gave the verdicts on the finishes of races at Newmarket for almost a century and a quarter between 1806 and 1928 when Mr Malcolm Hancock received the appointment.

It was John F. Clark who persuaded the Jockey Club to erect the artificial bank that runs parallel to the Devil's Dyke for four furlongs, thus forming the gallop Between the Ditches. The purpose of this construction was to foil the touts but proved an utter failure as Mr Clark had overlooked the fact that a right of way runs along the top of the Devil's Dyke, and the men of observation readily availed themselves of the facilities it offered.

Bill Chifney never recaptured any vestige of the prosperity that he had known at Newmarket. Whenever he could afford the third class railway fare he would return to the town where he had lived in much the same style as the peers and other wealthy men for whom he had trained. There, he was to be seen walking across the Heath, in the midst of Queen Victoria's reign, a relic of the days of the Regency with his memory stretching back to the Escape affair the previous century. Curious eyes stared at the tall old man in his well-worn blue coat and broad-brimmed hat held down by a coloured bandanna, still retaining dignity in the face of adversity.

Eventually William Chifney, who had trained Sam, Sailor and the the beautiful Priam to win The Derby, died in Pancras Square, just off London's St Pancras Road, at the age of 78 on 14 October 1862. Of his two sons, one, also William, became an army officer. The other had a short career as a jockey and married a daughter of Lord Jersey's trainer William Edwards.

At the same time as success had ebbed away from the Chifney stable, Newmarket began to go out of fashion as a training centre. To a large extent this was a matter of cause and effect. While he was undoubtedly a superb trainer, Bill Chifney must necessarily have broken down many horses by the severity with which he sweated them, thereby creating the erroneous impression that the ground on which he worked them was unsuitable for that purpose. Consequently owners began to send their strings to Lambourn, Findon and elsewhere on the Downs of Berkshire, Wiltshire and Sussex to be trained, complaining that the going at Newmarket became far too firm in summer.

For a time even the racing at Newmarket went out of vogue. As early as the year before the Chifney brothers had their last unavailing plunge on Shilelagh a correspondent wrote in *The New Sporting Magazine* "...things at Newmarket are come to a pretty pass, when with 500 horses in training they can only muster six races for one meeting, miss an entire day in the next, and dock the third of its 'fair proportions' by omitting the Saturday altogether! They were in fact a practical definition of the three degrees, the First October being dull, the second very dull, and the third extremely so".

One of the few influential owners to continue to have his horses trained at Newmarket in those years when it was so much out of fashion was Brownlow Cecil, second Marquess of Exeter, whose magnificient home, Burghley House, on the outskirts of the Lincolnshire town of Stamford, was within convenient travelling distance from the Heath. The Marquesses of Exeter are the senior branch of the Cecil family, being descended from the son of the first marriage of Queen Elizabeth I's great minister Lord Burghley, whereas their cousins, the Earls and Marquesses of Salisbury, of whom the second Earl owned the winner of the first recorded match at Newmarket, descend from the son of the second marriage of the statesman.

A small man, usually dressed in black, the Marquess of Exeter entertained no false modesty with regard to his position in society. Full of pride in his ancestry and vast possessions he would walk the length of Newmarket High Street without deigning to acknowledge any of the many greetings that he received. Exeter House, in which his horses were trained by Harlock, had been known as Foley House in the days when Lord Foley had been its principal patron. On the instructions of Lord Exeter the first covered ride ever built for racehorses was constructed on a paddock adjoining the stable. That novel amenity, which has become so commonplace, gave his early season runners a big advantage on the score of fitness, especially if the latter part of the winter had been particularly harsh, as they would have been able to canter while horses in other stables were confined to light work on straw beds. Although progressive in that respect Lord Exeter was by no means an easy man for whom to train as he did his horses no good by his insisting that any over whom he had lost money should be tried the day after running in order to ascertain whether earlier trials had been correct.

Lord Exeter had inherited the title at the age of nine and commenced racing on coming of age in 1816. He won his first classic when Jem Robinson rode Enamel to beat Mr Wyndham's unnamed bay colt in The 2,000 Guineas in 1825. He also owned three subsequent winners of that race, the last of which was Stockwell, who was to consolidate his reputation in the St Leger in 1852. In addition he won The 1,000 Guineas with Galata in 1832 and The Oaks on three occasions.

Lord Exeter was obliged to sell his horses to Mr Simpson, a banker of Diss, Norfolk, in 1855 to pay the price of his own stubbornness and lack of vision. A few years earlier he had refused to allow the Great Northern Railway to cut across a corner of his Burghley estate. As a result Stamford became isolated and the trade of its inhabitants, most of whom were his tenants, was badly hit. To rectify the situation Lord Exeter reluctantly constructed a twelve-mile spur to connect Stamford with the main line at Essendon at the cost of £75,000.

While the standard of racing at Newmarket deteriorated in those years that followed the heyday of the Chifneys, much of the excitement in the town emanated from the gambling hell run by William Crockford, the former fishmonger. Crockford's house, which had once belonged to Thomas Panton, stood on the corner of the High Street and Old Station Road, while his gaming rooms were at Rothesay House, a few doors up from the White Hart in the middle of the High Street.

He built Crockford's farm, which is still to be found near the Links, and also owned Park Lodge with its surrounding 45 acres including Park Paddocks, where Messrs Tattersalls built their impressive modern sale ring in 1965 and extended the complex surrounding it in 1980. In Crockford's day the stabling at Park Lodge consisted of a single range facing the house, the two wings of boxes that give the establishment a rectangular aspect being added some years afterwards. 'Old Crocky' died on 24 May 1844, "dead of a Derby favourite", so they said. His colt Ratan, who started second favourite for The Derby two days earlier, had been nobbled on the eve of the race and then pulled by Sam Rogers for good measure.

In the decade or so that followed the death of Crockford, racing at Newmarket carried on in an almost desultory way. Races still finished at the various winning posts situated along the Rowley Mile and July Courses, making mobility of prime importance to bookmakers and backers alike. The bookmakers drove their carriages from post to post, formed them into a ring for the transaction of business and then used their roofs as grandstands from which to bet in running. For their part, most racegoers were mounted on hacks in order to follow the peregrination of the bookmakers while their womenfolk were ensconced in carriages, parked at strategic points around the Heath, that afforded a great deal more comfort than the small, rudimentary stands. Racing having commenced in the morning, as was the custom in the middle of the last century, the men of title, wealth and fashion would join the women for lunch in the carriages where the menu would consist of such dishes as salmon cutlets, curried prawns, *chaud-froid* of quails, lobster cutlets, galantine of chicken and plovers' eggs in aspic.

Bookmakers, the grooms in charge of the hacks and carriages, stablelads, racecourse workers and the smaller backers had to make do with the primitive catering offered by Jarvis's booth, which was situated near the Birdcage. This was run by a member of the well-known training family and did a brisk trade in 'thumbers', thick cheese sandwiches held between thumb-size pieces of beef, pork or mutton, which the customer would hack off the joint with his own clasp knife. Those who did not fancy 'thumbers' used to bring their own food, in most cases thick steak sandwiches, which were long regarded as traditional racecourse fare.

While excitement on the Rowley Mile and the July Course rarely reached a particularly high pitch during those middle years of the last century, activity on the training grounds was very much less than it had been while the likes of Robert Robson, James Edwards and Richard Prince had worked their big strings on the Heath back in the Regency. For season after season stableyards stood empty and neglected as falling roofs left boxes open to the skies and doors swung off their hinges.

Between 1788 and 1832 all but three of the Derby winners had been trained at Newmarket. Between 1833 and 1862 only three came from the town.

4 The Great Races of the Heath

No less an authority than Sir Gordon Richards has acclaimed the courses at Newmarket as the best and fairest in the world.

There never was a jockey who could proffer a remotely valid excuse for being beaten on either the Rowley Mile or the July Course. Both afford all the room for manoeuvre that any rider could ever need while providing an absolutely fair and true test of a horse of any conformation whatever.

The Rowley Mile Course, upon which the Spring and Autumn Meetings are held, is in fact, a straight mile and a quarter. For a mile it rolls along almost absolutely level, then at a little clump of bushes on the right, begins the furlong downhill run to the dip, that gradient on which Charlie Smirke stole a memorable race for The 2,000 Guineas in 1950 by using the speed of the non-staying Palestine to set up a lead the luckless Prince Simon could not quite cut back. Leaving the dip, the horses climb the last furlong, with the stands on the left, to the winning post, an ascent that so often provides the final test of stamina as it did when Cider with Rosie fought like a cat to claw away at the lead of The Admiral and beat him in the Cesarewitch of 1972.

Races of more than a mile and a quarter at the Spring and Autumn Meetings start behind the Devil's Dyke way over to the half-right of the stands. Passing the Running Gap, through which it is briefly visible, the field races in a dead straight line until making the gentle turn to the right onto the Rowley Mile just behind the mile-and-quarter starting post. That same part of the course behind the Devil's Dyke is used at the meetings in the summer, but shortly before reaching the junction with the Rowley Mile the runners make a graduated right-hand turn to race the final mile straight up to the stands of the July Course, where the horses walk round in the cool of a belt of trees before being led into the parade ring. The atmosphere on the July Course, which attracts holidaymakers from far afield, is always more relaxed than it is in that of the utter professionalism on the Rowley Mile.

Almost as though they are at a garden party racegoers on the July Course wander amongst the vivid floral decoration and the thatched bars that surround the stands, or sip drinks in the welcome shade of the trees nearest those bars.

But when Newmarket's classics, The 2,000 Guineas and The 1,000 Guineas are run on the other side of the Heath in late April or early May the weather is by no means certain to be as kind as it generally is on the July Course. Considering that Newmarket is, and always has been the headquarters of British racing it is surprising that its classic

The start of The Rowley Mile in the days of the barrier

races were the last to be instituted. The St Leger, the oldest of the five, was founded in 1776, The Oaks in 1779 and The Derby in 1780 but The 2,000 Guineas was not run for the first time until 1809 and its sister race The 1,000 Guineas not until 1814. Thus came about the completion of a series of championship races for three-year-olds that are extended in distance as the season progresses. The 2,000 Guineas and The 1,000 Guineas, for fillies only, are both run over a mile, the two Epsom classics, The Derby and The Oaks, the latter also confined to fillies, over a mile and a half a month later, and finally The St Leger is run over a mile and three quarters at Doncaster in early September. The Park Hill Stakes is the fillies' equivalent of The St Leger but has never enjoyed classic status.

The first winner of The 2,000 Guineas was a chestnut colt called Wizard ridden by Billy Clift in the colours of Mr Christopher Wilson of Oxton Hall near Tadcaster. Mr Wilson was one of the most popular racing men of the day and such was the faith in his integrity that his services as an arbitrator were in constant demand. He had hardly missed any of the principal meetings at Newmarket, or elsewhere, for sixty years before he died at the age of 78 at Christies on the morning of Derby Day 1842.

The fourth Duke of Grafton dominated The 2,000 Guineas in the 1820s winning with Pindarrie in 1820, Reginald in 1821, Pastille, the first filly to be successful in the race, in 1823, Dervise in 1826 and Turcoman in 1827. The following decade pre-eminence in the race belonged to the fifth Earl of Jersey, who won with Riddlesworth in

1831, Glencoe in 1834, Ibrahim in 1835, Bay Middleton in 1836 and Achmet in 1837.

Bay Middleton, who also won The Derby, was one of the best of the early winners of The 2,000 Guineas, and another was Lord Exeter's Stockwell, though he only beat the favourite Homebrewed by half a length in 1852. A fine, strong chestnut trained by Harlock at Exeter House, Newmarket, Stockwell completed the classic double in the St Leger in the autumn and on being retired to stud became known as 'The Emperor of Stallions', siring the Derby winners Blair Athol, Lord Lyon and Doncaster, as well as a host of other good horses.

The year after Stockwell had won, West Australian became the first winner of the Triple Crown by supplementing his success in The 2,000 Guineas with those he obtained in The Derby and The St Leger. He was a bay, trained for Mr John Bowes by John Scott in the Whitewall stable at Malton, Yorkshire.

When Wizard won the first running of The 2,000 Guineas in 1809 there were eight runners. Five years later, when Mr Wyndham's Olive was the winner in 1814, 14 went to the post and that remained the record for almost half a century until West Australian's son The Wizard, bearing almost the same name as the first winner, was suc-

Bay Middleton

cessful in a field of 15 in 1860. The two factors that contributed to the small fields in the early history of The 2,000 Guineas were the manner in which wealthy owners like the Duke of Grafton and Lord Jersey were able to dominate the big races and the relatively few horses there were in training during the first half of the last century.

Since The 2,000 Guineas began to attract bigger fields following the success of The Wizard it has been won by a great many horses who were to consolidate their reputations as real champions. Among those of recent times have been the late Mr J. A. Dewar's Tudor Minstrel, trained by Fred Darling at Beckhampton in 1947, Crepello, Royal Palace and the Irish-trained Sir Ivor.

Still more recently Nijinsky, trained like Sir Ivor, by M. V. O'Brien in Ireland, went on to become, at the time of writing, the 16th and last winner of the Triple Crown in 1970. Brigadier Gerard used his brilliance to beat the subsequent Derby winner Mill Reef in 1971, Wollow won in 1976 and To-Agori-Mou triumphed for Guy Harwood's Sussex stable in 1981.

Having owned Champion, who had become the first horse to win both The Derby and The St Leger in 1800, and Wizard, first winner of The 2,000 Guineas, the Yorkshire sportsman Christopher Wilson brought off a remarkable treble when he won the first race for The 1,000 Guineas with Charlotte, ridden by Billy Clift, in 1814. In the early years of its existence fields for The 1,000 Guineas were even smaller than those for The 2,000 Guineas. There was actually a walkover in 1825, the fortunate filly being Tontine, whose owner, the fourth Duke of Grafton, won the race eight times in nine years between 1819 and 1827. Not until Sagitta was successful in a field of 13 in 1860 did more than a dozen runners go to the post after the field had only reached double figures in five of the 46 previous years.

Two of the most notable of the early winners of The 1,000 Guineas were Lord George Bentinck's Crucifix, ridden by John Barham Day and trained by him at Stockbridge in Hampshire, and Virago. The 1840 winner Crucifix, who started at 10-1 on in a field of four, had also won The 2,000 Guineas and went on to win The Oaks. On being retired from racing she exerted considerable influence as a broodmare, becoming the tail-female ancestress of the 1929 Cambridgeshire winner Double Life. The latter was to be the foundation mare of the late Lady Zia Wernher's Someries Stud, one of the most consistently successful breeding establishments in the Newmarket area.

Virago was also trained by John Barham Day, though after he had left Danebury to take over the private stable of Henry Padwick at Findon in Sussex. Padwick, the most extortionate moneylender of the era, ran Virago under the *nom-de-course* of 'Mr Howard'. A rich, dark chestnut combining power and elegance, Virago was endowed with remarkable vitality. She had already been heavily raced in the spring of 1854 before beating her only two rivals in The 1,000 Guineas, having completed the double in the City and Suburban and the Great Metropolitan at Epsom on the same day and then gone up to York to win two more races.

Great fillies to win The 1,000 Guineas later in the last century included Formosa in 1868, Hannah in 1871, Apology in 1874 and La Flèche in 1892, all of whom went on to complete the fillies' Triple Crown in The Oaks and the St Leger. Yet another notable winner of The 1,000 Guineas was Lord Lonsdale's Pilgrimage, who had initiated the Newmarket classic double in The 2,000 Guineas in 1878.

At the age of 19 Pilgrimage was sold for a mere 160 guineas while carrying the future Derby winner Jeddah. Another of her sons was Loved One, sire of Gondolette.

Both the great fillies of the early years of this century, when the English jockeys were pulling up their stirrup leathers in imitation of the Americans, were successful in The 1,000 Guineas. Sceptre owned and trained by the professional gambler Bob Sievier, won in 1902 and then came the turn of Pretty Polly two years later.

Sievier had been determined to buy Sceptre when Tattersalls sold the recently deceased Duke of Westminster's yearlings at Newmarket in July 1900. As the firm had none of the complex of buildings they have in Park Paddocks today, old Somerville Tattersall rented an office in the Rutland Arms. Sievier's problem was that he doubted whether Tattersall would accept his bids as he had no account with

Captain Boyd-Rochfort's String in April 1955. Meld brings up the rear

the firm. Accordingly he went to the Rutland after the banks had closed on the day before the sale and deposited £20,000 in cash with a highly embarrassed auctioneer who was as nervous by disposition as he was apt to be pompous in manner. As it happened Sievier had no need to spend the whole sum as Sceptre was knocked down to him for 10,000 guineas and a much relieved Somerville Tattersall repaid the balance of his deposit. As well as bringing off the double in The 1,000 Guineas and The 2,000 Guineas, Sceptre won The Oaks and The St Leger.

Two recent winners of The 1,000 Guineas to earn comparison with Sceptre and Pretty Polly have been Crucifix's descendant Meld, who landed the fillies' Triple Crown in 1955 and the grey Petite Etoile, who was to prove herself superior to the colts of her generation.

In the same way that the classics are the principal features of racing at Newmarket in the spring, two handicaps, the Cambridgeshire and the Cesarewitch are the races that capture the public imagination and engender the heaviest betting in the autumn. The Cambridgeshire is run over the straight nine furlongs at the October Meeting as September merges into October and the Cesarewitch one of the races that starts behind the Devil's Dyke away across the Heath over twice that distance at the Houghton Meeting a fortnight later.

Up to, and including 1968 the Cesarewitch was run first, and until 1961 the Houghton Meeting was held in late October, so a touch of winter was already coming to the Heath and the days were drawing in by the time that the Cambridgeshire was run. That the county of Cambridgeshire should give its name to a race run on the outskirts of a town with a Suffolk postal address is accounted for by Newmarket being situated on a spur of the west of Suffolk almost entirely surrounded by the Cambridgeshire countryside, much of the town, in fact, actually being in the latter county.

The Cambridgeshire was run for the first time on Monday 28 October 1839. Twelve of the 55 entries ran and Mr Ramsay's four-year-old brown colt Lanercost was the winner. Lanercost was trained by Tom Dawson at Middleham and ridden by Billy Noble, who lived to be a very old man in the closing years of the century.

It was not long before the Cambridgeshire acquired an enormous popularity among owners. The size of the field grew rapidly and it came to be regarded as the best betting race of the end of the season. When Prior of St Margaret, owned by Mr Nun, won in 1846 there were 23 runners and the following season The Widow, a 30-1 chance, won in a field of 37. In Prior of St Margaret's year the fog on the Heath was so dense that men were stationed at intervals along the Cambridgeshire course to guide the jockeys. Later in the day, 26 October, the course was marked out by tan and sawdust.

Two factors gave the Cambridgeshire of the nineteenth century a very different character to the race we know today. The first was that the lack of opportunities to exploit high class horses made the Cambridgeshire one of the relatively few attractive engagements for them.

Thus La Flèche was to win the Cambridgeshire in 1892 after having won The 1,000 Guineas, The Oaks and The St Leger earlier in the season, while Hannah, who won the same three classics in 1871, was unplaced in the Cambridgeshire in both 1872 and the following year and her stablemate Favonius was unplaced in the Cambridgeshire in 1871, the year that he won The Derby. Another Derby winner to fail in the Cambridgeshire was Gladiateur. He started 13-2 favourite in 1865 and finished unplaced to Mr Richard Sutton's filly Gardevisure, to whom he was giving no less than 52 lb, after the start had been delayed half an hour by the disobedience of certain jockeys. The starter reported the culprits to the stewards who suspended Sammy Kenyon Barker and Jarvis until 12 November and taking a still poorer view of the behaviour of Charlie Maidment and Ward stood them down until 2 April of the following year.

The second difference between the Cambridgeshire of the nineteenth century and today's race is accounted for by many of the horses of that period being so very much more versatile than their specialist descendants. Mr Frederick Gretton's great horse Isonomy for instance, won the Cambridgeshire as a three-year-old for John Porter's Kingsclere, Hampshire, stable in 1878 before being successful in the Ascot Gold Cup over more than twice the distance, in each of the two following seasons.

Lester Piggott on Petite Etoile

Stayers running in the Cambridgeshire gave rise to the possibility of the double in that event and the Cesarewitch being completed, and Rosebery, in 1876, Foxhall in 1881 and Plaisanterie in 1885 did win both races.

Rosebery was owned by the brothers James and Sidney Smith, who were course bookmakers in a small way. Ridden by Fred Archer he went to the post for the Cesarewitch, an apparently moderate maiden four-year-old, without even a previous race that season and won in a canter by four lengths. As Archer was claimed for Skylark in the Cambridgeshire it was in the hands of Harry Constable that Rosebery defied a 14 lb penalty by beating Sir John Astley's Hopbloom by a neck. The brothers Smith won something like a quarter of a million pounds over the double.

Unlike his compatriot Iroquois, the American horse Foxhall had not been entered for the classics so he had to make the best of the opportunities offered by the handicaps. He was trained at Woodyates in Wiltshire by William Day, son of John Barham Day, for the American financier James R. Keene and also won the Grand Prix de Paris.

Among the outstanding handicappers to win the Cambridgeshire towards the end of the last century was Mr H. T. 'Buck' Barclay's Bendigo, trained by Charlie Jousiffe in the Seven Barrows stable at Lambourn. He carried only 6 st 10 lb when winning as a three-year-old in 1883, but had 9 st 8 lb on his back when second to Plaisanterie, to whom he was giving 10lb, with the Derby winner St Gatien unplaced in 1885. In the intervening season he had also been second, beaten a head by Florence, then he was runner up for a third time in 1887 when he carried 9 st 13 lb and failed by just half a length to give 35 lb to Gloriation.

In the year that Bendigo won the Cambridgeshire his lightweight jockey Harry Luke had the greatest difficulty in riding the big strong brown colt who wandered badly once in front. After the race little Luke, full of self-satisfaction, said to the Newmarket trainer Joe Cannon, "Well, I pulled that race out of the fire!"

"Did you?" replied Cannon. "Then the fire must have been all over the course."

Bendigo was extraordinarily unlucky not to win again the following year instead of being beaten that head by Florence, as his jockey Jem Snowden was, not uncharacteristically, drunk.

Soon after the turn of the century the Druid's Lodge Confederacy, who cost the bookmakers fortunes during their heyday, engineered some of their most spectacular coups in the Cambridgeshire. The Confederacy, which comprised Captain Wilfred Purefoy, Captain Frank Forester and other owners, had their horses trained in the utmost secrecy in the Druid's Lodge stable on a remote part of Salisbury Plain, by Jack Fallon and then later by Tom Lewis. Fallon won them the Cambridgeshire with Hackler's Pride in 1903 and 1904 and Lewis with Christmas Daisy in 1909 and 1910.

In between these two successes for Druid's Lodge the bookmakers were also given a bad time by Polymelus in the Cambridgeshire of 1906. Having paid 4,200 guineas for Polymelus in late September the diamond millionaire Solly Joel set about getting his money back with interest by backing him for the Cambridgeshire. Starting at the extraordinarily short price of 11-10 Polymelus brought off the gamble by beating Kaffir Chief by three lengths and Mr Joel took £30,000 out of the ring. Polymelus was to become an immensely influential stallion as the sire of Phalaris, whose sons included the brothers Pharos and Fairway. In turn Pharos was sire of Nearco, whose descendants in tail male line have been enjoying such enormous success in the United States and Europe during recent years.

Bendigo who captured the imagination of the late Victorians by his feats in the Cambridgeshire, had his modern equivalent in Mrs P Harris's Baronet, trained by John Benstead at Epsom and usually ridden by Brian Rouse. Having run in the Cambridgeshire for the first time as a five-year-old this tough and utterly honest bay gelding by Huntercombe was second under 8 st 5 lb then twelve months later he won with 9 st. In 1979 he was sixth when carrying 9 st 8 lb, then after winning for a second time with 9 st 3 lb in 1980 he was runner-up again with 9 st on his back as a nine-year-old in 1981. Thus Baronet has been the principal beneficiary of the sponsorship of the Cambridgeshire by the William Hill Organisation, one of the four big firms of nationwide bookmakers, who have made a substantial contribution to the prize money for the race since 1977. Previously the Cambridgeshire had been sponsored by the Irish Hospitals Sweepstakes between 1971 and 1976.

The Cambridgeshire has been likened to a cavalary charge because a large field thunders down a straight course in almost line abreast. Unless the going is distinctly soft, which is rare on heathland with well-drained chalky subsoil, jockeys prefer to be drawn low on the stands side. Why the draw should make any difference on a dead

Horses in training on Warren Hill in the early 19th Century.

..t the start of the Warren Hill canter today.

J. ROBINSON. WON THE DERBY ON BAY MIDDLETON.

R. BOYER: THE DUKE OF YORK'S JOCKEY.

ARNULL

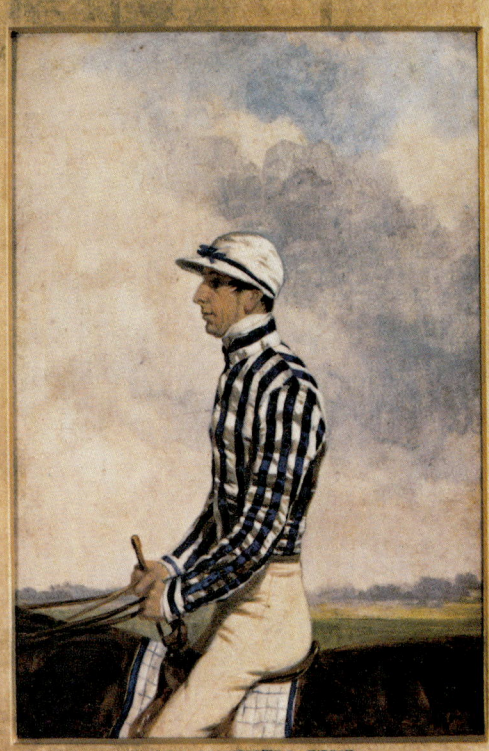

SAM CHIFNEY, SEN^R

*Mr Christopher Wilson's Lurcher beats
Sir Frank Standish's Kit Carr and
Mr Wentworth's Ormond for £500
Sweepstake Ditch In (2 miles 97 yards)
April 15th 1793.*

E *View of horses going to the start on the Round Course at Newmarket in about 1720.*

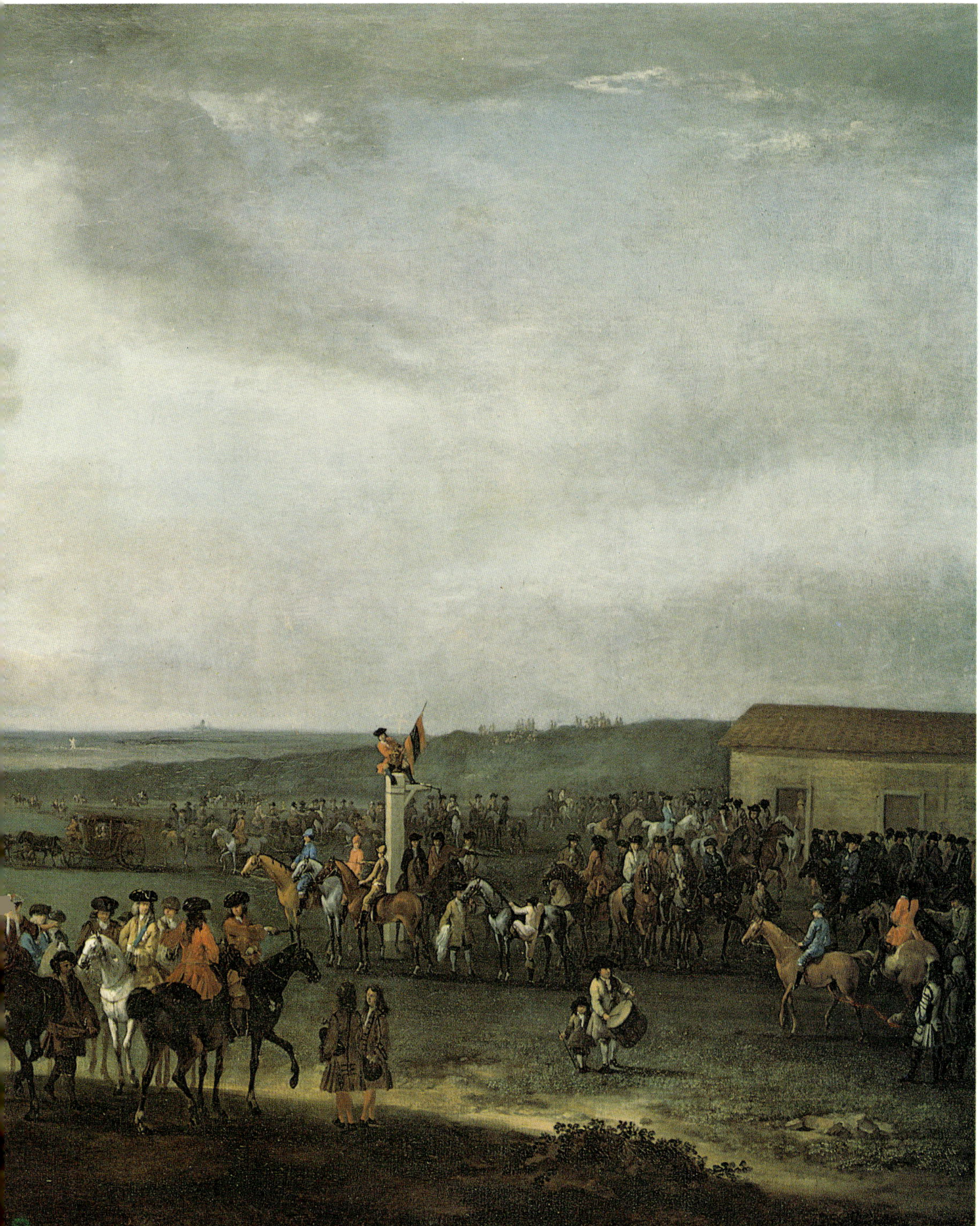

F *Eclipse, the most influential sire of the eighteenth century*

G

Admiral Henry John Rous (1795-1877) The third great dictator of the English Turf, who brought handicapping to a fine art.

H *Flying Childers, a bay by the Darley Arabian foaled in 1715, acknowledged as the first great racehorse, though he only ran twice. In April 1721 he beat Speedwell in a match for 500 gns over four miles at Newmarket and in October 1722 Chanter for one of 1,000 gns over six miles there.*

straight course would seem to be inexplicable but experience has shown that horses drawn on the stands side on the Rowley Mile enjoy a considerable advantage. And although the race is only nine furlongs it generally takes a horse that gets a mile and a quarter well to win the Cambridgeshire as that final furlong uphill from the dip can prove too much for runners who stay little further than a mile, let alone the specialists at that distance.

The Cesarewitch is a very different race from the first leg of Newmarket's great autumn double. Run over a gruelling two and a quarter miles across a landscape that is all but featureless it provides a far sterner test of stamina, and a horse's powers of mental concentration, than the Chester Cup, which is over the same distance, or Britain's two longest races, the Queen Alexandra Stakes and the Brown Jack Stakes, which are both run over four furlongs further at Ascot. The course on the Roodeye at Chester is only seven furlongs in circumference so that the field for the Chester Cup is constantly on the turn, checking slightly from full gallop on the bends, and while the course at Ascot is not as tight as that at Chester the bends there afford the stayers more respite than they enjoy at Newmarket. On the Cesarewitch course there is just the one turn round which the pace slackens before the field sets out up the stark, staring straight of more than a mile.

Like the Cambridgeshire the Cesarewitch was run for the first time in the autumn of 1839. While visiting Newmarket a short time previously, the 21-year-old Tsarevich, the future Emperor Alexander II of Russia, made a gift of £300 to the Jockey Club, who put up the money as first prize for a new long distance handicap, bearing the name of the donor in the anglicised form of Cesarewitch. The first winner of the race was Lord Milltown's chestnut mare Cruiskeen, ridden by a boy called Stag at 6 st 6 lb on Wednesday 16 October when ten of the 26 entries went to the post.

The heir to the throne of Russia was so pleased by having an English race named after him that he continued to sponsor it until 1849, by which time the differences between Britain and Russia that would lead to the Crimean War were becoming apparent. The winner of the Cesarewitch the last time that Tsarevich Alexander gave his £300 was Lord Stanley's three-year-old filly Legerdemain who slipped a foal by Ion on the evening of the following day.

The Cesarewitch was not long in attracting a top class horse, for when the outsider Clarion won the second running in 1840, the runner-up was Bloomsbury, winner of The Derby of the previous year. Twelve months later, in 1841, the race was won by Iliona, owned by Lord Palmerston, the future Prime Minister, and trained by John Barham Day. Thus twice in a decade the Cesarewitch was won by a man destined to become Prime Minister, as Legerdemain's owner was to hold that office after succeeding his father as Earl of Derby.

When The Cur, owned by William Stirling Crawfurd was successful in the Cesarewitch in 1848 he won by a length from Dacia, carrying a mere 4 st 13 lb, with Ellerdale third and 3-1 favourite Surplice unplaced in a field of 32. Surplice had won The Derby a few months previously, while Ellerdale, who was third in that Cesarewitch, was to become the dam of the 1856 Derby winner Ellington.

There was a minor tragedy when Mr E. R. Clark's half-bred horse Mr Sykes won the Cesarewitch in 1855 as Baron Rothschild's King Tom broke down. Fortunately King Tom, a half-brother to Stockwell, was saved for stud. He was twice champion sire, his offspring including the Derby winner Kingcraft, and his grateful owner erected a statue to him at Mentmore.

In 1858 there was a triple dead-heat between Pryoress, El Hakim and Queen Bess. The bookmaker George Hodgman, who had watched from the top of a coach in the betting ring, was sure that Pryoress would have won had she been competently ridden. Shouting to a colleague, Tubby Morris, to put £100 on her to win the run-off, he dashed over to Pryoress's American owner Mr Richard Ten Broeck and convinced him he should exercise his right to replace his jockey Tankesley, also an American, in the deciding heat and engage George Fordham. Ridden by Fordham, Pryoress vindicated Hodgman by beating El Hakim, whose original rider had also been supplanted, by a length with Queen Bess a head away, third.

Curiously enough Pryoress was also involved in a dead heat in the Cesarewitch of the following year as she and The Brewer shared second place behind Rocket, and there was the second heat for first place within three years when Sir W. Booth's Artless was inseparable from Tom Parr's Gaspard in 1859. Another decider was run and Artless won by three lengths.

Having been a good winner over the success that George Fordham had obtained on Pryoress in 1857, the betting man George Hodgman had a less happy experience as a result of the great jockey being unable to do the weight for his horse John Davis, who was set to carry only 6 st 12 lb in 1869. Obliged to engage the moderate lightweight Sammy Mordan, who lisped badly, Hodgman told him to jump John Davis off smartly and let him run through his hands to make the pace. By way of interpretation of these instructions the rider held up John Davis at the back of the field singing to himself, "Mithith Thammy Mordan'th huthband will win the Thetherwitch today. Mithith Thammy Mordan will have her thewing mathine tonight." When at last John Davis was given his head it was too late and he was beaten a length and a half by Mr Richard Naylor's Chérie, trained by Jem Godding and ridden by 16-year-old Fred Webb at 5 st 7 lb.

Another success for American interests had materialised in 1881 when Foxhall had won by way of a prelude to completing the autumn double in the Cambridgeshire. Earlier that year the Emperor Alexander II, who had given the money to found the race 42 years earlier, had been assassinated by the Nihilists in St Petersburg.

Derby winners met with mixed luck when they made sporadic appearances in the Cesarewitch during the second half of the last century. Blue Gown was unplaced in 1868, as was Kingcraft in 1871 and Sefton in 1878 but St Gatien gave the four-year-old Polemic 38 lb and a beating of four lengths in 1884.

Lily Langtry won the first of her two Cesarewitches with the Australian horse Merman in 1897 when she was still using the *nom-de-course* of 'Mr Jersey'. By the time that Yentoi brought off a gamble for Sam Darling's Beckhampton stable in 1908 she was racing in her married name of Lady de Bathe.

Three years later Sam Darling won another Cesarewitch with Mr C. E. Howard's Willonyx, who carried the then record weight of 9 st 5 lb. Willonyx was a really good, game and consistent stayer. Earlier on in the same season he had completed the double in the Ascot Stakes and the Gold Cup at the Royal Meeting and won the Chester and the Jockey Club Cups. At stud, though, he proved a bitter disappointment before being sent to Uruguay, the best of his offspring being Air Raid who won the Cesarewitch a few weeks before the end of the First World War in 1918.

An even better horse than Willonyx won the Cesarewitch in the restricted war-time conditions of 1915. This was Sir Abe Bailey's four-year-old Son-in-Law, who was destined to become an outstanding sire of stayers, his sons including such stout-hearted horses as Foxlaw, Trimdon and Epigram.

Willonyx's feat of winning the Cesarewitch under 9 st 5 lb remained a record for more than half a century, not being broken until the late Lord Astor's chestnut gelding Grey of Falloden, one of the most popular horses of the day, carried 9 st 6 lb to beat Magic Court by three parts of a length in 1964. Grey of Falloden was trained by Major Dick Hern at West Ilsley and ridden by Joe Mercer, who obtained his second success in the Cesarewitch on Halsbury in 1981. Halsbury was trained by Peter Walwyn in Lambourn's historic Seven Barrows stable, which had quartered Bendigo almost exactly a century earlier. Peter Walwyn, leading trainer in 1974 and 1975, had embarked upon his career as assistant to Major Geoffrey Brooke in Newmarket's Clarehaven stable.

George Fordham

Whereas the Cambridgeshire and the Cesarewitch pack the stands and arouse intense speculative interest amongst the racing public, racing's professional element, apart from that concerned exclusively with betting, attaches more importance to Newmarket's three principal two-year-old races of the back-end — the Middle Park Stakes and the Cheveley Park Stakes run over six furlongs at the Autumn Meeting, and the seven furlong Dewhurst Stakes at the Houghton Meeting. By way of generalisation one can say that the Middle Park Stakes is a rehearsal for The 2,000 Guineas and the Cheveley Park Stakes a trial for The 1,000 Guineas, while the extra furlong of the Dewhurst Stakes makes it an attractive end-of-term proposition for colts thought to have the potential to win The Derby.

The Middle Park Stakes was first run on Wednesday 10 October 1866, when William Blenkiron put up the £1,000 prize money. William Blenkiron, a Yorkshireman, owned the Middle Park Stud at Eltham in Kent. The Middle Park Stud, where Blenkiron kept some 120 broodmares, was the first commercial breeding establishment of any considerable importance, and the sale of its yearlings, conducted by Tattersalls on the premises, one of the principal features of the racing year. After William Blenkiron died in 1871 his son and namesake carried on the stud until obliged to close it in 1882 when a railway line was laid across the paddocks.

As £1,000 was a very large prize at that time the Middle Park Stakes attracted top class two-year-olds from the outset. When Mr T. Pryor's The Rake, ridden by Jack Loates, was successful in the first running in 1866 he won by three lengths from Colonel Pearson's wonderfully good filly Achievement. She won eleven of her other twelve races as a two-year-old and was successful in the St Leger of the following season.

John Porter won the second and third races for the Middle Park Stakes for Sir Joseph Hawley with Green Sleeve and Pero Gomez, subsequently second in The Derby, in 1867 and 1868 respectively. Amongst those unplaced to Green Sleeve was Formosa, who was to win The 1,000 Guineas, The Oaks and The St Leger and dead heat in The 2,000 Guineas. Hannah, another destined to win the fillies' Triple Crown, was third to Albert Victor in 1870. The following year the Middle Park Stakes was won by that great Newmarket course specialist Prince Charlie.

It was appropriate that the Bedford Lodge trainer Joe Dawson, who revolutionised the handling of young stock, should have won the Middle Park Stakes three times in the first six years of its existence. As well as with The Rake and Prince Charlie he was also successful with Frivolity in 1869. Subsequently he won it for a fourth time with Peter in 1878.

William Blenkiron produced the £1,000 prize money for the Middle Park Stakes again in 1867, in 1868 and for a fourth and last time in 1869. The following year the Jockey Club took over responsiblity for the provision of the prize money, though reducing it to £500.

Colonel Harry McCalmont's 1893 Triple Crown winner Isinglass, with trainer Jimmy Jewett in the background

During the last quarter of the nineteenth century the Middle Park Stakes was won by no fewer than nine horses destined for classic honours, namely the Triple Crown winners Isinglass and Galtee More, Melton and Donovan, both of whom completed the double in The Derby and The St Leger, The Derby winner Ladas, Petrarch winner of The 2,000 Guineas and The St Leger, The 2,000 Guineas winners Chamant and St Frusquin, and Busybody, winner of The 1,000 Guineas and The Oaks.

It is perhaps an indication of the specialisation of modern racing that no winner of the Middle Park Stakes between the end of the Second World War and 1981 won any other English classic save The 2,000 Guineas. The five horses to win the two races over that period were Nearula, Our Babu, Right Tack, Brigadier Gerard and Known Fact. By contrast to those five Middle Park winners that graduated to success in The 2,000 Guineas eleven more were runner-up in that classic and three more third so that 19 out of 36 Middle Park winners finished in the first three in The 2,000 Guineas.

Until 1899 any owner or trainer desirous of giving a filly championship status as a two-year-old was obliged to take on the colts in either the Middle Park Stakes or the Dewhurst Stakes. This rather unsatisfactory state of affairs was changed when the Cheveley Park Stakes, named after Colonel Harry McCalmont's Newmarket estate, was staged for the first time on Wednesday 12 October 1899. The winner was Lord William Beresford's Lutetia, ridden by Tod Sloan and trained by John Huggins at Heath House.

Within a very short time the Cheveley Park Stakes was already enjoying a status comparable to that of the Middle Park Stakes as Pretty Polly enhanced its prestige by her success in 1903. Her daughter Molly Desmond emulated her while the British Empire was in the throes of war in 1916 and in the last year of the war the Cheveley Park was won by Bayuda, who was to be successful in the first peacetime Oaks.

In between the wars the race was won by a number of notable fillies. These included Lord Derby's Selene, dam of Hyperion, in 1921, Scuttle, who was to give King George V his only classic success by taking The 1,000 Guineas in 1928, little Tiffin in 1928, whose almost unbelievable speed was developed by Fred Darling at Beckhampton, the Oaks winners Brown Betty in 1932 and Light Brocade in 1933 and Stafaralla, dam of Tehran, in 1937.

Still more high class fillies have won the Cheveley Park Stakes since the end of the era. Of the 36 to be successful between 1945 and 1980, six, Belle of All, Zabara, Night Off, Fleet, Humble Duty and Waterloo, went on to win The 1,000 Guineas, five more were second in that classic and another two third.

The Dewhurst Stakes was run for the first time in 1875 when Mr T. Gee donated the £300 prize money. Mr Gee was the proprietor of the Dewhurst Stud at Wadhurst in Sussex, where he stood the 1857 2,000 Guineas winner Vedette and three other stallions. He provided the £300 for the Dewhurst Stakes again in 1877 and then the Jockey Club maintained the race at the same value.

Mr Gee's hopes of establishing a race in which owners could run two-year-olds with the potential to reach the top class was realised immediately as each of the first four winners of the Dewhurst Stakes went on to success in one or more of the classics. The initial running was won by Mr Alexander Baltazzi's Kisber, ridden by Charlie Maidment and trained by Joe Hayhoe at Palace House. In the light of a tragedy to occur more than a decade later it was ironic that Kisber should have been bred on the Hungarian Royal Stud, which was the property of the Emperor Franz Josef, as Alexander Baltazzi, a Levantine merchant, was the uncle of Baroness Marie Vetsera, who shared the mysterious death of the Emperor's only son, the Crown Prince Rudolf, at Mayerling in January 1889.

As a three-year-old Kisber won The Derby and in the autumn of that season Chamant, already the winner of the Middle Park Stakes, completed a notable double in the Dewhurst Stakes as a prelude to his success in The 2,000 Guineas. The third and fourth winners of the Dewhurst Stakes were amongst the greatest fillies of the era. Pilgrimage was to win both The 2,000 Guineas and The 1,000 Guineas while Lord Falmouth's Wheel of Fortune triumphed in The 1,000 Guineas and The Oaks in 1878. Other classic winners to have won the Dewhurst Stakes between then and the end of the century were Dutch

Oven (St Leger), Ormonde, Rêve d'Or (Oaks), Donovan and St Frusquin.

The Dewhurst Stakes was very much a favourite race of that great trainer Alec Taylor, who made the Manton, Wiltshire stable one of the most powerful in the country. Of the six winners of the race he saddled during the first quarter of this century four went on to take classic honours, namely Bayardo (1909 St Leger), Lemberg (1910 Derby), Kennymore (1914 2,000 Guineas) and My Dear (1918 Oaks).

A trainer with a still more impressive record in the Dewhurst Stakes was Frank Butters. While at Stanley House he was responsible for the success of Lord Derby's subsequent Oaks winner Toboggan in 1927 then on moving to Fitzroy House he won it five times in six years with Firdaussi in 1931, Mrs Rustom in 1933, Hairan in 1934, Bala Hissar in 1935 and Sultan Mahomed in 1936. During the war he won with Umiddad in 1942 and Paperweight in 1944 and then for a ninth and last time in 1946 with the late Aga Khan's Migoli.

During the 1950s both Pinza and Crepello followed up successes in the Dewhurst Stakes by winning The Derby for the late Sir Victor Sassoon and in the last dozen years or so the race has proved an equally reliable guide to the classics. Nijinsky in 1969 went on to be the 15th and most recent winner of the Triple Crown. Mill Reef in 1970, Grundy in 1974, and The Minstrel in 1976 also won The Derby while Wollow in 1975 won The 2,000 Guineas.

Like Alec Taylor and Frank Butters, the Irish trainer Vincent O'Brien has shown a great propensity for running his top class two-year-olds in the Dewhurst Stakes. As well as with Nijinsky and The Minstrel he has won it with Cellini in 1973, Try My Best in 1977, Monteverdi in 1979 and Storm Bird in 1980.

The oldest two-year-old race run at Newmarket, and in the world for that matter, is the July Stakes over six furlongs at the three-day July meeting. When run for the first time back in 1786 the winner was Lord Clermont's Bullfinch, a chestnut colt by Woodpecker. The Prince of Wales won with Cymbeline in 1792 and a number of other prominent owners such as the Dukes of Grafton and Bedford, Sir Charles Bunbury, Lord Grosvenor and Mr Christopher Wilson won it during the same era, but not until 1814 was there a winner of any consequence. This was the fourth Duke of Grafton's Minuet, who won The Oaks in 1815. Five years later the July Stakes was won by Gustavus, the winner of the Derby the following year.

No other horse of any note won the July Stakes until Crucifix in 1839 then nine years later Lord Eglinton's colt The Flying Dutchman came down from Middleham to win in 1848 before returning south to win The Derby in 1849. The July Stakes was always very much a favourite race of Lester Piggott's forbears John Barham Day and his son John Day the younger. As well as with Crucifix, the father won it with Old England, Sweetheart, Grecian, Spindle and Drumour after turning to training, while his son sent out Lady Elizabeth to win in 1867. Lady Elizabeth also won eleven of her other twelve races as a two-year-old but after such intensive activity during her first season

Sir Victor Sassoon at the sales

failed to train on and her defeat in The Derby finally broke her high betting young owner the Marquess of Hastings. Two other really good fillies to win the July Stakes in the same era were Achievement and Hannah and some 30 years later Sceptre, perhaps the greatest filly of all time, was successful.

Hammerkop was the winner of the July Stakes in 1902 and her subsequent career is another example of the versatility of horses in times gone by. Three years later she won the Cesarewitch then on retiring to stud became the dam of the Derby winner Spion Kop.

Five subsequent classic winners — Diophon, Apple Sammy, Fairway, Mr Jinks and Four Course — won the July Stakes in eight years during one period between the wars. After the Second World War the prestige of the race continued to ride high, Masaka was successful in the season before her triumph in The Oaks and Nimbus won as a prelude to bringing off the double in The 2,000 Guineas and The Derby. Darius, who was to land The 2,000 Guineas, became the last future classic winner to have been successful at the time of writing when he beat that high class sprinter Princely Gift by a short head in Coronation Year 1953.

More good horses have won the July Stakes in the meantime. Sir Noel Murless's four winners included that fast filly Abelia in 1957 and Lorenzaccio in 1967, who was a successful sire until being exported to Australia. Auction Ring in 1974, with whom the West Ilsley trainer Major Dick Hern won his second July Stakes, proved a great success on being retired to stud, his first crop including that high class miler Belmont Bay.

Soon after being appointed Clerk of the Course at Newmarket at the age of 34 on New Year's Day 1974, Captain Nick Lees set about enhancing the importance of the July Meeting so that it became the focal point of that part of the season between Royal Ascot in the middle of June and the opening of Goodwood's big meeting in late July. One part of that process has been the raising of the prestige of the July Stakes which was worth £15,108 when Anglia Television sponsored it for the first time in 1981. The winner was End of the Line, trained by Barry Hills at Lambourn, and the field of eleven was the biggest since King George V's Runnymede won in 1924.

Another of the long established races of Newmarket's principal summer fixture to have become still more competitive since being sponsored is the six furlong July Cup. Now the William Hill July Cup, this event is amongst the most important weight-for-age sprints of the mid-season. As opposed to the £14,247 it was worth when Gentilhombre was awarded the race on the relegation of Lester Piggott's muzzled mount Marinsky to second place in 1977, it was worth £23,225 when Marinsky's trainer Vincent O'Brien obtained compensation with Solinus, also ridden by Lester Piggott, twelve months later as a result of the William Hill Organisation having underwritten the value. By the time Mr Edmund Loder's remarkably fast filly Marwell beat the previous year's winner Moorestyle in 1981 the first prize had risen to £37,098.

The July Cup was introduced as an all-aged race in a somewhat inauspicious manner in 1876. There were only three runners, of which Count de Lagrange's Echanson bolted, leaving Mr J. H. Houldsworth's Springfield, ridden by Tom Osborne, to win by a dozen lengths from the Duke of Albans's two-year-old Crann Tair.

In the early days of existence the July Cup was used by high class hourses for the demonstration of their remarkable versatility. Melton, for instance, won it in the season after his success in The Derby, and the Duke of Portland's 1890 Oaks winner Memoir also won it as a four-year-old. In the present century, though, it has been the specialist sprinters who have given the July Cup its importance. Sundridge completed the hat-trick by winning in 1902, 1903 and 1904 while subsequent winners of comparable calibre include Diadem in 1919 and 1920, Tetratema in 1922, Myrobella in 1933, Bellacose in 1935 and 1936, the flying grey Abernant in 1949 and 1950, Right Boy in 1958 and 1959, Lucasland in 1966 and the French-trained Lianga in 1975.

The third important weight-for-age race at the July Meeting is the Princess of Wales Stakes, run over a mile and a half for three-year-olds and upwards. This was first run in 1894 and named after the Queen's great-grandmother who was to become Queen Alexandra as the consort of King Edward VII seven years later. The race became an instant success with the first running being won by Colonel Harry McCalmont's great horse Isinglass who had carried off the Triple Crown the previous season. Isinglass had to win that first Princess of Wales Stakes on the firm ground that he absolutely detested so that it was by no more than a head that he beat the 50-1 outsider Bullingdon with that year's Derby winner Ladas three lengths away third. Isinglass, who started at 100-12 in a field of seven, carried 10 st 3 lb and gave 12 lb to the 15-8 on favourite Ladas.

Ironically both the Derby winners owned by King Edward VII as Prince of Wales were beaten in the Princess of Wales Stakes. Persimmon lost out to his old rival St Frusquin in 1896 and his foul-tempered brother Diamond Jubilee was second to Merry Gal in 1900 and again to Epsom Lad in 1901. Between then and the outbreak of the First World War Derby winners continued to meet with mixed luck in the Princess of Wales Stakes. Ard Patrick won in 1903, so did Rock Sand in 1904, but Lemberg had to take second place to Swynford in 1910. The best horses to win the race between the wars were Blandford, arguably the outstanding stallion of the first half of the century, in 1922, Solario in 1925 and Fairway in 1928. Post war winners of the Princess of Wales Stakes include Lord Derby's great stayer Alycidon in 1948, Primera, who was to become a successful stallion after his successes in 1959 and 1960, the Queen's Hopeful Venture in 1967, and Mrs Stanhope Joel's Oaks winner Lupe by Primera in 1971 when she became the first classic winner to take the race since Airborne in 1946. Still more recently Mr H. J. Joel's 1980 St Leger winner Light Cavalry has helped maintain the reputation of the Princess of Wales Stakes as one of the great races of the Heath by getting up close home

The irascible Diamond Jubilee, winner of The Triple Crown in 1900

to beat Castle Keep by a neck as a four-year-old.

Like other racecourses Newmarket has been indebted to sponsors for the maintenance of the value of prize money in recent years, and its great popularity with a wide variety of commercial interests was fully reflected when Clerk of the Course, Captain Nick Lees was able to claim it was the best sponsored course in the country in 1982. Of the record prize money of £1,455,500 on offer that year £386,500 (about 27%) came from sponsors while the Levy Board contributed £513,800, £278,700 of which comes from the Board's pattern allocation (about 35%).

The big bookmaking companies, William Hill and Ladbrokes, have both made substantial contributions to underwriting the values of some of the Heath's most important races for a number of years now. From 1974 to 1982 Ladbrokes has sponsored the Craven Stakes, and the Nell Gwyn Stakes at the Craven Meeting with the name of the firm used as a prefix to each event. The Craven Stakes is always regarded as an important trial for The 2,000 Guineas and though no winner of it has graduated to success in the classics while sponsored, its running shed light on The Guineas on at least one occasion as To-Agori-Mou went on to win the latter race after being runner-up to Kind of Hush in the Craven in 1981.

The Nell Gwyn provided a great deal more accurate pointer to The 1,000 Guineas than the Craven did to the colts' classic. Two years after Ladbrokes undertook its sponsorship Flying Water won the Nell Gwyn and then went on to success in The 1,000 Guineas. Subsequently One in a Million in 1979 and Fairy Footsteps in 1981 have emulated her. One in a Million and Fairy Footsteps were trained by Henry Cecil who also won the Nell Gwyn with Evita in 1980 and Chalon in 1982, making four successes for the Warren Place stable in as many years. Another notable winner of the Nell Gwyn Stakes while sponsored by Ladbrokes was Rose Bowl, who was to return to Newmarket to win the Champion Stakes for Fulke Johnson Houghton's Blewbury stable later in 1975.

Ladbrokes continue their sponsorship of the Abernant Stakes, also begun in 1974, and in 1983 took over the underwriting of the Free Handicap from The Tote thereby changing their pattern of sponsorship on account of the Free Handicap being a stronger betting race than either the Craven Stakes or the Nell Gywn. The Abernant Stakes, named after the flying grey Sir Noel Murless trained at Beckhampton shortly before coming to Newmarket, has served its purpose of bringing about a clash of top class sprinters remarkably well, and was dominated by that popular performer Boldboy in the early years of sponsorship. Trained at West Ilsley by Major Dick Hern for Lady Beaverbrook, Boldboy had a great deal more ability than most sprinters rated good enough to make stallions but had to be gelded after displaying waywardness as a two-year-old in 1972. Two years later Boldboy won the Ladbroke Abernant Stakes for the first time. He won it again in 1976 and 1977 then for a fourth time by beating Ubedizzy by two lengths as a eight-year-old in 1978. The following year the sponsoring firm underwrote the six furlong Wisbech Handicap at the same meeting, renaming it the Ladbrokes Boldboy Handicap in his honour. The first running was won by Son of Shaka, ridden by Brian Taylor and trained by Captain Ryan Price in Sussex.

Winners of the Abernant Stakes since the near monopoly of Boldboy came to an end include the previous season's Ayr Gold Cup winner Vaigly Great in 1979 and Gypsy Dancer twelve months later. Gypsy Dancer was one of those good sprinters whose achievement made such an enormous contribution to the success of Bill O'Gorman's Graham Place stable in the 1970s and early 1980s.

Two other betting organisations to provide important sponsorship at the Newmarket Spring Meeting have been The Tote and Heathorns, the bookmakers. The Tote began sponsoring the Free Handicap in 1969, when Mr H. J. Joel's Welsh Pageant won for Noel Murless's stable, and amended the name of the race to The Tote European Free Handicap in 1981 after changing the conditions to allow horses that had raced exclusively on the continent to be included in the official assessment of the previous season's two-year-olds. Although a handicap, this race has provided a good guide to the classics on several occasions since its institution in 1929. Pay Up was successful in it before winning The 2,000 Guineas in 1936 and Mid-Day Sun prior to winning The Derby the following season. Since sponsorship, the northern filly Mrs McArdy won it as a prelude to winning The 1,000 Guineas in 1977 while Remainder Man, who won in 1978, was placed in both The 2,000 Guineas and The Derby.

The Heathorn Stakes, run over a mile and a quarter at the Guineas Meeting, is intended to test potential top class middle distance three-year-olds. The first running attained this objective to the full when Shirley Heights beat Ile de Bourbon by a short head in 1978. Within a few months Shirley Heights had won The Derby and Ile de Bourbon the King George VI and the Queen Elizabeth Stakes. Shirley Heights was trained at Arundel, Sussex, by John Dunlop and carried the colours of the late Earl of Halifax, who frequently acted as a steward at Newmarket and was Senior Steward of the Jockey Club in 1950 as well as 1959.

Whereas Ladbrokes make the most significant contributions to the prize money at the Craven Meeting, the William Hill Organisation is the principal sponsor at the autumn fixtures. Since 1973 the firm has underwritten the value of the three important two-year-old races, the Middle Park Stakes, the Cheveley Park Stakes and the Dewhurst Stakes and in 1977 they took over the sponsorship of the Cambridgeshire from the Irish Hospitals Sweepstakes, heavy commitments that make the firm the biggest of Newmarket's sponsors. The Cesarewitch has been sponsored by the The Tote since 1978.

Other sponsors at the autumn meetings include Tattersalls, Bloodstock and General Insurance, a company with offices in Newmarket High Street, and Bisquit Cognac. Among the events to which Tattersalls contribute are the Somerville Tattersall Stakes, a seven furlong race for two-year-olds, which Wind and Wuthering won in 1981 before being second in The 2,000 Guineas the following spring. The five furlong Bloodstock and General Insurance Nursery was run for the first time in 1978 when the winner was Bucco Bay, ridden by Brian Rouse and trained by Richard Hannon at East Everleigh in Wiltshire. In 1981 the BGI Nursery was won by My Lover, one of several useful horses to have been owned by syndicates organised by Newmarket resident Squadron-Leader Alan Milsom and trained by Michael Jarvis in the Kremlin House stable.

The Bisquit Cognac firm sponsored the Challenge Stakes for the first time in 1979. The initial running of the Bisquit Cognac Challenge Stakes was won by Lord Howard de Walden's Kris, and Moorestyle was successful in each of the two following seasons.

Newmarket acquired another important sponsor in 1982 when the Maktoum family, who are the rulers of Dubai, undertook to add £50,000 to the Champion Stakes for five years as a 'gift to British horse racing'. The Maktoum brothers are amongst the many Arab owners who have made substantial investments in the British Turf over the past decade, and have horses with Thomson Jones and Michael Stoute. Tom Jones trained Maktoum al Maktoum's Touching Wood who was second in The Derby in 1982 before winning The St Leger, while Michael Stoute sent out the same owner's Shareef Dancer to beat Dalmane in the Park Lodge Stakes on the July Course in the late August of 1982. Shareef Dancer, who had cost 3,300,000 dollars, thus became the most expensive horse to have won in Great Britain up to that time.

As mentioned elsewhere the Champion Stakes was first run in 1877, the first winner of it being Mr J. H. Houldsworth's Springfield ridden by Tom Cannon and trained by Jimmy Ryan at Green Lodge. It soon became established as the last of the season's important middle distance weight-for-age races by the successes in it of the classic winners Janette, Robert the Devil, Bend Or, Ormonde and La Flèche before the turn of the century. Those great fillies Sceptre and Pretty Polly both enhanced the standing of the Champion Stakes by winning in 1903 and 1905 respectively, while notable recent winners include Pretty Polly's descendant in tail female line Brigadier Gerard, who was successful in both 1971 and 1972.

Among other sponsors who made important contributions to maintaining the standard of racing on the Heath in the early 1980s were the local bookmakers, Laurie Wallis, Child and Co, the London bankers, who underwrite the prestigious race for three-year-old fillies on the July Course, formerly known as the Falmouth Stakes, Tolly Cobbold, the East Anglian brewer, Philip Cornes and Company, the Owens Group of New Zealand, Ward Hill, the bookmaker who sponsors the Banbury Cup and two other races, Holstein Distributors and Sir Kenneth Butt who puts up money for the Petition Stakes.

5 The Jockey Boys, Newmarket's Crew – Sam Chifney to Nat Flatman

In the course of a poem to commemorate the death of that famous old reprobate the Duke of Queensberry in 1810 the elegist refers to "The Jockey boys, Newmarket's crew, who know a little thing — or two".

The first of the riders to whom these lines could be properly applied was Sam Chifney the elder. Before his appearance in the saddle in about 1770 horses were ridden in their races, as at exercise, by grooms who knew nothing at all about what was to become the highly developed art of race riding. Sam showed that he knew a little thing or two by introducing tactics into his riding, and demonstrating the elemental subtleties of jockeyship. Instead of sending his horses on at as strong a pace as possible all the way and relying upon the liberal application of the whip to exact any vestige of reserves on approaching the winning post, he developed the art of saving up his mount for a challenge, and was the first rider to come from behind to win his races. In due course this late run was to become famous as the 'Chifney Rush'.

Sam Chifney was to race riding what his contemporary George Stubbs was to the portraiture of horses. Stubbs brought an end to the Primitive period by his analysis of the anatomy of the horse through dissection, so that his pantings of horses were so much truer to nature than those of his predecessors. Similarly Chifney made a close study of the action and mentality of the racehorse and introduced rudiments of jockeyship that would survive until Tod Sloan brought about the second revolution in race riding more than a century later.

A superb horseman by any standards, Chifney would relax his horses by riding on a loose rein, and though he was no more than 5 ft 5 in. in height, weighing out at 7 st 12 lb all the while he was riding, his wonderful hands enabled him to hold the hardest puller in a snaffle. On one occasion at Guildford, due to ride a horse, notorious for the hard hold he took, he was handed a heavy bridle with a curb. "Take away that silly gimcrack, and bring me a plain snaffle" demanded Chifney before going out to ride the horse as if it were an aged hunter. A quiet and unspectacular, although immensely effective, rider, he took the greatest care never to jerk a horse's mouth while pulling up. That should be done, he wrote, "as if you had a silken rein, as thin as a hair, and you were afraid of breaking it".

The distribution of his weight while riding in a race was another thing to which he paid close attention. Rather than sit well back in the saddle all the way, he would change his seat at various stages with the idea of reducing the demands made upon his mounts by affording them periodic respites, which must at least have reduced the mon-

Sam Chifney sen, W. Wheatly and Jem Robinson

otony of those slogs around the four miles and a furlong of Newmarket's Beacon Course.

His enormous conceit about his horsemanship, which can scarcely have made him an agreeable companion, was matched by his personal vanity. So much of a dandy that he was almost effeminate, he trailed lovelocks from beneath the front of his cap, was fond of affecting ruffs and frills and even brought a little colour to the tops of his boots by decorating them with bunches of ribbons.

Sam Chifney was born in Norfolk in 1753, and having commenced his apprenticeship in Foxe's stable at Newmarket in 1770 soon found his services in demand. In 1782 he won The Oaks on Lord Grovensor's Ceres. He won the same classic for the same owner on Maid of the Oaks twelve months later and brought off the Epsom double on the Duke of Bedford's Skyscraper in The Derby and Lord Egremont's Tag in The Oaks in 1789. The following season he received the appointment of first jockey to the Prince of Wales and a retaining fee of 200 guineas a year.

In the early summer of 1790 Chifney won The Oaks for a fourth time on the Duke of Bedford's Hippolyta but by the autumn of 1791 his career had come to its dramatic and disastrous end. Having been accused of cheating on the Prince's Escape at Newmarket in October 1791 by no less influential a man than Sir Charles Bunbury, Sam Chifney could find no other owner prepared to employ him after the Prince had retired from racing in understandable disgust. It was to compensate a man he deemed the victim of injustice whilst in his service that the Prince converted the 200 guineas he had been paying Chifney as a retainer into an annuity. In doing so 'Prinny' acted with consideration and generosity that were not always characteristic of him. As it happened he had hardly chosen the right man to whom to show the better side of his nature as Chifney sold the annuity for a lump sum of £1,260 and left Newmarket for London.

Having quit the racecourse Sam Chifney indulged in a bout of self-justification by writing his autobiography which he entitled *Genius Genuine* and published at £5 in 1795. Not only the title showed that misfortune had done nothing to diminish his enormous conceit. "In 1773" he wrote, "I could ride horses in a better manner in a race... than any person ever known in my time, and in 1775 I could train horses for running better than any person I ever yet saw. Riding I learnt myself, and training I learnt from Mr Richard Prince, training-groom to Lord Foley". Another passage reads "If the Jockey Club will be pleased to give me 200 guineas I will make them a bridle as I believe never was, and I believe never will be, excelled, for their lightweights to hold their horses from running away".

The feature of that bridle was the Chifney bit, which was to be used in racing stables throughout the world, but proved of no interest to the Jockey Club nor profit to its inventor. Having run up a bill for £350 with a saddler called Latchford, Sam Chifney was committed to the Fleet Prison for debt. And it was within the rules of that establishment that the first great jockey died on 8 January 1807 aged 53.

Sam Chifney married the daughter of Frank Smallman, a Newmarket trainer. As well as their two sons William and Sam junior, they had four daughters. One of the daughters married a Mr Weatherby of Newmarket and another a trainer in the town by the name of Butler. The latter became the mother of the successful jockey Frank Butler.

By contrast to Sam Chifney who was so much of a dandy as to be almost effeminate, Dick Goodisson was the most slovenly and unkempt of the Newmarket jockeys of the late eighteenth century and his turn of phrase was no more pleasing than his mode of attire. To have assumed from his appearance that Dick was perennially short of funds would have been a grave error for he always carried £500 in ready cash. He had once been unable to make a bet for that amount through not having the stake and was determined never to miss a second chance.

Dick Goodisson, who was born in Selby in about 1750, won the first three races for The Oaks on Bridget in 1779, Teetotum in 1780 and Faith in 1781. Although lacking the subtlety of Sam Chifney, Dick Goodisson was a strong, vigorous rider, who could be relied upon to squeeze the utmost out of a horse. He was the favourite jockey of the Duke of Queensberry for many years until that nobleman retired from The Turf in 1806. On his death four years later the Duke left Dick Goodisson £2,000. Dick Goodisson himself died at Newmarket on 9 September 1817.

The first of many brothers who have made their names at Newmarket were John and Sam Arnull. It was Sam Arnull who won the first Derby on Diomed in 1780. He was regularly employed by the founder of the race, the 12th Earl of Derby, for whom he won it on Sir Peter Teazle in 1787. He also won The Oaks for Lord Derby on Hermione in 1794 and rode two other Derby winners. Sam Arnull was a modest and retiring man, whose only pride was in his hunters and the groom that accompanied him when he rode to hounds. He would have been about 40 when he died in 1800.

John Arnull, Sam's elder brother, rode regularly for the Prince of Wales for a number of seasons. He won the first of his five Derbies on Colonel O'Kelly's Sergeant in 1784. Although he had such great trouble maintaining a racing weight that he lived on no more than the occasional apple for eight days at a time, John Arnull lived to be 62, dying in 1815.

John's son William Arnull also rode successfully, relying upon his strength and fearlessness rather than anything resembling guile. Much of his early success was for the stable of his brother-in-law Richard Boyce, their wives being sisters. William Arnull won each of the Newmarket classics three times and The Derby the same number of times.

Bill Arnull took good care of his money and spent it sparingly. Having to pay out £400 for an unsuccessful action in a Cambridge court hurt him greatly, so that it was not infrequently that he was heard to say, "I've never swallowed that £400 yet". His fondness for money, his irritability, accentuated by chronic gout, and the pride he took in being an Overseer of the Poor, made him a natural butt of the wags of Newmarket. They took great delight in telling itinerant tramps of Bill's unstinting generosity and watching the vagrants being rebuffed by a rider whose temper was never improved by the necessity for constant wasting.

His propensity to boast did little to help enlist sympathy for the irascible Bill Arnull. On one occasion he had made much of the large hamper of wine that he was expecting from a grateful owner. Finding a hamper on returning from riding work one morning he opened it eagerly, and out jumped the dwarf known as 'Little Peter'. Chased by an absolutely infuriated jockey that diminutive specimen of humanity dashed across the road to seek refuge amongst his friends in The Horse Shoe Inn.

Bill Arnull, who had been apprenticed to Frank Neale, went on riding until 1833, when he won the Gold Cup on Lord Exeter's Galata at the age of 48. He had just commenced to train for Lord Lichfield when he finally succumbed to gout on 29 April 1835.

Frank Buckle, whose record of riding 27 classics winners is still unbroken at the time of writing, was born the son of a Newmarket saddler in 1766. He was apprenticed in the Hon Richard Vernon's private stable at Newmarket and weighed out at a mere 3 st 13 lb when he rode his first winner in 1883. By the time he came to the end of his long career almost half a century later at the age of 65 in 1831 he could still go to the scales at 7 st 11 lb. He soon came to appreciate the efficacy of Sam Chifney's waiting tactics, which he adopted most effectively. He had a quite perfect seat in the saddle and was seen to particular advantage on a lazy horse.

Although he did have the wit to model himself upon Sam Chifney, Frank Buckle was a long way from being the most intelligent of riders. They said that if you turned him round once after a race he became so disorientated that he forgot what had happened in running and if you turned him round twice he forgot what horse he had just ridden.

Having come out of his apprenticeship Frank Buckle was retained by the first Earl Grosvenor, on whose John Bull he obtained his first classic success in The Derby of 1792. Following the death of Lord Grosvenor in 1802 he became attached to the stable of Robert Robson, that first in a long succession of great Newmarket trainers. Most important of Robson's patrons was the fourth Duke of Grafton, in whose all scarlet Buckle won The 2,000 Guineas four times and The 1,000 Guineas five times between 1820 and 1827.

Having achieved prosperity Frank Buckle ran a farm near Peterborough, where he bred greyhounds, bull-dogs and fighting cocks as well as fatstock. Mounted on an immaculate hack and wrapped in a voluminous white cloak with his racing saddles strapped across his back he would make the 92-mile round trip to Newmarket in a day being back in time to have tea with his family at six o'clock.

There was never a breath of suspicion about the riding of Frank Buckle, who survived his retirement by no more than a matter of weeks, and died in February 1832.

John Barham Day can scarcely be called a Newmarket jockey, but it was on the Heath that he belatedly laid the foundations of his reputation. He was still an unknown provincial rider of 32 years of age when he brought off the double in the Guineas on Dervise and Problem in 1826. Talking about the way he won his first classic on Dervise in The 2,000 Guineas when in reminiscent mood in later life John Day used to say, "I saw Buckle preparing to go, and it seemed as if something told me that if I went first I should beat him. And I did. I got first run and I beat him". Subsequently John Day rode three more 2,000 Guineas winners and another four of The 1,000 Guineas. His son and namesake, who was to succeed him in the Danebury stable, obtained his only riding success in the classics on The Ugly Buck in The 1,000 Guineas of 1844.

Frank Buckle's rival William Clift made Newmarket history by winning the first 2,000 Guineas on Wizard in 1809 and the first 1,000

Frank Buckle (1766-1832) stable jockey to Robert Robson, first of the great Newmarket trainers

Guineas on Charlotte in 1814. He had begun life as a shepherd boy on the Marquess of Rockingham's Yorkshire estate, but impressed his employer so much by the way he rode in some impromptu pony races staged for the amusement of visitors that he was taken into the stables. Not long afterwards Lord Rockingham transferred his string to Newmarket and Billy Clift was amongst the staff that accompanied the horses.

Although, on his arrival at Newmarket, he inevitably came into close contact with men, who spoke, dressed and in all other respects lived in the very height of fashion, Billy Clift allowed none of their style to rub off on him. No wonder that one of his more than ordinarily outraged contemporaries called him a 'wild uncultivated Indian'.

Blunt and uncompromising, he showed scant respect for the wealthy and influential men who employed him. On the Duke of Dorset enquiring whether he liked a horse he replied, "Hang me! won; That's enough for ye".

As a race rider he demonstrated no more polish than he did as a conversationalist. Unlike Sam Chifney and Frank Buckle he had no time for restraint. He liked to win his races from pillar to post, punishing his horses hard and running neck and neck from the start with anything that wanted to go along with him. Despite his reliance on these elementary and unsophisticated tactics Billy Clift was enormously successful, and enjoyed the patronage of almost all the leading owners. As well as winning The 2,000 Guineas, The 1,000 Guineas, The Oaks and The St Leger twice apiece, he won The Derby no fewer than five times — on Waxy in 1793, Champion in 1800, Ditto in 1803, Whalebone in 1810 and Tiresias in 1819. It was thus the lot of Billy Clift to win The Derby on two colts who were to take their place amongst the most influential stallions in international breeding. Waxy founded one male line that has been perpetuated so effectively in the present day by Northern Dancer through the likes of Nearco, Cyllene and Stockwell. Another of the male lines of Waxy flourishes through Bustino, whose forebearers include Blandford and Isinglass. For his part, Whalebone became the grandsire of the 1834 St Leger winner Touchstone, from whom descend Hampton, Hyperion, Vaguely Noble and the latter's son Empery.

The esteem in which Billy Clift was held was reflected in his having three pensions when he retired, £30 a year from Lord Fitzwilliam and £50 from both the Duke of Portland and Mr Christopher Wilson. Almost to the end of his long life he remained fit and active, thinking nothing of walking the 28 miles from Newmarket to Bury St Edmunds and back, just for a bit of exercise, when nearly 80. He was 78 when he died in 1840.

Whereas Billy Clift was a little human dynamo of a man, almost incapable of keeping still, whether in the saddle or on his feet, Sam Chifney the younger was quite unbelievably idle. All too often he would be seen wandering around the flat East Anglian countryside with a sporting gun under his arm and his lemon-and-white pointer Banker, at his heel when he should have been on the racecourse

Rather than enter into an agreement to exert himself with any regularity he declined the plum retainer from Lord Chesterfield, even though he would only have been required to ride the best horses, and missed winning The Oaks on Industry and The St Leger on Don John in 1838.

Had he been more ambitious, and of a more energetic disposition, Sam Chifney would almost certainly have been one of the outstandingly successful jockeys of the first half of the last century. By common consent he was an even better race rider than his father. A really brilliant judge of pace, he perfected the use of the 'Chifney Rush', and was as strong as any rider in a finish, or a set-to as they called it in those days.

As stable jockey to his elder brother Bill he obtained a large number of his most notable successes on horses owned by Squire Thomas Thornhill, of Riddlesworth, Norfolk, and Lord Darlington. For Squire Thornhill he won The Derby on Sam in 1818 and on Sailor two years later.

Even at the age of 18 Sam Chifney could not go to the scale at less than 7 st 9 lb and throughout his career he had difficulty in controling his weight, for at 5 ft 6 in. he was an inch taller than his father and somewhat larger of frame. All the same he went on riding intermittently until he was 57 in 1843 when he won The 1,000 Guineas on Squire Thornhill's Extempore, his last mount in public. The following year Squire Thornhill died, leaving his house and stables at Newmarket to Sam Chifney for life.

In November 1851 Sam Chifney finally left Newmarket to spend his last few years on the Sussex seaside at Hove. His final visit to a racecourse was to see his nephew Frank Butler win The Derby on West Australian in 1853. When he died in 1854 the stone erected at the head of his grave in the churchyard at Hove simply described him as 'Of Newmarket'. It was as eloquent a tribute as a great jockey could wish.

Old Dick Goodisson had two sons to follow him in the jockey's profession, though one of them, Charles died at the early age of 26 in 1813. The other, Thomas, was one of the most successful riders in the days of the Regency. Having had his first mount on the Duke of Bedford's Cub at the age of twelve at the Newmarket Houghton Meeting of 1794 little Tom Goodisson weighed out at just 4 st 1 lb when he rode the Duke of Queensberry's Pecker to beat Mr Wilson's Bennington in a match for 500 guineas a side over the Beacon Course in the May of the following year. A mile from home in that famous contest Goodisson senior jumped in to shout advice and encouragement to his son.

For a number of seasons Tom Goodisson had a retainer from the Duke of York, for whom he won The Derby on Moses in 1822. He never won either of the Newmarket classics but won The Derby on three other occasions — on Pope in 1809, Smolensko in 1813 and Whisker in 1815 — as well as The Oaks on Music in 1813 and Minuet in 1815 and the St Leger on Barefoot in 1823. Tom Goodisson was still living at Newmarket when he died in 1840.

John Barham Day on Lord George Bentinck's Crucifix

The most prolific father of jockeys in the early part of the last century was Lord Chesterfield's trainer James Edwards. When King George IV was watching 'Tiny' Edwards's string exercising one day he kept asking the names of the riders. On receiving the answer "Edwards" for about the sixth time the King exclaimed, "Bless me! What a lot of jockeys that woman breeds". The royal assumption was in fact, slight awry as the boys came variously from the three marriages of Tiny Edwards.

All those Edwards boys could ride well. There was Bill, who was to train for King George in the last years of his reign, Harry, George, Charlie, Edward and Freddie.

Harry Edwards was the best of them all, and better than almost all the rest of his contemporaries too. He had only one eye and no morals whatsoever. Had he been honest, Harry Edwards would have established himself as one of the outstanding jockeys in the whole history of the British Turf.

His enormous strength in a finish was his greatest asset. Sitting well back in the saddle, he spurred hard in front of the girth and made full use of his rather unusual length of arm as he swung his whip from quarters to shoulders and back again. Unfortunately he was an absolutely compulsive cheat who would rather stop a horse for £25 than earn a £100 share in the prize money. Early in his career he was second jockey to John Scott's powerful Malton stable for a number of seasons until he stopped Epirus at Wolverhampton, forgetting that the trainer's brother Bill had a mount in the same race and was able to witness at first hand that particular piece of malpractice.

Harry Edwards obtained his most important successes on Lord Egremont's Caroline in The Oaks in 1820 and the Duke of Grafton's Pastille in the same race two years later. Unlike the vast majority of jockeys of his own or even later times he had a remarkable knowledge of veterinary surgery, which could be of great value to his employers. When he was booked to ride Lord Chesterfield's Don John, winner of the previous season's St Leger, for Scott's stable at the Newmarket First Spring Meeting of 1839, owner and trainer were undecided as to whether to risk the colt's legs on the testing circuit of the Beacon Course. Eventually they consulted Edwards, who whipped off his white gloves, and having run his hands down the suspect limbs pronounced, "He'll pull through, but only just". Events proved him exactly right. Riding one of the finest races he had ever done, Edwards got Don John home from Lord Exeter's Almedar, the mount of Patrick Connolly, but by the time he pulled up both Don John's hind tendons had gone so badly that it was nearly an hour before they had him back in his box.

When at last he had completely lost the confidence of the English trainers Harry Edwards crossed the channel to France. The rigging of races was more or less common in that country, but even so local standards of integrity proved too high to permit the one-eyed English rider to flourish. Returning home he settled in Carlisle where he lived by his veterinary skill for a while before dying in dire poverty. They buried him in a pauper's grave.

George Edwards was a good jockey without the brilliance of his renegade brother Harry. He won The Oaks on Variation in 1830, The Derby on Lord Berner's Phosphorus in 1837 and The 1,000 Guineas on Cara two years later before General Jonathan Peel, brother of the Prime Minister Sir Robert Peel, secured him the position of trainer to the Duke of Orleans in France. The Duke was eldest son and heir of Louis Philippe, King of the French, and a great deal better liked than his grandfather, whom the Prince of Wales had so unceremoniously deposited in the goldfish pond. He was the owner of the Meudon Stud and was largely responsible for the laying out of the Chantilly course in 1834. The best horse that George Edwards trained for him was Beggarman, whom he sent over to win the Goodwood Cup in 1840. Two years later the Duke of Orleans was killed when thrown from a runaway carriage in the Avenue de la Grande Armée. George Edwards never really got over the death of the Duke and died in about 1850.

Two other sons of 'Tiny' Edwards also rode classic winners. Edward was successful in The 2,000 Guineas on both Sir John Shelley's Antar in 1819 and Lord Jersey's Asmet in 1837, as well as in The 1,000 Guineas on Lord Albemarle's Barcarolle in 1838, while Bill won The Oaks on Mr Craven's Bronze just after the beginning of the new century in 1806.

George Edwards's brother-in-law Arthur Pavis had the great asset in a jockey of being a man able to ride at a boy's weight and went to the scales at 6 st 10 lb right to the end of his career so that he could always ride against mere children on level terms. Such was the demand for his services that he had more mounts than any other rider season after season. That widespread patronage, together with the fuss made of him by grateful owners, combined to make him dreadfully conceited.

Lightweight jockey Arthur Pavis (1807-1839) surveys Archibald

He had his first mount in public on Nightshade at Exeter in 1821 when he weighed out at 3 st 11 lb and was beaten a head. Subsequently he spent a spell in Ireland riding for Lord Rossmore.

By the end of 1836 he had ridden 592 winners from 1,501 mounts. His only classic success was on General Peel's Archibald in The 2,000 Guineas in 1832 but he always maintained that he would have won The Derby on Caravan in 1837 instead of being beaten a head by Phosphorus had not his brother-in-law George Edwards on Phosphorus struck Caravan. For his part George Edwards was adamant that there were no grounds for family friction arising from the race.

Always smartly dressed in a sightly old fashioned way, wearing knee-high boots, rather than pantaloons, little Arthur Pavis had a fine collection of sporting prints in his fashionable home — described as 'a villa come down on a week's visit from Cheltenham' — somewhere in the vicinity of the White Hart. There he died after two days' illness at the early age of 32 on 15 October 1839. His brother Edward rode for the Duke of Orleans in France.

Poor Frank Boyce lived little longer than Arthur Pavis. A good jockey but an unlucky one, who invariably had his mounts fast away, he rode very few good horses, though he did win The 2,000 Guineas on Lord Exeter's Patron when there was only one other runner in 1825 and The Oaks on the Duke of Richmond's Gulnare in 1827. He should have won The Oaks again on Lord Berners' May-Day in 1834 had the filly not been killed when she broke a leg while well clear of the field with the race at her mercy. Two years later, on 4 November 1836 Frank Boyce died of consumption at Newmarket at the age of 38, a mere fortnight after the death of his wife from the same disease.

James Robinson, the son of a Newmarket stable lad, was in Robert Robson's stable for 13 years, during which time he received valuable tuition from Frank Buckle. By winning his sixth and final Derby on Bay Middleton in 1836 Robinson set a record for the number of Derby winners ridden at Epsom that stood for more than a century until equalled by Lester Piggott on Roberto in 1972 and then broken by him on The Minstrel in 1977.

At the age of 31 in 1824 Jem Robinson reached a memorable stage of his career and a turning point in his private life by winning a bet that he would bring off the double in the Epsom classics and marry within the week. He landed the wager by winning The Derby on Cedric on the Wednesday, The Oaks on Cobweb on the Friday and being wed to Miss Powell on the Saturday.

A thoroughly honest jockey, Jem Robinson was far too generous to amass a fortune. As with the £1,200 he was given after winning the St Leger on Matilda in 1827 he would gladly share his presents with his family, or just about anybody else. As easy going as he was open handed he always took rooms in London as soon as racing was over for the year so that he could spend the winter emptying his pockets of the not inconsiderable amount of money that he had earned in the course of the season.

On reaching manhood Jem Robinson rode many matches against

his mentor Frank Buckle. The most famous of these was for 300 guineas over the mile and a quarter Across the Flat on Monday 15 October 1821, the opening day of the Newmarket second October meeting. Robinson rode an unnamed bay colt by Ardrossan out of Vicissitude for Lord Exeter and Buckle, Mr John Udny's brown colt Abjer, who was giving 7 lb. As the Vicissitude colt had savaged him in the Ditch stables the previous week it was with no compunction that Robinson plied his whip with the utmost liberality to force a dead heat. The Vicissitude colt never forgot that thrashing. When Robinson was visiting Lord Exeter's Burleigh stud two years later he entered the horse's box on being given to understand that he had quite lost his temper, but the mere sight of the jockey was enough to make him savage again so that Robinson had to beat a very hasty retreat.

As well as The Derby six times Jem Robinson won The 2,000 Guineas nine, still a record for the race, The 1,000 Guineas five times, and The Oaks and The St Leger twice each. Thus until the advent of Lester Piggott he had ridden more classic winners than any other jockey save Frank Buckle.

The first of those 24 classics that he won had been on Azor in The Derby of 1817. Thirty-five years later his long career came to an end when his stirrup leather snapped and he was thrown as Lord Clifden's two-year-old Feramorz swerved after going just 30 yards in a match at Newmarket on 26 April 1852. Robinson broke a thigh and was left with one leg four inches shorter and a bad limp for the remainder of his life. Feramorz, who was running for the first time, turned out to be a notoriously hard ride and anything but a suitable mount for a veteran jockey just a year short of 60. Five months later he was to bolt with Frank Butler at the Houghton Meeting.

Characteristically Jem Robinson had no savings on which to support himself when he had finished riding, but was saved from poverty by pensions from the Dukes of Rutland and Bedford. For another 13 years he lived on at the red-brick cottage he had built in Old Station Road, now much enlarged and known as Machell Place. He died on 3 April 1865 and is buried in the cemetery at the top of the High Street.

Frank Butler, who had fared little better with the headstrong Feramorz than Jem Robinson, was the son of a successful Newmarket trainer and, as already mentioned, a grandson of Sam Chifney senior. He was apprenticed to his uncle Bill Chifney. Predictably he developed a partiality for waiting tactics and then winning his races with the famous 'Chifney Rush'. At times he was inclined to delay his challenge too long as was the case when Springy Jack failed by half a length to catch Surplice in The Derby of 1848.

When the luck of his Chifney relatives began to run out as he was approaching manhood in the 1830s Frank Butler was forced to go the rounds of the smaller meetings looking for spare rides until appointed first jockey to John Scott's great Malton stable in succession to the trainer's brother Bill. That year he rode his first classic winner on Poison in The Oaks.

In the course of just eleven years Frank Butler was successful in 14 classics, bringing his career to its climax by riding West Australian which became the first horse to wear the Triple Crown by winning The 2,000 guineas, The Derby and The St Leger in 1853.

Like all too many of his contemporaries in the weighing room Frank Butler was a long way from being incorruptible, so that the bookmaker Harry Hill and a bunch of his associates were able to bribe him to stop West Australian in the St Leger. With their suspicions aroused by the way the colt was drifting in the market John Scott's owners deputed Lord Stanley to appraise Butler of his fate should his riding give rise to even the faintest suspicion, and straightaway the willingness to lay against West Australian disappeared.

At the time of his triumphs on West Australian Frank Butler was only able to maintain a racing weight of 8 st 7 lb with the utmost difficulty, and was drinking heavily. It was hardly surprising, therefore, that he did not ride after that season.

A large fund of anecdotes about racing, recounted in a husky voice, made Frank Buckle an amusing companion, who liked to join in a sing-song after dinner. He did not enjoy his retirement from the saddle for long, dying after a lingering illness at the age of just 38 in 1856.

Few jockeys contributed more to the bad reputation that attached to racing in the middle of the last century than the foul-mouthed Sam Rogers. He was born at Newmarket in 1818 where his father, Joseph, was then private trainer to Lord Lowther.

A strong, rough jockey and a heavy gambler, Sam Rogers never hesitated to stop a horse if it suited his betting. Retribution eventually overtook him for laying against Ratan whom he rode for William Crockford in The Derby of 1844. His principal employer, Lord George Bentinck, who had backed the colt, demanded to see Rogers's betting book, and having obtained it stood on the steps of Epsom's Spreadeagle Hotel (then known as Lumley's) and addressed an assembly of bookmakers and professional backers as follows, "Gentlemen, I am going to call over my jockey Samuel Rogers's book, and will thank you to answer to your names and your bets".

Despite the ensuing revelations as to where Sam Rogers's interests lay he was nevertheless allowed to ride Ratan in The Derby a few days later — probably because the horse was trained by his father and the owner was a dying man. After being unplaced on Ratan to the ringer Maccabeus, racing in the name of Running Rein, in what was probably the most villainous of all Derbies, Sam Rogers was warned off though it was not until October that the Stewards of the Jockey Club passed sentence.

Largely through the influence of Lord George Bentinck, who was not usually the most forgiving of men, Sam Rogers was reinstated three years later in 1847. The following season he won the Cesarewitch on The Cur, trained by his father for Mr William Stirling Crawfurd.

When Joseph Rogers died in 1854 Sam Rogers took over the stable while continuing to ride, and won The 1,000 Guineas on the Duke o

West Australian, Frank Butler up, first winner of The Triple Crown in 1853

Bedford's Habena in 1855. His only other classic success had been on Lord George Bentinck's Firebrand in the same race in 1842.

Nat Flatman was a rider of very different moral calibre to Sam Rogers. Discreet, modest and utterly honest, he even earned the good opinion of Admiral Rous, who loathed jockeys as a species, regarding them as pampered, overpaid and by and large, untrustworthy. Nat would never accept a retainer of more than £50 a year from General Peel, his first employer, nor one in excess of £50 from Mr George Payne.

He was born at Holton St Mary in Suffolk in 1810, the son of a small farmer, and came to Newmarket as a boy of 15 weighing less than 4 st, to be apprenticed to General Peel's trainer William Cooper.

Nat was said to be "a good jockey by profession, rather than a brilliant horseman by intuition". Unlike most riders who reach the top of the tree, he made an extraordinarily slow start to his career, not having his first mount in public until he was 19 in 1829. Six years later he obtained his first classic success on Mr Charles Greville's Preserve in The 1,000 Guineas, winning the same race again on Clementina in 1847 and Imperieuse 1857. He also won the 2,000 Guineas three times — on Idas in 1845, Hernandez in 1851 and Fazzoletto in 1856 — and The St Leger on the same number of occasions. He was never first past the post in either of the Epsom classics though Orlando, on whom he finished second in the infamous Derby of 1844, was awarded the race on the disqualification of the ringer, Maccabaeus.

The great handicaps of the Newmarket autumn meetings were fully established long before Nat Flatman came to the end of his career, and he won them both more than once. In 1845 he brought off the double on The Baron, owned by Mr Watts, in the Cesarewitch and Mr Greville's Alarm in the Cambridgeshire while he was also successful on Vulcan in 1841 and Evenus in 1844 in the Cambridgeshire as well as on the 3-1 favourite Muscovite in the Cesarewitch in 1854.

As had been the case with Jem Robinson, Nat Flatman had his career brought to its end by an injury sustained on the Rowley Mile Course. He had just dismounted from the Duke of Bedford's Golden Pippin after being beaten three parts of a length by Alf Day on Apollo in a four furlong match on 29 September 1859 when the filly lashed out and kicked him hard in the body. He was far too badly injured to be able to weigh in and soon became seriously ill. By the following spring there were good prospects that he would recover, but he suffered a relapse after a drive in his carriage and died on 20 August 1860. He is buried beneath the tower of All Saints Church, Newmarket.

While Nat Flatman had been at the peak of his ability, proper records of the number of winners ridden by the leading jockeys were kept for the first time and he became the first acknowledged champion with 81 winners accredited to him in 1846. He was also champion for the next seven seasons, achieving a personal record on 104 winners in 1848.

Soon after the institution of the Jockeys' championship a new era of race riding opened. Largely due to the efforts and strength of character of Admiral Rous the authority of the Jockey Club was to be enormously increased so that the kind of villainy to which Harry Edwards and Sam Rogers had so lightly turned their hands would be no longer tolerated. Until the middle of the century absolutely honest jockeys like Frank Buckle and Jem Robinson were few and far between. The career of Nat Flatman marked the beginning of a tradition of integrity that would be maintained by such great jockeys as George Fordham, Fred Archer and Tom Cannon, though the strain of black sheep would never be completely bred out.

6 James Godding, Macaroni and Palace House

When James Godding started to give Macaroni his preparation for The Derby of 1863 on the Heath at Newmarket, he became the laughing-stock of the racing world. The pundits were loud in the opinion, which it had been so conventional to hold for 30 years, that the going at Newmarket was far too firm to allow horses to be properly trained on it. Moreover they pointed out that it was a particularly dry spring and this heightened the folly of not sending a colt with a chance in The Derby to do his work on the fashionable South Downs of Berkshire, Sussex and Wiltshire.

But 48-year-old Godding, 'rubicund Jem Godding' as one contemporary recalled him many years later, was impervious to the almost universal criticism of his faith in the Heath as a working ground. Unlike the critics he remembered how many good horses had been trained to win The Derby and other big races on it in years gone by, while in more recent history he himself had trained Feu de Joie to win The Oaks from Newmarket's Palace House stable the previous season. He declared that if he could not train a Derby winner on the Limekilns he could not train one anywhere.

Macaroni fully vindicated his trainer at Epsom, where he was engaged in a gruelling duel with Lord Clifden up the straight. Close home the strain told upon Lord Clifden for a fraction of a second in which he faltered, and Macaroni, making one more gigantic effort in response to the strong riding of Tom Chaloner, got up on the post to win by a head.

When the news that Macaroni had won The Derby reached Newmarket, the town went almost delirious with delight for reasons that went far deeper than mere enthusiasm for a local success. In short, the end of serious unemployment, which must have been a running sore in the town since the days of the Chifneys 30 years before, was at last in sight. Newmarket was saved as a training centre. Jem Godding had proved how a Derby winner could be trained on the Heath and his fellow Newmarket trainers would no longer have to go cap in hand for horses, while yards in which no trainer had had his string for many a year would soon be full again. This meant jobs for lads, farriers, saddlers, cornfactors and everybody concerned with racing, to say nothing of the business it offered the local shopkeepers and innkeepers. The welcome prospects held out by Macaroni's triumph in The Derby seemed endless. No wonder the bells of All Saints Church, next door to the Palace House yard, rang out to proclaim it.

Macaroni was owned by Richard Christopher Naylor, a Liverpool banker, who became Master of the Pytchley Hounds. He was not a very easy man to get on with; at least that was the view of his son-in-law Lord Rossmore, for he could be very mean and hard to please. As a result he made himself and many of those closest to him very unhappy. He would pay £300,000 for a piece of property as casually as though he were buying a new hat and then walk miles for the purchase of a box of pills if he thought he could save a farthing by doing so.

Naylor was not the only difficult cutomer to have horses with Jem Godding. For a short time the Earl of Glasgow, one of the most eccentric peers of his day, patronised Palace House.

As he was going round stables with the Earl one night they came to a handsome horse called Volunteer. "It is a curious thing," said the trainer, "but the owner and breeder has never seen this colt although he lives only four miles from here".

"Indeed," replied Lord Glasgow, "I should certainly have thought a gentleman would have come such a short journey to see such a good-looking horse".

"Yes," said Jem Godding, "but you see, my lord, the owner was born blind".

The joke was wasted upon the humourless Lord Glasgow, who reacted by chasing the luckless Jem around the Palace House yard calling him a 'red-faced scoundrel' and a lot else besides. A few days later he removed his horses, sending them back to Tom Dawson at Middleham's Tupgill yard, who had already had one dose of the Glasgow temperament.

Jem Godding had been born in 1815, the year of Wellington's victory over Napoleon at Waterloo, and, of more local interest, of work beginning on the building of the Rutland Arms. He had been seriously ill and confined to a wheelchair for some two years before he died at the comparatively early age of 58 on 14 June 1873. Although it was then ten years since he had won that memorable Derby with Macaroni, the people of Newmarket had not forgotten all that he had done for them. Above his grave in the cemetery at the top of the town stands a memorial inscribed: 'This monument was erected by a few friends as a testimonial of their respect and esteem. Though dead he still lives in the memory of those who loved him'.

James Kealey Godding was survived by a son, his namesake, who died at the age of 83 in 1944 and three daughters. Of these, one married the Waterwitch trainer Bill Jarvis and became the mother of Sir Jack, Willie and Basil, and another third married Tom Chaloner junior, son of Macaroni's jockey.

Macaroni's rider, Tom Chaloner the elder, had been born in Manchester in 1839 and apprenticed to John Osborne senior at Ashgill Middleham. Osborne always liked to recruit his apprentices from Manchester as he considered the lads from that city sharper and more intelligent than others. One might also add that they were lighter as well, on account of so many of its inhabitants having been reduced to something near starvation by the conditions produced by the Industrial Revolution. Judging by the novelist Mrs Gaskell's account of life in Manchester during the middle of the last century, the place must have been a breeding-ground for natural lightweights.

After having wed Nellie Osborne, the daughter of his master, Tom Chaloner came to Newmarket to ride for Richard Naylor, for whom he won The 2,000 Guineas as well as The Derby on Macaroni.

His other classic successes were obtained in The 2,000 Guineas on Moslem in 1868 and Gang Forward in 1873, in The Oaks on Feu de Joie in 1862, and in no fewer than five St Legers — on Caller Ou in 1861, The Marquis in 1862, Achievement in 1867, Formosa in 1868 and Craig Millar in 1875.

Tom Chaloner senior had already begun to train when he died at the early age of 47 in 1886, leaving his widow, Nellie, with sons Tom junior, Dick, Harry, George and Phil. Considering the difficulty that women had in getting the Jockey Club to grant them licences to train a few years ago, it may seem strange that as long ago as 1886 Nellie Chaloner was able to carry on her late husband's stable. Trainers did not have to be licensed in those days, but those at Newmarket needed the permission of the Jockey Club to use the Heath, so the Jockey Club must have given Nellie Chaloner full recognition.

On the death of their father, the indentures of the younger Chaloner boys were transferred to their mother. When George claimed the apprentices' allowance on a winner called Jacob at the now-extinct Hampton Court meeting one day, Charlie Wood, the rider of the second, objected on the grounds that the horse had carried the wrong weight. His argument was that a boy could not be indentured to a woman and as only properly indentured apprentices were entitled to the riding allowance George Chaloner could have no right to claim it, so Jacob had carried underweight.

This objection raised a point of law that put the Stewards in a quandary. Finally the matter was resolved in favour of the Chaloners by a sporting lawyer finding a precedent of a boy being apprenticed to a woman plumber and the courts recognising it as good legal practice. As is mentioned elsewhere, George Chaloner subsequently trained with great success at Newmarket.

Tom Chaloner junior trained at Newmarket's Stockbridge House stable, which is 192 High Street. He won some hefty bets when he landed the Cambridgeshire with Marco in 1895 and was able to retire shortly afterwards.

After riding many winners as a steeplechase jockey, Dick Chaloner took over the Osborne House stable from his mother and remained there until 1901 when he handed over to his brother Phil.

As for Nellie Chaloner, she lived on at Osborne House for many a year after her sons had finished training, and it was not until 1944 that the widow of the man who had ridden the Derby winner 61 years previously, died at the great age of 97.

Nellie Chaloner's brother was the celebrated Johnnie Osborne who was the leading jockey in the north throughout the second half of the last century. Among his classic successes was The Derby of 1869 on Pretender the last northern horse to win The Derby at Epsom.

Osborne House, named after Nellie Chaloner's family, still stands at the bottom of Warren Hill opposite the stable of Sir Mark Prescott.

7 Joe Dawson, Prince Charlie and Bedford Lodge

In terms of achievement, Joe Dawson must rate some way beneath his elder brother Mat. Yet although he did not do as much to make history as Mat and some of their other contemporaries, Joe played a more decisive part in the shaping of Newmarket's destiny and developing the art of training racehorses than ever Mat did. Whereas posterity has readily given Mat the credit he deserved for his many brilliant training successes, it has never really accorded Joe his due as an originator in more than one field.

Not only did Joe Dawson show great independence of mind by coming to Newmarket at all, for there he was, a young Scot, flying in the face of the opinions of the large majority of the most experienced English trainers — they were quite convinced that it was impossible to train horses at Newmarket — but in two other respects he showed the way along the road that others were to follow. He was the first Newmarket trainer to work his horses without sweating them, and he also revolutionised the methods of rearing young stock so that they were stronger and more forward when they came to be trained as two-year-olds.

Joseph Dawson was born on 27 December 1825, the son of George Dawson of Stamford Hall, Gullane, Scotland, and was one of four brothers to follow their father into the training profession, the others being Thomas, Mathew and John.

Like the others, he served his apprenticeship with his father, but he was still a young man when he left Scotland to train at East Ilsley in Berkshire. After a short while there he became private trainer to the Earl of Stamford, whose large string he took to Heath House at Newmarket. This is not the stable of the same name in which Sir Mark Prescott trains today, but the one that stood on the site of the hotel adjoining it.

The Earl of Stamford, a first class cricketer as well as a racehorse owner, was not an easy man for whom to train. He bet heavily, losing, for instance, £70,000 over Hermit's Derby, and made himself most unpopular with other owners by employing touts to watch the work of their horses so that he could punt on them. He paid big prices for his horses, was never niggardly when things were going well, but expected substantial returns from his investments in bloodstock.

In 1861 Joe Dawson won him The 2,000 Guineas with Diophantus but soon afterwards they fell out. To obtain money still owed to him, Joe Dawson had to take Lord Stamford to court.

With the proceeds of the successful litigation and his own savings Joe Dawson bought Bedford Lodge, which came on the market after the death of the seventh Duke of Bedford in 1861. That Duke had had very little interest in racing, nor had his father, but his uncle, the fifth Duke, had won The Derby with Skyscraper in 1789, Eager in 1791 and Sister to Pharamond in 1797.

The first purchaser of Bedford Lodge had been Sir Joseph Hawley, who passed it on to the old Duke's trainer William Butler on hearing he had set his heart on it. Had he not done so the great stable he and his trainer John Porter were to found would have been at Newmarket instead of Kingsclere.

William Butler did not avail himself of Sir Joseph's generosity for long, as he had sold Bedford Lodge for £6,500 within a year or two. As the stabling had been sold separately, Joe Dawson's first task was to build himself a yard. When this was completed in 1864, it was acclaimed as a model training establishment with every possible amenity.

Bedford Lodge and the stables that Joe Dawson erected on the eastern side of it became separate properties some 50 years ago. The house is now an excellent hotel, retaining the original name, while the yard has been renamed Highfield. John Winter trains there today.

As well as Bedford Lodge, Joe Dawson acquired the range of paddocks that ran from there to the top of the Limekilns, the land along the north of the Bury Road which was to become the site of the Stanley House, Freemason Lodge, Carlburg and Clarehaven stables. These paddocks he stocked with the broodmares, which were the foundation of the stud that he ran on lines far more enlightened than the majority of his contemporaries.

While Joe Dawson was developing this stud, the racing of two-year-olds was becoming a more important feature than hitherto. Joe Dawson and his contemporary William Blenkiron, of the Middle Park Stud at Eltham in Kent, were the first men to recognise the need for developing the strengths and physique of young horses from their earliest days if they were going to be capable of maximum two-year-old performance.

Nothing was too much trouble, and nothing was too expensive for Joe Dawson when it came to feeding his foals and yearlings in the paddocks behind Bedford Lodge. If they would have eaten gold he would have fed it to them. To provide a more practical diet he had the best of the oats sent down from the Carse O'Gowrie in his native Scotland. Moreover, he reared the foals on the richest Alderney milk and was always careful to mix vetch and carrots with their feeds to make them more appetising. After the much more haphazard methods that had been prevalent in the studs at Newmarket and elsewhere during the previous 50 years or so, these measures were completely revolutionary.

The great care that Joe Dawson took to bring on the produce of his stud had all the desired effects. A writer in the volume on racing in the Badminton Library, published in 1887, remarks that the foals at Bedford Lodge looked like yearlings before Christmas. When these carefully reared and well-matured youngsters were ready to go into training they enjoyed a great advantage over those in other stables and Joe Dawson soon acquired a well-deserved reputation for his outstanding successes with two-year-olds. He won the first running of the Middle Park Plate with The Rake in 1866 and won it again with Frivolity in 1869, Prince Charlie in 1871, and Peter in 1878.

Prince Charlie, a gentle giant of a chestnut colt standing 17 hands high, was the best horse that Joe Dawson ever trained and was a great favourite with the public on account of his being almost unbeatable on his home course at Newmarket. They dubbed him 'The Prince of the T-Y-C', that being the abbreviation for Newmarket's two-year-old course, and a poem of eight stanzas was written in his honour.

When this great tall colt was first led into Bedford Lodge by a smock-clad farm labourer, no-one formed a very favourable opinion of him. Joe Dawson's initial reaction was to declare that he should be sent straight back home while his head lad Billy Greaves contented himself with the remark that they were going to need a ladder to get on to his back. Not without misgivings they decided to give him a chance but consigned him to some boxes the lads called the 'Hovels', that stood on the boundary with what is now Stanley House, along with the rest of the less promising yearlings.

By the summer Prince Charlie had started to muscle up and develop the strength to match his enormous frame, so that Joe Dawson entertained the idea that he might conceivably be something. Accordingly he allowed the colt to make his debut in the Middle Park Plate. He was obviously still backward and started at 100-9 in a field of 16 without a trace of confidence behind him, but to everybody's surprise he got home by a head from Laburnum. That first outing and another fortnight's work did wonders for Prince Charlie who showed great improvement when beating Nuneham by a length with Cremorne another two lengths away third in the Criterion Stakes. After that Prince Charlie went into winter quarters, but not in the 'Hovels'. He was now promoted to the splendid new stables his trainer had built seven years before and commanded the respect due to a horse with classic pretentions.

Prince Charlie thrived during the early weeks of the close season and his prospects of winning The Guineas looked brighter and brighter. Then it happened. Early in January 1872 they heard him make noise in his work, so there they were with a champion on their hand and that champion a roarer. He was going to be difficult if not impossible to train, and things looked no brighter when later in the month Jo Dawson was taken seriously ill, probably from the diabetes that was to prove fatal, and Bill Greaves had to take over the stable.

A slight inflammation of the knee in Craven week caused serious alarm about the colt but this cleared up in a day or two and as Prince Charlie had had all the work he needed there was no shortage of condition about him. Better still, from all that could be learned from his work, the infirmity in his wind did not impair his ability, so it looked as if the great chestnut might yet win The Guineas.

There were 16 runners for The Guineas that year. Before long it was apparent that the race lay between Prince Charlie and Cremorne with the rest out of the back door, and at the post the verdict went to Prince Charlie by a neck. On the strength of that success he was made a hot favourite for The Derby despite the fact that a horse of his great size was most unlikely to be at home on the switchback course on the Surrey Downs. Not only was Prince Charlie unsuited to the Epsom course, but he did not stay it either and was unplaced to his old rival Cremorne, trained by William Gilbert at Newmarket.

His defeat in The Derby was one of only four that Prince Charlie suffered during his four seasons in training. As a four-year-old in 1873 he won ten times from as many starts and in his final season he was eight times successful from nine attempts. By the end of his career this popular and lovable horse had won 25 of his 29 races, been runner-up twice, third once, and unplaced in one race — The Derby, his earnings amounting to £14,025.

Perhaps the most widely acclaimed of all Prince Charlie's successes was his final one in a match with the French horse Peut-Etre over the Rowley Mile. Four days earlier Peut-Etre had won the Cambridgeshire and the cock-a-hoop Frenchmen boasted that he could beat any horse on earth at weight-for-age over a mile.

The gauntlet was picked up on Prince Charlie's behalf, and the French, who had won a small fortune over the Cambridgeshire, went for still more, while English backers would not hear of their idol being beaten on his favourite course. National honour seemed to become more and more involved as the stakes of the two camps mounted. The bookmakers asked 2-1 about Prince Charlie. This looked a giveaway price about a Guineas winner conceding 12 lb to a horse that had just won the Cambridgeshire under 6 st 13 lb, but the French were amazingly confident and kept the market alive. After all the excitement that preceded this famous match, the running of it came as a great anti-climax. Prince Charlie simply hacked up without the Frenchman having ever delivered anything like a challenge. English backers went mad with delight and so did all the stable lads in Newmarket, not just those from Bedford Lodge. They cheered Prince Charlie to the echo. Rarely can there have been such a scene on Newmarket Heath. The crowd was still cheering when his owner, Mr Jones, a Littleport farmer, insisted on mounting the successful favourite and riding him in triumph back to Bedford Lodge on the other side of the town.

A visitor to Newmarket High Street that afternoon might have supposed he had happened upon a carnival. As the gigantic Prince Charlie, with his joyous owner on board, made his way through the centre of the town he was escorted by a huge following of lads and successful punters still huzzaing the horse, patting him and even pulling hairs from tail. It was a good thing that Prince Charlie was endowed with the most placid temperament imaginable or somebody might have been hurt!

Prince Charlie was not a great success at stud during the few seasons he stood in England. On the death of his owner he was sold to

America. Across the Atlantic he did a great deal better, the good horses that he sired including Salvator, who won the Great Futurity Stakes. His death at the age of 21 in 1890 was regarded as a major calamity by American breeders.

As well as pioneering ways of rearing horses, Joe Dawson also adopted methods of training them that were new, at least as far as Newmarket was concerned. As has already been mentioned in passing, it was Joe's elder brother, Tom, trainer of the Derby winners Ellington and Pretender as well as a host of other good horses at Middleham's Tupgill yard, who first omitted sweats from his work schedule. But while he was obtaining brilliant results from the new methods he was employing on Middleham Moor in the north, the Newmarket trainers still employed the traditional ones that had commended themselves to the Chifneys, the Edwardses and the Arnulls in the first half of the century.

When Joe Dawson trained his horses by confining them to galloping and routine cantering he became the laughing-stock of the Heath. The older and conservative Newmarket trainers, with all the prejudice bred of following one routine for a lifetime, roundly declared that horses could never be made fit by such molly-coddling. Joe Dawson, who was always seeking improvement in the ways of preparing horses both on the training ground and the stud, was indifferent to their ridicule. Elder brother Tom had made these methods work, and before long Joe, in his turn, was able to prove that horses could indeed be trained on far less drastic preparations than those that they had had hitherto.

When the Bedford Lodge horses began to win very much more than their share of races, the new ways by which they were trained could no longer be ignored and the apostles of sweating were laughing on the other sides of their faces. Inevitably, first one of the old-time trainers and then another gave up sweating his horses, while those that were just setting up their stables probably adopted the new methods from the start, so that before he died at the early age of 54 in 1880, Joe Dawson had the satisfaction of seeing that sweating no longer had any part in the work done by horses on the Heath.

Other important successes obtained by Joe Dawson besides those already mentioned included The St Leger with Mr T. V. Morgan's Hawthornden in 1871, The 1,000 Guineas with Lord Stamford's Lady Augusta in 1863 and Elizabeth in the year of his death, and the Royal Hunt Cup with Thuringian Prince in 1875 and Julius Caesar in 1878. Had the Middle Park Stakes winner, The Rake, not broken down in the final stages of his preparation for The Derby of 1867, he might well have been returned the winner of that race instead of Hermit, thus postponing if not averting the ruin of the Marquess of Hastings.

For a man who showed so much originality in his professional life, it is surprising that Joe Dawson should have been somewhat dominated by his wife, Harriet, at home. Yet this does seem to have been the case. She was a niece of the Middleham trainer John Fobert, who had won The Derby with The Flying Dutchman in 1849.

During the closing years of his life Joe Dawson was a chronic sufferer from diabetes, and was able to play little active part in the running of the Bedford Lodge stable. As a result most aspects of the training of the horses were left in the hands of his head lad, Richard 'Buck' Sherrard. Eventually Joe Dawson succumbed to the disease that had been torturing him for so long on 23 July 1880, when Sherrard took over the stable. The redoubtable Harriet survived him until 1902.

Although other men have trained more winners and won more of the important races than Joe Dawson did, few have exerted so much influence on the development of the twin arts of rearing and training horses. His achievements are all the more remarkable for their having been accomplished in a relatively brief life span.

8 Tom Jennings, Phantom House and Lagrange

For the last 40 years of the nineteenth century taciturn Tom Jennings controlled the international interests of one of the most powerful stables in Newmarket. It was, in many ways, only natural that he should have taken a stable there when he brought over a contingent of French-owned horses to be trained for their English engagements. Many another man might have given the half-forsaken Newmarket a wide berth and followed the fashion to the South Downs, but Tom Jennings was born and bred in East Anglia only a few miles from the Heath.

When Tom was born in 1823 his father, John Jennings, was farming at Shelford near Cambridge. Shortly afterwards John Jennings became landlord of the Swan at Bottisham on the road between Cambridge and Newmarket. As this was a posting house for the stage coaches, accommodation had to be given to as many as 40 horses at a time and it must have been amongst these roadsters that Tom Jennings learned the rudiments of stable craft. At the same time he must have heard the travellers discussing the racing at Newmarket and all the gossip of the town, for when Tom Jennings was a boy the Chifneys were still at the height of their fame and Newmarket one of the hubs of the fashionable world in the England of bumbling old King George IV.

Maybe it was because the standard of racing at Newmarket declined and the number of horses trained there was sharply reduced that Tom Jennings did not go literally down the road when he was ready to be apprenticed, or maybe it was just because of the better opportunities offered by family connections. At all events, he and his elder brother Henry, whom they called 'Hat' Jennings, went over to France to be indentured to their relative, Tom Carter, at Chantilly near Paris in 1836.

In 1841 Tom was riding for brother 'Hat' and that year they were responsible for Nativa winning the first running of the Prix de Diane, the French Oaks. About a year later the brothers quarrelled. Neither spoke to or acknowledged the other for 18 years. After they had split Tom Jennings went further afield to train at Piedmont in northern Italy. In 1850 or 1851 he returned to France and a few years later he had charge of the stable of Comte Frédéric de Lagrange, the son of one of Napoleon's marshals, and his partner Baron Niviers. In 1857 Lagrange and his partner decided to split their racing interests between their own country and England. Accordingly Tom Jennings was sent to Newmarket with a string with which to start a stable at Phantom House and his elder brother 'Hat' had charge of those left in France.

The French horses soon made their presence felt in England.

Monarque, the son of the once despised Poetess, won the Goodwood Cup in 1857, and other successes followed. Much as one would like to think of one's ancestors as good losers, it would be idle to pretend that there was a healthy and friendly spirit of Anglo-French rivalry on The Turf in mid-Victorian times or that the English accepted the triumphs of the French invaders gracefully. On the contrary, the French horses and their connections were unpopular both with English owners and with racegoers in general. It became very much the thing to do to object to a French winner on any conceivable pretext and the crowd could always be relied upon to give a successful French horse a pretty rough passage to the winner's enclosure. As a result Tom Jennings was obliged to hire an assortment of prize fighters to provide an escort for his horses when they appeared in public.

Matters came to a climax and the pugs really had to earn their wages after Fille de l'Air had won The Oaks in 1864. The Epsom crowd went nearly berserk and it seemed as though they would have torn horse and jockey limb from limb had they been able to get near them. Poor Fille de l'Air may have deserved no such treatment but the same could not be said about her rider, Arthur Edwards, who would have incurred the same displeasure had he ridden an English-trained winner in similar circumstances. At Newmarket Fille de l'Air had finished last in The 2,000 Guineas, and not only many members of the public but Tom Jennings thought that Edwards had pulled her. The trainer had wanted to put up another jockey in The Oaks but Comte de la Grange would not hear anything against Edwards. The Count soon changed his ideas about Edwards. A few weeks after The Oaks he stopped Fille de l'Air again in the Grand Prix de Paris at Longchamp. When Tom Jennings went to have matters out with him he locked himself in the jockeys' lavatory and refused to weigh in.

One evening when Tom Jennings was showing a party of Frenchmen around the Phantom House yard they came to a great ugly raking bay colt with hardly a vestige of quality about him. That, the trainer informed them, was his cab horse and they believed him. On the completion of their tour one of the visitors expressed the disappointment they all felt at not having seen Gladiateur, the winner of that year's Derby. Thereupon Tom Jennings assured them that they had and took them back to see the animal that had been dismissed as a cab horse saying, in characteristic manner, that he had not supposed that even they would have been such fools as to believe him.

To be fair, one can hardly blame the Frenchmen for failing to acclaim Gladiateur at first sight. This great ungainly horse hardly looked like a Derby winner and, as often as not, he did not move like one. He was almost chronically lame and suffered from navicular disease. Moreover, he had been trodden on as a foal by his dam, who had herself been too unsound to be trained, and throughout his life he carried an enlargement of his off fore. Thus not only did Gladiateur's appearance do him no favours, but in far more important respects he was a trainer's nightmare. Yet Tom Jennings prepared this inelegant giant to win the Triple Crown (The 2,000 Guineas, The Derby and The

St Leger), and he also sent him across the Channel to win the Grand Prix de Paris in his native France in 1865.

When Gladiateur won The Derby, with the short-sighted Harry Grimshaw in the saddle, the ranks of Tuscany could scarce forbear to cheer. Whether or not he was French, everyone at Epsom was prepared to give a really good horse the reception that he deserved and the atmosphere was very different to what it had been when Fille de l'Air had won The Oaks on the same course twelve months previously. For their part, the French went mad with delight and spoke more than figuratively when they declared that Gladiateur was the avenger of Waterloo.

However well the crowd at Epsom may have behaved, at least one man at Doncaster still had the old entrenched attitude of hostility to the French runners. After Gladiateur had beaten The Oaks winner Regalia by three lengths in The St Leger, Regalia's owner, Mr Graham, objected to him on the score of his being a four-year-old. Understandably the Stewards took the view that had Gladiateur been any older than he was alleged to be the matter would have been brought to their notice after he had won The Guineas or The Derby.

Kept in training as a four-year-old, Gladiateur crowned his brilliant career by beating Regalia by 40 lengths in the Gold Cup at Royal Ascot. As the ground was as hard as a road, that was a great achievement by a horse with such bad legs. When he had finished racing, Gladiateur retired to William Blenkiron's Middle Park Stud at Eltham in Kent at a fee of 100 guineas but he was never anything like as good as a stallion as he had been as a racehorse.

In his work on the Heath at Newmarket, Gladiateur was always ridden by George Barbee, who had been born in Norwich. In 1872 Barbee was persuaded to go to America by Mr John Chamberlain and ten years later his riding was almost dominating the long-distance races in that country. It was this English jockey who rode the first winner of the Preakness Derby, John Chamberlain's Survivor in 1873. George Barbee was still living in America when over 80 in 1930.

Needless to say Tom Jennings had made a lot of money over Gladiateur, whom he had backed to win The Derby at £30,000 to £1,000 as early as 1863. In those days of heavy wagering on the big events long before they took place, it was possible to do this as the leading layers were accustomed to make a yearling book on The Derby of two seasons ahead.

A large part of his winnings over Gladiateur Tom Jennings used to purchase a derelict mansion called Cockfield Hall some 20 miles from Newmarket. This he pulled down and rebuilt with bricks from his own brickyard which he had established nearby.

With the outbreak of the Franco-Prussian War in 1870, Baron Schickler, M Delamarre, M Lupin, M Delatre, Baron Niviers, who had left the Phantom House stable in 1863, and other patriotic French owners transferred their racing interests to the safety of English stables.

Comte Frédéric de Lagrange, who was already established in

England, did the very opposite, putting up his entire stud, including Gladiateur, for sale. Not only was the Count a Bonapartist in politics, as became a son of one Napoleon's generals, but he was a close friend of the Emperor Napoleon III. Thus the fall of the Second Empire in 1871 left him not only much impoverished but sad and almost broken in spirit. The debonair and immaculately turned out man of the sixties became one who had aged fast in a few years, whose hair and moustache had a bedraggled look about them and whose clothes were old and ill-fitting.

The Count tried to put his troubles behind him and resumed racing in England, but things were never really the same again. Eventually his affairs were put into the hands of the Public Liquidator in Paris, though when that official sent his agents to collect the Count's horses in England shrewd old Tom Jennings refused to hand them over until he had received payment of their owner's outstanding training fees. That same year, 1883, Comte Frédéric de Lagrange, once the owner of the greatest horse France had produced up to that time, died at the age of 67 as he tottered on the brink of brankruptcy.

The Count was not the only Frenchman associated with Phantom House to encounter financial trouble in the seventies. As a result Tom Jennings was left with a great many bad debts on his hands.

Despite the misfortunes that the Frenchmen encountered, their unpopularity in English racing circles remained undiminished. As late as 1879 Tom Jennings and Mat Dawson came to blows at their lodgings for the Epsom Derby meeting, after Dawson, in characteristically forthright fashion, had declared that the French horses and all their connections should be bundled back to France. The upshot of the affair was that old Mat collected a black eye. Rather than let the same be seen in public he stayed in bed the following day instead of saddling Lord Falmouth's Wheel of Fortune to win The Oaks.

Tom Jennings had six sons. One of these, Tom Jennings junior, rode with considerable success, first on the flat and then over the sticks. One of the highlights of his career came when he won the Sandown Grand Prize hurdle on the 20-1 shot Rifle in 1879, but although he was still only 24 by the following year it was already becoming evident that young Tom would soon be too heavy for riding and would have to turn to training.

At about the same time his mother was hankering after a new and modern house to be designed and built in the highest fashion of late Victorian times. Falling in with his wife's ideas, Tom Jennings senior built a house and yard a little way up the Fordham Road from Phantom House at the joining with the Snailwell Road. Having done this he handed over Phantom to the younger Tom, who was then ready to begin his career as a trainer.

His new stable Tom Jennings senior named Lagrange to perpetuate the memory of the man whose patronage gave him his first chances in English racing, and who owned Gladiateur, the greatest horse he ever trained.

The deep red bricks with which the establishment was built all came from Tom Jennings's own kilns at Cockfield. From the same source also came the bricks for the construction of Warren Towers.

In the tradition of the old school of Newmarket trainers, Tom Jennings was a hard man on his horses. He believed in giving them plenty of work, especially the stayers, and those that stood up to his methods were generally something out of the ordinary. For the new-fangled equipment for giving support to horses' legs he had no time. One of his favourite sayings was, "Take off those boots and bandages and give nature a chance and you will have less horses break down by far than is the case now".

It was as a trainer of stayers that he was most famous. As well as winning the Goodwood Cup with Monarque and the Ascot Gold Cup with Gladiateur he won both events on several other occasions. Perhaps the best of his other Ascot Gold Cup winners was Tristan who was successful in 1883. At the Royal Meeting of 1878 he brought off one of the most remarkable trebles in the history of racing, for not only did he win the Cup with Verneuil but the Vase and the Alexandra Plate with the same horse.

In 1890 he won the Cesarewitch with Sheen for Prince Soltykoff, whose horses he had taken over on the death of Charlie Blanton in 1887, and he obtained one of the last important successes in his long career when Cypria dead-heated in the Cesarewitch of 1893.

Tom Jennings was essentially a reserved man, who kept his own counsel at all times. He never asked a question and he never answered one. He knew how to look after his own interests, but was as straight as a dye in all his dealings and in the privacy of his family circle he was an admirable father, all of whose children prospered.

In his relationship with the rest of the inhabitants of Newmarket, and even with most of his training colleagues, he was apt to hold himself aloof. True he would go down to the White Hart for a glass or two of whisky with Bill Jarvis and other trainers in the evenings, but even then he was hardly convivial. In *The Sportsman* of 1883 the Special Commissioner wrote, "Cold in his deportment, and with, shall I say a 'dignity of soul' that has kept him rather too much above familiarity even with his equals, Mr. Thos. Jennings senior is nevertheless without any superior in his business of a trainer".

As he was never entirely sociable with the other trainers, it almost goes without saying that Tom Jennings's relationship with the racing press was totally non-existent. Later on in the article just quoted, Special Commissioner wrote "In his [Jennings's] opinion of the capabilities of his many great winners of the past he was as undaunted as a rock but he was also as silent as a gravestone, and few, if any, members of the sporting press ever succeeded in gaining any information from him that was likely to be of any benefit to himself... that his line of policy with regard to members of the fourth estate has been popular with these gentlemen, on the whole, it would be hypocrisy to admit".

Although Tom Jennings was so often unforthcoming to the individual inhabitants of Newmarket, he was far from indifferent to the well-being of the town and its community. It was through his efforts almost as much as through anyone else's that the two hospitals were built, for ever since he had had smallpox during his days in Italy he had been keenly interested in the question of health. He was also tirelessly insistent on the necessity of everybody drinking clean water and, to the embarrassment of many in authority, never left the matter alone for long until the Newmarket Waterworks were built. Because of his great preoccupation with these issues, Tom Jennings became generally known as 'Old Waterworks' amongst the stable lads and others in Newmarket during the closing years of his life.

Along with Joe Dawson, Joe Hayhoe, Baron Meyer de Rothschild, James Godding and Captain Machell, Tom Jennings was one of those who helped make Newmarket great again during the middle of the nineteenth century. When he died at the age of 77 on 12 December 1900 he had outlived all those others, most of them by the best part of a quarter of a century or more. His eldest daughter married her cousin William Carter of the famous French-based training family, and their daughter Catherine married Major Eric Rickman, who wrote as 'Robin Goodfellow' of the *Daily Mail* for 20 years. One of Major Rickman's sons was John Rickman, 'Gimcrack' of the *Daily Sketch* and a popular interviewer on ITV's racing programmes.

9 More about Palace House, the Rothschilds and their Trainers, the Hayhoes

Another sign of recovery in Newmarket's fortunes was the arrival of Joseph Hayhoe with the horses of Baron Meyer Rothschild in 1857. These were possibly trained at Exeter House for about ten years, but when Jem Godding retired the Baron bought Palace House, installing Hayhoe in the trainer's house in the corner of the yard on the opposite side of the road. For more than half a century this establishment was the racing headquarters of the English branch of the Rothschild family in whose possession it remains to this day. Bruce Hobbs, the present Palace House trainer, leases the yard from Mr Evelyn de Rothschild.

Baron Meyer Rothschild was a grandson of that Meyer Rothschild who had laid the foundation of the immense fortunes of his family at Frankfurt-am-Main towards the end of the eighteenth century. This first Meyer secured the lucrative position of banker to the Landgrave of Hesse-Cassel, who obtained huge sums of money by hiring out his subjects as mercenaries to the other European powers. Whenever one of these Hessians was killed in action his employer was obliged to compensate the Landgrave in hard cash.

The original Meyer had five sons whom he set up in financial houses at strategic points throughout Europe. While Amscher, the eldest remained in Germany, Nathan, the second came to London, Carl was based in Italy, Salomon in Vienna and Jacob in Paris. It was through the complicated financial network these five brothers controlled that the British Government was able to pay Wellington's troops in the Peninsular War.

Baron Meyer Rothschild, who purchased Palace House, was the fourth and youngest son of Nathan, the first of his family to come to England. The title of baron was an Austrian one. In 1822 the House of Rothschild made a large loan to the all-powerful Austrian minister Prince Metternich. By way of appreciation, Metternich persuaded the Emperor to confer the title of baron on the five brothers, already mentioned, and all their male descendants.

The Baron first registered his colours as amber with lilac sleeves and red cap in 1842. The following year he changed them to dark blue and yellow cap, the colours that are carried by horses belong to the owner of Palace House today.

Until 1856 the Baron's horses were trained by Joe Hayhoe at Russley Park near Lambourn in Berkshire. Joe Hayhoe had been head lad to the great John Scott, who is credited with having trained 16 winners of The St Leger, at Malton's Whitewall stable. On coming to Russley Park he thought that he had reached the end of the world, so remote was that property from most other human habitation, and he persuaded his employer to move the stable to Newmarket. The town might have been unfashionable amongst the racing world in general but at least it provided a rather more congenial atmosphere than that prevalent at Russley Park.

As money was more or less unlimited, it is hardly surprising that Baron Meyer Rothschild was able to build up a powerful stud which supplied him with a regular flow of winners. As a result 'Follow the Baron' became the motto of a very large section of the racing public.

The greatest season that this, the first of the racing Rothschilds, enjoyed was that of 1871, which has gone down in history as 'The Baron's Year'.

The bay filly Hannah, whom he had named after his daughter and heiress, brought off a wonderful treble in The 1,000 Guineas, The Oaks and The St Leger, while Favonius won him The Derby by beating the dead-heaters Albert Victor and King of the Forest by a length and a half.

In all three of her classic triumphs, Hannah was ridden by Charlie Maidment. He also won The Derby on Cremorne and Kisber and obtained a number of other important successes but he was a poor man by the time he retired from the saddle in 1891. To supplement his tiny income he continued riding work at Newmarket for a good number of years, eventually dying in the town at the age of 82 in 1926.

After Hannah had completed her classic treble by beating Albert Victor by a length in The St Leger, Baron Rothschild outraged all the professional instincts of his excellent trainer by ordering the filly straight back to Newmarket, not for a well-earned rest, but so that she could play the humble role of trial tackle for the stable's Cesarewitch candidate Corisande! Joe Hayhoe remonstrated for all he was worth but nothing he said could make any impression on the Baron, who was determined to know whether or not he had the Cesarewitch in safe-keeping, for if he had, he was determined to have the cream of the market. He was perfectly agreeable to the public following the Baron, and not a little flattered that it should want to, but when it came to betting he had no intention of allowing the public to precede him.

Thus it was that on the Friday after the St Leger Corisande came to be tried with the winner of three classics at level weights over two miles on the racecourse side. Hannah won the gallop, but by no more than a head. That made Corisande a moral certainty to win the Cesarewitch with 7 st 12 lb.

With all the best horses away at Doncaster, most of the touts took no interest in what took place on the Heath that Friday morning, but one, by the name of Sam Quince, more conscientious that the rest, saw exactly what went on. There was nothing for it but to offer to let him stand in with the stable's commission provided he told nobody of what he had seen Corisande do. Sam Quince was as good as his word and the Baron was able to get £10,000 to £300 about the filly. The following month the form of the gallop worked out to perfection when Corisande won the Cesarewitch very easily, so the Baron got his

Baron Meyer de Rothschild (1818-1874), owner of the Palace House Stables in which Joe Hayhoe trained him the 1871 Derby winner Favonius

Leopold de Rothschild (1845-1917), owner of the 1904 Derby winner St Amant, trained at Palace House

money as well as his way over that race.

Favonius remained in training as a four-year-old in 1872. After he had won the Goodwood Cup in a canter, Joseph Hayhoe declared he, "would not take a thousand pounds for a hair of that horse's tail". Subsequently Favonius was retired to the Baron's Mentmore Stud but he died at the early age of nine in 1877.

Baron Meyer Rothschild did not long survive the year in which his horses almost swept the board in the classics, dying on 6 February 1874 at the age of 55. The first Jew to be elected a member of the Jockey Club, he was universally popular both on account of his genial personality and his great generosity to private individuals as well as public charities. He was survived by his daughter Hannah; she married Lord Rosebery, who was to become Prime Minister towards the end of the century. Their elder son, the late Lord Rosebery, carried on his grandfather's Mentmore Stud with conspicuous success, as is mentioned elsewhere.

After the death of Baron Meyer Rothschild, his nephew Leopold de Rothschild took over Palace House, where Alfred Hayhoe continued to train. About this time the Baltazzi brothers, sons of a Levantine merchant, joined the stable. It was for them that Hayhoe trained Kisber to win The Derby in 1876. Although foaled in Hungary, Kisber came of exclusively English stock.

Three years later, in 1879, Palace House won The Derby for the third time within a decade when Mr Leopold de Rothschild's Sir Bevys provided that great jockey George Fordham with his only successful ride in the race. Sir Bevys ran in Mr de Rothschild's assumed name of 'Mr Acton'. He had been using this *nom-de-course* since the death of his uncle five years previously but after he became the owner of a Derby winner he registered the dark blue jacket and yellow cap in his own name. 'The Acton', under which he had concealed his identity, was the name of the place where he had a stud just north of London. It is now the site of one of the suburbs of the capital and a less likely place to be suitable for the rearing of racehorses is unimaginable.

When Joseph Hayhoe died in 1881, his son Alfred, who was then only 29, succeeded him as trainer to Leopold de Rothschild and his friends. Like his father, Alfred was a first-class man at his job, but we have it on the authority of George Lambton that he tended to be hard on his horses, who needed constitutions of iron to stand up to the work he gave them.

An ideal subject for the training of Alfred Hayhoe was that hard and sturdy brown colt St Frusquin, who won The 2,000 Guineas for Leopold de Rothschild in 1896.

10 A Pair of Gamblers – Captain Machell and Jack Hammond

No man made a greater contribution to the rehabilitation of Newmarket as a training centre in the middle of the last century than Captain Machell, whose formidable character and successful management of the Bedford Cottage stable made him one of the most important personalities in the town for a period of almost 40 years.

James Octavius Machell belonged to an old Westmoreland family, but it was at Beverley in Yorkshire that he was born in 1838, the youngest son of a clergyman. As a very young man he was commissioned into the 14th Regiment of Foot and subsequently transferred into the 59th Foot. An outstanding athlete, he excelled as a runner, and on one memorable occasion won a bet in Makin's Hotel, Dublin, that he could jump onto the mantlepiece from a standstill, making a full turn in mid-air and landing with his back to the wall.

While stationed at The Curragh he acquired his taste for racing. When still only a subaltern he owned a useful sprinting mare in Grisi, who won three races at The Curragh and two more at Bellewstown in 1862. Promoted Captain the following year he won with his two-year-old Bacchus, a well-named bay colt by Claret, at Bellewstown and rode another of his horses, Little Nelly, to beat Master Richard on the Heath of Maryborough the following year.

Already bitterly disappointed at having been too young to serve in the Crimean War, he was soon disillusioned by the monotony of peacetime soldiering, and resigned his commission to make a living from his understanding of horses and knowledge of racing, in particular the intricacies of handicapping. Although he had been able to ride at little more than 10 st in 1863 he soon grew into a large man, and with his walrus moustache and ramrod back, long retained his military demeanour. In character as unbending as he was in appearance, he had a coldness about him that was better calculated to generate respect than affection, while his inbred suspicion ruined more than one of the few friendships that he did make, and ultimately brought him much unhappiness. In his early days at Newmarket George Fordham was his favourite jockey, but after he had backed a horse despite the latter's protestation that he could not win, he accused the rider of not trying after he had been beaten. Fordham, who was immensely jealous of his reputation for integrity, would never ride for him again. "That damned horse" an aggrieved Machell used to say, "was no good and I lost the best jockey in the world".

By the early months of 1864 Captain Machell was established at Newmarket with two or three horses that he had brought over from Ireland, and went for his first big coup when he ran Bacchus, who had cost him 19 guineas, in a field of 24 for the Prince of Wales Stakes over the Rowley Mile on the opening day of the First Spring Meeting, 25 April. Machell backed his horse to win something like £10,000 and the adage about fortune favouring the bold was, on that occasion at any rate, borne out to the full. Count Batthyany's well fancied Suburban, the mount of Harry Custance, was travelling like the probable winner until a stirrup leather snapped and Bacchus, ridden by a boy called Tomlinson at 6 st, got up to win by a neck. Even then Machell's money was not safe as Custance objected to Bacchus for crossing, but having heard the evidence after racing the stewards upheld the result.

Captain Machell's eminently successful exploitation of those few horses that he trained for himself brought him to the notice of the wealthier patrons of racing and the third Earl of Lonsdale and Lord Calthorpe were only too pleased to appoint him to manage the stable they shared a mile or two outside Newmarket. Before long the demands for his services in this capacity had become so great that he was able to open his own stable at Bedford Cottage (now known as Bedford House and occupied by Luca Cumani), with the brothers Charles and George Bloss, both tall men like himself, as his trainers, while retaining the patronage of Lords Lonsdale and Calthorpe.

Sketch of Captain Machell by Finch Mason

Several members of the Bloss family trained at Newmarket and elsewhere during the course of the last century. Alfred Bloss, who died in August 1876, had run a stable in Prussia before retiring to Newmarket to be proprietor of The Crown Hotel. In those days there was a range of stabling behind The Crown in which runners from other training centres were quartered during the Newmarket meetings. Three years before the death of Alfred Bloss the Derby winner George Frederick had been stabled behind The Crown prior to being unplaced in the Middle Park Stakes.

Among the wealthy young men to entrust their horses to Captain Machell was the Lincolnshire Squire Harry Chaplin. As though seeking consolation for a romance that had turned into a sensational disaster he "bought horses as though he were drunk, and backed them as though he were mad". In the summer of 1864, when still only 22 and just down from Oxford, Harry Chaplin had become engaged to Lady Florence Paget, the enchanting daughter of the second Marquess of Anglesey, but what was to have been the wedding of the year never took place as she eloped with the Marquess of Hastings, also aged 22, who was already becoming notorious for his reckless gambling and heavy drinking.

It was on behalf of Harry Chaplin that Captain Machell bought the colt by Newminster out of Seclusion, who was to be known as Hermit, for 1,000 guineas at the sale of the Middle Park Stud's yearlings in 1865. A rangy chestnut with an elegant head and great strength behind the saddle Hermit raised hopes that he might win The Derby by his successes at Royal Ascot and in three of his other five races as a two-year-old. While his owner and Captain Machell backed him steadily throughout the winter of 1866/7 the Marquess of Hastings laid heavily against the colt as though unable to bring himself to contemplate the man he had wronged winning The Derby.

On the Monday of the week before The Derby Custance was at Newmarket to ride Hermit in a gallop with the four-year-old Rama, to whom he gave 16 lb, over the mile and a half from the Ditch to the Duke's Stand. After a mile Hermit was going so easily that Custance called on to the lad on the older horse to draw his whip, but still Rama could make no impression on Hermit, then suddenly Hermit coughed, blood streamed from his nostrils, and he all but dropped to the ground.

When he heard that his colt had broken a blood vessel Harry Chaplin had wanted to scratch him from The Derby straightaway, but was dissuaded from doing so by Lord Calthorpe on the grounds that it would not be fair to Captain Machell, who stood to lose so much. Neverthess he released Custance to ride The Rake and the bookmakers laid Hermit for all that they could take. Meanwhile Hermit began to recover and Captain Machell was able to give him a couple of canters the reverse way of the Rowley Mile on the Saturday before Derby. Harry Chaplin tried to reclaim Custance but Mr Pryor, owner of The Rake, was not agreeable to losing his services so the matter was referred to the Stewards of the Jockey Club, who ruled in favour of Mr

Pryor. Thereupon Captain Machell engaged lanky, young John Daley, whose father trained for Sir Robert Clifton and other owners, and hardly had he done so than The Rake, too, broke a blood vessel, but, like Hermit, was able to run in The Derby.

The weather on Derby Day has rarely been more unpleasant than it was on 22 May 1867 and flurries of snow and sleet blew across Epsom Downs, though the skies were clearing by the time the runners for The Derby were being saddled. With his coat staring, and tail tucked between his legs, Hermit looked poor value even for the 66-1 that the ring was still laying against him, though Harry Chaplin, Captain Machell and the Bloss brothers still thought he could win. As Marksman came to the stands with a decisive lead those hopes seemed singularly unfounded until Daley asked his mount to make the run for which he had been saved, and producing the acceleration that had characterised his two-year-old career Hermit beat Marksman by a neck.

The Marquess of Hastings had lost £120,000, yet with typical flamboyant courage was the first to pat Hermit in the winner's enclosure. When he died, worn out by the pace of his profligacy, at the age of 26 just over a year later his last words were, "Hermit's Derby broke my heart, but I didn't show it, did I?"

To John Daley, whose riding career was soon to be terminated by increased weight Harry Chaplin gave £1,000 and on hearing that George Bloss had slept in Hermit's box every night during the three months preceding The Derby as a precaution against nobbling he sent that faithful man a cheque for £5,000. The little iron bed on which Bloss kept his vigil was long preserved at Bedford Cottage to be shown to visitors.

Hermit eventually retired to the stud that Harry Chaplain had built up on his Blankney estate in Lincolnshire. He was champion stallion seven times, sired the Derby winners Shotover and St Blaise, and died in 1890.

After having spent freely and bet heavily in early manhood, Harry Chaplin faced considerable financial embarrassment that necessitated his curtailing his racing interests drastically and selling property. Eventually he settled down to be a highly respected Conservative Member of Parliament deeply committed to the agricultural interest. He served as Minister of Agriculture, led a titular opposition to the Asquith Government after the outbreak of war in 1914 and was raised to the peerage as Viscount Chaplin in 1916. A member of the Jockey Club for nearly 60 years he never lost his enthusiasm for racing and paid his last visit to Newmarket to see Drake win the Middle Park Stakes in October 1922 before dying the following year.

Having consolidated his reputation by enabling Hermit to win The Derby after having met with such a serious setback, Captain Machell engineered one of his next coups over Lord Lonsdale's King Lud in the Cesarewitch in 1873. A four-year-old bay colt by King Tom, King Lud was so gross an individual that he looked more like a broodmare about to foal than a horse in training.

Hermit

Using the sort of subterfuge that was almost second nature to him, Captain Machell arranged for his own three-year-old Feve, who was also in the Cesarewitch, to do a series of impressive gallops in full view of the touts while King Lud was worked discreetly elsewhere. In consequence the touts were extolling the achievements of Feve to the bookmakers and sporting papers that employed them while Captain Machell, old Lord Lonsdale and the other patrons of the Bedford Cottage stable were backing King Lud at 40-1. Eventually starting at a shade over 20-1 (1000-45) King Lud was ridden by Tom Bruckshaw to win by two lengths from Stirling Crawfurd's Royal George with Marie Stuart, fresh from beating the Derby winner Doncaster in The St Leger, unplaced in a field of 34.

As well as managing the string of high class flat racers in the Bedford Cottage yard Captain Machell had a number of steeplechasers in training with the amateur rider John Maunsell Richardson at Limber Magna in Lincolnshire. Many people regarded Machell as an even better judge of a jumper than he was of a flat horse and 'Cat' Richardson, who had ridden over some of the fastest hunting country in England since early boyhood, had few equals in a steeplechase even amongst the professionals.

Towards the end of March 1873 'Cat' Richardson had ridden Captain Machell's six-year-old Disturbance, a little bay by Commotion, to win the Grand National. The Captain's first bet had been £200 at 500-1 and he was reckoned to have won even more over that race than he had done over Hermit's Derby.

The following year Captain Machell had three runners in the Grand National, namely Disturbance professionally ridden by Joe Cannon, Reugny, the mount of Richardson, and Defence ridden by Lord Melgund. Richardson tried Reugny as almost sure to win and advised Machell to back him, but the Captain did nothing until the horse was down to a very short price. As furious as he was disgusted by the odds offered him Machell informed Richardson that he did not keep horses for Lincolnshire farmers to back and had a good mind to scratch Reugny and rely on Defence. Richardson replied that the Lincolnshire farmers were the friends amongst whom he had lived and ridden all his life and he did not care if they did back his mounts, adding that if Machell carried out his threat to scratch Reugny he would ride Furley for the Baltazzi brothers and beat Defence. By way of compromise Captain Machell suggested that 'Cat' Richardson forbore from informing the press as to which of the three Limber Magna runners he would ride at Aintree, while their owner got what he could from the market. As much disgusted by all this manipulation as Captain Machell was adept at it, Richardson declared that Reugny would be the last horse he would ever ride in public. Reugny, who was favourite at 5-1, duly won, but it was the end of the association between the Lincolnshire hunting man and the professional racing man from Newmarket.

Having taken his jumpers away from Limber Magna Captain Machell had them trained by Joe Cannon on the schooling ground that he had laid out at Kennett. After Captain Prime's Trappist, ridden by Fred Archer, had won the Stewards Cup for Bedford Cottage in 1875 Joe Cannon trained and rode Regal to give Captain Machell his third success in the Grand National. Once again the Captain confused the issue by having a second runner in Chandos. Chandos was very fast but knowing Regal would be much the safer over the big Aintree fences, Machell had his own money on Regal. All the same Chandos ridden by Jimmy Jewett started favourite at 100-30 only to fall, just as his owner had suspected he would, leaving Regal to win at 25-1. Later in 1876 Joe Cannon, still only 27 years of age, left Kennett to take over the training of the Bedford Cottage horses, and the same year the third Earl of Lonsdale died and was succeeded by his eldest son. St George Lowther, fourth Earl of Lonsdale was a very different man from his courtly old father. When he arrived in Cumberland to take possession of his huge estates the local militia lined the route from Clifton Station to Lowther Castle and a huge crowd of civic notabilities and tenantry turned out to welcome him. Unfortunately he had spent almost the entire railway journey drinking so all that the crowd saw of the six foot three inch peer was his recumbent figure being borne upon an improvised stretcher the short distance between the station and his carriage.

Although a great deal more fascinated by the vagaries of the Gulf Stream and other aspects of oceanography than those of the race course the new Lord Lonsdale greatly increased the string of horses he had inherited without making any change in the training arrangements. Most important of his acquisitions was the chestnut filly by The Earl or The Palmer out of Lady Audley whom he bought from Mr Cookson for 200 guineas. Given the name of Pilgrimage she won the Dewhurst Plate and three of her other four races as a two-year-old and was then ridden by her trainer's elder brother Tom Cannon to complete the double in The 2,000 Guineas and The 1,000 Guineas. The only other time she ran she started at even money for The Oaks but though breaking down was only beaten a length by Janette. Eighteen years later her daughter Canterbury Pilgrim avenged her by winning The Oaks before becoming one of the foundation mares of the Stanley House Stud as the dam of Swynford and Chaucer.

Four years after Pilgrimage had triumphed in the Newmarket classics the fourth Earl of Lonsdale died, while his brother and heir whom the sporting world would known as 'The Yellow Earl' sat in an adjoining room, calmly smoking cigarette after cigarette as he waited to enter upon his inheritance. Right to the end of his life the fourth Earl had caused embarrassment. As his decease had taken place in a house he had bought for the entertainment of actresses, his servants had to perform their final duty to him by smuggling his body into his own residence in Carlton House Terrace.

The year after the retirement of Pilgrimage Captain Machell won the Royal Hunt Cup, always a favourite race with him, with his bay horse The Mandarin. Starting at 33-1 and ridden by Charlie Wood The Mandarin beat Sir Joseph by a length. Four years later Bedford

Cottage turned out another Royal Hunt Cup winner in Mr W. Gerard's three-year-old Elzevir, who was also ridden by Wood but 5-1 favourite. In the same year Joe Cannon left Bedford Cottage to become private trainer to the Earl of Rosebery and was succeeded by his former fellow steeplechase jockey Jimmy Jewitt who had ridden Chandos in the Grand National.

Among the patrons of the Bedford Cottage stable paying high prices for horses and betting in the same proportion during that era was Sir John Willoughby, who had celebrated his 21st birthday in 1880. In company with Captain Machell he attended the dispersal sale of Lord Falmouth's bloodstock in the Heath House paddock in late April 1884 and paid 8,600 guineas for the three-year-old colt Harvester, a brown son of Sterling, who had won two races at Newmarket the previous autumn.

Although the stable already had two fancied contenders for The Derby in Queen Adelaide, also owned by Sir John Willoughby, and Mr Gerard's St Medard it was decided that Harvester should run, though serious doubts about whether he would be able to do so arose after he was found slightly lame the previous Saturday.

The Bedford Cottage horses dominated the betting on the 15 runners in The Derby that year. Queen Adelaide, ridden by Fred Webb, started favourite at 5-2, St Medard, ridden by Fred Archer, was second in the market at 6-1, and Harvester, the mount of Sammy Loates, the outsider of the trio at 100-7. Not for the first time Captain Machell gave the betting public an unpleasant surprise as it was Harvester who made a dead heat of it with Mr Jack Hammond's St Gatien, a bay colt by Rotherhill or The Rover, with Queen Adelaide two lengths away third. Jack Hammond declared he was ready to run his horse in a deciding heat or to divide the stakes according to whatever suited Bedford Cottage, and Machell, mindful of Harvester's doubtful leg, quickly accepted the offer to divide. The following day Sir John Willoughby rather churlishly objected to St Gatien on the grounds that he was incorrectly described on account of there being two stallions by the name of The Rover, but then showed better sense by withdrawing his objection.

Fred Archer, who had the mount on St Medard, was a longstanding friend of Captain Machell and valuable confederate both by reason of the winners he rode for the stable and the advice he gave periodically. The incurable suspicion of Machell, however, was the ruination of their relationship just as it had been in the case of George Fordham so many years earlier. Having lost heavily during the Houghton Meeting of 1886 Machell was advised by Archer to get out on Queen Bee, whom the champion jockey was to ride for Bob Peck in the two-year-old seller, but asked to keep the information to himself. After Queen Bee had been beaten by a head, Machell became enraged at hearing a lady, usually in Archer's confidence, state that she knew Queen Bee would not win as Archer had told her not to back the filly, as indeed he had, because he had no intention of advising anyone except Machell of the stable's confidence.

Meeting up with Archer shortly afterward Captain Machell cut him dead, though not without seeing the look of sad reproach on the rider's face. Within a fortnight Archer had shot himself with the rift between them unhealed, though Machell had learned the truth of the matter and was bitterly reproaching himself for the treatment of his old friend. Machell continued to be haunted by the memory of the sad, hurt expression on Archer's face the last time he had seen him, until, so he assured Lord Rossmore, the ghost of Archer appeared by his bedside one night and patted him reassuringly on the shoulder.

Although he could be absolutely charming, and was capable of showing quite disinterested kindness, Captain Machell was little mellowed by success. In consequence, many harsh things were still spoken of him, often with a great deal less than justice. It was said, for instance, that he encouraged irresponsible young men to gamble and thereby brought about their ruin, when the truth of the matter, in almost every case, was that they lost their money, not by taking his advice, but by ignoring it.

Few of the young men who had horses in the Bedford Cottage stable ventured into folly more fully than the seventh Lord Rodney, whose forebear, the great admiral, defeated the Spanish Fleet off Cape St Vincent in 1780. The seventh Lord Rodney commenced racing at the age of 30 in 1887 and the same year won The St Leger with Bendigo's bad tempered brother Kilwarlin, ridden by W. T. 'Jack' Robinson. Knowing the waywardness of the colt Captain Machell sent his travelling head lad down to the start with a long tom to ensure that he jumped off, but that ploy failed to produce the desired result and Kilwarlin was left more than half a furlong. Fortunately for Robinson the pace was steady enough to enable him to make up his ground gradually and at the other end of the race the luck was on his side as the Derby winner Merry Hampton was baulked with the result that Kilwarlin held him by half a length.

The following month Lord Rodney backed his three-year-old colt Humewood down to favouritism for the Cesarewitch and although Robinson was obliged to put up 5 lb overweight at 7 st 6 lb he won by a length from Bendigo, who was giving him 29 lb. The ruin of Lord Rodney lay in his persistence in backing horses from other stables instead of restricting his betting to those trained at Bedford Cottage. Thus despite the success of Kilwarlin and the enormous amount of money he won over Humewood he finished the season of 1887 owing large sums to various bookmakers. In the March of 1888 Lord Rodney made one last attempt to square accounts with the ring. After his black mare Ringlet had finished fourth to Playfair in the Grand National he pulled her out again for the Champion 'Chase, in which there were only two other runners, and went along the rails backing her at 7-4 on for all that he could. As she jumped the last fence in the lead the race seemed in safe keeping but then her effort in the Grand National took its toll and Johnny Longtail ran her out of it by a length to write finis to the racing career of Lord Rodney. He was subsequently obliged to sell his ancestral home, Berrington Hall in Herefordshire, and died in 1909.

Soon after the retirement of Lord Rodney from The Turf Captain Machell was managing the horses of a very much wealthier young man. This was Harry McCalmont for whom he won the Royal Hunt Cup with Suspender and the New Stakes (now the Norfolk Stakes) with Isinglass, both ridden by George Chaloner at Ascot in 1892.

Like his employer, the Bedford Cottage trainer Jimmy Jewett was a man with a very short temper, and as neither was at any pains to conceal his opinions their rows were to be heard almost all over the Heath on many a morning. One of their most violent disagreements was over the preparation of Isinglass for the classics of 1893. Fiery little Jimmy Jewett maintained that it was quite impossible to train the big bay for The 2,000 Guineas on the firm ground that persisted throughout the exceptionally dry spring and was all for scratching him. As had been the case with Hermit just over a quarter of a century earlier Captain Machell refused to allow circumstances to deny him a classic, and insisted Isinglass could be made fit enough for the race. Twice a day he had the horse out for a series of short canters on the tan on Bury Hill and thus enabled him to beat Ravensbury by three parts of a length in The Guineas. As the drought continued throughout the summer and early autumn it was due to his class and the clever training of him by Captain Machell that Isinglass overcame the disadvantage of having the ground against him in both The Derby and The St Leger and completed the Triple Crown. Isinglass had been bred by Harry McCalmont by the mating of Isonomy with Dead Lock, a mare that Captain Machell had bought from Lord Alington for just 19 guineas. Machell bred two colts from Dead Lock, House of Lords and Gervas, and then sold her before Gervas had won five times as a two-year-old in 1886. Determined to be repossessed of the mare he failed to locate her until recognising her between the shafts of a trap in which a farmer had driven to Bedford Cottage to inspect the carthorse stallion Marvellous. On Machell proposing the exchange of the mare in harness for a colt by Marvellous the farmer readily agreed to the deal and 12 months later Dead Lock, with a colt foal at foot, was sold to Harry McCalmont for £500.

Horses carrying Captain Machell's colours, white jacket and dark blue cap, played leading parts in the long distance races in 1895, the year in which Isinglass crowned his career by winning the Ascot Gold Cup on his only appearance. The five-year-old Ravensbury, who had been bought out of Bill Jarvis's Waterwitch stable, brought off the double in the Ascot Stakes and the Alexandra Stakes at the Royal Meeting before being retired to Machell's Kennett Stud at a fee of 100 guineas. Kilsallaghan won both the Chester Cup and the Doncaster Cup while Campanjo was successful in the Goodwood Stakes prior to being sold to South Africa.

The triumphs of those stayers were really the swan song of Captain Machell. He had first been taken ill while staying at the Adelphi Hotel, Liverpool for the autumn meeting at Aintree in 1893, and by 1895 was being caused excruciating pain by gout. In an attempt to regain his health he went to Genoa, having sold the Bedford Cottage stable to

Harry McCalmont, and returning to England, still an invalid, divided his time between Hastings and Newmarket until dying at the age of 64 in 1902. He is buried in the cemetery at the top of the town a few yards from the grave of Fred Archer.

Although racing brought Captain Machell little in the way of happiness by reason of his incurable suspicion of other people's motives, his betting made him a great deal of money. In consequence he was able to buy back Crackenthorpe Hall, the family home in Westmoreland, and acquire the Chetwynd House stable and a good deal of other property in Newmarket. It was in Chetwynd House that he installed as trainer George Chaloner, one of his former jockeys. Shortly afterwards the name of the stable was changed to Machell Place, and as such keeps the memory of him alive in the town today.

There was a strong note of irony about Harvester, second of the three Derby winners managed by Captain Machell, having to settle for a dead heat with St Gatien, as St Gatien was owned by that remarkable character John Hammond, who had begun his working life in the employment of Machell as a stable lad in the Bedford Cottage yard. John Hammond was born in the village of Barrow, a few miles from Newmarket, in about 1845. He was the nephew of George Rosbrook landlord of the Five Bells at Newmarket, and as a boy helped his uncle in the bar during the evenings.

Having used his very considerable intelligence to learn all that he could of horses and racing while at Bedford Cottage Jack Hammond bought a little cottage by the roadside at Newmarket and entered the employment of John Robinson, Charlie Hibbert and other Nottingham bookmakers as a tout, sending them daily reports of the work done by the Newmarket horses, and his assessment of their current form. As his confidence in his own judgement increased he backed it with his own money ever more frequently, so that he was soon making his living as a professional backer, with the friendship and confidence of Fred Archer an invaluable asset. In due course he acquired a reputation for integrity and discretion that ensured him regular employment working the commissions for a number of stables, particularly Bedford Lodge, in which the horses of the Duchess of Montrose and her second husband Stirling Crawfurd were then trained privately.

Relying heavily upon the evidence of his own eyes, both on the racecourse and the gallops, Jack Hammond developed something akin to an instinct for divining the difference between reliable information and mere rumour while divulging nothing at all of his own knowledge. When asked about how one of his horses would run he would reply, "Yes, I fancy him, put me £500 on, will you?" even though he thought it sure to get beaten. More money would follow the lead he had given and then the horse would start at a short price only to run the way its owner had supposed it would. It was rarely that the £500 Hammond invested in such circumstances would prove wasted. When the horse was properly fit people would be wary of backing it because of its apparently disappointing previous running, and Hammond could back it at the sort of price that he liked. And if the

Stewards asked him to explain its earlier performance, he would blandly reply that he was quite baffled by it as he had backed it on that occasion too — and could prove that he had.

By and large Jack Hammond bet modestly on horses that were at short odds and plunged when he thought he was getting good value for money from an outsider. Rarely was that almost unshakeable confidence in his own judgement better vindicated than over The St Leger of 1882. After Fred Archer had ridden Lord Falmouth's Dutch Oven to win the Yorkshire Oaks, Hammond was amongst those who backed her at 8-1 for The St Leger. Two days later she ran an appalling race to be third to Peppermint over the full Leger distance, which seemed to test her stamina too severely. Archer declared she had not a 1,000-1 chance in The St Leger and tried to beg off her to ride the favourite Geheimniss while the bookmakers offered 66-1 against her. Hammond was the only one of the big backers to stand by the impression he had formed after the Yorkshire Oaks by backing her again at that price, and after Dutch Oven had beaten Geheimniss a length and a half at Doncaster he gave Archer a present of £10,000.

By the time that Geheimniss won The St Leger Jack Hammond already had horses with Joe Cannon but their brief association ended acrimoniously. When Hammond wanted to run a two-year-old Cannon advised against doing so as it was not fit enough to warrant backing but might be good enough to win. Hammond insisted on it running and as the trainer feared it won unbacked, whereupon Hammond, uncharacteristically, lost his temper. He blamed Cannon for not having given him sufficient encouragement to have a bet, and Cannon asked him to remove his horses. The following day Hammond apologised for the way he had behaved, but Cannon still insisted he should take his horses out of the yard. For all the success that he was to enjoy subsequently Jack Hammond always blamed himself for losing the services of the man he rated the best trainer in the country, just as Captain Machell had reproached himself continually after George Fordham had refused to ride for him again.

On being obliged to part company with Cannon, Jack Hammond sent his horses to Bob Sherwood at Exeter House. As well as sending out St Gatien to dead heat in The Derby of 1884 Sherwood brought off the autumn double for Hammond later that year, winning the Cesarewitch with St Gatien and the Cambridgeshire with Florence.

St Gatien, who shared second favouritism for the Cesarewitch at 9-1 by the time Hammond had finished with the market, used his class to win in a canter from Lord Rosebery's four-year-old Polemic, to whom he was giving no less than 38 lb, with Archiduc third and Florence fourth. The following Monday the bookmakers had £90,000 to pay out to Hammond. A fortnight later the ring had another £75,000 to find after Fred Webb had ridden Florence to win the Cambridgeshire.

Like their owner, both St Gatien and Florence were of modest origins. The Rover, who was almost certainly the sire of St Gatien, had once pulled a cab, while Enigma, the dam of Florence, had been driven in harness by a Shropshire farmer before he sold her with Florence at foot for £15.

As a result of having owned one of the dead-heaters in The Derby, and also having won the Cesarewitch, the Cambridgeshire, the Gold Vase, the Manchester Cup and 15 other races in 1884, Jack Hammond, the former stable lad, was the leading owner at the end of the season.

Bob Sherwood was a fine trainer but with his passion for secrecy and quick temper anything but an easy man with whom to maintain a harmonious relationship. In the circumstances it is not altogether surprising that Jack Hammond failed to establish one with him and sent his horses to Jimmy Waugh at Meynell House. It was Jimmy Waugh therefore who was responsible for St Gatien becoming the first horse to win the Jockey Club Cup for a third time in 1886, a feat that was not emulated until High Line, currently enjoying a most successful career at stud, won the race in 1969, 1970 and 1971.

In 1887 Jimmy Waugh won the Ascot Stakes and the Alexandra Plate for Hammond with Eurasian, who was ridden by Fred Barrett in both races, and in 1889, the Cambridgeshire with Laureate, on whom Billy Warne beat Harry McCalmont's Claribelle, ridden by George Chaloner at 6 st 7 lb. Laureate, a chestnut colt by Petrarch, was then retired to Newmarket's Scaltback Stud but on his proving infertile Hammond put him back into training in 1891, and backed him for the Royal Hunt Cup, telling his commissioner, "It does not matter how much you put on, just let me know on Monday". Hammond took a very different attitude when told his agent had averaged no more than 20-1 to £1,000. "You had better keep it," he said disagreeably. "I don't want it", leaving the poor man with no time to get out of the money. A few days later he could well repent those words when Laureate, ridden by Morny Cannon at 2 lb overweight, won the Royal Hunt Cup by half a length from Captain Machell's Rathbeal.

The last of the good horses to carry Jack Hammond's white jacket with red collar, sleeves and cap was Herminius, whom he bought out of a seller for 240 guineas at Derby in the autumn of 1897. The following season Herminius won him another Ascot Stakes and two years later in 1899 justified 7-4 favouritism in the Manchester Cup.

Utter fearlessness combined with that absolute confidence in his own judgement made Jack Hammond the greatest gambler on the racecourse during the last two decades of the nineteenth century. Totally unemotional on the course he was never seen to let his poker face slip. Registering neither pleasure, disappointment nor disgust he would watch a tight finish from his usual place on one of the lower tiers of the stands as though he did not have a penny depending on the outcome. Far from shouting a horse home, he would never react by so much as a flicker of a muscle and saunter away as though thoroughly bored by proceedings. That apparent indifference to all form of sentiment he cultivated so assiduously on the course was in sharp contrast to another side of the character of Jack Hammond. While living in his fine house, The Lawns, during the days of his prosperity, he never forgot the people from whom he came, and gave a great deal of money to help alleviate the plight of the poorest inhabitants of Newmarket.

With the opening of the new century, the luck began to turn against Jack Hammond so that he could hardly afford to bet. Not so long before he died in 1910, he confided to Charlie Morton, then private trainer to Mr Jack Joel at Wantage, "I never back a winner now. I worked for years and years and never lost. Now I never win. I can't tell you how much I have lost these last few years".

HEADQUARTERS

11 Mathew Dawson

Mat Dawson was big in everything but physical stature. He thought on a grand scale, he set his sights on the highest targets and he achieved success such as no other Newmarket trainer had enjoyed since Robert Robson in the early years of the century.

His only concern was to develop the ability of top-class horses to its fullest. At this he was a genius. He had no time for second-class horses or second-class men — whether they were rich and titled owners or stable-lads. Both went the same way — out of his yard. He was absolutely straightforward himself, and expected everybody else to be the same. He was also autocratic. Once an owner had sent him a horse, he insisted on having complete control over that horse. He made the entries. He engaged the jockeys. He gave the riding orders. All he offered the owner was results. But if Mat was autocratic, he was anything but arrogant. On the contrary, he had abundant charm which he did not reserve for those he regarded as his social superiors.

All his life Mat strove to produce the very best in all that he did. And he had his reward, for his name will for ever be associated with St Simon, the greatest horse of the century, and Fred Archer, its greatest jockey. Moreover, in the second half of his career he had the satisfaction of training for great owners like Viscount Falmouth, the Duke of Portland and the Earl of Rosebery, who bred and raced their horses for the pure pleasure of the sport, not for punting.

Mat Dawson was born at Stamford Hall, Gullane, in Scotland on 9 January 1820, the son of George Dawson, a trainer, and his wife Jean. Like many of the Scottish children of that time he received a better education than he would have done had he been born in similar circumstances in England. This was to stand him in good stead throughout his life.

Having served an exacting apprenticeship at Gullane with his father, who showed no paternal favours, Mat went to his elder brother Tom at Middleham. There he became head lad at Tom's Brecongill stable when still only 18 in 1838. Two years later he was back at Gullane training a string of his own under the watchful, and doubtless critical eye of his father. It was with great pride that Mat set forth from Gullane to take his first Derby runner, Pathfinder, to Epsom. Overnight he stopped with Tom at Middleham. When he left the village in the morning he was followed by the mocking voice of his brother crying "There goes Cocky little Mat to win the Derby". Pathfinder finished last, 200 yards behind his nearest rival. Twenty-year-old Mat must have been bitterly disappointed, but then he did not know that he was to send out six Derby winners in the years to come.

Mat Dawson (1820-1898) trained at Heath House before going into semi-retirement at Melton House, Exning

Soon afterwards Mat became private trainer to Lord Eglington at Bogside, where he stayed a couple of seasons before returning to Gullane for a second time. During the next two or three years he began to win more important races than hitherto, though his activities were largely confined to Scotland and the north of England. In 1843 he won the Cumberland Plate with William le Gros, in 1844 the Northumberland Plate with The Era, and in 1845 a second Cumberland Plate with Pythia.

His father, George Dawson, died in November 1846. Shortly afterwards Mat quit the family home to train for Lord John Scott and his partner Sir John Don-Wauchope. Where he was based for the next ten years it is hard to say. Perhaps he had no headquarters. Lord John's stud was at Cawston Lodge near Rugby, but his horses spent much of their time while in training at Yew Tree Cottage at Compton in Berkshire, though during the height of the season they were quartered at Newmarket for weeks on end. It looks as though Mat spent time at Rugby, Compton and Newmarket according to the needs of the season.

Before long he was winning the big races in the south. In 1851 he took the New Stakes at Royal Ascot and the July Stakes at Newmarket with Hobbie Noble; the Stewards Cup he won with Kilmeny in 1852 and the following year he obtained the first of his 29 classic successes when Catherine Hayes landed The Oaks. To the end of his long life Mat thought the world of Catherine Hayes. Even after he had had all those other famous horses through his hands he still rated her very nearly the best.

In 1856 Mat won the Great Metropolitan with Cannobie. The following year the partnership between Lord John Scott and Sir John Don-Wauchope was dissolved. When Lord John sold his share of the stud Mat found him a buyer in the Scottish ironmaster, James Merry. For a mere £5,000 Merry became the owner of Catherine Hayes, as well as priceless yearlings, foals and other broodmares. To put the final touch to his great bargain he even secured the services of the trainer, whom he installed at Russley Park, Wiltshire. Mat Dawson had known Merry for some years as his father had had his horses at one time. One would have thought that acquaintanceship with Mr Merry was proof against any desire to train for him. Not to put too fine a point on it, he was greedy, narrow-minded and deeply suspicious of anyone with whom he had dealings. Having James Merry's horses was one of the occupational hazards of trainers who were on the way to the top of what was only just becoming a profession during the second half of the last century. Mat emerged from the furnace of Mr Merry's nastiness tried and true, just as Jimmy Waugh and Bob Peck, both of whom play their own parts in the story of Newmarket, were to do afterwards.

By winning The St Leger with the filly Sunbeam in 1858, Mat got off to what should have been a flying start. Two years later, and 20 after his first attempt, he saddled a Derby winner, Thormanby. These were the highlights of his nine years at Russley Park. In 1866 he parted company with James Merry to go to Newmarket, leaving his friend and protégé, James Waugh, as his successor at Russley.

During his early days at Newmarket, Mat lived in a house opposite St Mary's rectory; then he moved to Heath House. This is not the present Heath House, which is occupied by Sir Mark Prescott, but the big house that stood beside the Hyperion Garage on the right hand side as you leave the town by the Bury Road.

The highlight of Mat's first season there in 1867 was the success of the Duke of Newcastle's Julius in the Royal Hunt Cup. In those days the Dukes of Newcastle and Hamilton were the principal patrons of the stable. Both were heavy plungers and despite all their trainer tried to do for them it was not long before they had to pull in their horns.

Just as the Dukes were retiring hurt, Viscount Falmouth, who had had his horses with John Scott at Malton, sent them to Heath House. On all counts he was a much more satisfactory owner. He was extremely rich and could afford to breed from the cream of the stud book. The classic races and the other important weight-for-age events were the only ones he wanted to win. Handicaps never entered into his reckoning. More important still from the point of view of his trainer, he was totally uninterested in betting. In fact he is said to have made only one bet in his life.

Mrs Scott, the wife of his first trainer, was quite convinced that Queen Bertha would win The Oaks of 1863. Lord Falmouth, who thought otherwise, made a sixpenny wager about where the filly would finish. Queen Bertha won and Lord Falmouth settled by giving Mrs Scott a sixpenny bit — set in a diamond brooch.

Even though Lord Falmouth seems to have been the ideal owner, the strong-willed Mat would only train for him on his own terms. After one of the Falmouth horses, Wheatear, had been beaten because Tom French did the very opposite of what Mat had told him to do, the furious trainer demanded an explanation. On being told that Lord Falmouth had given completely different orders that the rider thought he was bound to obey, Mat immediately asked Lord Falmouth to remove his horses from Heath House. It was a staggering request to make of one of the richest owners in the kingdom. Yet such was Mat's prestige, he could not only make it but hold the upper hand. Rather diplomatically, Lord Falmouth asked Mat's brother Joe if he would have his horses at Bedford Lodge, knowing that Joe would refuse to train for anyone who had fallen out with his brother. What Joe did do was to offer to act as an intermediary with the usually adamant Mat, who changed his mind for once, and a chastened Lord Falmouth kept his horses at Heath House.

In those first few years at Heath House, Tom French was the stable jockey. He stood five foot eight-and-a-half inches in his stockings and, as was natural, he had great trouble with his weight. This led to consumption and the poor man died at the early age of 29 in the summer of 1873. His successor was already at hand and riding the stable's light-weights, for Fred Archer had been apprenticed to Mat Dawson on 10 February 1868.

The 6th Viscount Falmouth (1819-1889), whose horses were trained by Mat Dawson at Heath House

The 1870s were great days for Mat Dawson and Heath House. No fewer than 15 classics were won during the decade. Kingcraft took The Derby of 1870 and Cecilia The 1,000 Guineas in 1873, the first year it was run over the Rowley Mile. (Previously it had been run on the Ditch Mile.) Atlantic won The 2,000 Guineas in 1874 thereby providing the new stable jockey, the 17-year-old Fred Archer, with his first classic success. He weighed out at 6 st 1 lb that day and it speaks volumes for the regard in which Mat held him that he gave such a light and inexperienced lad the ride.

In 1875 Caballo won The 2,000 Guineas and Spinaway The 1,000 Guineas and The Oaks, while Silvio was successful in The Derby of 1877.

The following year Janette, who had been second in The 1,000 Guineas, won both The Oaks and The St Leger. That the Derby winner Silvio was kept in training to lead work in 1878 gives some idea of the magnificent scale on which Mat Dawson did things. And even after the end of that year, Mat had still not finished with Silvio for he had him to do the donkey work for yet another great filly, Wheel of Fortune, in 1879.

Wheel of Fortune won The 1,000 Guineas and The Oaks and a third classic came to Heath House in 1879 through the medium of Charibert in The 2,000 Guineas. Wheel of Fortune was one of the greatest fillies in the history of racing. Archer was inclined to rate her the best horse of either sex that he had ever ridden, after St Simon. She was neither beaten nor extended in ten races until she broke down in the Great Yorkshire Stakes. For all his regard for his old favourite Catherine Hayes, Mat was forced to admit that Wheel of Fortune was the best filly he ever trained.

Of those classic winners that came from Heath House in the 1870s Kingcraft, Cecilia, Atlantic, Spinaway, Silvio, Janette, Charibert and Wheel of Fortune all carried Lord Falmouth's colours, while Camballo belonged to Mr H. C. Vyner.

In 1882 Mat Dawson won The St Leger for Lord Falmouth with Dutch Oven and the following year The 2,000 Guineas with Galliard. Although a hot favourite for The Derby, Galliard could finish only third to St Blaise and Highland Chief. Tongues were quick to wag, for it was said that Archer stood in over Highland Chief with his brother who trained the horse. When Lord Falmouth announced his decision to give up racing and sell off all his horses in the following year, it was said it was out of disgust and disillusionment with Archer's riding of Galliard. It is highly unlikely that it was anything of the sort. Much more probable is that Lord Falmouth retired from The Turf because he was growing old and sick.

The sale of the Falmouth horses was held by Mr Edmund Tattersall in the paddock at Heath House on 28 April 1884. Seeing so many of his old favourites going under the hammer must have made it one of the saddest days of Mat's life. The lovely Wheel of Fortune was bought by the Duke of Portland for 5,000 guineas, Janette by 'Mr Manton' (the *nom-de-course* of the Duchess of Montrose) for 4,200 guineas, Spinaway for 5,500 guineas on behalf of 'Abington' Baird, but the Derby winner Kingcraft cost Lord Rossmore only 500 guineas. Of the three-year-olds the colt Harvester fetched 8,600 guineas and the filly Busybody 8,800 guineas. About a month later Harvester had dead-heated for The Derby and Busybody had won The Oaks. The grand total paid for Lord Falmouth's racing empire was 11,880 guineas.

Just before his association with Lord Falmouth came to its sudden end, Mat had acquired a still wealthier patron in the young Duke of Portland, who had come of age in 1878.

In 1883 Prince Batthyany had dropped dead in the Rowley Mile stands on 2,000 Guineas day because he was so excited about the chance of the aforementioned Galliard in the Classic. Galliard was a son of the Prince's 1875 Derby winner, Galopin, and the old man followed all the stock of Galopin with as close an interest as he would have done had he owned every one of them himself.

About three months later came the dispersal sale of the Prince's horses. The Duke of Portland attended with hopes of buying a three-year-old called Fulmen, for whom he was willing to go up to 4,500 guineas. In an unraced two-year-old called St Simon he had only a secondary interest. Fulmen fetched 5,000 guineas and Portland acquired St Simon for 1,600 guineas. With a courtly bow, Mat said to his owner "I think I may congratulate Your Grace on a good morning's work". The shrewd old Scot was guilty of understatement. The Duke had obtained the greatest bargain in racing history.

By Galopin out of St Angela, St Simon was a bay colt, whose only marking was a star on his forehead. His claims to being the best racehorse of his own time or any other, Ormonde not excepted, were very strong indeed. On the racecourse he was never challenged, let alone beaten, and at stud he was to acquire a reputation that was, if anything, still greater than that which he had enjoyed during his racing days. Mat always declared that St Simon was completely different from any other animal he had ever trained. He used to say the colt had more 'electricity' about him than any other horse he had known; that even the way in which he moved about his box made him different.

In these days when horses are custom-bred for specialisation as sprinters, stayers and so on, it is staggering to think that St Simon had the speed to be a top-class two-year-old and the stamina to win the Gold Cup as a three-year-old.

As the rules stood then, all St Simon's engagements became void on the death of his nominator. This meant he was out of the classics, but it can have made much less difference to his career than has sometimes been suggested, for he was only entered for The 2,000 Guineas. He was also ineligible for the top-class juvenile races like the Champagne Stakes, the Middle Park Stakes, the Dewhurst Stakes, and others for which the entries had closed before Prince Batthyany had died.

Thus St Simon was obliged to fulfil an unconventional programme in his five races as a two-year-old. Perhaps his most sensational performance during his first season was in the Princess of Wales Nursery at Doncaster, where he was giving between 17 lb and 44 lb to his rivals. Despite the concession of these huge weights, and even in spite of Archer's efforts to restrain him from winning by much further than was necessary, St Simon came storming home by eight lengths.

St Simon's first appearance of his second season was in an extraordinary affair called the Trial Match, which was neither a trial as it was held in public at a Newmarket meeting, nor a match as there were three other participants. In this, St Simon was up against the previous year's Gold Cup winner Tristan, a six-year-old trained by Tom Jennings, each of them having a pacemaker. The outcome of this unique event was that St Simon slammed Tristan by six lengths at weight-for-age. It was a magnificent achievement.

When St Simon renewed rivalry with Tristan in the Gold Cup at Royal Ascot, Fred Archer was unable to do the weight so Charlie Wood came in for the ride. Mat Dawson's orders were that Wood was to win by no more than two lengths, but once again he had reckoned without St Simon, who never did anything by halves. After they had turned into the straight for the second time, Wood let out a reef and St Simon simply sprinted away to win by 20 lengths — not two. After having established himself as the champion stayer he reverted to running over a mile in a Gold Cup at Newcastle, where he made light work of beating his only opponent. Finally St Simon landed the odds of 100-7 laid on him for the Goodwood Cup in which he beat Dutch Oven, the St Leger winner of two years previously, by 20 lengths without being out of a canter.

St Simon, owned by the 6th Duke of Portland, trained by Mat Dawson and ridden by Charlie Wood to win the Gold Cup by 20 lengths as a three-year-old in 1884.

However near to perfection St Simon came in most respects, his temperament left much to be desired. Charlie Fordham, the one-eyed lad who did him, used to say "Talk about the patience of Job! Job never did no St Simon". One evening Charlie was forced to take refuge under the manger and was only rescued by Mat Dawson just as St Simon was about to drag him out with his teeth.

Charlie Fordham had been apprenticed to Mat Dawson at the same time as Fred Archer, with whom he became close friends. It was while cleaning a shotgun for Archer that he lost his eye. After Mat Dawson reduced his string and moved to Exning, Charlie was employed as a tout by the *Sporting Chronicle* and became one of the greatest characters at Newmarket. In season he could find mushrooms with almost second sight while watching work on the Heath in the mornings, while in the evenings he would yarn on about racing in the olden times, taking a pinch from his snuff-box with almost every sentence he uttered.

When St Simon retired to the Duke of Portland's Welbeck Stud, Lambourn, his new *valet-de-chambre* found him as much of a handful as ever Charlie Fordham had done. The only thing that would quieten the great champion and make him as tractable as a lap-dog was the sight of an open umbrella. On the occasion when there was no brolly to hand John Huby, the stud goom at Welbeck, used to improvise by putting his hat on a stick. This usually had the desired effect on St Simon, who mistook it for the dreaded umbrella.

St Simon was leading sire for seven consecutive years between 1890, the season in which he had his first three-year-old runners, and 1896 as well as in 1900 and 1901. Perhaps his greatest year was in 1900 during which each of the five classics fell to his offspring. His overall record as a sire of classic winners was to get ten colts and fillies who landed 17 of the races between them.

St Simon, the greatest horse to be trained at Newmarket Heath or anywhere else, was 27 when he dropped dead after returning from exercise on 2 April 1908.

The season of 1885 must have seemed something of an anti-climax to the previous one without the excitment of having St Simon at Heath House. It was also the last that Mat Dawson spent in the yard and he wound up his tenancy of it in characteristic manner by winning The Derby and St Leger with Melton.

In his heyday at Heath House, Mat had had more than 100 horses under his care at one time. Obviously the boxes behind the house were hopelessly insufficient in number and even when, in about 1881, his landlord, Edward Weatherby, built a new range, probably that which constitutes the main block of Sir Mark Prescott's yard today, Mat still had need of overspill yards.

To meet these requirements, Mat Dawson built the St Albans stable and rented that at Queensberry Lodge on the racecourse side of the town. With so many horses in so many places he needed a first-class staff to whom he could delegate responsibility, and he had it. Many of those who were to make their names as trainers in the years to come did their groundwork either as assistant to Mat Dawson or as head lad in one of his yards. Those who began in this way include Felix Leach, George Blackwell, Billy Walters junior, and John Dawson. Richard Waugh was assistant trainer at Heath House while St Simon was there, but as he trained for the Kaiser at Graditz in Germany for many years he was not so well-known in this country as the others just mentioned.

By the time that Melton won The Derby of 1885, Mat was 65 years old, and after a busy and demanding life he longed for retirement. Accordingly he purchased the Manor House at Exning and renamed it Melton House after his most recent classic winner. But if Mat was bent on going into retirement there were plenty of influential and wealthy owners determined that he should do nothing of the sort lest his genius should be lost to them.

For another twelve years Mat tried in vain to retire, but the horses and the owners would not leave him. In his first year at Exning, 1886, he won the Grand Prix de Paris with Minting. Later successes included The Derbies of 1894 and 1895, with Ladas and Sir Visto, both of whom belonged to the Prime Minister, Lord Rosebery. He also won The 2,000 Guineas with Ladas and The St Leger with Sir Visto, The 1,000 Guineas with Minthe in 1889 and both The 1,000 Guineas and The Oaks with Mimi in 1891.

For close on 30 years Mat was a familiar figure on the Heath where he supervised the work of his horses every morning. From the crown of his top hat to the shine on the toes of his boots his little figure was immaculate. Only after he had had a particularly good night on the whisky, sent down especially for him from his native Scotland, was the topper replaced by some softer headgear. That was the danger signal to the lads that he was unlikely to be in the best of moods that morning. Otherwise he was unfailingly polite to all and sundry while remaining the complete autocrat in his own domain, where he insisted on manners as perfect as his own. Even when his former apprentice Fred Archer was stable jockey and enjoying the income of a cabinet minister, old Mat would reprimand him for failing to open the gate of the yard for the Duke of Portland by saying, "Archer, mon, where are your manners? Are ye no going to open the gate for his Grace?"

Towards the end of his life Mat became painfully afflicted with gout, and could only walk with the aid of a stick. Riding a hack being out of the question, the Jockey Club did him the signal honour of allowing him to drive a brougham on to the Heath to watch his string work. One morning the Prince of Wales rode over to talk to him. Not wishing to show discourtesy to the Prince by turning his back to raise a window through which a cold draught blew behind him, the old trainer just carried on the conversation, and while he did so he caught the chill that was to prove fatal. On 18 August 1898, Mat Dawson died at the age of 78.

After Mat had left Heath House in 1885, the Duke of Portland took over the lease so that he could use it as his Newmarket residence, and

George Dawson, son of Mat's younger brother John, was installed as trainer. It was for George Dawson that the present Heath House, in which Sir Mark Prescott lives, was built.

George Dawson's position was that of private trainer to the Duke, Lord Portland, owner of the 1885 Derby winner, Melton, Lord Londonderry and Lord Lascelles. Unlike so many other members of his family, George Dawson had not been in stables since boyhood. Originally he had been involved in the management of a brewery at Burton-on-Trent, but indifferent health obliged him to follow an occupation that enabled him to spend more of his time in the open air. Accordingly his Uncle Mat made arrangements for him to take over the Heath House stable.

George Dawson won The Derby for the Duke of Portland with Ayrshire in 1888 and Donovan in the following year. Ayrshire must have been one of the laziest horses that has ever worked on Newmarket Heath. When he was sent to Windsor to run in the Royal Plate as a two-year-old, he was standing on the floor of his box, the lad having heaped the straw neatly into a corner. On opening the top of the door half-way through the morning George Dawson was astonished to see that Ayrshire had spread the bedding back on the floor of the box and was sound asleep on it. Donovan began racing far earlier than a horse with top-class potential usually does and won the Brocklesby Stakes at the opening meeting of the season in 1888.

The Duke of Portland's lease of Heath House terminated in 1898. As he was not going to renew it, the Duke sent his string to John Porter at Kingsclere in the late autumn of that year. After leaving Newmarket the owner of St Simon did not enjoy anything like the success he had done during his association with the Dawsons. During the last part of his life he lost much of his enthusiasm for racing and kept only a few horses in training. He was 85 when he died in 1943.

Shortly after the break-up of the Heath House stable, George Dawson took over that at Warren House on the retirement of his father in 1900. He retired to live in Cambridge in 1905 and died of a paralytic seizure while on a visit to Newmarket at the age of 54 on 14 June 1913.

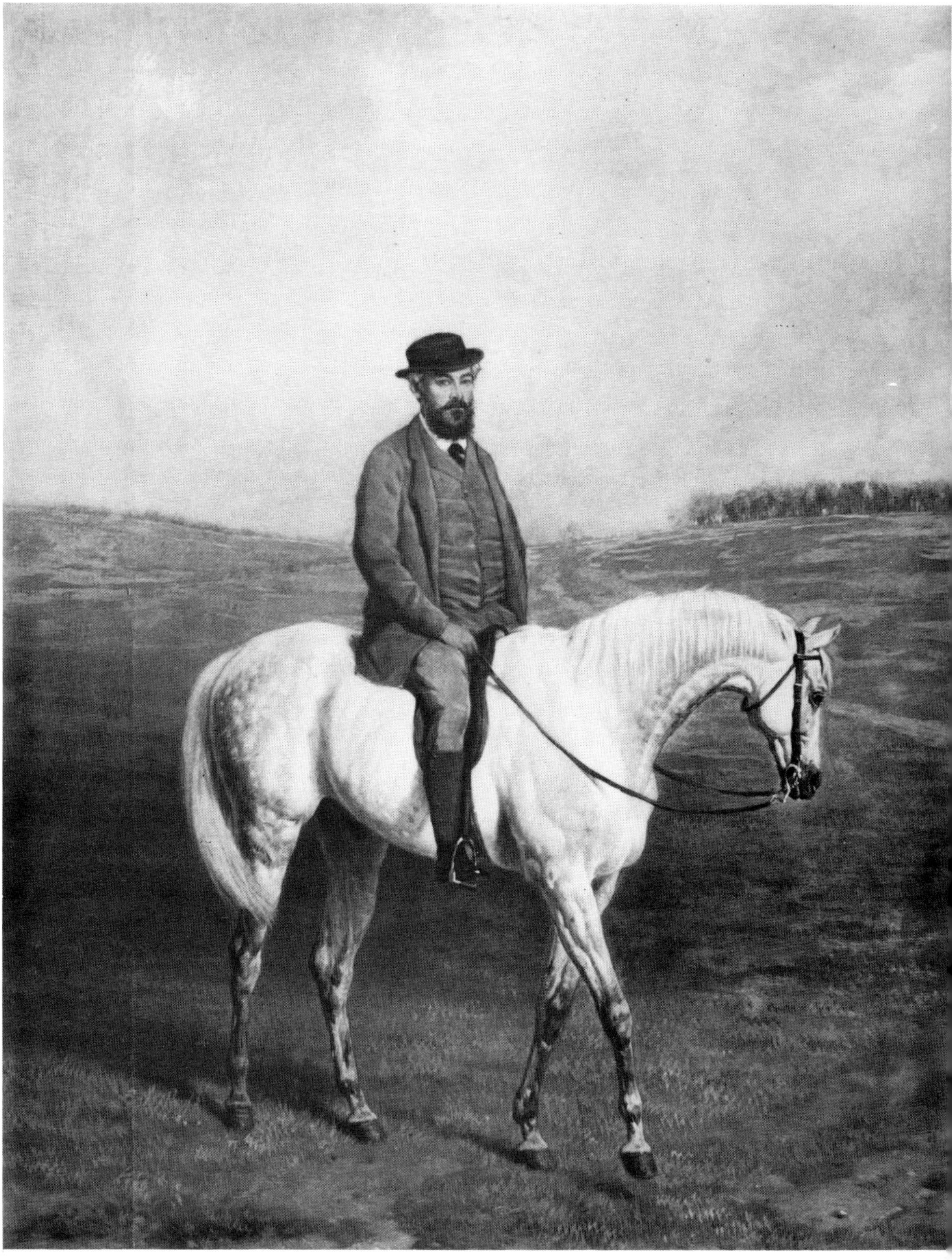

12 Sir John Astley

One of the most picturesque characters at Newmarket during the middle part of Queen Victoria's long reign was Sir John Astley. A well-built man with a heavy beard, he had a distinctly nautical appearance so that he acquired the nickname of 'The Mate', although he had been a professional soldier of some distinction during the early years of his adult life.

Never a very rich man, and often a very poor one, he was devoted to almost every other form of sport as well as racing. He was a fine athlete and excelled at pedestrianism, foot racing being particularly popular in those days before the invention of the motor car and the bicycle, and was a good cricketer too. He was also an enthusiastic follower of the fortunes of the prize fighters and even the attendance at an illicit cocking main came as anything but amiss to him.

Sir John Dugdale Astley, third baronet, of Everleigh, Wiltshire, was born in 1828. On leaving Eton he joined the Scots Guards, rising to the rank of lieutenant-colonel. During the war with Russia he saw active service in the Crimea, where he was severely wounded in the neck in the battle of the Alma in 1854.

Sir John was always prepared to wager on almost anything. His entry upon the racing scene was largely due to the happy belief that he would be able to increase his bank balance by successful betting. As a young man his racing activities had been confined to visits to Royal Ascot and the other big meetings for social reasons. It was not until his return from the Crimea that he became a regular racegoer in 1856.

In the spring of 1862 he was much taken by the style in which Caractacus won the Somersetshire Stakes at Bath and promptly secured 40-1 to a large sum against that colt winning The Derby. After Caractacus had justified the confidence by beating The Marquis, a raging hot favourite, by a neck, Sir John, for just about the first time in his life, found himself very much in funds. Some part of his winnings he invested in purchasing his first racehorse, Hesper, whom he sent to be trained by Dick Drewitt at Lewes.

Throughout the flat racing season, Sir John travelled from meeting to meeting, taking rooms for the shorter and less important ones and sharing a rented house with a friend or two for the longer and more fashionable fixtures. For the Newmarket meetings he had a lease on the cottage that had been built by Jem Robinson, the jockey. This property has been much enlarged and is today known as Machell Place. In 1870 Sir John bought this house with the paddock of an acre at the back, the site of the present Machell Place yard, for £3,000.

Sir John Astley (1828-1894)

In his wonderfully readable autobiography, *Fifty Years of My Life*, Sir John wrote:

> ...we kept our hacks at Mrs Flatman's (the widow of old Nat) next door... and I do not think I ever enjoyed any period of my life so much as those pleasant meetings at Newmarket; for we did the thing 'proper'. We each (wife and I) had two hacks, and never missed a morning, when it was fine, but were out on the Limekilns, or wherever the horses were doing their work, by 8.30, and came in for a delicious breakfast, with plenty of appetite, at 10.30. An hour or so before the races we mounted our fresh hacks, and with a fly to carry our coats, cloaks and convey our two grooms, we caracoled down to the races, seldom dismounting, but riding from saddling-paddock to betting-ring, and backwards and forwards between different courses. If it rained real hard, we hopped into our fly... Ah! those were happy days and no error.

Sir John's favourite hack was Ruskie, a grey of half Arab and half Russian breeding. When this old faithful died, Sir John had him buried in the paddock behind the cottage and in the wall beside the grave he placed a plaque inscribed:

> Beneath this yer sod lies my poor old quad
> He was very fond of me and I of he you see
> J.D.A

This memorial to a much-loved mount can be seen behind Tony Hide's yard today.

In 1869 Sir John was elected to the Jockey Club and in 1875 he embarked upon a three-year period as one of its Stewards. In his second year of office he was both chairman of a committee for revising the rules of racing, and responsible for rebuilding the stands at the end of the Rowley Mile, a project that was undertaken at the instigation of Lord Falmouth.

Not only did the existing stand provide hopelessly insufficient accommodation, but even those who secured a position on it availed themselves little. The structure was so unsafe that nobody was allowed on top, but that was the only place from which a good view of the running could be obtained. In the course of its demolition it was found that only a miracle had prevented the members of the Jockey Club and its other *habitués* collapsing amidst a heap of rubble. The walls of the old stand were constructed from bricks laid lengthwise on both its inner and outer faces with no proper bonding between them

When the new stand had been completed the betting ring was placed beside it whereas previously it had been by the Bushes some way down the course. This change was resented by many of the seasoned racing men, who missed the hack down to the ring, but as increasing age rendered them less energetic they became reconciled to the way Sir John had reorganised things, especially on the not infrequent days when the wind drove the rain across the Heath.

The cost of erecting the new Rowley Mile stand and laying out the paddock amounted to some £20,000. A few years later the Jockey Club was receiving an income of £25,000 in admission fees to it every season, so the stands paid for themselves many times over, enabling the Club to make a considerable increase in the prize money it put up for racing at Newmarket.

Although Sir John was very much more conversant with the Rules of Racing and the weight-for-age scale than he was with the intricacies of the British constitution and the niceties of political in-fighting, this popular sporting personality agreed to stand as Tory candidate for North Lincolnshire on condition that he was unopposed. He was duly returned to the House of Commons by that division in 1874.

As Sir John was quite incapable of understanding that he could not say exactly what he liked in the political arena just as he did on the racecourse, he caused more than one minor sensation. In the course of a speech to his constituents he remarked that the Irish members of the House of Commons included "forty of the most confounded rascals ever seen". Asked to apologise he stood half-way across the floor of the House, in direct contravention of its rules, with his hands thrust deep into his trouser pockets and declared that he had been a soldier and was not afraid of any Irishman!

On another memorable occasion a campaigner for teetotalism asked 'The Mate' his opinion of Sir Wilfrid Lawson's Liquor Bill. As Sir John never troubled himself with matters concerning total abstinence either in theory or practice, he was taken aback for a moment but recovered himself to reply, "I don't know much about Sir Wilfrid Lawson's Liquor Bill, but mine was a deuced sight too high when I paid it last".

It must be admitted that 'The Mate' was not cut out to be a legislator. No doubt he was profoundly thankful that he lost his seat at the general election of 1880.

Sir John was just about as complete a sportsman as this country has ever seen. Although plagued by an acute shortage of money almost throughout his life, nothing would ever tempt him to do something underhand or abuse a trust. Furthermore he was utterly loyal to his friends and those whom he employed. That loyalty could cost him dear, as it did in the case of Peter.

Peter, with whom the Bedford Lodge trainer Joe Dawson won the Middle Park Stakes in 1878, was probably the best horse of his generation. He was also an incorrigible rogue on whom it was impossible to rely. Had he been in the right mood he might well have asserted his superiority over his contemporaries by winning The Derby of 1879, but his entry for the race became void by the death of his owner, General Peel. (This would not happen today, as the rules have been changed.) At the sale of the General's horses Peter was bought for 6,000 guineas by a man called Gee, who gave Sir John first refusal of the horse.

For two impecunious years 'The Mate' sought to raise the necessary £6,300 for the purchase of Peter. At last he came within sight of his goal when he won £5,000 over the success of his filly Windsor in the

Chester Cup in 1881. Borrowing the balance, Sir John was the owner of Peter on the following Saturday. By this time the colt's original trainer, Joe Dawson, had died and had been succeeded at Bedford Lodge by his head lad, 'Buck' Sherrard, for whom Charlie Wood continued to ride as first jockey. After purchasing Peter, Sir John Left him with Sherrard.

In the early part of 1881 the American three-year-old Foxhall was at Bedford Lodge being prepared for the Grand Prix de Paris. One morning Peter was asked to give that horse 35 lb over a mile and half on the Limekilns. He won the gallop as easily as if he could have given the younger one another stone and still come out on top. The form looked good and would have looked still better had Sir John and his trainer known that after he had been sent to William Day at Woodyates a few weeks later, Foxhall would go on to win the Grand Prix de Paris and both the Cesarewitch and the Cambridgeshire as well.

Even without foreseeing what the future held for Foxhall, Sir John knew that in Peter he had something with which he could go to market in a big way. The Manchester Cup was selected as the objective and Charlie Wood was told he would have the ride.

A few days after the gallop on the Limekilns, Fred Archer went up to Sir John at Kempton Park saying, "I will ride Peter if you wish, Sir John", and, handing him a piece of notepaper, added, "This will interest you". On the paper was a note that Captain Machell had written Archer: "If you will ride Valour in the Manchester Cup, I will run him; if not, I shall not send him to Manchester".

It looked as though Sir John was in the happy position of being able to secure the services of the champion jockey and, at the same time, eliminate Valour from the opposition. Yet this could only be done at the expense of Charlie Wood, and the very last thing that Sir John Astley would do was to obtain an advantage for himself if it meant going back on a previous obligation. One of the unwritten rules of racing is that you never supplant the stable rider unless he has proved himself unsuitable for the horse concerned, and to a man so completely straightforward as 'The Mate' that rule was very nearly Holy Writ.

When Archer asked Sir John what reply he should make to Captain Machell's note Sir John told him he could ride Valour and much good it would do him as Peter would win the Manchester Cup.

In a field of 14, Fernandez started 3-1 favourite; Peter, over whom Sir John stood to win £12,000, was at 9-2; while Valour seemed generally regarded as holding as much chance as Sir John gave him, for he was freely offered at 25-1. This was a huge price for one of Archer's mounts, but it was thought that a mile was Valour's distance and that he had absolutely no hope of getting a mile and a half.

What Valour's stamina might not have achieved, Archer's brilliant jockeyship did. By setting off to make the running, then giving the non-stayer a vital breather while still in front of his field, Archer was able to produce a refreshed Valour for the final set-to with Peter. Riding as strong a finish as ever he did, Archer kept Valour going long enough to hold Peter by a neck.

Instead of winning £12,000 over the Cup, Sir John was out of pocket to the tune of more than £2,000, and all because he refused to stand down Wood. By this time Sir John had a wealth of experience of racing and even if it had not made him a rich one it had made him a wise man in its ways. His head told him that Archer would give the wayward Peter a far better ride than Wood, but his heart would not permit him to desert the stable jockey. Even in the moment of defeat, he gave not the faintest sign of disappointment with Wood, who had been outgeneralled and outridden by the champion, but consoled him with a pat on the back as he went to weigh in.

Sir John resolved to recover his Manchester losses by winning with Peter at Royal Ascot, where the Royal Hunt Cup was the five-year-old's target. In those days many horses were considerably more versatile than their present-day counterparts, and, what is more, they undertook much more arduous programmes than they do today, so it was decided that Peter would also go for the Queen's Vase on the opening day of the meeting and for the Hardwicke Stakes on the final one too. As Charlie Wood was required by another of the Bedford Lodge patrons in the Hunt Cup, Sir John was able to book Archer for his horse in that race without any misgivings.

The first day of the Royal fixture found Peter in the very worst of moods. As they were going up the hill after passing the stands in the Vase, he decided that he had had enough for one afternoon, and that with the paddock in the immediate vicinity it was a good point at which to pull up. And that was exactly what he did. Resisting his rider's efforts to get him going again, with an ill-tempered exhibition of bucking and kicking he was eventually allowed to return to the paddock.

Despite Peter's unpropitious antics on the previous day, the ring was taking no chances with him in the Royal Hunt Cup, for which he was made favourite at 5-1. Knowing that he was quite as capable of refusing to start as he was of giving up racing half-way through the proceedings, Sir John left Archer to deal with the latter contingency and tried to reduce the likelihood of the former by sending a jockey called Giles, who had no mount in the race, down to the post with a long tom to make him jump off. As it turned out, no such encouragement at the start was required. Peter got away all right, but hardly at racing pace. By the time they reached the half-way stage he was sulking some way behind the rest of the field with no apparent chance of winning. Had Archer not been as consummate a horseman as he was a jockey, he would never have won that race. Somehow he managed to coax Peter into taking hold of his bit. Having done so, the horse almost flew past his rivals and despite the 9 st 3 lb on his back, he actually won with something in hand. It was an amazing performance that stamped Peter as being a truly great horse when in the mood.

After the way in which Peter had won the Royal Hunt Cup, he looked a good thing for the Hardwicke Stakes, provided he were in a co-operative frame of mind. Over this race Archer used the sort of intelligence that distinguishes a brilliant jockey, who takes the most minute detail into consideration, from the competent one, who confines his responsibilities to giving his mount a good ride.

Before racing began on the Friday he went to Sir John and pointed out that on the way to the mile and a half start he would have to pass the point where Peter had given up the ghost in Tuesday's race. To take him to it again, Archer continued, could invite a repetition of his tantrums, so it might be as well to obtain the permission of the Stewards for the horse to be taken to the start the reverse way, that is anti-clockwise, so that no memories were stirred in that unbalanced equine brain. The Stewards' permission was obtained and everything went according to plan. Sir John did not have his bet until he saw Peter safely off, when he obtained an even £1,500 from the bookmaker, beside whom he had stationed himself. For the nonce Peter decided to enjoy his racing and won hard held by eight lengths.

Another good horse that 'The Mate' owned was Ostregor. Until the day of his death he never really got over the way in which he had come to part with that old favourite. At the Goodwood meeting of 1867 he was more financially embarrassed than even he was accustomed to being, and had to find £3,000 by the following Monday morning, with which to repay Sam Lewis, the money-lender.

Two Austrian generals, looking for horses for the Emperor Franz Josef, offered him exactly £3,000 for Ostregor. Seeing no other way out, Sir John reluctantly accepted on condition that the horse should run in the Chesterfield Cup, in which he had been runner-up the previous year. Ridden by Harry Custance this time, Ostregor went one better with a vengeance by coming home five lengths clear of his field, thereby landing Sir John £5,000 in bets.

The first thing Sir John did was to seek out the Austrian generals to cancel the sale. He offered them £1,000 to let him have his pet back. He offered them £2,000. He appealed to their sportsmanship. He called them every kind of foreigner he could think of. They remained adamant. What had been done on behalf of the Emperor could not be undone.

For a long time Sir John was inconsolable about the loss of Ostregor. When he paid Sam Lewis he declared he was doing it with blood money. When still worse financial catastrophes forced him to sell his plate many years later he refused to part with the Chesterfield Cup that Ostregor had won. On it he had had engraved, 'The best-looking, best-tempered and gamest horse of his day. We ne'er shall see his like again'.

As well as by supervising the building of the Rowley Mile stands, Sir John left his own memorial in Newmarket by founding the Astley Institute for stablemen.

Unlike so many of the richer owners, Sir John was deeply concerned about the hard-worked lads. The boys in other industries were able to continue to live at home after they had gone out to work, but racing lads had, of necessity, to leave their homes if they were to go into stables, except for the small minority who were Newmarket born and bred. As a result they found themselves in a strange town, with low wages and no opportunities for recreation. About the best thing they could do with their leisure hours was to haunt the pubs hoping to be bought a beer or a cheap cigar in exchange for divulging information about the horses in the stables in which they worked.

To remedy a thoroughly unsatisfactory state of affairs that should have been tackled many years previously, Sir John launched a fund to build the stablemen and stud hands a club in which they could relax over a game of billiards or a hand of cards or go into a quiet room to read in comparative comfort.

Lady Wallace gave the site of the Institute, and of the £3,000 that it cost to build Sir John himself collected about £2,500. Most of this he raised by making rapid approaches to owners directly one of their horses had won an important race, or by obtaining the promise of a donation from the owner of the favourite in the event of success. The Astley Institute was opened by the Prince of Wales in July 1883. Sir John took his place on the board of managers and played his part in arranging concerts and other activities for the entertainment of the lads. These enterprises proved a huge success.

One lad in whose life Sir John played a decisive part was Joseph Lewis. One April morning in 1886 Sir John, mounted on a hack, was chatting with Lord and Lady Zetland as they were watching work on Racecourse Side. Suddenly a horse called Catastrophe became perfectly unmanageable and bolted. Galloping headlong at a post on which a notice board was nailed it dislodged its rider as it passed underneath. The lad, who was Joseph Lewis, broke his thigh so badly that the bone protruded through his trousers and he also broke his left arm.

Immediately he saw the lad was off, Sir John rode over to see whether he was hurt. Finding him in such a terrible state he borrowed Lord Zetland's carriage to take him to the Rous Memorial Hospital. On arrival Lewis was still unconscious and the doctors had almost given up hope of saving his life when he responded to artificial respiration. Thereafter he improved gradually but it was inevitable that his leg should be amputated. Thus even though he recovered his health the loss of the leg meant that Lewis could no longer earn his living in stables. He was unemployed and the best that the future seemed to hold for this unfortunate young man was a life dependent upon charity.

Once again, Sir John, always one to help people in difficulty came to the rescue. Organising a subscription, he raised enough money to pay for Lewis to take a course in shorthand and typewriting. When he had completed it he was fully qualified for secretarial work and was able to take a job again. Needless to say it was to Joseph Lewis that Sir John dictated his autobiography, quite one of the best books on the sporting, military and social aspects of its period.

Like all great characters Sir John had some little mannerisms that were entirely his own. For instance he would refer to himself alternately in the first and third person, and always mispronounced his own name, persistently calling himself Ashley. Lord Rossmore recalled how Sir John described his watch being stolen at Epsom races as follows:

Ashley went to the Derby, and I'm blessed if Ashley's ticker wasn't stolen from him. As it had been given me, and I prized it, I went to the head pick-pocket, with whom I was acquainted, and said, 'See here, they've taken Ashley's ticker'.

The man blushed. 'Good Lord, you don't mean it, Sir John?' he stammered. 'Will you 'ave the goodness to just wait 'ere? I'll be back in a jiffy'.

He was back in three minutes with Ashley's ticker, which he handed over, saying most humbly as he did so 'I 'ope Sir John, you'll accept the apologies of the 'ole fraternity; it was quite a mistake, and it was done by a noo beginner!'

When Sir John Astley died on 10 October 1894, the whole racing community, from the stable lads of Newmarket to the Jockey Club had reason to mourn a great sportsman. His own troubles were never far away from him, yet he spent much of his time and energy helping other people, and whether they were rich or poor they could all be his friends.

A string of horses taking a turn in the High Street. Modern traffic makes such an operation impracticable – even with the by-pass!

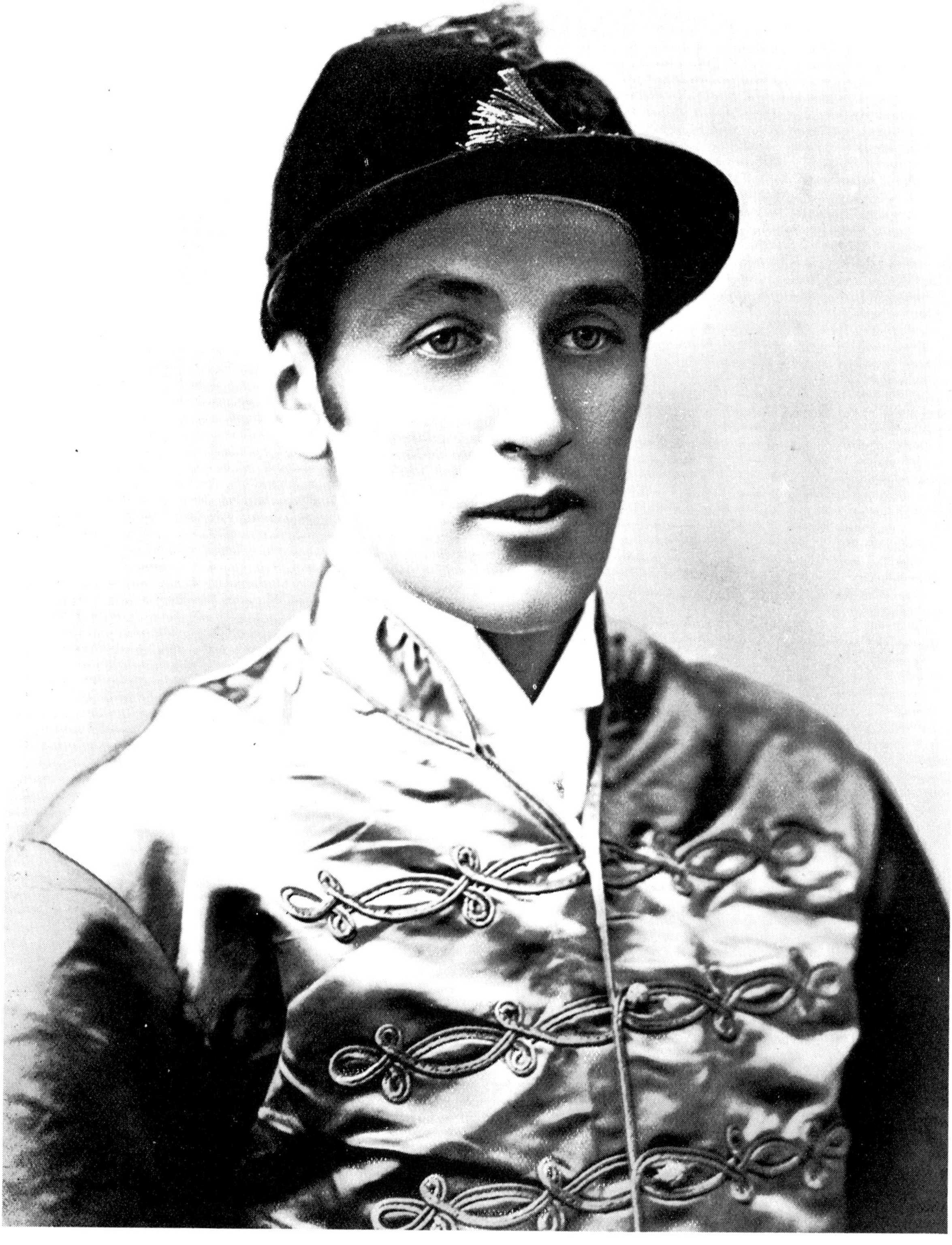

13 The Death of Fred Archer

Never was there such a sensation as on that cold November day of 1886 when Newmarket was swept with the news that Fred Archer had shot himself in his fine new house up on Fordham Road. It seemed so fantastic that few can have believed it at first. When they did their senses were numbed, such was the gap that was left in the life of Newmarket and the rest of the racing world. For many a day afterwards, owners, trainers, his fellow jockeys and all the stable lads would be asking each other why he did it. Not only these people in whose life he had been an integral part, but throughout the British Empire and across the Atlantic in America, men and women who had only the faintest knowledge of the affairs of racing were shocked.

At first no-one could understand how the greatest and most successful jockey that the world had seen up to that time should take his life at the age of 29. He was at the height of success, commanding a huge income and the respect of all who knew him. Yet those who knew him best recalled that behind all the glittering triumphs the world saw there lay two spectres. The first was the death of the lovely wife he had adored and the second the struggle to maintain his health while reducing to an unnatural weight. These two things preyed on his mind continually.

Unlike Sir Gordon Richards, but in common with Lester Piggott, Fred Archer came from a racing family. He was born at St George's Cottage, Cheltenham, on 11 January 1857, and the following year his father, William Archer, won the Grand National on Little Charlie.

Billy Archer was a hardbitten horseman of the old school. His life was rough and tough and he liked it that way. By contrast to this squat little steeplechase rider, his wife Emma presented a taller figure with not a little elegance and gentility about her.

After having spent the early years of his life with these parents, his brothers, Billy and Charlie, and the jumping jockeys and stable lads of Cheltenham, Fred Archer went to Newmarket to become apprenticed to Mat Dawson at Heath House. He had just turned eleven when he signed indentures on 10 February 1868.

Archer had his first ride on Honoria at the Newmarket Second October Meeting of 1869 but had to wait almost another year before he rode his first winner under Jockey Club rules on Athol Daisy at Chesterfield on 28 September 1870. This was not the first winner he ever rode, as his Cheltenham connections secured him the offer of a ride on a pony called Maid of Trent in a steeplechase at Bangor. Mat Dawson's permission for acceptance having been obtained, the future champion weighed out at 4 st 11 lb to win on her.

Fred Archer (1857-1886), apprenticed to Mat Dawson at Heath House

Before long Fred Archer was in greater demand than any other lightweight, and his winners, unimportant at first and then in more notable events, began to accumulate. His first big race success was on Salvanos in the Cesarewitch in 1872. The following year he came out of his apprenticeship and by the end of it he was second in the list with 107 winners to his credit; then in 1874 he obtained his first classic success on Atlantic in The 2,000 Guineas. By the end of the season he was champion jockey for the first time while still only 17 years of age.

In those days while he was making his name, Fred Archer was displaying some characteristics from both his parents. In his riding he showed all the relentless determination to win that his father had had to show while he was struggling to earn every crust he could give his family. There was just about nothing he would not do to bring a winner home and a bit of rough riding here and there was something in which he was perfectly prepared to indulge.

When he was not riding, this tallish lad, with large brown eyes set above a slightly protuberant upper lip in a pale face, showed that he had inherited much of the gentility of his mother. His manners were a great deal better than those of the other jockeys, who came from the slums of the great cities or the rough farms of the countryside, and his intelligence was certainly superior. Anyone seeing the sombrely dressed young man going into Mat Dawson's study to discuss the week's running plans would take him for an accountant, auditor or some other clerk instead of the most dashing jockey of the day.

Quite possibly Fred Archer, for all his natural brilliance, would not have made quite such rapid progress if it had not been for the death from consumption of Mat Dawson's stable jockey, Tom French, at the age of 29 in 1873. Archer was still going to the scale at little more than six stone, and Mat Dawson and his principal patron, Lord Falmouth, were at first reluctant to retain a rider who would often need to carry two or three stone dead weight, but after Archer had become champion without the benefit of the retainer from Heath House in 1874, he was given the job of first jockey to Mat Dawson's stable.

When Archer was not required by Mat Dawson, he was sure to be on a good present from anyone else for whom he rode a winner. Owners and trainers were falling over themselves to secure his services, and for his part the jockey had no doubt about their value. It would be going too far to describe him as greedy, or even ungenerous, but one can see why they began to call him 'The Tinman'. Restless in his determination to excel all rivals he would go anywhere for a successful mount, so that he was not long in amassing a fortune. Having done so, he made sure it remained intact by shrewd investment and frugal living.

On top of the vast revenue he earned from his riding fees and his presents, Fred Archer also received handsome sums from his punters. For instance, John Hammond gave him £10,000 after he had won the 1882 St Leger on Dutch Oven, and Arthur Cooper gave him £5,000 over the same race.

The extent to which Archer captured the imagination of the general public is hard to conceive. In those days there was no popular press to keep the people in touch with their idol, yet he commanded an immense following, so much so that by the time he was at the height of his fame his name had become part of the English language. When people asked each other how they were, if all was well, the reply would be "Archer's Up", and, as the most casual of punters knew, nothing could be better than that.

In the early years of the 1880s Fred Archer carried all before him, and every aspect of his private life seemed equally satisfactory. It looked as though years and years of uninterrupted success and complete happiness lay before him.

On 31 January 1883, Fred was married to Nellie Dawson, daughter of Mat's younger brother John, who trained at Warren House. The ceremony took place at All Saints Church, where Tom Jennings junior was best man. All Newmarket rejoiced that day and people from the outlying villages flocked into the town to join in the celebrations. The crowd that assembled to watch the bride and groom leave the church lined each side of Palace Street right up to the Rutland Arms.

That evening Mrs John Dawson gave a ball for the two families and their friends at the Rutland. On the opposite side of the High Street all the lads in the stables of John Dawson, Mat Dawson and Charlie Archer were given a party in the Wagon and Horses, while there were more jollifications on the Severals, where an ox given by Lord Hastings was roasted whole.

Up to the time of his marriage Fred Archer had led a spartan life in a room over the stables at Heath House. On becoming engaged to Nellie he built a large house amongst the paddocks that lie on the left of the Fordham Road as you leave the town. This he named Falmouth House in honour of the owner for whom he had ridden so many of his most important winners, and Lord Falmouth, who always took a keen interest in his welfare, made several practical suggestions about its design and construction. It was to the newly completed Falmouth House that Fred and Nellie Archer returned from their brief honeymoon in Torquay during the early spring.

The first disaster in a marriage that had looked perfect came when their son died within a few hours of his birth in January 1884. On 8 November of the same year Nellie gave birth to a daughter.

Fred first heard news of the little girl while he was riding at Liverpool races. He had just won the Autumn Cup on the Duchess of Montrose's Thebais when he received a telegram to say that both mother and daughter were doing well at Falmouth House.

As he travelled back to Newmarket on the train from Liverpool Fred felt happier than he had ever done before. In his profession he had achieved almost everything he could possibly wish and even at that very moment he was assured of being champion jockey for the eleventh year in succession. Now at last he was a father, so the tragedy of the early part of the year could be forgotten.

Remembering how much Nellie always loved to see him dressed up for a meet of the Newmarket drag, Fred decided to cheer her up by greeting her and their newborn child in his hunting clothes. The first thing that he did on arrival at Falmouth House was to change into these. Just as he was finishing, his sister Mrs Coleman rushed into the room screaming, "Fred! Fred! Nellie is dying!"

He ran to his wife to find her writhing in agony. The convulsions ended and she died without recognising him.

With the death of his beloved Nellie ended the last day of happiness Fred Archer ever knew. That winter he took a holiday in the United States, returning refreshed in body if not in soul and in 1885 he won The Derby on Melton. The winners still came the way they had always done but they were ridden by an automaton to whom nothing could bring real pleasure any more. For what it was worth, he was champion jockey for a twelfth time at the end of 1885, and the following season, when the battle against increasing weight added more than ever to his misery, his successes included yet another Derby on Ormonde, trained by John Porter at Kingsclere, and the Grand Prix de Paris on Mat Dawson's Minting.

In the early autumn of 1886 he agreed to ride St Mirin for the Duchess of Montrose in the Cambridgeshire (one of the few important races he had not won) even though it seemed that he was sure to have put up a pound or two overweight on that colt, to whom 8 st 6 lb had been allotted.

In October he went across to Ireland to ride Cambusmore for the Lord Lieutenant, Lord Londonderry, at the Curragh, travelling in company with former jockey Harry Custance, who was to act as starter.

When he arrived at Dublin on Tuesday, 19 October, he could not weigh out at an ounce less than 9 st 4 lb, yet two days later he was due to ride Cambusmore at 9 st and, worse still, a rather smart two-year old called Isidore at 8 st 12 lb. Making the lower weight he delighted the Irish by winning on both horses but by now he was beginning to look a very sick man indeed.

Custance, who knew him well, told him he had never looked half as ill as he did then. Raising a laugh Fred replied, "Well, if I look bad now what shall I look like next Wednesday when I ride St Mirin in the Cambridgeshire?"

The effect on Archer of reducing to St Mirin's weight preyed on the mind of his friend Custance. While they were returning to England by the packet steamer, Custance tried hard to dissuade the champion but Fred Archer had not risen to the top of his profession by being easily influenced. "Cus", he said, "I am sure to ride St Mirin at 8-6 or 8-7. I shall win the Cambridgeshire and then be able to come down to your country and enjoy myself this winter". However much deprivation may have weakened his body, the iron will remained as strong as ever.

For three days before the running of the Cambridgeshire, Fred Archer never ate a thing. He told a friend, "I have never ridden the winner of the Cambridgeshire and if I don't succeed this time I shall never try again". The words were prophetic.

For all his wasting, Archer still had to put up a pound overweight on St Mirin even though he was wearing the thinnest of silk shirts that did nothing to protect his weakened body from the cold of that bleak autumn day. As he took the lead inside the distance it looked as though all these privations would be repaid, but from out of the blue something came up on the far rails. Archer rallied St Mirin to answer the challenge and the two horses passed the post almost dead level. At first Archer thought he had won, then doubts assailed him so that by the time the judge had given a verdict of a head to the other, an unconsidered outsider called Sailor Prince, he was already reconciled to defeat.

As Fred Archer sat alone in Falmouth House that evening, he must have felt more despondent than he had done for months, and felt it without hope of any consolation. Defeat had been something that he had always found hard to accept at the best of times, but in those circumstances it was more bitter than it had ever been. He had set his heart on winning that Cambridgeshire, backed himself heavily to do it, and, perhaps worst of all, had endured a painful ordeal in an unsuccessful attempt to make the exact weight. Had he shed that last pound he might well have won, or at least made a dead-heat of it. On top of all these things he had caught a severe chill while riding on the Heath that afternoon.

Despite the deterioration in his condition, Archer took the rides for which he had been booked during the rest of the Houghton Meeting. On the Friday he rode five winners, and the fifth of them, Blanchard, provided him with his last success on a racecourse. Appropriately, Blanchard was one of the few horses that Lord Falmouth still kept in training.

As he showed no sign of recovering from the chill, Archer missed the meeting at Lincoln early the following week. This in itself was a minor sensation. In the general run of things if there was racing on, Archer would be there to ride. As he had promised to take mounts at Brighton he rode there on both the Wednesday and the Thursday, and though he was feeling terribly ill by the end of the meeting he went on to Lewes for a fancied ride on Tommy Tittlemouse. Despite the immense confidence behind him, Tommy Tittlemouse ran unplaced, and Archer, now near a state of collapse, made the belated decision to return to Falmouth House.

So weak did he feel that he asked Martin Gurry, then training in Newmarket's Park Lodge yard, to accompany him in case he should need assistance. Gurry agreed. When they reached Liverpool Street Station he made Archer take a basin of arrowroot with brandy in it. This seems to have been some benefit to the sick man, for he slept throughout the train journey. On arrival at Newmarket he declared he felt better. Gurry saw him to Falmouth House, where his sister, Mrs Coleman, who kept house for him, put him to bed immediately. That was on Thursday, 4 November 1886.

On the following day, Archer was more desperately ill, and Mrs Coleman sent for his medical adviser, Doctor Wright, who was so seriously perturbed, after making his examination, that he sent for Dr Latham of Cambridge for a second opinion.

As Fred Archer was a national figure, and concern about his condition was felt all over the country, there was no question of treating his illness as a private matter. Consequently the following statement was issued on the Saturday: "Falmouth House, November 6th, 1886, 6.0 p.m. Mr. F. Archer has returned home suffering from the effects of a severe chill, followed by a high fever. (signed) P. W. Latham and J. R. Wright".

On the Sunday he seemed slightly better but signs that he was suffering from typhoid were detected. The improvement was maintained overnight and the next morning a second statement was issued. This read: "Newmarket, November 8th, 1886. Mr. Fred Archer is suffering from an attack of typhoid fever. There is an improvement in his symptoms today. (signed) J. R. Wright".

But though rest and warmth may have brought about an improvement in his physical condition by Monday, his poor distracted mind was still in the grip of the fever. Even in his brief moments of lucidity he could no nothing but torture himself. He was still obsessed by the defeat of St Mirin and, worse still, he must have recalled that they were coming to the second anniversary of Nellie's tragic death.

Late on Monday morning he became more coherent and held a long conversation with Mrs Coleman, though not without wandering off from time to time. About two o'clock in the afternoon he requested the nurse to leave the room as he wished to speak to his sister alone. Mrs Coleman was standing at the window with her back to her brother when he suddenly asked the totally irrelevant question, "Are they coming?" Almost immediately she heard a noise behind her. On turning round Mrs Coleman saw that Fred was out of bed and had pulled out the revolver he kept in the drawer beside his bed in case of burglary. Rushing towards him, Mrs Coleman tried to prevent him using the revolver which he was holding in his left hand. Thereupon he threw his right arm round her neck and fired into his mouth. He died instantly.

Even the tragedy of the death of the greatest of all jockeys could not silence the scandal-mongers. They said that he had shot himself because he had been in a ring with Charlie Wood and others and was unable to face an enquiry by the Stewards of the Jockey Club. Others had equally fantastic theories to account for the fact that he had taken his own life, yet who can really doubt the coroner's verdict that he shot himself "whilst in a state of unsound mind"?

Whether his final words "Are they coming?" meant anything nobody will ever know. If they did have a meaning, could it not be that the poor distracted man was asking about the wife and son he was so soon to join?

As had been the case with regard to many other men and women who have met with strange or violent deaths, there have been many reports of Fred Archer's ghost having been seen over the years. For instance Captain Machell said that when he was unable to sleep on night he saw Archer standing by his bed. After a few minutes Archer put out his hand to touch him. He felt unaccountably soothed and contented and went straight to sleep. There have also been various reports from time to time of his ghost being seen riding along the lanes in and around Newmarket.

Falmouth House, now demolished, the home of Fred Archer

14 Sir George Chetwynd versus The Earl of Durham – A Case of Libel

In 1887 Britain celebrated the Golden Jubilee of Queen Victoria. Meanwhile the town was more preoccupied than usual with retailing gossip and scandal. Everywhere, in the public houses and the clubs, in the trainers' houses and in the stable lads' dormitories, they were discussing how the leading jockey, Charlie Wood, was pulling horses he rode for the Chetwynd House trainer, 'Buck' Sherrard. Moreover, popular rumour had it that he was able to do this because he was acting in concert with the stable's principal patron, Sir George Chetwynd, a leading member of the Jockey Club and former senior steward.

Things came to a head at the Gimcrack Dinner at York in December 1887, when no less a person than the Earl of Durham implied in the course of his speech that the way in which a certain Newmarket stable was run was nothing short of a disgrace to the good name of racing.

Asked to which establishment he had been referring, Lord Durham made no secret of the fact that he had Chetwynd House in mind. Nailing his colours to the mast still more firmly he wrote to Lord Lurgan to say, "It is quite correct that I gave George Lambton my authority to inform you, or any other gentleman, with the exception of Sir George Chetwynd, that I have no wish or intention to make any imputation against you in my remarks at the Gimcrack dinner on the subject of Sherrard's stable".

On realising the futility of his first reaction in challenging Lord Durham to a duel, Sir George sued him for £20,000 damages for libel. Both sides embarked upon the lengthy process of preparing their cases. Soon it was apparent that it would be nearly impossible to obtain a fair trial of the action before a High Court judge, who would almost certainly be hampered by his ignorance of racing and betting, so both parties agreed to have the case tried by three assessors. These were to be the Stewards of the Jockey Club, Mr James Lowther, Lord March and Prince Soltykoff. When proceedings eventually opened in 1889 Sir Henry James represented Sir George and Sir Charles Russell appeared for Lord Durham.

The central figure of this drama, Sir George Chetwynd, of Grendon Hall in Warwickshire, had been born in 1849. A tall spare man of considerably dignity, Sir George wore a moustache that twirled into curls at the ends, but no beard. Never popular, though always respected on account of his strength of character, Sir George had a coldness of demeanour that became the more unpleasant when it was tempered by that streak of arrogance that was never far below the surface. When things were going well, and his horses were winning, he was apt to be particularly haughty. On the other hand, there were times when he could be the most agreeable of companions.

Like so many young men of his time, he began racing under the guidance of Captain Machell, and even before he came of age he had runners in the assumed name of 'Mr Mortimer'. As soon as he became 21 in 1870 he registered his colours as straw with sky-blue sleeves and cap. In the same year he married, of all people, the beautiful widow, Florence, Marchioness of Hastings, whose husband had been ruined by Hermit's Derby in 1867. In 1871 Sir George was elected to the Jockey Club.

Before long Sir George decided that Captain Machell was not having much luck with his horses, so he took them away from Bedford Cottage and sent them to Billy Saunderson at Hednesford, which was nearer his home. This arrangement did not last long, either. In 1873 he became a patron of Harry Woolcott's Beckhampton stable, but after three or four seasons he made yet another move and had his horses with Joe Dawson at Bedford Lodge.

In 1877 Joe Dawson won him the Ascot Stakes with Chypre, who provided a young jockey called Charlie Wood with one of the first important successes of his career. The following year Sir George Chetwynd became Senior Steward of the Jockey Club.

By comparison with most other members of the Jockey Club, Sir George was a man of slender means. His income was quite sufficient to enable him to be comfortable, but nothing like large enough to live as extravagantly, or to own horses, on the scale that he did.

In order to make ends meet, Sir George Chetwynd relied upon betting. Thus the unfortunate situation arose in which a member of the Jockey Club was nothing less than a professional punter. As it happened, Sir George was a good judge of horses and could read a race better than most men, so his betting prospered. Furthermore, he soon began to be able to take advantage of the knowledge imparted to him by the jockey Charlie Wood, a character as shrewd as himself.

Charlie Wood was born in 1856 and came to Newmarket to be indentured to Joe Dawson. After a successful apprenticeship he became one of the leading riders and first jockey to Bedford Lodge. In 1880 he obtained his first classic success on Elizabeth in The 1,000 Guineas. Three years later, in 1883, he won The Derby on St Blaise and the following year he rode St Gatien to dead-heat with Harvester in The Derby. On six occasions he was runner-up to Fred Archer in the jockeys' list while in the season that ended just before Lord Durham made his speech at the Gimcrack dinner he had succeeded Archer as champion jockey.

Unlike so many of his fellow jockeys, Charlie Wood had a sound sense of business and full realisation of the value of money, of which he accumulated as much as he could. Through riding fees and presents he earned huge sums, which he invested in property and became the owner of a stud just outside Newmarket as well as one or two hotels and houses in the town. He bought Suffolk House, and from Sir John Astley he purchased the house that Jem Robinson had built in

Sir George Chetwynd (1849-1917), was at the centre of the greatest of all the Victorian racing scandals

about 1850. As has already been mentioned, this is now known as Machell Place.

From the above it will be seen that Sir George and Charlie Wood had ample reason for making common cause. Both needed money; Sir George to maintain his social position amongst some of the richest men in the world, and Charlie Wood so that he could acquire the property that would give him security against returning to the poverty in which he had been born, when his riding days were finished.

Clever though Sir George was, he inevitably experienced the times when the luck ran against him in his betting, and then he had to apply to the famous money-lender, Sam Lewis, of Cork Street, London. To mend his finances he had to bring off a coup. The engineering of a coup eventually had to lead Sir George into breaking the rules that as a member of the Jockey Club he was bound to uphold and entering into the underhand arrangements with Charlie Wood which Lord Durham denounced.

After Joe Dawson had died in 1880 and his head lad 'Buck' Sherrard had taken over Bedford Lodge, Stirling Crawfurd and his wife, the Duchess of Montrose, who was still known by that title, became the principal owners in the yard with Sir George Chetwynd managing their horses. This arrangement did not last very long, for the Duchess soon took exception to the way in which Sir George went about a spot of horse-dealing with a notorious American gambler called Walton. On the pretext that she and her husband wished to turn Bedford Lodge into a private stable, she wrote to Sir George in 1882 asking him to take his own horses elsewhere.

Sir George did more than oblige. Not only did he remove his horses, but he took their trainer 'Buck' Sherrard and jockey Charlie Wood as well, and between them they set up their own establishment at the Nunnery stables. That was the yard in which William Gilbert had trained Cremorne to win The Derby for Henry Savile in 1872. Henry Savile had died in 1880, leaving his trainer the choice of any five of his horses.

The move of Sir George's horses to the Nunnery stables was no more than a temporary expedient. While they were there, Charlie Wood was busy enlarging the cottage that he had bought from Sir John Astley and building a thoroughly modern stable yard in the paddock immediately behind it. When this was finished he named the new establishment Chetwynd House in honour of his patron. The latter's horses moved into the boxes, and 'Buck' Sherrard was installed as trainer.

Other owners, most of them heavy gamblers, soon sent their horses to Chetwynd House. These included Lord Lurgan, Sir George Arthur, General Owen Williams and Ernest Benzon, the 'Jubilee Plunger' who soon brought ruin on himself by his reckless betting.

Secure, as he thought, under the powerful protection of Sir George Chetwynd, Charlie Wood seems to have played fast and loose with the rules of racing. For his part Sir George made sure that his betting showed a profit from the misdemeanours of his jockey. Wood was Sir

George's jockey only in a technical sense. Apart from the statutory riding fees of three guineas for a loser and five for a winner, that were automatically paid through Weatherby's, Wood did not even receive the normal presents when he rode a winner for Sir George, let alone his nominal retainer of £300 a year. Moreover, after the Jockey Club had forbidden jockeys to own horses by a notice published in the *Calendar* in December 1883, Charlie Wood avoided complying with the new rule by selling his horses to Sir George in what was no more than a paper transaction. So it was that Charlie Wood, accomplished jockey and shrewd businessman, was the real power behind Chetwynd House, while Sir George became more and more of a figurehead.

First of all the bookmakers, who were the real victims of the policy of the Chetwynd House stable, and then other owners and trainers began to talk about the way the horses ran. Bit by bit the matter became an open scandal so that every stable lad and even the casual racegoers were talking about Sir George Chetwynd and Charlie Wood. With Lord Durham's Gimcrack speech the storm broke.

When the case opened Lord Durham entered 27 points of justification of what he had said and written about Sir George. His main themes were that Sir George was fully aware of, and profited by, Wood's dishonest riding and that he knew perfectly well that the jockey was the real owner of several horses at Chetwynd House.

One of the main planks in Lord Durham's case was the way in which a horse called Fullerton had been run. He contended that Fullerton had run in the Lincoln, the Kempton Park Jubilee Stakes, the Manchester Cup, the Stewards Cup and four other races in 1887 without attempting to win any of them — a prodigious feat of non-trying. In those races, Lord Durham alleged, Fullerton's connections were trying to throw dust in the eyes of the handicapper and Sir George had small bets on the horse for the sake of form. On the other hand, when Fullerton won three races at Newmarket in the same year, the Crawfurd Plate, the Babraham Plate and the Select Handicap, Sir George had a heavy bet each time.

Cool and self-assured, Sir George Chetwynd made an excellent witness. In the early part of the trial it looked as though he would win easily, so readily did he answer all the questions that were put to him, and Lord Durham and his supporters began to lose heart. But Sir Charles Russell probed and probed so that gradually Sir George's financial reliance on Wood began to emerge in this passage of cross-examination:

COUNSEL: Now I want to call your attention to another matter. You were paying at first a retaining fee of 100 guineas to Wood. Afterwards it was increased to £300. I see from the accounts that you have given us that at the end of 1884 you owed Wood £651.

SIR GEORGE: Yes, that is his account.

COUNSEL: That would be exclusive, would it not, of the fees which he would be paid through Weatherby — the five guineas for the winning and the three guineas for the losing mounts?

SIR GEORGE: Yes.
COUNSEL: These would pass through your account? They would go to the debit of your account at Weatherby's?
SIR GEORGE: Yes.
COUNSEL: Did you pay anything in 1885?
SIR GEORGE: I do not know, I am sure.
COUNSEL: What was the £651 account for?
SIR GEORGE: I forget what it was for.
COUNSEL: It is to the end of 1884?
SIR GEORGE: I did not pay anything for 1885. He never sent in his account at all.
COUNSEL: Am I not right in saying you paid nothing in 1885?
SIR GEORGE: I think that £651 was for 1883 and 1884.
COUNSEL: Quite right.
SIR GEORGE: So he sent me the bill for two years in one. You may take it I paid the two years in one.
COUNSEL: I want to get this clear. You paid him nothing in 1883 and 1884?
SIR GEORGE: I do not think so.
COUNSEL: You paid nothing in 1885?
SIR GEORGE: I do not think I did.
COUNSEL: You paid him nothing in 1886?
SIR GEORGE: That I cannot tell you.
COUNSEL: You paid him nothing in 1887?
SIR GEORGE: Then when did I pay him the £651?
COUNSEL: I will come to that in a moment. You paid nothing in 1887?
SIR GEORGE: I say I do not know when I paid the money.
COUNSEL: Then kindly look and see.
SIR GEORGE: I find I did not pay it till 11 January 1888.
COUNSEL: So that in 1883, 1884, 1885, 1886 and 1887 you paid nothing?
SIR GEORGE: I paid all his winning and losing mounts.
COUNSEL: I began by saying that, Sir George.
SIR GEORGE: Quite so.
COUNSEL: That was through Weatherby. You yourself paid nothing?
SIR GEORGE: No, I paid nothing.
COUNSEL: And you were aware by the date January 1888 that severe strictures, well or ill-founded, were made upon your relations with Wood...

A few minutes later Sir Charles Russell said to Sir George:

Now again I must put it to you — do you think that relation which is disclosed by the non-payment of these accounts was consistent with thorough independence between master and servant?
SIR GEORGE: Certainly. I was not obliged to pay him at all.
COUNSEL: Not the retainer?
SIR GEORGE: Certainly not: the retainer was simply a nominal thing. I begged Wood several times to get another master who would give him more money than I could afford to do, and he said he would rather ride for me first call than anybody else who would give him £1,000 a year. I

said I would try to give him £300 a year retainer, but that it must not be considered that I might not have to throw him over.

COUNSEL: Then am I to understand that instead of your being under an obligation to pay £300 a year, it was a fast and loose engagement to pay him what you pleased, or pay him nothing if you pleased?

SIR GEORGE: No, I meant fully to carry it out if I could afford it.

Even in examination by his own counsel, Sir Henry James, Sir George had to admit that he had played the part of front man to enable Charlie Wood to buy one horse.

COUNSEL: Did Wood on one occasion purchase a horse called Portnellan, or direct it to be purchased?

SIR GEORGE: Yes, at Derby in November 1886. I was not present.

COUNSEL: When did you first learn that he had bought the horse?

SIR GEORGE: The next day at Northampton.

COUNSEL: What was your pecuniary position at the time as regards your balance at your bankers? Was it in a good condition or not?

SIR GEORGE: I had no balance at my bankers. I could not write a cheque. I did not write a cheque for six months, I suppose.

COUNSEL: You have an income dependent on your agricultural estate?

SIR GEORGE: Yes.

COUNSEL: Did you tell Wood your position?

SIR GEORGE: Yes, I told him I had no money.

COUNSEL: What did Wood say or do?

SIR GEORGE: Wood offered to lend it to me, and he sent me a cheque two or three days afterwards. Meanwhile I had paid for the horse at Weatherby's. I had only £300 at Weatherby's at the time. Weatherby's of course, had paid for the horse.

COUNSEL: That same sum, £315, for which Portnellan had been purchased, which you had to pay to Weatherby's, was that sum sent in a cheque from Wood to you?

SIR GEORGE: Sent by a cheque from Wood to me.

COUNSEL: Is that the only transaction that ever took place of money advanced or payment between you and Wood?

SIR GEORGE: Yes.

Unfortunately the assessors did not really believe that answer. Bit by bit, the full story came out and it became apparent how Wood had been able to manipulate affairs with the full consent and knowledge of Sir George, who should have made him keep the rules of racing. Even when he had his back to the wall, Sir George was completely unruffled. Furthermore, he made no effort to shift the blame on to Wood by so much as a word, gesture or intonation of his voice. Throughout the action he stoutly maintained that the jockey was as innocent as himself of the charges levelled by Lord Durham, but it was no good. Even though the assessors found that Lord Durham had libelled Sir George they made it plain what they thought of Sir George's character and conduct by awarding him a farthing damages.

The contemptuous award made to Sir George spelled out his ruin. Racing had been his life and henceforth he was to be an exile from its world following his obligatory resignation from the Jockey Club.

Few people had liked Sir George before the beginning of the case, but by the time it had finished there was nobody who did not admire him for the brave fight he had made to clear his name, even when his cause seemed hopeless, and his dignified bearing in defeat. Most of all he gained fresh respect by his unswerving loyalty to his jockey and his refusal to make a scapegoat of Wood.

Sir George Chetwynd lived on for nearly 30 years after this famous libel action, dying at Monte Carlo in 1917, but not before a reconciliation between him and Lord Durham had been effected through the good offices of Mr Leopold de Rothschild.

It almost goes without saying that as a result of what had come out at the trial, Charlie Wood was warned off. After a few years the Jockey Club decided that he had been sufficiently punished and his licence was restored to him. To show that all was forgiven and old scores completely wiped out, Lord Durham insisted upon providing him with his first mount.

Charlie Wood soon showed that he was as good a jockey as ever he had been. In 1897 he won the Triple Crown on Galtee More trained by Sam Darling senior at Beckhampton, and the following year he won The St Leger on Wildfowler for the same trainer. In 1899 he gave up riding for good at the age of 43 and began training for Lord Rosebery. In the year that he retired from the saddle Charlie Wood obtained a notable success on Autoscope at Alexandra Park. That was the first winner trained by his 22-year-old son, Jim. The latter had begun training so early in life as Charlie Wood would never hear of his becoming a jockey, possibly because of disillusionment or disappointment caused by the Chetwynd affair that had blow up when Jim was ten years old.

Charlie Wood only trained for a few years and later retired to live at Eastbourne. He continued to show good sense in the way he handled his financial affairs and was still comfortably off when he died at the great age of 89 in 1945.

'Buck' Sherrard, who trained for Sir George Chetwynd, was a first-class stableman and absolutely doted on his horses, but had little or no say in stable policy. This the Stewards of the Jockey Club accepted and after the Chetwynd case was over they imposed no penalty on him other than obliging him to move his stable from Newmarket. Before long this honest little man was training again with a useful string of horses at Royston. In 1902 he was back in the news in a more pleasant light when he won the Ascot Stakes with Scullion.

Lord Durham was in racing purely for the sport. Most of the horses that he raced during a period of some 40 years he bred from his own mares and stallions, rarely buying a yearling. As most of the horses that he bred were moderate or worse, this policy was far from protfitable, but when he did have a winner it afforded him immense pleasure. His only classic success came when he won The Oaks with Beam in 1927, the year before he died at the age of 73, but, being a north-eastern magnate, he probably obtained less satisfaction from that success than he did in winning the Northumberland Plate with Drizzle in 1889, Sherburn in 1899 and Osbech in 1902.

Lord Durham lived at Harraton Court, Exning, where his horses were trained by Percy Peck for many years. The great sorrow of Lord Durham's life was that his wife became incurably mad within weeks of their marriage in 1882. As he had no children, he was succeeded by his twin brother.

15 Robert Peck, Barcaldine and Beverley House

One of the most influential men in Newmarket during the final 20 years of the nineteenth century was Robert Peck, a fearless better and a wonderful judge of a horse. Not only did he control the Beverley House stable, where he had Jim Hopper as his trainer, but he also had a big say in what happened at Park Lodge. In the latter yard his former head lad, Martin Gurry, was private trainer to General Owen Williams, who had several horses in partnership with Peck.

Bob Peck was born on 4 March 1845 at Malton, where his father trained at Grove House. After having been apprenticed to William I'Anson senior at Malton's Spring Cottage stable he went to Enville at the age of 21 to be private trainer to Lord Stamford. Shortly afterwards he returned to Malton to take over his father's stable, from which he sent out his first important winner in Fichu, who took the Stewards Cup at Goodwood in 1869.

A year or two later he accepted an offer to become private trainer to the surly Scottish ironmaster, James Merry, at Russley Park, where Martin Gurry was his head lad. In 1873 he had an outstandingly successful season, during which he brought off the Epsom classic double with Doncaster in The Derby and Marie Stuart in The Oaks, and the filly also went on to land The St Leger. After the death of James Merry in 1877 Russley Park became a public stable with the Duke of Westminster among its patrons. It was with the Duke's Bend Or that Bob Peck won his second Derby in 1880.

In 1881 Bob Peck retired from training at the amazingly early age of 36. By then he was a relatively wealthy man and in due course he went to live at Howbury Hall in Bedfordshire, where he had a stud with accommodation for five stallions. The produce of this stud, together with Peck's other horses, was sent to Newmarket to be trained by Jim Hopper at Beverley House, where Martin Gurry continued to carry out the duties of head lad until he went to Park Lodge.

The most notable horse that Hopper trained for Bob Peck was Barcaldine. A large and muscular bay standing nearly 17 hands high, Barcaldine, who was foaled in 1878, was one of the best horses bred in Ireland during the second half of the last century, and one of the worst-tempered too.

As a two-year-old he was the unbeaten winner of four races in Ireland. The following year he was entered in the Northumberland Plate, for which he became much fancied. His owner, a Scot called George Low living at Birtown, County Kildare, informed Sir John Astley that for the consideration of £1,000 he would not run at Newcastle. Why he should have done this is not at all clear. Possibly he thought that Si

John would be only to pleased to pay for information that would enable him to make a nice killing by laying a leading public fancy that was certain not to run, and if a member of the Jockey Club were to do that, no action could be taken against the owner if he followed suit.

If this was Low's motive, it was unfortunate for him that, however-much Sir John was in need of money, he remained incorruptible. Consequently he reported the offer to the Stewards of the Jockey Club, who decided that English racing would be better without the patronage of Mr Low and forbade the running of Barcaldine in the Plate.

The following year, 1882, Barcaldine was entered for the Cambridgeshire in the name of another owner. The Stewards were not to be taken in by that one. Rightly supposing that the horse was still Low's property, they once again forbade his running.

Giving up hope of hoodwinking the Stewards, Low sent Barcaldine to the sales and Edmund Tattersall knocked him down to Peck for 1,300 guineas. More than six months later Barcaldine had his first outing in England in the Westminster Cup at Kempton Park in May 1883. So much flesh was this big, gross horse carrying, it seemed unlikely that he would win anything until he was a lot straighter in condition. Certainly it seemed impossible that he was ready to beat such a good horse as Tristan who was destined to win that season's Gold Cup. But Barcaldine was an even better horse than everybody supposed. Starting at 10-1 he beat Tristan without the wily Bob Peck having a penny on him.

Soon afterwards Barcaldine won again at Epsom and Ascot. From Ascot he returned very sore and it became evident that it would be difficult to train him for his belated bid for the Northumberland Plate, in which he had been allotted the crushing weight of 9 st 10 lb. In the circumstances Peck and Hopper confined the horse to walking exercise, keeping a leg, in which he had developed weakness, in a bucket of ice for hours on end. The day before the race he was given the only gallop that he did between winning at Ascot and the Plate. Bookmakers, armed with the reports of their touts, became convinced that, far from winning the Northumberland Plate on this abnormaly light preparation, he would not even put in an appearance at Newcastle. The day before the race 50-1 was being laid against Barcaldine, but when it was known that he had reached the course the bookmakers were falling over themselves to cover the liabilities. Many of those who had been sceptical about the way in which Barcaldine had been trained must have burned their fingers badly. With Archer in the saddle he won the Northumberland Plate, thereby maintaining his unbeaten record.

Later in the summer Barcaldine was tried for the Cambridgeshire on the Racecourse Side with the Lincoln winner Fulmen and others. So well did Barcaldine win that trial that he looked something to bet on in the Cambridgeshire, but when he pulled up it was found that his leg had gone. As a result he never ran again.

On being taken out of training, Barcaldine was sold for £8,000 to Lady Stamford. She stood him at the Park Paddocks Stud, now part of

Robert Peck (1845-1899), managed the Beverley House stable

Tattersalls sale paddocks, until he died at the early age of 15 in 1893. During his comparatively brief career at stud, Barcaldine got the Derby winner Sir Visto and Marco, who landed a big gamble for Tom Chaloner junior in the Cambridgeshire of 1895. Today the male line of Barcaldine is carried on by the Derby winner Santa Claus and the St Leger winner Premonition.

One of the biggest coups that Bob Peck ever brought off was with a four-year-old filly called Hackness in the Cambridgeshire in 1882. Much earlier in the year he had a very big bet on her in, of all things, a hunters' flat race at Sandown Park in February. Even then he had it in mind that he would win a much bigger race with her later on, but he thought that the handicapper would not take much notice of winning form shown in a hunters' race. As it happened, the gamble at Sandown did not come off and Hackness was beaten by a head. However, there was a silver lining to that particular cloud, as her defeat was one of the things that ensured that the filly got into the Cambridgeshire with a light weight.

Came October and Hackness was a raging hot favourite for the Cambridgeshire on a day when the wind was blowing so hard that it seemed determined to sweep men, horses, stands and everything else off Newmarket Heath. It was not just a case of hats and sheets of newspaper being blown about. Even the cabs were overturned by the gale. By the time the field had got down to the start for the Cambridgeshire, the experienced starter Tom McGeorge had reached the conclusion it was impossible to race, and sent a messenger to inform the Stewards, who decided to postpone the race till the following afternoon. When the messenger set off on the return jouney he was unable to make his horse face into the storm. Edward Weatherby, then an old man, set off on his hack to contact the starter, only to be blown bodily out of the saddle before he had gone many yards.

In the end George Lambton and Arthur Coventry, a couple of the best amateur riders of the day, volunteered to take the Stewards' decision to McGeorge. Somehow these two skilful horsemen managed to reach the start, where they found chaos reigning. Some horses, driven frantic by the elements, were careering all over the place while others stood and shivered in sheer dejection and misery. Of those in the second category, none looked sorrier than Hackness. Both Lambton and Coventry decided that this was one favourite that was not going to win. The following day they were proved completely wrong as Hackness took the Cambridgeshire and won a lot of big bets for Bob Peck. The name of the winner is commemorated by the Hackness stable close to Beverley House on Exeter Road, in which Gerry Blum has his horses today.

The two-year-olds of 1885 came from a vintage crop. By the end of the season the Duke of Westminster's Ormonde, trained by John Porter at Kingsclere, Mr R. C. Vyner's Minting, trained by Mat Dawson, and The Bard, owned in partnership by General Owen Williams and Bob Peck, and trained by Martin Gurry at Park Lodge, were all unbeaten.

The connections of each of this trio acclaimed their horse a champion. They were certain he would win The Derby.

The Bard, a dapper little chestnut ticked with white and full of quality, had started off by landing the Brocklesby Stakes at Lincoln in the spring and by the end of his first season he had had 16 successes to his credit. After he had completed this remarkably long sequence in the Tattersall Sale Stakes at Doncaster, General Williams announced that he would not run again until The Derby. This plan was adhered to, and even though Ormonde had won The 2,000 Guineas by beating Minting, there was immense confidence behind The Bard's ability to maintain his unbeaten record in the face of the Duke of Westminster's colt. But Ormonde was something out of the ordinary. At every stage of the race he was going far better than The Bard, whom he beat by a very comfortable length and a half with St Mirin a bad third.

The Bard's next race was the Manchester Cup, in which he was set to carry 8 st 4 lb. On arrival at Manchester, Bob Peck was horrified to see how high the grass had been allowed to grow on the New Barns course, and decided it would do a great deal to reduce the chance of a little horse like The Bard saddled with such a large weight for a three-year-old. Consequently he made the unusual request to the Executive that the course should be mown before the Cup was run. This was done but the weight proved too much for The Bard, game as he was, and he failed by a length of give 31 lb to Riversdale.

The Derby and the Manchester Cup were the only races in which The Bard was ever beaten. His subsequent successes included the Doncaster Cup and he was given a walkover in the Goodwood Cup.

Even in boyhood, Robert Peck's favourite reading was the General Stud Book. By hard work and concentration he had acquired immense knowledge of a thoroughbred by the time he was 20. On top of what he knew about horses he had that genius that almost enables men such as he, Mat Dawson or George Lambton to X-ray a horse whilst they look at it. As has already been noted, he trained a Stewards Cup winner at the age of 24 and a Derby winner at 28.

There is no knowing what he might have achieved had his life covered anything like a normal span and his training career not been so incredibly brief. One cannot but suspect that it was indifferent health that obliged him to give up training while a young man of 36, and he was still only 54 when he died at Scarborough on 17 August 1899.

His two sons, Charles and Percy, both became successful trainers. Charlie Peck's most notable successes were with Pommern in The wartime Derby in 1915, Bachelor's Button in the Gold Cup, and that wonderful handicapper, Priory Park, who won the Lincoln, the Stewards Cup, the Royal Hunt Cup and City and Suburban amongst other races. For many years he was private trainer to Jack Joel, first at Wantage and later on at Foxhill. He died in 1941.

Percy Peck, who died at the age of 68 in 1938, was only 19 when he trained Millstream to win the Chester Cup in 1889. Later he became private trainer to Lord Durham at Harraton Court, Exning, and when Lord Rosebery joined the stable he won The Derby for him with Cicero in 1905.

16. More Scottish Trainers – John Dawson, Jimmy Waugh and Jimmy Ryan

John Dawson, the younger brother of Tom, Mat and Joe, trained for Prince Batthyany and later other owners at Warren House. That was the establishment that Bill Chifney had built for his wife, Mary, to assuage her jealousy of her brother-in-law's new place at next-door Cleveland House in the 1820s. Few stables have been run on more magnificent or ostentatious lines than Warren House was in the days when Prince Batthyany was its principal patron. The lads rode out in dark blue livery and stove pipe hats and the horses wore opulent scarlet rugs.

Prince Batthyany, a Hungarian nobleman, came to England as a young man and was soon thoroughly anglicised. He began owning horses in 1843 and in 1859 he was elected to the Jockey Club. Following a number of seasons, in which his runners achieved little or nothing of note, John Dawson was appointed to be his private trainer. Soon afterwards the Prince's luck took a decided turn for the better.

John Dawson had been born at Gullane in 1827. For some years he was attached to the stable of his elder brother Tom, who became his guardian on the death of their father, at Middleham. Later he went south and trained at Roden House at Compton in Berkshire until he took over the horses of Prince Batthyany a few years later, when he was still little more than 30 years old.

The outstanding horse that John Dawson trained for Prince Batthyany was Galopin, a bay colt by Vedette out of Flying Duchess.

The last thing that old Prince Batthyany ever allowed to influence his attitude to his horses was any commercial consideration. All his horses were his pets and his racing policy was always dictated by sentiment. When they won a good race he became so excited that his doctors feared for his weak heart, and he simply hated to see them beaten. Thus it was that he absolutely refused to fall in with his trainer's plan to have a crack at Prince Charlie with Galopin when the latter was still a two-year-old in 1874. The Prince was scared stiff of taking on such a good horse, but John Dawson held a high enough opinion of Galopin to be convinced that he could beat Prince Charlie at weight-for-age.

Such was John Dawson's confidence in Galopin that he never even tried him for The Derby although on his only appearance as a three-year-old before going to Epsom he had done no more than give a moderate filly called Stray Shot 10 lb and a comfortable beating at the Newmarket Second Spring Meeting. But John Dawson knew the time of day all right and needed no trial or testing preliminary race to tell it to him. He was quite sure that so long as Galopin was himself he would

John Dawson (1827-1903) trained the 1875 Derby winner Galopin in the Warren House stable, now demolished

win The Derby and in the weeks approaching the race there could be no doubting the colt's well-being. Even though he was giving away lumps of weight to some decidely smart older horses in one of his final gallops, it was all that his jockey John Morris could do to hold him.

In The Derby Galopin vindicated his trainer's high regard of him to the full. So confident was Morris that he indulged in the luxury of taking Galopin round the wide outside to avoid trouble at Tattenham corner, and riding the most confident of races from thereon he won by a length from Claremont with an unnamed colt belonging to Lord Falmouth six lengths away third.

It was only by an even-money chance that Prince Batthyany came to own Galopin. When he and his trainer were attending the sale of the Middle Park yearlings in 1873, John Dawson had to leave to catch the five o'clock train before they had made a purchase so he marked the two colts he thought most promising on his owner's catalogue. Fortunately the Prince bought Galopin — and for the bargain price of 520 guineas — instead of the other colt, who, as it turned out, never saw a racecourse.

By the time that Galopin won The Derby, other owners, including Lord Dupplin, had joined the Warren House stable. It was for Lord Dupplin that John Dawson trained an elegant bay colt called Petrarch. Trained at Findon as a two-year-old, he beat 29 others in the Middle Park Plate at Newmarket the only time that he ran at that age, and on the strength of that success Lord Dupplin bought him for £10,000, an enormous sum for those days.

As a three-year-old in 1876 Petrarch won The 2,000 Guineas, greatly to the surprise of his connections as he had just been badly beaten in a trial, and later on he landed The St Leger, while in The Derby he was fourth to Kisber. At Epsom Petrarch nearly drove his trainer distraught as he positively refused to come out of his box, and John Dawson was on the point of sending for a mason to dismantle a wall when the colt walked out quite unconcernedly.

After Galopin had retired to stud, Prince Batthyany would become excited about the chances of any of his progeny, whether or not he owned them himself, winning a big race as he had been about their sire. Eventually it became too much for his heart and he dropped dead at the door of the Jockey Club luncheon room on the Rowley Mile the day that Galopin's son Galliard was to run in The 2,000 Guineas.

During the last decade of the century John Dawson was private trainer to Mr Wallace Johnstone with about 25 horses in the Warren House string each season. The most notable success that he obtained during that period was with Disraeli in The 2,000 Guineas of 1898.

In 1900 John Dawson retired and handed over Warren House to his son, George, who had been training at Heath House since his uncle, Mat Dawson, had moved to Exning in 1886. Of John Dawson's other children, John junior trained at St Albans and Nellie married Fred Archer.

James Waugh was the first member of his family to come to Newmarket. He was born at Jedburgh, Roxburghshire, on 13 December 1831, and prided himself on his descent from the celebrated Scottish outlaw, Rob Roy McGregor. When he came to register his colours in 1881 they were Rob Roy tartan, yellow sleeves and black cap.

From hunting in the Lothians as a boy he graduated to riding in steeplechases and then to training. Even before he came of age he controlled the stable of the Scottish banker, Mr Grainger, at Cessford Moor, then after a most successful season in 1855 he became trainer to Sir David Baird and Sir J. Boswell at Gullane's Stamford Hall, which had, until a few years previously, been the home of the Dawson family.

Through the influence of his compatriot, Mat Dawson, Jimmy Waugh was able to come south to train for an Australian called Wybrow Robinson at East Ilsley in Berkshire. For that owner he won

Jimmy Waugh (1831-1905) trained at Meynell House (now Hurworth House)

the Royal Hunt Cup with Gratitude in 1865 and the following year the Queen's Vase with Eltham, who had been third to Gladiateur in The Derby. Shortly after Eltham's success at the Royal Meeting, Wybrow Robinson sold all his horses to the Duke of Hamilton, and Jimmy was out of a job.

Once again Mat Dawson proved a friend. Mat was on the verge of moving to Newmarket to open a public stable and arranged for Jimmy to succeed him as private trainer to James Merry at Russley Park. While employed by Merry, Jimmy won The 2,000 Guineas of 1870 with McGregor, in whose naming he must have had a say, and shortly afterwards he left Russley.

On parting from Merry, Jimmy Waugh accepted an offer to train for Count Henshel at Carlburg in Hungary. This was the beginning of the long connection between the Waugh family and continental racing.

With the horses that he ran in Hungary, Austria and the neighbouring German states, Jimmy achieved outstanding success. So often did his candidate win the Franz-Friedrich-Renner, that the Duke of Mecklenburg, whose wife gave a cup for the race, sent his chamberlain to ask Jimmy to agree to its being made a handicap to prevent the field from cutting up. The trainer sent back word to say that he was quite happy with arrangements as they stood. Some time later, as a gesture to local susceptibilities, he himself presented a cup that was to be run for as a handicap.

In 1880 Jimmy Waugh returned to England on account of the deterioration of the health of his wife, who had borne him about a dozen children. The return did not have the desired effect and Isabella Waugh died at Newmarket on 5 July 1881 when she was only 47.

On arrival at Newmarket, Jimmy Waugh settled down at the Middleton Cottage stables, and continued to bid for the big races in Europe. With Gondolic he won the Grosser Preiss von Baden-Baden and with Ovaszar the Hamburg Derby.

At the age of 62 the much-travelled Jimmy Waugh made his final move when he took his string from Middleton Cottage to Meynell House (now Hurworth House) on the Fordham Road. In his new yard he trained The Rush to win the Chester Cup and Phoebus Apollo the Chesterfield Cup in 1896, Piety the Manchester Cup in 1897, and Refractor the Royal Hunt Cup in 1898.

Born in the reign of William IV, Jimmy Waugh survived that of Queen Victoria and the turn of the century to die at the age of 73 on 23 October 1905, mourned by a far larger family than most men leave behind.

His eldest son, Richard, who was assistant to Mat Dawson as a young man, trained for the Kaiser at Graditz for many years, dying in Berlin in 1931. Four of Jimmy Waugh's younger sons trained at Newmarket. Willie was at Balaton Lodge, Dawson (christened Mathew Dawson after his godfather) at Somerville Lodge, and Charlie at Carlburg, while the youngest, Tom, followed their father at Meynell.

Of Jimmy Waugh's daughters, two became the wives of trainers. Grace married John Dawson junior of St Albans, and Janet, Joe Butters of Kremlin House.

Jimmy Ryan (1836-1915) trained at Green Lodge

Like the Dawson brothers, James Ryan came from Gullane, where he was born in 1836. He began his career as a professional steeplechase jockey and, on becoming too heavy, trained at Irving in Ayrshire for seven years. When that period ended in 1871 he came to Newmarket with Mr J. Houldsworth as his patron and bought Green Lodge. This stable, which stands on the Severals, had been built by John F. Clark in about 1855, and on acquiring it Jimmy Ryan enlarged it considerably.

Although he trained The 2,000 Guineas winners Enterprise (1887) and Enthusiast (1889) and Briar Root, who won The 1,000 Guineas in 1888, the best horse that Jimmy Ryan ever had was Springfield, whose 17 successes did not include a classic.

It gives some idea of the excellence of Springfield that he was 28 lb in front of Coltness when they were both two-year-olds in 1875. Coltness was something more than useful himself, as he won the New Stakes at Royal Ascot, and later in life took the Great Yorkshire Stakes at York in 1876 and the Alexandra Plate at the Royal Meeting the following year.

In 1877 Springfield won the first race for the Champion Stakes with that year's Derby winner Silvio amongst those he beat. Springfield also made history by running out the first winner of the July Cup at Newmarket in 1876 and the next season he won it a second time. His other successes included the Gimcrack Stakes. At stud Springfield got the 1890 Derby winner Sainfoin, who, in turn, sired Rock Sand, winner of the Triple Crown in 1903.

Another good horse that Jimmy Ryan trained was the sprinter, Eager, whose owner, Mr A. W. Cox, an Australian, went by the *nom-de-course* of 'Mr Fairie'. In 1894 Cox wanted a foal to run in the paddocks with one on whom he was building great hopes. The trainer's wife, Rosa Ryan, obliged by selling him Eager as the price was right and she thought he was never likely to make up into much. This is one of the countless instances in the history of racing where the ugly duckling became the swan. The colt of whom 'Fairie' Cox thought so much turned out to be useless while Eager developed into a top-class sprinter. He landed the Portland Plate at Doncaster as a four-year-old in 1898 and the next season he carried 9 st 7 lb to victory in the Wokingham Stakes at Royal Ascot before winning the July Cup at Newmarket. To commemorate the achievements of Eager, 'Fairie' Cox gave Mrs Ryan a beautiful statuette of the horse which has become an heirloom in the family of her nephews, the Jarvises. It used to stand in the hall at Park Lodge when it was in the possession of the late Sir Jack Jarvis.

Rosa Ryan, sister of the Waterwich House trainer Bill Jarvis, was a woman of considerable talent. Without any help from an architecht she designed Woodlands, which was built to accommodate her husband's owners when they were visiting Newmarket. Woodlands is one of the stables of Harry Thomson Jones.

It was at the expense of the owners in Jimmy Ryan's stable that the Green Lodge Draghounds, of which Jimmy was master for many years, were kept. Enthusiastic followers of the drag included Fred Archer, another good jockey in Fred Webb, who won The Derby on Doncaster in 1873, and the royal trainer Dick Marsh.

As might be expected of a former steeplechase jockey whose recreation was a run with hounds, Jimmy Ryan could never quite get jumping out his system and generally had the odd National Hunt horse at Green Lodge. The best of these was probably Coronet. A fast and brilliant fencer, he started a hot favourite at 3-1 for the Grand National of 1886, but he did not stay and finished only sixth to Old Joe.

The only child of Jimmy and Rosa Ryan was called Jimmy after his father. After leaving Charterhouse he went as a pupil to the famous vet, Professor Pritchard, and then returned to Green Lodge to assist his father. It was a great sorrow to many outside his immediate family circle when this charming boy died at the age of 19 in the typhoid epidemic that swept Newmarket in the autumn of 1895. Memory of him and his father is kept alive today by the christian name of his cousin, the former Phantom House trainer, Ryan Jarvis.

A true sportsman as well as an able trainer, Jimmy Ryan senior was one of the most popular men in Newmarket. At the end of the 1902 season he leased the Green Lodge Yard to Mr John Musker's trainer, A. J. Gilbert, and was 79 when he died in 1915.

17 Caroline, Duchess of Montrose

Caroline, Duchess of Montrose (1818-1884), lived at Sefton Lodge, and built St Agnes's Church, Newmarket

Of the society hostesses who entertained at Newmarket during the 1880s, none made a greater impact than Caroline, Duchess of Montrose. Defying the convention that restricted the ownership of horses to men, she kept several in training, running them in the assumed name of 'Mr Manton', her trainer being old Alec Taylor at Manton.

Gifted with a vivid turn of phrase, and at times a very acid one, she could be the terror of her jockeys, trainers and social circle alike. About the only man who would not put up with her nonsense was Alec Taylor. When she asked him what he regarded as the danger to her runner, the gruff old man thought nothing of replying, "Damned to hell if I know, your grace". The Duchess could be an incredibly tiresome woman, but essentially she was good-natured and there were not many people who disliked her. Behind her ample back she was known as Carrie Red because of the colour of her hair.

Born the Hon Caroline Agnes Beresford, daughter of the second Lord Decies, she married the fourth Duke of Montrose in 1836. The Duke died in 1874 and two years later she remarried, her second husband being William Stuart Stirling Crawfurd. He was already a well-known owner. Three years after their marriage he won The Derby with Sefton, who was trained at Manton.

Subsequently Stirling Crawfurd and his wife (who continued to style herself Duchess, as widowed peeresses are entitled to do irrespective of remarriage) had horses with Joe Dawson at Bedford Lodge. Shortly after 'Buck' Sherrard had taken over the yard on the death of Joe Dawson, they turned it into a private stable, the other owners taking their horses elsewhere.

In 1881 Stirling Crawfurd won The 1,000 Guineas and The Oaks with Thebais, who remained in training with Sherrard as a four-year-old in 1882. That year Stirling Crawfurd landed the Cesarewitch with Corrie Roy, and Thebais became a raging hot favourite to complete the double for him by taking the Cambridgeshire a fortnight later. To the consternation of a large section of the betting public, however, the Duchess insisted on Thebais being scratched the day before the race. As a result Martini was booed loudly when, on the day after the Cambridgeshire, he carried the all-scarlet Crawfurd colours successfully. After the ugly scene that ensued round the unsaddling enclosure, the Duchess herself was booed by disgruntled punters as she left the course.

Contrary to what was thought by those who spoke through their pockets, the Duchess had not scratched Thebais to spite the public. The Rowley Mile does not often ride soft but after all the rain that had fallen that autumn it was actually beginning to become holding. In the circumstances, the heavily-weighted Thebais would have stood no chance.

After Corrie Roy had won the Cesarewitch, one of the sporting papers came with out the following piece of doggerel about Stirling Crawfurd, who was generally known as 'Craw', and his spouse:

> Isn't Craw a lucky boy?
> With Carrie Red and Corrie Roy
> With Corrie Roy and Carrie Red,
> One for the course and one for the bed.

At the end of 1882 or early in 1883 the Duchess removed her horses and those of her husband from Bedford Lodge and took them across the Bury Road to Sefton Lodge. This establishment was built by a Frenchman called Lefèvre, in all probability the same C. J. Lefèvre who set up a record by winning 110 races with his horses in 1873. It was the Duchess who named the stable after her second husband's 1878 Derby winner, Sefton.

Hardly were the horses installed in Sefton Lodge than Stirling Crawfurd died in Cannes at the age of 64 in the spring of 1883. His death came as a severe blow to the Duchess, who was devoted to him. She had his body returned to Newmarket and it was eventually buried behind the church that she built as a memorial to him next door to Sefton Lodge. This church she dedicated to her own name-saint, St Agnes.

As builder of the church the Duchess was its patron, with the right of nominating the rector, a matter of which she was not unmindful. Attending service in it one Sunday in late summer, she was horrified to hear the Reverend Colville Wallis pray for fine weather in which the farmers could gather the harvest. Storming out there and then she afterwards informed the clergyman that he had better start looking for another living as he should have known that her St Leger candiate could only go on soft. The Reverend Colville Wallis knew her ways. As he expected, the Duchess was soon back in a better humour and he stayed at St Agnes for many years.

After the death of Stirling Crawfurd, the Duchess took over his long string of horses, keeping it in training along with her own at Sefton Lodge, Gray, Golding and Day being her trainers at various periods. Another man with whom she had horses was the Lambourn trainer, Peace, whom she was accustomed to refer to as "the Peace that passeth all understanding".

A formidable figure generally dressed in a rather masculine manner with her outfit crowned by a homburg hat, the Duchess had a deep knowledge and understanding of racing. All the same, she could exasperate her jockeys. She once remonstrated with Harry Huxtable, who rode her lightweights, saying, "Why on earth did you not come when I told you to?"

"Beg your pardon, your Grace," replied the little man, "but I should have had to come without the horse".

The royal trainer Dick Marsh was more than a match for the Duchess when it came to bandying words. One day when she asked him what he expected to win he mentioned a couple of horses, whose form suggested they would be hard to beat. "Pooh," she said, "those are just newspaper tips," and off she stalked. Both horses won, and next morning she went up to him, saying, "Oh, Marsh, what will win today?"

"I regret, your Grace," replied the suave Marsh, "I have not yet read the newspapers today".

The real bane of the Duchess's life were the handicappers. She hated them, being absolutely convinced that they went out of their way to give her horses far more weight than they deserved. Reginald Mainwaring, a tall saturnine man who could not help a slight resemblance to a stage villain, she used to call "the man who murdered his mother". To another handicapper, Major Egerton, she was heard to say, "I see from the way you handicap my horses that you are desirous of riding them yourself. I only intend to say that on no account will your wish be gratified".

In 1888, five years after she had been widowed for the second time, the unpredictable Duchess amazed everybody by marrying a young man of 24 called Henry Milner. For a time the horses ran in his name, but the marriage does not seen to have been a complete success, and soon they raced as the property of 'Mr Manton' again and carried the all-scarlet that she had taken over from her second husband. Rather more recently, the celebrated scarlet jacket has been carried by that fine chaser Cool Customer, who won the Great Yorkshire 'chase under the crushing weight of 12 st 7 lb in 1948. Trained by Captain Jack Fawcus at Middleham, Cool Customer was owned by Major R. Stirling Stuart, a nephew of Stirling Crawfurd.

The Duchess of Montrose died in 1894. On her death the stock at her Sefton Stud was put under the hammer and the land sold to become the site of Stanley House.

18 Two Big Spenders – George Alexander Baird and Colonel Harry McCalmont

Newmarket has almost invariably extended a warm welcome to millionaires. In the case of George Alexander Baird, though, it was perfectly prepared to make an exception. Although his undeniable talent as a Gentleman Rider, which made him a match for all but the best of the professionals, should have done as much to ensure him popularity as his willingness to pay almost any price for a horse for the Bedford Lodge stable, he was totally unacceptable to a town desperately anxious to share in the respectability of the late Victorian era and live down the unwholesome reputation racing had earned from the scandals of the middle of the century.

A brief spell at Eton and a rather longer one at Magdalene College, Cambridge, where he never attended a lecture, did nothing to provide George Baird with the faintest veneer of culture or the semblance of education. On coming down from Cambridge in 1881 he was nearly as petulantly uncouth as he had been when running wild in boyhood on the Stichil estate on the Scottish border under the utterly inadequate supervision of a doting, widowed mother. The redeeming feature of his character was a real generosity. Ironically it was that cardinal virtue, rather than his many shortcomings, that was to bring about his destruction. Rejected by those who should have been his social equals he readily fell under the influence of some really deplorable cronies, whose continual requests for loans, that were never to be repaid, he could rarely refuse.

The enormous wealth of George Baird came from ironworks in Glasgow that were fed from mines elsewhere in Scotland and the North of England, all owned, or leased, by the family firm of William Baird and Co. His grandfather, Alexander Baird had begun life as a small farmer, but giving up the struggle of trying to earn enough from the land to keep his wife and seven sons, he turned to mining, first for coal and then for iron, just as the construction of the first railways was creating an insatiable demand for the latter commodity. Rather than receive payment for the contracts they undertook, old Alexander Baird and his sons accepted shares in the newly formed railway companies, thereby laying the foundations of fortunes that were soon to transform them into landed gentry of independent means.

George, the sixth son and father of George Alexander Baird, bought the 18,000 acres of the Strichen estate from the 14th Lord Lovat in 1855, and David, the youngest brother, the Stichil property, just north of Kelso in Roxburghshire, for £155,000. On the early death of David in 1860 he left Stichil to his brother George, who died in 1870 leaving a great inheritance to his nine-year-old son, George Alexander Baird.

Thus the latter was the heir of two of the seven of these immensely wealthy sons of a once poor crofter, and on coming of age on 30 September 1882 entered into control of £3,000,000 worth of shares in Scottish railways, Stichil, Strichen and other estates in Scotland, with a rent roll of £100,000 a year, and three quarters of a million pounds in ready money that had accumulated during his minority.

Having acquired a taste for fast horses while following the Cambridge Drag, George Baird began to indulge it by riding in hunters' flat races and intermittently over hurdles, some time before he came of age, but in order not to arouse the displeasure of the trustees of his father's will assumed the name of 'Mr Abington'. In those days it was a not unusual practice to register a *nom-de-course* and George Baird was to race as 'Mr Abington' throughout his life. While filled with an exuberance of youth, and the arrogance of his millions, he was never averse to rough riding, and compounded the offence he gave in the saddle by philandering with the womenfolk of his victims. In consequence the establishment resolved to teach 'Mr Abington' Baird a lesson and found their opportunity when he threatened to put the Earl of Harrington over the rails during the running of a Hunters' Selling Flat Race at Birmingham's Four Oaks Park in April 1882. His behaviour towards Lord Harrington was construed as foul riding, for which offence he was warned off for two years.

On being declared a disqualified person George Baird put his horses into the name of 'Stiffy' Smith, the most rapacious of his many friends, and retired to Paris. Shortly afterwards he learned that Mrs Montague Tharp, of Chippenham Park, was trying to sell the Limekilns, the greatest of all the Newmarket gallops, on which the going never becomes firm no matter how dry the summer.

"They can be bought, can they?" asked George Baird appreciating the opportunity for mischief. "But I wonder what the Stewards would say if they knew that I was the owner?"

Realising the damage that could be done to Newmarket as a training centre if the Limekilns were to be acquired by somebody who was warned off, or inimical to racing for any other reason, the Jockey Club quickly negotiated a lease of that vital strip of land, that lies in the fork of the Bury St Edmunds and Thetford roads on the eastern side of the town. It was not until nearly 50 years later, in 1930, that the Club eventually purchased the freehold of the Limekilns.

On being reinstated on The Turf in the spring of 1884 George Baird decided to race on a level befitting his wealth. To that end he attended Lord Falmouth's dispersal sale conducted by Edmund Tattersall in the paddock of the Heath House stable at the foot of Warren Hill on 28 April 1884 and came away the biggest buyer. As well as paying 8,800 guineas for the three-year-old filly Busybody, winner of the Middle Park Plate the previous season, he acquired four other animals for a total outlay of £17,587, having selected as his trainer the former champion jockey Tom Cannon, who was running the Danebury stable near Stockbridge in Hampshire while continuing to ride.

Disappointed at the cool reception given him after Busybody had

George Alexander Baird (1861-1893),

won both The 1,000 Guineas and The Oaks, George Baird abandoned his ambition to be a leading owner and set his heart upon becoming the most accomplished Gentleman Rider in the country. Accordingly he leased the Bedford Lodge stable from Captain Machell, took up residence in the house, which is now the Bedford Lodge Hotel, and installed Martin Gurry as his private trainer. In addition he had horses with William Stevens at Compton in Berkshire, Bob Armstrong at Penrith and in a good many other stables so that he could provide himself with a locally-trained mount at almost any meeting in the country.

Martin Gurry, who had been head lad to Robert Peck at Russley Park, was a wonderfully good stableman but hardly the ideal trainer for George Baird. A puritanical little man, who had come up the hard way, even having had to sleep with the stable dog while apprenticed to William Oates at Middleham, he believed that rich men had a moral obligation to set a good example and was inevitably disappointed by his employer. He deeply disapproved of the idle, drunken cronies that George Baird brought down from London for house parties at Bedford Lodge. Sycophantically they addressed their host as 'Squire' and disrupted the routine of the stable by lounging round the yard, exchanging risqué stories with the lads, and showing no respect at all for the authority of the trainer.

Race riding may have been the principal sporting interest of George Baird, but it was far from being the only one. The 'Squire' was also strongly addicted to cock fighting, which flourished long after being made illegal in 1849, prize fighting and dog fighting. Whenever Baird was expected to come into residence at Bedford Lodge his henchmen would scour Cheveley, Fordham, Saxon Street and other villages in the vicinity for stray dogs to be matched against his favourite bull terrier, a ferocious beast by the name of Donald, while the keepers of his fighting cocks prepared them for the main.

Among the favourite Newmarket haunts of George Baird and his friends was The Greyhound, the former coaching house that stood on the site of the old Doric Cinema, now the Cabaret Club, in the High Street until pulled down in about 1895. Behind its long narrow bar, with raftered ceiling and sawdust spread upon the floor beneath deal tables, the landlord, Bill Riley, ran a boxing saloon. Knowing of Riley's predilection for pugilism many a penniless prize fighter would fetch up at The Greyhound for a square meal and a night's sleep in return for putting on the gloves the following day. Word would go round the town that there was to be a fight behind The Greyhound in the evening and a large crowd of stable lads, jockeys and a number of trainers, not infrequently including Mat Dawson, would assemble to see it.

It was at The Greyhound that Jem Smith sparred with Charlie Mitchell while training for his fight with the American Jake Kilrain in 1887. Before long both Smith and Mitchell became prominent members of George Baird's singularly unselect circle of friends, and were largely instrumental in persuading him to extend his patronage of the ring by having his own stable of prize fighters. To provide his pugilists with the necessary facilities George Baird built a boxing saloon on to the western side of Bedford Lodge, the outside walls of this extension being tastefully decorated with medallions depicting classical scenes in relief.

It was to the boxing saloon that the 'Squire' and his guests would repair after a day's hard drinking and roistering to watch, and wager on, a bout or two or just to witness a couple of the better known fighters sparring. Not infrequently George Baird himself would climb into the ring to spar with a man who would take good care to ensure no harm befell his paymaster. In his book *Old Pink 'Un Days* J. B. Booth, one of the most able members of the staff of the *Sporting Times*, left a vivid account of proceedings at Bedford Lodge of an evening writing:

At a certain stage of the old brandy process of training, The Squire's opinion of his fistic capacity would rise to preposterous heights, and a turn-up with the pugilist was an inevitable demonstration. It was, of course, the pugilist's duty to flatter his patron's self-esteem, and there was the interesting spectacle of a half-intoxicated, half-lunatic millionaire feebly belabouring the professional boxer, who puffing artistically and simulating collapse, would gasp at intervals:

'edge a bit, Squire! 'edge a bit! we're on'y tappin''

And then The Squire would steady himself for a straight left, which the professional would carefully receive on a callous portion of his face, turning immediately to the crowd of trusty retainers with the anguished query:

'How long have we been at it?'

Whereupon the valet Monk ... would reply enthusiastically:

'Damn near twenty minutes' *and although the encounter had barely lasted a couple of hundred seconds, everybody was perfectly happy and more than satisfied.*

Although much of George Baird's life was passed in what was little better than alcoholic chaos he took his race riding very seriously indeed, and watched his weight as carefully as any professional jockey. No matter how late into the night he had been drinking he would be wakened by Monk as the lads were making the horses ready for first lot, and after a cup of weak tea and cod-liver oil, he was to be seen riding out of the yard, shortly after dawn, reins loosely held in the right hand, to accompany his string to the Heath where he would meet up with Jack Watts, Sammy Loates and other jockeys regularly associated with the stable to ride in a series of gallops. Back at Bedford Lodge he would deal with the day's correspondence according to the season of the year, putting it into the fire in winter or the wastepaper basket in the summer, in either case unopened. Having completed that undemanding task he would go to the station to catch the racecourse special, generally travelling, to the disgust of Martin Gurry, in the company of the lads in the horse boxes at the back of the train, rather than spend the journey discussing the riding tactics with his trainer.

To a large extent the high degree of proficiency that George Baird attained as a race rider was due to the coaching he received from Fred Archer, and with 'The Tinman' never having any doubts about the value of his services, it must have consisted of the most expensive riding lessons ever given on Newmarket Heath. As wasting left his strength unimpaired in early manhood he developed into a remarkably powerful finisher, who plied his whip with the same liberality as Archer himself, but was inclined to delay his challenge too long, a legacy, perhaps, of his first mentor, Tom Cannon, who loved to ride a waiting race.

In those days when the heart of George Baird was set upon riding as many winners as possible there was almost nothing he would not do or pay to achieve success in the saddle. Not only would he hire a whole train to take him to an obscure course in the north for a fancied mount in a selling plate, but he would reward one of his satellites with a substantial sum for bearing him company. Paying jockeys to stand down while putting the trainer onto the odds became common practice with him, and sometimes cost him even more dearly than expected. To secure the winning ride on Hungarian at the November meeting on Manchester's New Barnes course in 1889 he gave Fred Webb £200 and promised to put the Lambourn trainer Charlie Humphreys on the odds to the same amount, forgot to make the bet and ended up paying £1,000. There was an even more unfortunate outcome to his attempt to avoid Grand Composer being allowed to walk-over at Kempton Park in 1887. He paid the Berkshire trainer Tom Stevens junior £100 to start Country Boy against him and after Country Boy, ridden by Tom Cannon, had won, he treated everyone within earshot to a torrent of language that was so vivid as to raise doubts as to whether he could be properly termed a Gentleman Rider.

The bare statistics show how the combination of enormous financial resources and ability of a considerable order enabled George Baird to become the outstandingly successful amateur during the penultimate decade of the last century. When he was champion Gentleman Rider in 1889, for instance, he rode 61 winners whereas Willie Moore was second in the list with just three successes to his credit.

The dedication that George Baird brought to his race riding did nothing to make the cronies he brought to Bedford Lodge any more acceptable to Martin Gurry, and as he could never accept a sustained series of reverses in anything remotely like the stoical spirit of a sportsman, relations between owner and trainer were rarely good. Matters came to a head early in 1887. Baird dismissed Gurry but the latter refused to leave Bedford Lodge until paid for the full term of his contract. Unable to be rid of a man for whose services he no longer had any use George Baird was determined to ensure that at least he would not have any horses to train and removed his entire string to William Stevens at Compton, thereby providing the only instance of an owner being sent packing from his own private stable along with all his horses.

Some time in the spring of 1887 a reconciliation between George Baird and Martin Gurry was effected and the horses, including the unraced three-year-old Merry Hampton, a bay colt by Hampton, returned to Bedford Lodge. A few weeks later Merry Hampton won The Derby with Jack Watts up, but his owner, far from displaying any pleasure, just lounged against the rails and ungraciously refused to lead his colt into the winner's enclosure. The truth was he really would rather have ridden the winner of a selling race at Wolverhampton than own a Derby winner ridden by a professional with the credit for the training going to Gurry, though almost the whole of its preparation had been completed in Berkshire.

The triumph of Merry Hampton in The Derby on his first appearance in public heralded neither a brilliant racecourse career for the colt nor a permanent settlement of the differences between his owner and trainer. Having been unplaced in the Grand Prix de Paris Merry Hampton was second in The St Leger after being denied a clear run and unplaced in the City and Suburban the only time that he ran as a four-year-old before being retired to his owner's stud at Kentford, which like Bedford Lodge, was rented from Captain Machell.

By the time that Merry Hampton had reached the anti-climax of his brief career relations between George Baird and the punctilious Martin Gurry had deteriorated so far as to make a second *rapprochement* impossible. Once more George Baird dismissed Gurry without paying him his due in full, but rather than refuse to leave the stable as he had done the previous year, Gurry gladly took his leave of surroundings he found so uncongenial, determined to go to law to obtain the money still owed to him.

As successor to Martin Gurry at Bedford Lodge came Charles Morton, who had earned the good opinion of George Baird by providing him with a winning ride on a notoriously inconsistent sprinter called Bismarck at Windsor while conducting a small stable at Wantage. Then aged 33, Charlie Morton had served his apprenticeship at Wantage with that remarkable character Tom Parr, who had trained Fisherman, winner of 70 of his 121 races, the 1855 St Leger winner Saucebox and other good horses after beginning life as an itinerant tea pedlar between Weymouth and Plymouth.

A good stable man and absolutely loyal to his employers, though essentially secretive by nature, Charlie Morton had serious misgivings about accepting the appointment at Bedford Lodge. These at first, proved unfounded as George Baird was too engrossed with his race riding to be too much bothered with his drinking friends, while the likes of Pioneer, Snaplock, Juggler and King of Diamonds were winning regularly, as often as not with their owner in the saddle.

The most important horse that Charlie Morton trained at Bedford Lodge was a roarer who broke blood vessels and never won a race while he was in the yard. This was Gallinule whom George Baird bought for the large sum of 5,000 guineas after his previous owner, the disreputable fourth Marquess of Ailesbury, had been warned off for his complicity in the stopping of his horse Everitt at York in

August 1887. Lord Ailesbury and Baird had been friends until quarrelling over their claims to the affections of Lady Ailesbury.

Gallinule was a massive chestnut with conspicuous markings that made him a godsend for the Newmarket touts. As well as four white socks and a broad blaze he had a patch of white in the shape of an hour glass on the near side of his face. After he had been tried a certainty for Lincolnshire of 1889 Baird and his friends backed him so heavily that he started favourite only to break a blood vessel and finished unplaced. Determined to be out of such a bad bargain at any price Baird instructed Morton to find a buyer for him and he was bought by Captain Henry Greer for £900, with Baird greeting news of the deal by declaring he was "sorry for the fellow who bought him". The 'Squire's' concern was quite unnecessary as his cast-off was to become one of the outstanding sires of the early years of the next century. As well as earning immortality by getting Pretty Polly, he sired the 2,000 Guineas winner Slieve Gallion, the St Leger winners Wildfowler and Night Hawk and the 1905 Cesarewitch winner Hammerkop, dam of the Derby winner Spion Kop. Gallinule was champion stallion in both 1904 and 1905, getting, in all the winners of 663 races worth £316,963.

Of all the society women with whom George Baird dallied the one who shared his taste for The Turf to the most marked degree was Lily Langtry, who had made her appearance on the racing scene during the days in which she was mistress of the Prince of Wales. Being of an extraordinarily jealous disposition, Baird never hesitated to thrash her if suspecting he was having to share her favours. The more intoxicated he was the harder he beat her, and then by way of atonement he would shower her with jewellery, cheques for £5,000 or more and on one occasion a yacht called The Whyte Lady, that became known to all and sundry as 'The Black Eye'. Among the many gifts that avaricious woman accepted from him was the chestnut colt whom he had bred from the mating of Saraband and Colleen Bawn in 1890. Given the name of Milford he was put into training with Charlie Morton at Bedford Lodge and was a winner at Kempton Park first time out as a two-year-old in the May of 1892.

By the time that Milford won at Kempton, George Baird, still only 30 years of age, was displaying increasingly less interest in racing, and rarely taking a mount, being almost totally under the influence of Charlie Mitchell and even less desirable members of the boxing fraternity. Drinking harder than ever he roamed the West End of London with the fighting men acting as a body guard to protect him from the victims of his unprovoked assaults and crude practical jokes, such as pouring a drink over a stranger dining in a restaurant. Confident that he would never remember what he had done in his cups the previous evening his entourage used to tell him he had so little idea of his own strength that he had killed a man and asked to be reimbursed of the huge sums they had spent suppressing evidence of the supposed fatality.

Although George Baird spent most of his time in London as the season of 1892 was getting under way he had recently made a very considerable addition to his investment in racing by the acquisition of his own stud rather than continuing to lease that at Kentford from Captain Machell. Just after the turn of the year he had purchased Moulton Paddocks, just over the brow of Warren Hill, from Lord Gerard. There he stood Merry Hampton, whose fee was then 100 guineas, together with two other stallions, Juggler and Van Diemansland, and kept Busybody along with his other broodmares. W. Jugg, who had been stud groom at Kentford, continued to be employed in that capacity but the overall management of George Baird's greatly increased breeding interests and the horses in training at Bedford Lodge was entrusted to the 36-year-old former jockey Charlie Morbey, while Charlie Morton continued to run the stable.

Morbey had served his apprenticeship with Peter Price, who had the Somerville Lodge stable and stood the 1885 Manchester Cup winner Raffaello at the Fordham Road Paddocks. The first of Morbey's notable successes had been obtained on Lord Rosebery's Aldritch whom he rode at 6 st 4 lb to win the City and Suburban as a boy of 18 in 1874. Subsequently he made a good deal of money riding for the Nottingham bookmaker Charlie Hibbert and invested it in property in the village of Soham, a few miles from Newmarket.

Charlie Morbey was determined that the management of Baird's horses should be a thoroughly remunerative occupation, and had good cause to be satisfied with the results. Not only did the racing establishments provide him with a comfortable income but he was rarely a loser at the card parties he gave at his home, The Moat House, Soham, for the diversion of Baird and his guests at those Bedford Lodge house parties.

A remarkably resourceful little man, Charlie Morbey was quite capable of coping with all Baird's foibles, such as his extreme reluctance to settle his accounts despite the enormous funds at his disposal. On calling to collect a cheque for stable expenses one day Baird protested he was unable to give him one as he could not find a pen.

"I've thought of that," said Morbey, producing one from his waistcoat pocket. Taking the pen, Baird knocked over the inkstand.

"Oh! I've thought of that too, Squire," countered the ex-jockey pulling a bottle of ink out of the pocket of his jacket.

While George Baird drank and brawled in London in the company of the pugilists and the rest of his nefarious friends during the spring of 1892 Bedford Lodge had almost ceased to function as a racing stable. Whenever Charlie Morton took a horse to a meeting one of the owner's unpleasant henchmen was almost certain to appear on the course with a message to say that it was not to run. The 'Squire' was refusing to go racing unless he had a ride, and did not want any of his horses to run unless he was present, so that the Bedford Lodge horses were rarely seen in public in the early weeks of the season of 1892. By late May Charlie Morton could tolerate the situation no longer and when the inevitable messenger appeared at Epsom on the first day of the Derby meeting and told him that Baird did not want King of Diamonds to run in the Egmont Plate the exasperated trainer replied, "I don't care. The horse is going to run", and then, for good measure, brought him out again two days later. King of Diamonds won both times without doing anything to vindicate Morton in the eyes of his employer. Informed of the 'Squire's' displeasure by a gloating minion, Morton calmly remarked, "Then he had better get another trainer", and that was the end of their association.

The next trainer to enter the employment of George Baird was the 43-year-old former steeplechase jockey Joe Cannon, a genial, easygoing man whose inability to adopt the business like principles of his elder brother Tom consigned him to a long series of appointments as a private trainer until able to set up on his own comparatively late in life. Within almost a matter of days of taking over the Bedford Lodge yard Cannon won the Coventry Stakes with Milford for Lily Langtry at Royal Ascot, and with dreams of becoming the first woman to own a Derby winner she refused an offer of 20,000 guineas for the colt given her by her sporadically violent lover.

Ten days after the success of Milford at the Royal Meeting Baird's own two-year-old Meddler, a well-named brown colt by St Gatien out of the Oaks winner Busybody, beat Colonel North's Emita three lengths at Sandown Park. The following month Meddler consolidated his reputation by the impressive manner in which he won the Chesterfield Stakes on the July Course at Newmarket.

The potential of becoming top class shown by a colt that he had bred himself revived George Baird's enthusiasm for racing to such an extent that he began to take his riding seriously again. On 30 September, his 31st birthday, he was back in the city of his birth to win the Edinburgh Gold Cup on Alice and two months later Meddler beat the Duke of Portland's Raeburn in the Dewhurst Stakes.

When George Baird returned to London to spend the winter in his house in Curzon Street at the end of the flat racing season he was excited by the anticipation of his home-bred colt winning The Derby and genuinely determined to be quit of all his undesirable associates so as to be able to re-establish himself as the outstanding Gentleman Rider in 1893. For all his good intentions, though, the fighting men were soon to regain their ascendancy over him by their wheedling and flattery.

As part of an elaborate plan designed to relieve him of more money than ever before they persuaded him to accompany them to the United States to put up one purse for a fight between his protégé Jem Hall and Bob Fitzsimmons in New Orleans and a second one to enable Charlie Mitchell to challenge 'Gentleman Jim' Corbett for the Heavyweight Championship of the World in New York. Absolutely horrified at hearing of these proposals Joe Cannon went to London to bring Baird back to Bedford Lodge but found the door of 36 Curzon Street closed to him. The fighting men were not to be denied their prey.

Joe Cannon's worst misgivings about the expedition were only too fully justified when Baird caught malarial fever while acting as second to Jem Hall. Weakened by more than a decade of heavy drinking and wasting to ride, he had no resistance to the pneumonia that set in on top of it and died in the St Charles Hotel, New Orleans, on 18 March 1893.

Despite all those years of dissipating his fortune on "horse racing, prize-fighting and harlotry", to cite a disapproving obituarist, George Baird still proved to be worth £846,051 12s 11d. To the bitter chagrin of Lily Langtry, Charlie Mitchell and others he left it all to his mother.

The memorial to George Alexander Baird to be seen at Newmarket today is the Abington Place stable, which takes its name from his *nom-de-course*, while the stud at Kentford, where he bred the Dewhurst Stakes winner Meddler, is now known as the Meddler Stud. The present owner and manager of the Meddler Stud is Mr W. B. Leach, who stands Blue Cashmere and Bailidar there. Bill Leach is the son of H. B. 'Chubb' Leach, the Queensberry Lodge trainer.

The Abington Place stable, which Harry Wragg made such a powerful force in international racing for more than 30 years, was built by Martin Gurry, the first of George Baird's three private trainers. After failing to secure all the money due to him on being dismissed from Bedford Lodge, he quickly set in motion the machinery to bring George Baird to court to secure payment, but rather than defend a hopeless cause Baird displayed uncharacteristic discretion by settling in full. With the money thus obtained 'Smush' Gurry built the stable that he named after his reluctant benefactor. Most of the material and labour used for the building of Abington Place which was completed in 1890 came from Gurry's native city of Nottingham.

Martin Gurry, who never learned to read or write, trained Sir James Miller's La Sagesse to win The Oaks in 1895, but the only other race of any importance he won while at Abington Place was the Chesterfield Cup at Goodwood with Union Jack in 1904. In gratitude for a successful betting coup he proposed presenting a piece of plate to St Agnes's Church. Asked what inscription he would like on it he suggested the uncompromising legend 'From Gurry to God'. The wording, though probably not the gift, proved unacceptable to an embarrassed incumbent. When he retired in 1917 he sold Abington Place to Alfred Saddler, on the condition that he should occupy the house for the remainder of his life, and died in 1923.

A year after the death of George Baird, Joe Cannon opened a public stable at Lordship Farm, now one of three studs belonging to Lady Macdonald-Buchanan, and soon earned a reputation for the regularity with which he landed the big handicaps. In 1900 he won the Manchester November Handicap with Lexicon who beat Santoi by a short head, ridden by his nephew Kempton Cannon, and in 1904 the Royal Hunt Cup with Csardas.

Valet, ridden by Henri Jellis, won him a second Manchester November Handicap in 1910 and the following year he landed the Lincolnshire with Mercutio for the bookmaker Charlie Hibbert. In 1912 he obtained his most important success at home at Newmarket since Meddler's Dewhurst Stakes when Adam Bede beat La Bohème II by half a length in the Cambridgeshire. Subsequently he won the

Manchester November Handicap on two other occasions — with Dalmatian in 1913 and Planet in 1917. Joe Cannon handed the Lordship Farm stable over to his son J. H. S. 'Boxer' Cannon on retiring in 1919 and died at the age of 83 in 1933.

Meddler probably represented the best chance of winning a classic that Joe Cannon had, but even if the executors of George Baird had not been anxious to break up the Bedford Lodge stable as soon as they possibly could, the colt would not have been able to meet the engagements made for him as a three-year-old. As the rules stood until the novelist Edgar Wallace brought a friendly action against the Jockey Club in 1927 all entries became void on the death of a horse's nominator. Thus the early death of George Baird removed one of the very few serious dangers to Isinglass in the classics of 1893.

Harry McCalmont, the owner of Isinglass, had much in common with George Baird. Both were born in 1861, both were of Scottish descent, both went to Eton, both inherited large fortunes and both were essentially gregarious by nature, but whereas George Baird set his face against the establishment Harry McCalmont thrived on being one of its leading lights.

The McCalmonts migrated from Scotland to Ulster in the seventeenth century, and some hundred years later one of their number commanded a West Indiaman that sailed the lucrative Atlantic trade routes. His son Hugh, born in 1763, made a fortune from sugar plantations in the West Indies as well as from his interests in mercantile houses in the City and the United States and was still only 40 when he retired to the Abbeylands Estate in Northern Ireland. He had four sons, Robert, Thomas, Hugh and James, and set up Robert and Hugh as merchant bankers in London with capital of £100,000 and died in 1838, leaving another £200,000 to be divided between the four sons and their three sisters. Hugh (the younger) was very much the sleeping partner in McCalmont Brothers, but the energy and foresight of Robert made them the most important financial house in the City after the Barings. Their assets included a large holding in the railway line between Philadelphia and Reading, the indolent and cautious Hugh having only agreed to the highly speculative American investment on the condition that they made secret wills by which each left all his possessions to the other. Thus when Robert McCalmont died childless at the age of 73 in 1883 his nephews were more than a little disappointed by the whole of his estate being inherited by their other childless uncle, Hugh. Four years later, in 1887, Hugh McCalmont died at Abbeylands and most of the younger generation suffered another set back by his leaving his fortune of about £4,000,000 to Harry McCalmont strictly in accordance with the laws of primogeniture. Harry McCalmont was the only son of Hugh Barklie McCalmont, son of the first marriage of Thomas McCalmont, second son of old Hugh McCalmont.

Unlike George Baird, Harry McCalmont had aspired to considerable distinction at Eton. Twice he stroked the eight at Henley and he was also a member of the team that won the Football Cup twice while

Colonel Harry McCalmont (1861-1902) lived in style at Cheveley Park and had horses under the management of Captain Machell in the Bedford Cottage stable

on the academic side he was able to pass all his military exams before leaving.

At the time that he inherited the millions of his great-uncle, Harry McCalmont was serving as a subaltern in the Royal Warwickshire Regiment. Having transferrred into the more fashionable Scots Guards he set out on a spending spree to acquire the adjuncts he deemed necessary to his greatly altered circumstances. As well as a London house in St James's Square, he bought the yacht, Giralda, a sporting property in Herefordshire as well as the Cheveley Park estate on the outskirts of Newmarket from the Duke of Rutland while commissioning Captain Machell to buy him horses to launch his career upon The Turf.

Not content with the ducal residence in Cheveley Park, Harry McCalmont had it demolished and replaced by a grander building more to his taste. While this was being constructed he took up temporary abode in Sefton Lodge, which he bought from the Duke of Montrose for £12,000, almost opposite Captain Machell's Bedford Cottage stable. Once able to move into his new mansion in Cheveley Park, Harry McCalmont went to enormous expense to stock the estate with game, and quickly acquired a reputation for the lavishness of his hospitality, his guests being of very much greater social standing than those entertained by George Baird at Bedford Lodge. On more than one occasion Harry McCalmont, clad in large-checked suit and tyrolean hat, and his guests would finish a day with a bag of 2,000 head of game.

Rather than take the risk of buying yearlings for the latest patron of his stable, Captain Machell acquired the well-proven Timothy on his behalf. A chestnut four-year-old by Hermit, Timothy had won the Ascot Derby (now the King Edward VII Stakes) the previous season, and quickly kindled his new owner's enthusiasm for racing by bringing off the double in the Gold Cup and the Alexandra Plate (now the Queen Alexandra Stakes) at Royal Ascot in 1888. Four years later Harry McCalmont landed one of those betting coups that provided him with so much exhilaration when Suspender, ridden by the Bedford Cottage lightweight George Chaloner, won the Royal Hunt Cup at 25-1, and the same season Isinglass gave the first demonstrations of his excellence with his successes in the New Stakes at the Royal Meeting and the Middle Park Stakes.

As well as have Isinglass carry his scarlet and light-blue quartered jacket, the Eton football colours, to victory in The 2,000 Guineas, The Derby and The St Leger in 1893, Harry McCalmont won the Portland Handicap with Whisperer at Doncaster, while his chestnut filly Be Cannie won six of her eleven races as a two-year-old. At the end of the season he was leading owner after having been elected to the Jockey Club in October, the pleasant modesty with which he accepted the triumphs of his horses having done as much to contribute to his popularity with his fellow owners as his generosity as a host.

Largely as a result of Isinglass winning the Princess of Wales Stakes, the Eclipse Stakes and the first running of the Jockey Club Stakes as a four-year-old Harry McCalmont was leading owner again in 1894. The other important event that he won that year was the Dewhurst Stakes with Raconteur, a bay colt by St Simon out of that remarkable mare Plaisanterie, who had brought off the double in the Cesarewitch and the Cambridgeshire in 1885.

Although Raconteur was unplaced both when 6-5 favourite for The 2,000 Guineas and joint favourite for The Derby, the only times that he ran in 1895, the season was a satisfactory one for Harry McCalmont and the year a truly memorable one. Isinglass justified the decision to keep him in training as a five-year-old by winning the Gold Cup on his only appearance, thereby bringing his earnings to the £57,455 that remained a record until broken by Tulyar 57 years later in 1952. The same year Amphora won the Gimcrack Stakes and Emsworth the National Breeders Produce Stakes at Sandown Park.

What made 1895 a memorable year for Harry McCalmont was his election as Member of Parliament for East Cambridgeshire, the constituency that includes Newmarket, on 29 July. As a Conservative he commanded the support of the vast majority of the racing community, a notable exception being Bill Jarvis. He trained for Charles Day Rose, a banker and prominent Liberal Imperialist, who lived at Suffolk House, subsequently a cinema, opposite the site of the Edward VII Memorial Hall. Prudently supporting the party of his principa patron, Bill Jarvis took his small sons Willie, Basil and Jack to all the meetings of Harry McCalmont's Liberal opponent Sir George Newnes thereby subjecting them to the friendly derision of their contemporaries in the Conservative training families like the Hayhoes and the Waughs.

In a final effort to rally the Conservative vote the candidate made a lightning tour of the constituency by coach on polling day. The tour was long to be remembered as 'McCalmont's Drive'. With Alec Pennington on the box and Stanley Cave as guard, he started at Ely at 9.30 in the morning, passed through Soham, where he spent 18 minutes with the electors, on to Fordham, Chippenham and Snailwell, reaching the Clock Tower on schedule at noon, and changing horses at Newmarket, returned to Cheveley Park for lunch before setting out again half an hour later. Among the villages visited in the afternoon were Wood Ditton, Stetchworth, Dullingham, Brinkley and Balsham. Having changed horses at Linton between 3.38 and 3.45 he went on to Pampisford, Duxford, Sawston and Trumpington arriving on time at 5.45 at Cambridge, where the horses were changed for a third time. In the evening he drove through Cherry Hinton, Fulbourn and Great Wilbraham, called in at The Swan at Bottisham, then went on through Swaffham Bulbeck and Burwell before returning to Newmarket at 8.28, finally arriving home at Chevely Park at nine. In eleven and a half hours, including an hour and three quarters for refreshments, he had driven 87 miles and was rewarded with a majority of 343.

At about the same time as he entered parliament this enormously energetic man laid out a jumping course on that part of the Cheveley Park Estate, where the Newmarket-trained jumpers are schooled over fences and hurdles to the right of the road approaching the town from the direction of Cambridge. Despite the support that Harry McCalmont was able to give it, jumping never really caught on at Newmarket. It was discontinued after 1907 and the stands converted into the houses that are to be seen near the Golf Links.

After Knight of the Thistle, ridden by Fred Allsop, had become Harry McCalmont's second winner of the Royal Hunt Cup in 1897, important changes were made in the management of the Bedford Cottage stable in 1898. Jimmy Jewett died and as Captain Machell had become too ill to take any active part in racing Harry McCalmont purchased the yard and installed as trainer Major Charles Beatty, an old friend from his days in the Royal Warwickshire Regiment. Charlie Beatty was the son of Captain D. L. Beatty, a native of County Wicklow, with whom Harry McCalmont had a few jumpers in training soom after he entered into his inheritance. Of the brothers of Charlie Beatty, who was to die in 1917 after being severely wounded on the western front, David was the brilliant Admiral who commanded the battle cruisers at Jutland, and Major Vandy Beatty the Phantom House trainer.

Charlie Beatty's experience of racing when he took over Bedford Cottage at the age of 28 in 1898 was almost entirely confined to helping in his father's jumping stable and riding in steeplechases, rather than handling classic material. After obtaining his initial success on Radical at Rugby in 1892 he had won the Grand International 'Chase on Kestrel at Sandown Park in 1895 and had been fourth on Filbert in the Grand National of 1898 just before giving up riding to train.

The consensus of opinion on the racecourse was that Harry McCalmont was making a serious mistake in selecting Charlie Beatty as his trainer. "Everybody tells me I am wrong", he confided to his friend Alfred Watson, the racing journalist. "That it is ridiculous; that he does not understand the business; but I think I am right. If he doesn't understand now, he'll very soon learn."

The putting of the issue to the test was necessarily delayed by the outbreak of the Boer War in October 1898. Both Charlie Beatty and Harry McCalmont returned to the Warwickshire Regiment, of which the latter became commanding officer and Captain Machell came out of retirement to run Bedford Cottage on a somewhat low key for the duration of hostilities. Colonel McCalmont took great pride in commanding the first militia regiment to be sent outside Europe, and after a period at Capetown was transferred to garrison duties at Simonstown, the great naval base, writing home that South Africa was notable for nothing but south-easterly dust storms and north-easterly rain storms.

At the end of the War in 1901 Colonel McCalmont and his trainer returned to England determined to restore the prestige of the Bedford Cottage stables. Having taken over the yard again at the back-end of 1901 Charlie Beatty quickly showed his detractors the extent to which they had underestimated him by sending out St Maclou to win the Lincolnshire in 1902. In a desperate finish Harry McCalmont's four-year-old got home by a head from no less formidable rival than Sceptre, who was making a highly unorthodox seasonal debut for a three-year-old filly with obvious classic pretensions. Later in the season Sceptre was to have her revenge on the McCalmont colours by beating Glass Jug into second place in The Oaks and winning The St Leger from Rising Glass, who had also been second in The Derby. In the autumn Rising Glass, a well-named son of Isinglass and Hautesse, won the Jockey Club Stakes as well as three other races and finally St Maclou wound up a highly satisfactory season for the stable by landing another important handicap when Morny Cannon rode him to beat the Duke of Portland's Aldegonde in the Manchester November Handicap.

A few days after the success of St Maclou at Manchester, Colonel Harry McCalmont died of a heart attack on the doorstep of his London home. With his fine new mansion at Cheveley Park, his other sporting estate in Herefordshire, his private stable at Newmarket, house in the most fashionable part of London, sea-going yacht and membership of the House of Commons he had led the life of a true magnifico and it had cost him two million of the four million pounds that he had inherited 15 years earlier.

Although twice married, Colonel McCalmont died childless. His first wife Ann Hyacinth, daughter of Major-General Miller, had died in 1889 and in 1897 he had married Winifred, widow of William Atmar Fanning, two years before her brother became the second husband of Lily Langtry.

As had been the case with that of George Baird, the death of Colonel McCalmont had the effect of rendering void the classic engagements of a colt that might have been good enough to win The Derby. This was Zinfandel, a fine big chestnut by Persimmon. Trained by Charlie Beatty, he beat Sceptre and the previous season's Triple Crown winner Rock Sand in the Coronation Cup of 1904, while his other successes included the Gold Cup, the Gold Vase, the Queen Alexandra Stakes and the Jockey Club Cup. Like the rest of the bloodstock of Colonel Harry McCalmont, with the sole exception of Isinglass, Zinfandel was purchased from his executors by the eighth Lord Howard de Walden, who had succeeded his father in the title at the age of 19 in 1899.

Having neither brothers nor sons, Colonel Harry McCalmont had bequeathed his remaining two millions to his second cousin, Dermot McCalmont, son of Major-General Sir Hugh McCalmont, whose father James had been the youngest of those four sons of the founder of the family's fortunes. Major Dermot McCalmont will always be remembered as the owner of The Tetrarch, the unbeaten grey who showed such phenomenal speed as a two-year-old while trained by his owner's cousin Atty Persse at Stockbridge in Hampshire in 1913.

Twenty years after the triumphs of The Tetrarch differences arose between Major McCalmont and Atty Persse with the result that Major McCalmont renewed his family's association with Newmarket by sending his horses to George Lambton, who had just opened a public stable at Kremlin House. Most important of the horses that George Lambton trained for Major McCalmont was Lapel who won the Free Handicap and the Irish 1,000 Guineas in 1938 before becoming a successful broodmare.

Following the death of George Lambton in 1945 Major McCalmont resumed his patronage of Persse's stable until the retirement of that trainer in 1953 when he sent his horses back to Newmarket to be trained by Persse's brother-in-law Geoffrey Brooke at Clarehaven. Among the many winners Geoffrey Brooke turned out for Major McCalmont was that very consistent handicapper Durante, a chestnut gelding by Dante out of Lapel. Having won the Kempton Park Jubilee Handicap twice and the Liverpool Autumn Cup, a race of some consequence in those days, before coming to Newmarket, Durante won two more Liverpool Autumn Cups, Kempton Park's Rosebery Stakes and seven other races while with Brooke. Another notable success that Geoffrey Brooke obtained for Major McCalmont was with Zaleucus in the Royal Hunt Cup of 1964.

Major McCalmont died in 1968. At the present time two of the sons of his second marriage, Hugh and Patrick, play prominent parts in the life of Newmarket. With the idea of becoming a trainer Hugh McCalmont was assistant to Tom Jones while riding successfully as an amateur over the sticks, in which capacity he won the Princess

Royal Hurdle on his own horse Speedwell at Doncaster. Subsequently a deteriorating economic situation obliged him to abandon his plans to train and he is now involved in running a video cassette firm. In partnership with his mother and brothers he has a number of horses in training with Geoffrey Brooke's former assistant Peter Walwyn at Lambourn and during the time that he was a prominent member of the Bloodstock and Racing Industries Council played an important part in persuading Members of Parliament of all parties that the racing and breeding industries are a significant part of the national economy, both as employers and foreign currency earners.

Patrick McCalmont acquired some 100 acres of the Dalham Hall Stud from Major the Hon J. P. Philipps in 1970 to form the Gazeley Stud. As mentioned elsewhere that prolific mare Stilvi boards at Gazeley and Patrick McCalmont has been responsible for the rearing of Tachypous, Tyrnavos and her other winning offspring, while on his own account he has bred Free State, winner of the Waterford Crystal Mile in 1976. The Irish Derby winner Tyrnavos returned to Gazeley to take up stallion duties alongside Hotfoot, sire of Free State, Tachypous, Hot Grove, who was second in The Derby, and Count Pahlen.

19 The American Influence

American owners, as well as their trainers and jockeys, enjoyed appreciable success on the English Turf during the second half of the last century. What is even more important is that they exerted considerable influence on the development of English racing.

The first American to race on any scale on this side of the Atlantic was Richard Ten Broeck, who came from a family of Dutch extraction. He arrived in 1856 when he installed his trainer Brown in a stable in Newmarket. It was not long before Brown was being widely ridiculed for his relying almost entirely upon walking exercises to get his horses fit. Very rarely did he gallop any of them.

Critics of this system felt themselves well and truly vindicated when it looked as though Brown was never going to saddle a winner. The American horses were beaten in race after race in 1856 and for most of the following year. This was far from being the exclusive fault of Brown. Whatever the merits or defects of his methods of training might have been, it was quite certain that the standard of riding of the American jockeys of those days was deplorable.

At last the luck changed for Richard Ten Broeck when, in 1857, his filly Pryoress won one of the most dramatic races for the Cesarewitch in its history, (see The Great Races of the Heath p.57).

Once he had made a start it was not long before Richard Ten Broeck won other big races. He landed the Goodwood Cup with Starke and the Ascot Stakes with Optimist in 1861. Another high-class horse that he owned was Paris, who finished second to General Peel in The 2,000 Guineas in 1864.

During the next 15 years the American horses achieved little of note, then in 1879 Mr M. H. Sandford's Parole won the City and Suburban. The same year the tobacco millionaire, Mr Pierre Lorillard, sent over a consignment of yearlings and put them in the charge of his American trainer, Jacob Pincus at Newmarket.

Jacob Pincus was a good trainer but he looked askance at the English method of trying horses by the adjustment of weights. He believed that the clock was the only yardstick by which a horse could be tried. In much the same way as they had derided his compatriot Brown two decades previously, the conservative Newmarket trainers announced that he could not train ivy up a wall. They soon learned a healthier respect for Jacob Pincus.

In the season of 1881 the Americans dominated English racing. At Epsom Jacob Pincus turned out Mr Pierre Lorillard's Iroquois trained to the minute, and ridden by Fred Archer, the colt won The Derby by beating the favourite Peregrine by half a length. Jacob Pincus, who was born in Baltimore in 1838, commenced his career as a jockey at the age of 14. After early success in New Orleans, Charleston and elsewhere in the south he moved north to Saratoga, and established himself as one of the outstanding jockeys in the United States before increasing weight obliged him to turn to training. He came to Newmarket when Iroquois was a two-year-old in 1880 and on return to the United States took charge of the horses of Mr August Belmont, from whom he subsequently received a pension. He died at Mount Vernon on 23 January 1918.

In Mr J. R. Keene's Foxhall the Americans had an even better three-year-old than Iroquois in 1881. During the early part of the year he was with the Bedford Lodge trainer 'Buck' Sherrard, but by the time he began winning he had been transferred to William Day at Woodyates. Had Foxhall been entered for the classics it is more than possible that he would have won the Triple Crown. As it was he showed brilliant form by winning the Grand Prix de Paris and completing the autumn double in the Cesarewitch and the Cambridgeshire. As a four-year-old Foxhall confirmed his excellence by winning the Gold Cup, though so high was his reputation by that time that only two horses took the field against him at Ascot.

The Americans made their impact on English racing in two important ways. Firstly their jockeys introduced the modern method of riding with exaggeratedly short stirrup leathers and secondly they brought over from their own country the practice of doping. At first this was not against the rules of racing. Of secondary significance, the American trainers brought in their fashion of allowing more fresh air and a lower temperature in horses' boxes. This was in contrast to the practice of the English and Scottish trainers, most of whom were accustomed to stand their horses in something like hothouse temperatures.

Another improvement introduced by the Americans was the use of far lighter racing plates than those used for English horses. In the opinion of one American trainer, Huggins, the plates that he had sent over from the States gave a horse an advantage of four lengths in a mile.

Unlike most of these other innovations, the American method of galloping horses against the clock at home was not generally adopted in England. Nor is it widespread today.

The modern style of riding with short stirrup leathers was first employed by Negro jockeys at the rough-and-ready country meetings in the United States. These boys were never taught to ride. They were not even equipped with saddles. They were just slung on to the backs of horses and left to make the best of it. Naturally their first instinct would be to grab the horses' manes, and in doing so they would put their weight much further forward than a rider sitting in a saddle would do. Having done this they would have to tuck up their knees to obtain a better balance and thus evolved the crouch style used the world over today.

Obviously the trainers and jockeys in the fashionable sphere of

American racing did not appreciate the benefits of the new style immediately they saw it. What happened was that important trainers would buy horses after they had won on the minor tracks, confident that they could improve the animals. What surprised the trainers was that, far from improving, the horses did not even show the form they had done hitherto. Not until the despairing trainers gave the Negro boys, with their crouching style, a chance to ride the horses again did the latter return to form. Gradually the boys were given the chance to ride horses that had not been recruited from the up-country tracks and, to the surprise of almost everybody concerned, their mounts revealed enormous improvement when ridden with short leathers.

The first jockey to use the new style in England was a little coloured rider called Sims. Needless to say he was laughed at every time he appeared on a racecourse and everybody said he would have as much chance of winning a race if he jumped off and led his mount round the course. It was not until James Forman Sloan, for evermore Tod Sloan, came over here that the English fraternity began to take the new way of riding seriously. Tod Sloan may have lacked the style and elegance of Morny Cannon, Jack Watts, Fred Rickaby and Charlie Wood but the fact remained that he got more out of his mounts than their former partners had done. Time and again he beat the best of the English jockeys when he was riding horses with little or no apparent chance.

Tod Sloan first came to England to ride Saint-Cloud II in the Cesarewitch and the Cambridgeshire of 1897. He was unplaced in the former and beaten a head by Comfrey in the latter, but during the few weeks he spent in England he rode some 20 winners, which represented a very high percentage of success.

The following year Tod Sloan returned with a retainer to ride for Lord William Beresford. A younger son of the Marquess of Waterford, Lord William Beresford VC had an American-born wife in the former Duchess of Marlborough. In partnership with Iroquois' owner, Mr Pierre Lorillard, Lord William had about 50 horses in training with the American John Huggins at Heath House.

Tod Sloan was a brilliant jockey. He was also a conceited and tacless little man with a strong addiction to gambling and a genius for keeping the worst company he could find. In short, he was his own worst enemy. Despite his ability, despite even the patronage of such an influential owner as Lord William, he was doomed to failure in English racing almost from the start, if only because the Jockey Club had already set its face against jockeys betting.

Although his vulgar abuse of fellow jockeys in the weighing room and his rough riding on the course frequently invited severe punishment from the Stewards, Tod Sloan managed to rub along for two or three seasons, thanks, no doubt, to the intervention of his employers. In 1899 he won both The 1,000 Guineas on Sibola and the Kempton Park Jubilee on Knight of the Thistle for the Heath House stable, and wound up the season by landing the Manchester November Handicap on Proclamation, trained by John Dawson junior at St Albans.

In 1900 Tod Sloan had a good meeting at Royal Ascot, where he won the Ascot Stakes on Baldur and the Gold Cup on Merman. Later in the year he rated himself a certainty to win the Cambridgeshire on Codoman. Accordingly he sent his unpleasant set of friends and satellites about the task of getting his money on in the ante-post market. By the time they had finished it was estimated that he would have collected £150,000 if Codoman won the Cambridgeshire. On top of that he would have had about the same amount to come from a man called Frank Gardner to whom he had passed on information about the horse. Frank Gardner was a professional gambler with a singularly unsavoury reputation.

Now the only danger to Codoman was the Irish-trained Berrill, who was receiving 15 lb. At first Sloan and his associates tried to arrange for a friendly jockey to have the ride on Berrill. When that did not wash, and trainer Phil Behan remained adamant that Johnny Thompson would have the mount, they embarked on a course of intimidation and that did not work either. Finally they sent a couple of nobblers to the horse's box on the night before the Cambridgeshire. That final desperate piece of villainy achieved nothing as Behan had had the foresight to send Berrill to Newmarket with a strong bodyguard.

Having survived all these hazards, Berrill arrived at the post safe and sound and proceeded to win without being extended, Codoman finishing second. Never a good loser at the best of times, Tod Sloan was mad with rage at having lost one of the biggest bets of his life. What he called Johnny Thompson when they returned to the weighing room did not bear repeating. Even hardened riders, who had had three years of putting up with Sloan, had not realised the little American had such a wide range of coarse invective. In due course this offensive and one-sided conversation was relayed to the Stewards' Room.

Codoman was the straw that broke the camel's back. The Stewards were heartily sick of Tod Sloan and all his works. Investigations were put in hand and Sloan's betting activities as well as his relationship with Frank Gardner, and similar characters, came to light, to say nothing of a good few other things that did the American rider little credit.

Soon after Tod Sloan had returned to America for the winter he read in the newspapers that the Stewards of the Jockey Club thought it unnecessary for him to apply for a licence to ride in England in 1901. Because he was as vain as a film star, Tod Sloan may have been surprised by the announcement.

Richard Ten Broeck, J. R. Keene and Pierre Lorillard and their trainers, like Pincus and Huggins, were all men of unexceptionable integrity. By their patronage English racing was much the richer. Quite the opposite was the case with the second wave of the American Invasion that was operating in England during the second half of the nineties. This was headed by William 'Betcha-a-million' Gates, who had made his fortune out of the manufacture of barbed wire, and another heavy gambler by the name of James Drake. With them they brought something they knew would be the key to instant success in England – dope.

Diomed, a chestnut colt by Florizel foaled in 1777, owned by Sir Charles Bunbury of Great Barton, near Newmarket, and winner of the first Derby in 1780.

J   *Early morning in the Kremlin House yard, 1983.*

K   *Kremlin House trainer Michael Jarvis (right) with an owner on the Heath at first lot.*

Mr Michael Bramwell, Director of the National Stud, with the Stallion Moorestyle. Trained by Robert Armstrong at St Gatien, Moorestyle won 13 races from five to seven furlongs between 1979 and 1981 including the Bisquit Cognac Challenge Stakes twice, the Tote Free Handicap and the William Hill July Cup at Newmarket.

M *Newmarket 1885. l. to r. Lord Hastings, Mr. Henry Chaplin, Mr. Robert Peck, Lord Roseberry, Earl Spencer, Mr. W. G. Craven, Mr. Tattersall, Fred Archer, Mat Dawson, Captain Machell, The Duchess of Manchester, The Marquis of Hartington, The Prince of Wales, The Duke of Portland, The Marquis of Londonderry, The Dowager Duchess of Montrose, Mr. Leopold de Rothschild, Sir John Astley, The Duke of Hamilton.*

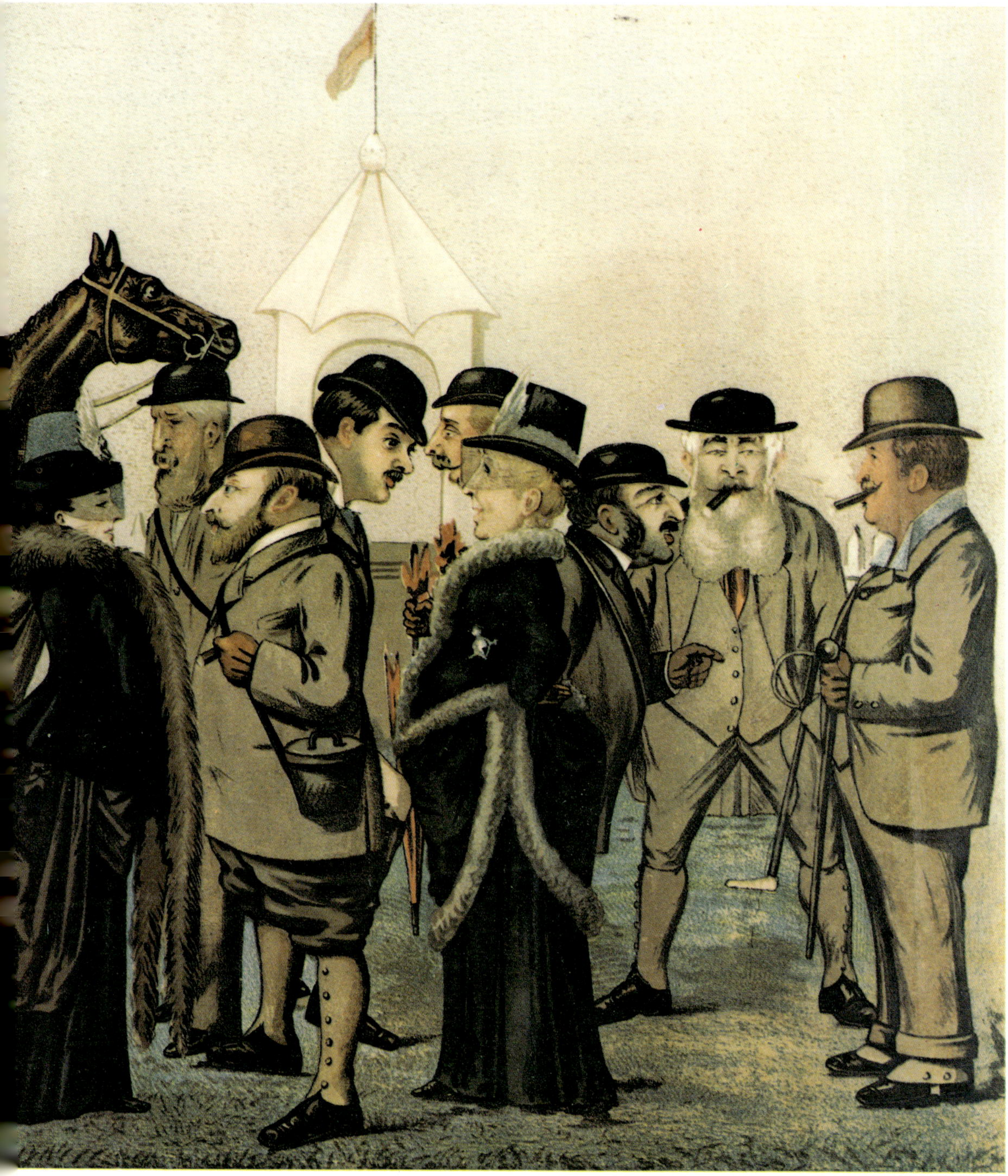

N *Sam, chestnut colt by Scud foaled in 1815, owned by Squire Thomas Thornhill and trained by Bill Chifney, was ridden to win the Derby of 1818 by Sam Chifney the younger.*

O *Persimmon, Jack Watts up, with his trainer Richard Marsh. A bay colt by St Simon foaled in 1893, Persimmon won the Derby and St Leger for the Prince of Wales (later King Edward VII) in 1896.*

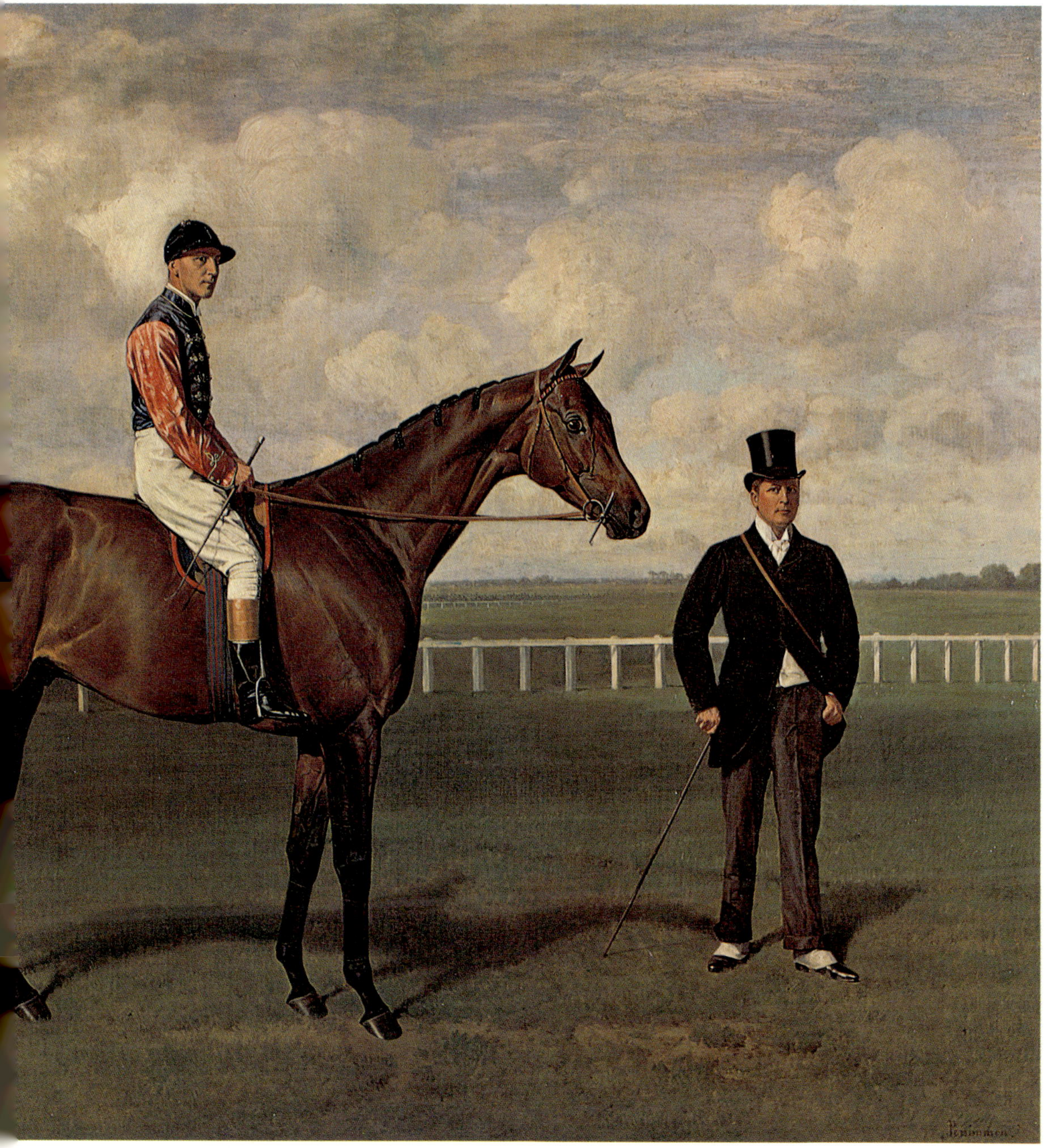

P *The Prince of Wales (George IV) on Warren Hill, 1790*

A general view of Warren Hill in Georgian times.

THE AMERICAN INFLUENCE

Gates and Drake took a lease on the Red House stable that used to stand near St Mary's Square before it was pulled down in the course of the redevelopment of that part of Newmarket in the early seventies. There they had Enoch Wishard, another American, as their trainer.

Wishard was a good stableman in his own right and his horses always looked wonderfully well, but first and foremost he was a past-master at the administration of dope. Whereas other trainers galloped their horses to put condition on them, Wishard galloped his in a series of experiments to ascertain how much dope needed to be given to them to obtain the desired standard of performance.

The usual routine was to buy a moderate horse that was fully exposed, run it way above its class, fill it with dope and back it off the board. The formula rarely failed. It is thought that Gates, Drake and the rest of them took something like £2,000,000 out of the ring between 1897 and 1901. Most of their horses were ridden by the brothers Lester and Johnny Reiff. In their knickerbockers and Eton collars they looked as innocent as choir-boys, but the fact of the matter was that either of them would stop any horse if it suited the gang who employed them.

The brothers also rode for those American stables who were above suspicion. Thus in the season of 1901, the first after the departure of Tod Sloan, Lester Reiff won The Derby on Volodyovski for John Huggins's Heath House stable. Lord William Beresford had died the previous December. His lease of the colt could not be passed on to his heirs, as was ruled in a court action over the matter, so when Volodyovski won the Derby he carried the colours of the American owner, Mr W. C. Whitney. The following season Whitney had taken over all the horses at Heath House.

A couple of the last coups that James Drake and the American gang brought off were with Royal Flush. This six-year-old had been trained by Steel near Pontefract and seemed well over the hill when he came up for sale. All the same, Enoch Wishard went up to 450 guineas to secure him.

Thereon the well-worn routine was followed. With the right amount of dope in him Royal Flush carried 7st to win the Royal Hunt Cup at Ascot and with a slightly increased dose he won the Stewards Cup at Goodwood under 7 st 13 lb a couple of months later. By this time the way in which the Americans were doping the horses to bring off coups and the riding of their jockeys had begun to be a crying scandal.

After Tod Sloan had been disposed of with the minimum amount of unpleasantness, Lester Reiff became the next recipient of some overdue justice from the Jockey Club. When he had stopped a horse in the New Barns Plate at Manchester the local stewards reported him to those of the Club and, the case against him proved, he was warned off by a sentence passed at the Newmarket First October Meeting of 1901.

Although Sloan and Lester Reiff were out of the way, the doping menace continued to play havoc with the form and the ring. What

Lester Reiff, the American jockey

made matters worse was that not all the members of the Jockey Club were convinced of its evil or its effect. Eventually George Lambton demonstrated both points by doping six horses after making known his intention of doing so. All six horses revealed unbelievable improvement. Lambton's contention was proved. Thenceforward doping of horses became an offence, the penalty for which was being warned off.

After all too long the game was up for James Drake and the rest and they departed *en bloc* for France to ply their trade on the Paris tracks. Johnny Reiff rode for them in France, making an occasional appearance in big races in England, but Lester Reiff never rode again.

A contrast in styles, England's Tommy Loates beats America's Tod Sloan at Newmarket in 1898

20 More about Victorian Newmarket

William Arthur Jarvis was Newmarket born and bred. Way back at the start of the nineteenth century, in the days of the Chifneys and the Arnulls, there were members of the Jarvis family with stables in Newmarket or its environs. One of them, Bill Jarvis's grandfather, had trained across the Heath at Six Mile Bottom and sent Gustavus to Epsom to become the first grey horse to win The Derby in 1821.

Born in 1852, Bill Jarvis had a short career as a jockey before he started training jumpers. Later he collected a useful string of flat racers at Waterwitch House with Charles Day Rose, later Sir Charles, as his principal patron. A member of the family banking firm of Morton, Rose & Co, Charles Rose belonged to the Jockey Club. His Newmarket home was Suffolk House, formerly the property of Charlie Wood.

The only classic that Bill Jarvis ever won was The 2,000 Guineas of 1892 with Mr Rose's Bonavista. He was desperately unlucky not to have won others. In Ravensbury and Cyllene he had two colts who were a great deal better than many classic winners.

Ravensdale had the misfortune to be foaled in the same year as Isinglass, one of the best horses of all time. In The 2,000 Guineas, in The Derby and again in The St Leger, Ravensbury was runner-up to Isinglass in 1893. His bad luck in the big races did not finish with the classics. Sent over to Longchamp for the Grand Prix de Paris he got home by a neck. Unfortunately the judge was more concerned with the honour of France than with giving a correct verdict, and awarded the race to Ragotsky.

As Cyllene was a late foal and very much on the small side, Charles Rose and Bill Jarvis made the fatal decision not to enter him for the classics. Had he been given the engagements, Cyllene might have won the Triple Crown. He grew into a sturdy individual of almost faultless conformation. More important still, he had the speed to win the National Breeders Produce Stakes in his first season and the Gold Cup as a four-year-old in 1899. Cyllene's achievements as a three-year-old included the winning of the Newmarket Stakes, in which the subsequent Derby winner Jeddah was only fifth.

In the sphere of handicaps, the most important won by Bill Jarvis were the Stewards Cup with Dog Rose in 1889 and the Cesarewitch with Scintillant in 1899. Bill Jarvis was married to a daughter of Jem Godding. By the time he died in the week of the December sales in 1921 their three sons, Willie, Basil and Jack were all training in the town.

The clock at the top of the High Street, which commemorates Queen Victoria's Golden Jubilee in 1887, was presented to the town

Cyllene, Sammy Loates up, trained by Bill Jarvis in the Waterwitch stable (now demolished) to win the Ascot Gold Cup in 1899

by the trainer, Charlie Blanton. Unfortunately he succumbed to a painfull illness in the same year.

'Nigger' Blanton was born in 1823. He trained in the stable on Old Station Road now known as Wroughton House. The outstanding horse that he had was Robert the Devil, which he owned in partnership with Charles Brewer the bookmaker. Because of the indifferent riding of Rossiter, Robert the Devil was unlucky not to have won The Derby in 1880 when Bend Or beat him in the last stride. In The St Leger Robert the Devil was ridden by Tom Cannon and won in a canter with Bend Or unplaced. A few weeks later Robert the Devil carried 8 st 6 lb to win the Cesarewitch. At the end of October 'Nigger' Blanton completed the autumn double by landing the Cambridgeshire with Lucetta.

On the death of Blanton his stable was taken over by a newcomer to Newmarket called Tom Leader. After being apprenticed to Jim Carter, Tom Leader managed the stud of Mr W. S. Cartwright, who owned coal mines in South Wales. Cartwright's horses were trained by the famous former steeplechase jockey Tom Oliver at Wroughton in Wiltshire. When Oliver died in February 1874, Tom Leader took over the

Wroughton stable and that year he won The Derby with George Frederick.

On arrival at Newmarket Tom Leader changed the name of the stable, in which Blanton had trained, to Wroughton House. The best horse he had during his early years there was Mr J. M. Hanbury's Cabin Boy, with whom he won 29 races between 1891 and 1893. Another good handicapper he had was Pitcher, who landed the Chesterfield Cup in 1895.

Tom Leader was 73 when he died in 1920. Of his four sons to become trainers Tom junior followed him at Wroughton House, Colledge was at Machell Place and later Stanley House, George Frederick, named after the Derby winner, at Warren House, while the youngest, Harvey, had the Bedford Lodge yard which he renamed Shalfleet. Ted Leader, who died in February 1983, was a son of Tom Leader the younger and trained at various stages of his career at Machell Place, Sefton Lodge and Wroughton House, as mentioned elsewhere.

W. H. Manser trained at Cadland House, the yard named after the horse who dead-heated for The Derby of 1828. So many tall stories did Manser tell about his adventures with horses abroad, the wits of Newmarket said that he should have been called R. O. Manser. After having run away from home to be apprenticed to Dick Drewett at Lewes he later found his way to Russia, where he trained for the Tsar Alexander II. On leaving Russia he went to Egypt to train for Ismail Pasha for three years. Returning to England he settled down at Newmarket and bought Cadland House, where he trained many winners under both codes though none of particular importance. This amusing little man was 85 when he died in 1921.

Kremlin House was completed in 1874, and as its name suggests its builder was a Russian. He was Prince Dimitri Soltykoff, who came to England after the end of the Crimean War in 1856 and remained for the rest of his life. He had his horses with Charlie Blanton and later Tom Jennings senior, who won him the Gold Cup with Gold and the Cesarewitch with Sheen in 1890. Shortly afterwards he decided to have a private trainer in his own Kremlin stable. This yard had been built on a parcel of land called the Gladiateur Paddocks which the Prince had bought off the Somerville Lodge trainer Peter Price.

Tom Fordham was the first trainer at Kremlin, but he was soon succeeded by Charlie Waugh, a younger son of Jimmy Waugh. Spending the seasons of 1895 and 1896 at Kremlin, Charlie Waugh won the Prince the July Cup with Woolsthorpe. After Charlie Waugh, T. Hammon was at Kremlin and he was still there when Prince Soltykoff died in 1903.

Joe Enoch trained for the Marquess of Zetland at Zetland Lodge, now the Equine Research Centre and known as Balaton Lodge. Joe Enoch had been head lad to John Day at Danebury when the Marquess of Hastings's horses were trained there. He left Danebury in 1874.

George Ashby, who had been apprenticed to Mat Dawson, trained for the brewer, Mr Hamar Bass, in the tiny Bloomsbury Cottage yard at the bottom of Fitzroy Street. Ashby only had about a dozen horses each season and won the Goodwood Stakes with Carlton Grange in 1896.

There was already a yard on the site of the St Albans stable before it was built by Mat Dawson. He had wanted to call it Bestwood Paddocks as a compliment to the Duke of St Albans, whose country seat was Bestwood Park, but the little Duke said, "Name it after me, not my house". When old Mat went into semi-retirement he sold it to his favourite nephew John Dawson, son of John Dawson senior of Warren House. The younger John Dawson married Grace, a daughter of Jimmy Waugh, and began training in 1880. Until he moved to St Albans in 1891 he had his string in Queensberry Lodge. During the period of more than 40 years that John Dawson trained at St Albans until he retired in 1934, he won many minor events but his only notable success was with Proclamation in the Manchester November Handicap in 1899.

Tom Jennings junior took over Phantom House from his father in about 1882. He won The Oaks with Lord Hindlip's Limasol in 1897 and the same race with Mirska in 1912. The following season, the last full one before the First World War, he took the Goodwood Cup with Catmint. He did not train again after the war and died at the age of 76 in Torquay in 1932.

Increasing weight brought the riding career of Charlie Archer, younger brother of Fred, to an early end, so he was still a very young man when he began training for Lord Ellesmere at Ellesmere House. At the age of 23 he won the Manchester Cup with Wallenstein, the Stewards Cup with Lowland Chief and the Manchester November Handicap with Boswell in 1882. Even then, Charlie Archer was already a heavy gambler and won £30,000 over Wallenstein alone. He was only 63 when he died in 1922. Ellesmere House, where he trained, was almost opposite the Conservative Club on Exeter Road. It was demolished about 1960 and the site is now used as a car park.

The Falmouth Lodge yard, built by Fred Archer and now known as Pegasus House, became the private stable of Sir John Blundell Maple, whose fortune came from his furniture store in Tottenham Court Road. He had between 30 and 40 horses in training each season. Percy Peck had charge of the string in 1894 and 1895 and John Day in 1896, after which Willie Waugh took over. He won The 1,000 Guineas with Nun Nicer and was still at Falmouth Lodge when Sir Blundell Maple died in 1903.

Bob Sherwood was at Exeter House when he trained St Gatien who dead-heated with Harvester in The Derby of 1884. His father Ralph had trained at Epsom, where Bob was born in 1835, and saddled Amato to win The Derby in 1838. In his brief career as a jockey Bob Sherwood won The Derby on Wild Dayrell in 1855.

After training for the English colony in Hong Kong, Bob Sherwood came to Exeter House in 1880. As well as dead-heating for The Derby, St Gatien won the Cesarewitch in 1884 and his trainer completed the autumn double by landing the Cambridgeshire with Florence.

On leaving Exeter House for the stable he named after St Gatien, Bob Sherwood had Lord Randolph Churchill, father of Sir Winston, amongst his owners. For Lord Randolph, who forsook politics for racing in 1887, he won The Oaks of 1889 with L'Abbesse de Jouarre, known to the bookmakers as 'Abscess on the Jaw'. Few men dressed as carelessly as Lord Randolph. Once after a race he dashed off the stands to ask Fred Rickaby how his runner had shaped. "What the hell is that to do with you?" retorted the jockey, having no idea that he was addressing the owner. Lord Randolph was furious and said Rickaby was never to ride for him again. Sir Frederick Johnstone tried to calm matters down by pointing out "with that old hat of yours, he took you for a tout", and in the end Rickaby was reinstated.

While Bob Sherwood was supervising work on Monday, 9 October 1894, he had an apoplectic fit. Four days later he died, a "stern keeper of stable secrets" as one obituarist recalled him. The St Gatien stable was taken over by his son, Robert Louis Vodoz Sherwood, then aged 34.

For a time Bob Sherwood senior had trained for the eccentric Colonel North. Inevitably he failed to give satisfaction and the 'Jolly Colonel' sent his horses to be trained privately by Charlie Morton at Chetwynd House.

John Thomas North was a self-made businessman, who had amassed millions out of nitrates in Chile without needing a great deal of acumen or ability but simply pushing himself forward. His colonelcy was a purely honorary one in an obscure unit called the Tower Hamlet Volunteers, which he equipped at his own expense. An ostentatious extrovert, and not an unlikeable one, he imagined that large sums necessarily bought good horses.

One of the Colonel's favourite tricks was to descend upon Newmarket with a host of friends, and, regardless of the time of day, order his trainer to have all the horses brought out on to the Heath so that he could stage private races for the amusement of his entourage when the poor animals should have been resting in their boxes. Colonel North died of a heart attack while attending a board meeting in London in May 1896.

After the departure of Bob Sherwood senior, young John Watson moved into the Exeter House yard to train a few horses for the Rothschild family, whose main interests remained at Palace House. The third son of the James Watson, who had had the Belle Isle stable at Richmond in Yorkshire, he had been born in 1870.

The feature of Exeter House is the covered ride, which is the oldest in the country. Putting this to the best possible use when frost and snow made the Heath unusable in February and March, John Watson soon acquired a reputation for the success of his early two-year-olds. Six times in seven seasons he won the Brocklesby Stakes at Lincoln's opening meeting — with Jest in 1896, Gay Lothair in 1897, Amurath in 1898, Hulcot in 1899, Fair Castle in 1901 and Skyscraper in 1902.

Alfred Brettle Sadler (not to be confused with his son, Alfred Day Sadler) trained at Graham Place, which was built in 1860. Born in

John Dawson the younger (1859-1942) trained at St Albans, built by his uncle Mat Dawson as an overspill yard. The House is now flats.

1848, he was the grandson of Isaac Sadler, who owned the 1833 Derby winner, Dangerous. After being at Rottingdean he moved to Stockbridge and then to Newmarket to take over Stockbridge House, to which he probably gave that name. In 1886 he was private trainer to Lord Durham, but by 1894 he was at Graham Place with Mr R. H. Combe as his principal patron. In 1901 he returned to Stockbridge House, where he remained until he retired in 1922. Seven years later he died of bronchitis at the age of 81.

After Mat Dawson gave up training all but his own horses in 1895, his head lad, Billy Walters junior, took over Lord Rosebery's horses which were installed in that owner's private stable at Primrose Cottage. The yard, in which W. Mumford had trained immediately previously, already bore the family name of the Earls of Rosebery. In 1897 Walters won The 1,000 Guineas with Chelandry, and the following season, his last at Primrose Cottage, the Eclipse Stakes with Velasquez.

After Lord Rosebery's horses had gone to Lord Durham's trainer, Percy Peck, at Exning, Billy Walters became a public trainer. By 1905 he was at Albert House, here he remained until the outbreak of the Second World War. The best horse that he had in those 34 years was Sir Richard Garton's Sir Cosmo, who won the July Cup in 1930.

The brothers Charles and George Bloss, who trained for Captain Machell in the sixties, came from an old Newmarket racing family. Another George Bloss, besides the one already mentioned, trained for Lord Westmoreland and later the Marquess of Hartington. In 1885 he won the Wokingham Stakes with Corunna and died of a protracted illness in the September of that year.

After having trained for Captain Machell and Lord Rosebery, Joe Cannon took over the tenancy of Lordship Farm from Dick Marsh in 1892. The son of a Windsor horse dealer, he was the brother of one champion jockey in Tom Cannon, the uncle of a second in Mornington Cannon and the great-great-uncle of a third in Lester Piggott. His lucky race while he was at Lordship was the Manchester November Handicap, which he won with Lexicon in 1900, The Valet in 1910, Dalmatian in 1913 and Planet in 1917. On retiring in 1919 he handed over the stable to his son, J. H. S. 'Boxer' Cannon. Joe Cannon was 84 when he died in 1933.

In 1893 the 16th Earl of Derby made the momentous decision to renew his family's association with The Turf. As his trainer he appointed the Hon George Lambton, a younger brother of the Earl of Durham. Lambton, who was then 33 years of age, still had his back in plaster after the final fall in his career as an amateur steeplechase jockey. An absolutely fearless rider over fences, whether on the racecourse or in the hunting field, George Lambton had held his own with the best of the professional jockeys. Always immaculately dressed, he was a man of great charm in whom a deep understanding of horses was almost inbred. While riding a horse called Hollington at Sandown Park in February 1892 he had had the final fall that left him with inflammation of the spine. Hollington took the paygate fence by the roots and gave Lambton a fall, the full impact of which was borne by his back. As a result he was almost a cripple for several years.

Soon afterwards he took what in those days was the extraordinary step of setting up as a trainer. At that time men of his social standing bred racehorses, owned them and rode them as amateurs, and they most certainly bet on them, but they did not train them. It must be remembered that less than a century previously trainers had been hardly more than grooms promoted to the positions of upper servants. By late Victorian times there was still a barrier of class consciousness between the aristocratic owners and their trainers. It could be argued that the opening of George Lambton's stable marked the end of the period in which the training of racehorses had graduated from a trade to a highly skilled profession.

At first George Lambton had a yard near St Mary's Square, where he trained Hettie Sorrel, an ancestress of Alycidon in tail female line. She started by being beaten in a seller, but was soon winning better races for Mr Reginald Brett, who eventually sold her to Lord Stanley.

On being appointed to train for Lord Derby, Lambton moved into Bedford Lodge, while the beautiful Stanley House stable was being built. Lord Derby had bought the Sefton Stud from the Duchess of Montrose, and it was on that property that the Stanley House training establishment and its private gallops were laid out.

While at Bedford Lodge, George Lambton trained his first classic winner for Lord Derby. This was Canterbury Pilgrim, who took The Oaks of 1896. As a two-year-old she had revealed little discernible promise, but even after she had finished unplaced in the Champagne Stakes at Doncaster that wonderful judge, Bob Peck, had consoled Lambton with the thought that she would probably win the Oaks. The triumph of Canterbury Pilgrim was the raising of the curtain on the great days that lay ahead of Stanley House and George Lambton in the coming 35 years.

21 The Newmarket of King Edward VII

King Edward loved Newmarket and Newmarket loved the King. The town lay within easy reach of Sandringham, the mansion he had purchased as his private home and the place in which he passed many of the happiest days of his life. In his mind Newmarket was associated with his beloved Sandringham, and by the same token totally dissociated from the stuffiness of his mother's court and the gloominess of her official residences.

Not only did he have his horses trained at Newmarket, both while Prince of Wales and then as King, but many of his friends had houses there and that also increased the pleasure he derived from his visits to the town. To begin with he used to enjoy the society of the Duke of Hamilton and others in the nineties. Later financiers such as Sir Ernest Cassel and Mr Leopold de Rothschild, both of whom were numbered amongst his close personal friends, used to entertain him at their Newmarket houses.

But the rich and the aristocratic were not the only ones who held the King in great affection. The man in Newmarket High Street adored this royal and flamboyant personage. Such was his popularity that huge crowds of the townspeople used to wait at the foot of the long flight of steps that led up to the front door of Palace House in the hope of a glimpse of the King as he arrived to dine with Mr Leopold de Rothschild.

People always knew when the King was due at Palace House as it was noticed that extra police would be stationed in its vicinity. As the loyal attentions of the crowd tended to interfere with the King's privacy, as well as to make Palace Street almost impassable to traffic, it was decided to take steps to prevent these assemblies. In the end a resourceful superintendent of police struck on the idea of stationing his men around the Rothschild house when a royal visit was not in the offing as well as when it was. After a series of disappointments at finding that the appearance of the constables did not necessarily presage the arrival of the King, the Newmarket people gave up surrounding the house whenever they saw policemen near it.

Lack of foresight and other factors made Queen Victoria stubbornly refuse to allow her eldest son, Albert Edward, Prince of Wales, to employ his not inconsiderable talents in the public service. As a result he was obliged to lead a life devoted almost entirely to pleasure. In these circumstances it was almost natural that the future King Edward VII should graduate to racing.

As likely as not he acquired his first taste for the sport while he was a student at Oxford, where he formed lasting friendships with Sir Fred-

King Edward VII on a hack

erick Johnstone and Henry Chaplin. Both these rich young men were soon to blossom forth as leading owners. Henry Chaplin, as has been said earlier, had his horses under Captain Machell's management, while Sir Frederick had horses with William Day at Woodyates and later with John Porter at Kingsclere in Berkshire.

Many things did not amuse Queen Victoria. Racing was one of them. Doubtless she did what she could to prevent the Prince from embarking upon ownership. All the same he registered his colours in 1875 but it was not until two years later that he had his first runners. To begin with, his interests were confined to having a few jumpers with Jack Jones at Epsom. No doubt it was largely through the influence of Sir Frederick Johnstone that he decided to widen his interests and have horses with John Porter in 1886.

During the seven seasons that John Porter trained the Prince's horses they obtained no significant success and by the end of that period they had won no more than 18 races. Yet though he accomplished little on the course on the Prince's behalf, the Kingsclere trainer laid the foundation of much of the success that the royal string was to enjoy in the following decade by the purchase of Perdita II as a broodmare for £900 in 1886. The value of Perdita II, who had won the Ayr Gold Cup after beginning her career in sellers, was not immediately appreciated by all concerned. Handing over the cheque for her, Sir Dighton Probyn admonished Porter, "You will ruin the Prince if you go on buying these thoroughbreds".

On becoming the property of the Prince, Perdita II was sent to his Sandringham estate, where he was building up his stud. In charge of this establishment was Edmund Walker, who had held a similar post at Fred Archer's stud at Falmouth House, Newmarket.

The ostensible reason for the Prince's horses leaving Kingsclere was that the stable was too far from their owner's Sandringham home, whereas Newmarket was eminently convenient. However, the real cause of their departure was probably more concerned with temperaments than geographical locations, for the Prince's racing manager, Lord Marcus Beresford and John Porter often failed to see eye to eye. In many ways this was hardly surprising. Lord Marcus was a charming man, who always seemed able to find the funny side to most things. By contrast John Porter was a serious-minded trainer, completely dedicated to his profession and endowed with very little sense of humour.

As a young man Lord Marcus was a competent rider over the sticks in soldiers' races — he was then in the 7th Hussars — and other events run under National Hunt rules. In 1875 he won the Grand Military 'chase on Chilblain at Croydon and the following year the National Hunt 'chase on Burford at Bogside.

At first Lord Marcus had his horses trained by Fothergill Rowlands, the legendary 'Fog' Rowlands, at Pitt Place, Epsom, but in 1876 he transferred them to Jack Jones, who had a stable in the same town. As often as not, Lord Marcus rode his own runners or gave the mount to his trainer, but on some occasions they were ridden by a young professional called Dick Marsh, who also trained a few jumpers belonging to Mr Hector Baltazzi at Banstead Manor near Epsom.

Born in 1851, Dick Marsh was the son of a hop farmer of Smeeth in Kent. While he was still at Folkestone Grammar School he rode as much work as he could on 'chasers trained by Ward at Sandgate. He was still at school in 1866 when, at the now defunct Dover meeting he rode his first winner on Manrico, who had been successful in the Lincolnshire three years previously. Soon afterwards Marsh joined Captain Machell's stable without ever becoming formally apprenticed. While at Bedford Cottage he rode the Derby winner Hermit in some of his work, and when difficulties in finding a jockey to ride him at Epsom began to arise, the idea of giving the mount to Marsh was entertained briefly.

On becoming too heavy for the flat, Dick Marsh graduated to riding over hurdles and fences with considerable success. During one of his occasional visits to the continent he won a race on Molly Bawn in Paris for the Duke of Hamilton, who was then living in France. Afterwards the Duke promised the rider that when he returned to England Marsh should become his trainer. Thus it was that Dick Marsh was established with the Duke's horses at Lordship Farm in 1876, the Duke being in residence at Lower Hare Park a few miles away.

The best races that Dick Marsh won for the Duke of Hamilton were The St Leger of 1883 with Ossian and The 1,000 Guineas with Miss Jummy three years later.

In 1890 Percy Heaton, who was Lord Ellesmere's land agent, conceived the idea of converting his employer's Egerton House Stud into the most modern training establishment in the country, if not in the world. As a result of the highly successfull stallion, Hampton, having stood there for many years, the Ellesmere estate was richer to the tune of some £50,000. It was this sum that was to be used to finance a massive modernisation programme.

Dick Marsh (1851-1933) trained for King Edward VII and King George V at Egerton House

Knowing that Dick Marsh's lease of Lordship had nearly expired, Percy Heaton approached him to see whether he would be interested in tenanting the sort of property into which they wanted to transform Egerton. Like almost every other man who has ever reached the top of any profession, Marsh thought big, and regardless of the cost that would be involved he leapt at the idea of having the use of a stable with all the amenities that Heaton had in mind for the new Egerton House.

The building of the Egerton House stable took two and a half years. In charge of its construction, as clerk of the works, was Walter Fenn, whose son Harold was a popular figure in the town. By the time it was all finished there were extensive ranges of boxes and other buildings that offered every possible facility required in a training stable, all this being set in an estate of 120 acres. Around the perimeter Marsh constructed a special moss litter gallop extending to a mile and a quarter on which he could work his horses without any fear of their breaking down or contracting sore shins, no matter how firm the going might be on other parts of the Heath. The idea of laying down a moss litter gallop came to Dick Marsh while he was hunting with the Duc d'Aumale's boarhounds in the forest of Chantilly. Noticing the perfect going afforded by the rides through the forest, he enquired how the effect had been achieved and noted the answer for future use.

To pay the rent and cover the other costs of running this equine palace Dick Marsh estimated that he had to earn £13,000 a year before he made a penny piece for himself. On 28 November 1892 he moved in with 54 horses in his charge. Of these, nine belonged to the Duke of Hamilton, 21 to the Duke of Devonshire, six to Lord Hindlip, nine to Noel Fenwick, three to Broderick Cloete, one to Lord Marcus Beresford, and five to himself.

Hardly were his horses installed in the brand new boxes at Egerton House than he received a call to meet Lord Marcus at Challis's Hotel in London. There Lord Marcus offered him the chance to train for the Prince of Wales. With characteristic candour that left him oblivious of the honour done him, Dick Marsh replied that he would have to consult the Duke of Hamilton. A more pompous courtier than Lord Marcus would have doubtless been flabbergasted by a reply that put the convenience of the Duke before that of the Prince, but the intensely human Lord Marcus met it with a laugh and the casual remark, "In the old days you would have had your head cut off for hesitating about such a thing".

This gentle chiding did not have the effect of preventing Dick Marsh from consulting his Duke, who expostulated, "For heaven's sake, wire off your grateful acceptance at once. You ought not to have said what you did".

Eventually the method of these negotiations came to the ears of the Prince, who said to his trainer, "I heard that you had to seek the Duke of Hamilton's permission before you accepted my horses". Poor Dick Marsh, who had done no more than try to do his duty to a generous employer of long standing, was too embarrassed for words, but the Prince put him at his ease by telling him, "You were quite right,

Marsh, in doing what you did. I am glad you had that respect for a good master".

In the matter of whether or not his trainer should accept the Prince's horses, the Duke of Hamilton had shown a more deferential attitude to the heir to the throne than was typical of him. A massive heavyweight of a man with flaming red hair in his younger days, he had no doubts about his own social status though he was far from certain about its being inferior to that of royalty. He must have constantly reminded himself that he was not only Duke of Hamilton in the peerage of Scotland and a descendant of King Robert III of that country, but he was Duke of Brandon in England, Duke of Chastellerault in France and, through the right of his mother, hereditary Prince of Baden, while his sister was married to the Prince of Monaco, so one way or another he ran the whole gamut of the *Almanac de Gotha*.

One afternoon he arranged to meet the Prince at Egerton House at five o'clock in order to go round evening stables. As usual the Prince was punctual to the minute, but to the intense distress of Dick Marsh there was no sign of the Duke. After some while the Prince went out on to the lawn to chat with other members of the party whilst Marsh kept anxious watch at the window for the arrival of the Duke. At half past five the Duke of Hamilton drove up in a dog cart and when the harassed Marsh reminded him that the Prince of Wales had been waiting for him for the past half hour he casually remarked that he had dropped in at the sales and bought a yearling. Worse still, he announced that he simply must have a whisky and soda, so, while the heir to the British Empire cooled his heels for a few more minutes, the Duke of Hamilton sat down to a drink.

The Duke's colours were cerise with French grey sleeves and cap, and his horses wore cerise rugs with grey borders. These rugs continued to be used after his death at the early age of 50 in 1895 and were still at Egerton House when Willie Jarvis took over the stable from Dick Marsh in 1924.

Amongst the eight horses that the Prince of Wales sent to Egerton House on New Year's Day 1893 was a bay colt by St Simon out of Perdita II, the mare that John Porter had bought for him. This colt was called Florizel II. During his two-year-old days Florizel II showed little or no ability, certainly not enough to win a race, and as none of the other seven royal horses were much better, Dick Marsh was sadly disappointed in them by the end of 1893. All that he won for the Prince that year were two small races worth £372 the pair.

The following season Florizel II revealed a great deal more than average improvement, so much so that he won the St James's Palace Stakes at Royal Ascot. By the following season, when he was a four-year-old in 1895, he had made up into a really good second-class stayer. That year his successes included the Manchester Cup, the Gold Vase, the Goodwood Cup and the Jockey Club Cup.

While the Prince's colours were coming to the forefront for the first time through the success of Florizel II in those long-distance races, that horse's two-year-old full brother Persimmon was beginning to show Dick Marsh signs of his being something out of the ordinary. When taken to the racecourse for the first time Persimmon readily substantiated the promise that he had shown in his gallops and trials by winning the Coventry Stakes at Royal Ascot, and when he reappeared at Goodwood he ran out a convincing winner of the Richmond Stakes.

During the early autumn Persimmon fell a victim to the cough but recovered so fast that about a fortnight before the Middle Park Plate was due to be run he was beginning to show his form again. In these circumstances, Lord Marcus Beresford became enthusiastic about the idea of running the colt in the Middle Park. The more cautious and professionally minded Marsh was anything but keen about the project, believing that a run before Persimmon had completely recovered from the cough could put the following year's Derby in jeopardy. Events were to prove Marsh was right although, fortunately, his worst fears were not be be realised in the long run. Starting 2-1 favourite for the Middle Park, Persimmon finished third to Mr Leopold de Rothschild's St Frusquin, trained by Alf Hayhoe at Palace House, and Omladina, beaten half a length and five lengths.

Now Persimmon was one of those horses who grow a coat like a teddy bear in the winter. Consequently he took much longer to come to himself in the spring than might have been the case and although he had made excellent physical progress over the close season, he was distinctly backward in the early part of his three-year-old days. By the beginning of April the prospects of beating St Frusquin, who was already in good work, seemed bleak. Dick Marsh and Lord Marcus gave the Prince the only advice they could. That was to miss the Guineas and to concentrate on the winning of The Derby. To this the Prince agreed.

As was generally expected, St Frusquin won The 2,000 Guineas and he then became a raging hot favourite for The Derby. Meanwhile, Persimmon started to come on in his work, and it was not long before Dick Marsh was able to ask Lord Marcus to come to Newmarket to watch him do a serious gallop.

The way Persimmon went in that gallop he could not have won a decent handicap. A moderate animal called Safety Pin made the pace Across the Flat on Racecourse Side. As they came to the Bushes Marsh expected Persimmon to go on, but the colt could not quicken, and kept on at the same pace to finish three lengths behind Safety Pin. "A nice Derby horse!" was the laconic comment of Lord Marcus.

Marsh was mystified, the more so as Persimmon continued to eat everything with which he worked in the following week just as he had done in his spins before that disastrous gallop. All the trainer could do was to have another gallop to prove the first one wrong. This took place on the private work ground at Egerton House and was watched by the Prince of Wales, the Duke and Duchess of York (later King George V and Queen Mary), other members of the royal family and Lord Marcus. The idea was that Persimmon was to give 21 lb to a useful sort of three-year-old called Balsamo and still more to Safety Pin and Courtier, who were to make the pace. A special stand was erected from which the Prince and his children could watch the work. This time Persimmon did all that was asked of him and beat Balsamo by three lengths without being extended. The form looked good enough to beat St Frusquin at Epsom.

Persimmon had already given Marsh one shock by the way in which he went in that gallop on the Racecourse Side and had another in store for his trainer. When they came to put him on the horse train at Dullingham Station the colt flatly refused to enter his box. Two of the three horse specials had already gone, and with only a quarter of an hour to go before the last was due to pull out, Persimmon remained intransigent. Eventually it took a dozen men to force him into the box, where the first thing he did was to walk over to his feed as if nothing had happened.

As Persimmon had not had an outing as a three-year-old he was nothing like as heavily backed as St Frusquin, who remained strong favourite. At starting St Frusquin was 13-8 on with Persimmon second in the market at 5-1. As St Frusquin led round Tattenham corner many of his backers were already counting their money, but Jack Watts on Persimmon still had a lot in hand. Once into the straight Persimmon began his run only to check in it before he had reached the leader. With the coolness of the great jockey he was, Jack Watts got him balanced again and with just 100 yards to go he asked his mount for the final, vital effort. Persimmon responded magnificently to the perfect handling of his rider and at the post he was a neck to the good of St Frusquin.

Because he had spent so long at the start, Dick Marsh, stuck in part of the huge crowd, never saw the colt win. Nor did he even know that he had won until he met Morny Cannon returning on one of the unplaced runners. Fighting his way back to the unsaddling enclosure he found even the heaviest backers of St Frusquin cheering the royal colours at the tops of their voices. The only person who seemed to derive no pleasure whatever from the situation was Jack Watts, surely the most undemonstrative man ever to have put a leg over a horse. "Well done, Jack," yelled Marsh as he walked up to his winner. Still the rider registered no emotion so Marsh slapped him on the thigh exclaiming, "Do you know you have just won The Derby for the Prince of Wales?" At last the ghost of a smile passed over Jack Watt's usually impassive face.

Although the last thing he intended to do was to show it, Jack Watts was as pleased and as proud of being associated with the Prince of Wales's Derby winner as Dick Marsh or anybody else. Moreover, in his case the success came as a reward for considerable personal sacrifice. By that stage of his career he was having such trouble with his weight that he even had to waste to do nine stone. The previous winter he had seriously considered giving up riding and it was largely because of the cajoling and persuasion of Dick Marsh, and regard for the high promise of Persimmon, that he decided to persevere instead of setting up as a trainer.

Jack Watts I (1861-1902), won the Derby on the Prince of Wales's Persimmon in 1896 and on three other occasions

Born on 9 May 1861, Jack Watts was apprenticed to Tom Cannon at Danebury and rode his first winner on Aristocrat who dead-heated with Sugar Cane at Stockbridge in 1876. About two or three years later he fell out with Tom Cannon. One day he approached Dick Marsh, who did not know him, at Alexandra Park and asked for a job at Lordship Farm. Marsh told him he could have one if he wanted to work hard and do his horses. Within a year Marsh had become so impressed by his horsemanship that he persuaded the Duke of Hamilton to give him a retainer.

The remainder of Persimmon's career can be summarised briefly. After winning The Derby he failed by half a length to give St Frusquin 3 lb in the Princess of Wales Stakes at Newmarket which meant that Derby form worked out to an ounce. Two months later Persimmon accounted for a weak field in The St Leger. Kept in training as a four-year-old, he won the Gold Cup over two and a half miles before proving his versatility by reverting to half that distance in the Eclipse Stakes and winning that too.

Retired to stud, Persimmon became as great a success in that sphere as he had on the racecourse. By far the greatest of his offspring was his daughter, Sceptre, who survived the amateurish training of her owner, the professional gambler Bob Siever to win four classics, and he also got the St Leger winners Your Majesty and Prince Palatine. From Prince Palatine the Derby winners Arctic Prince and Charlottown descend in tail male line.

In 1897 Britain celebrated the 60th anniversary of the accession of Queen Victoria, and when his priceless mare Perdita II bred a third colt to St Simon, the Prince of Wales named him Diamond Jubilee. Everything conspired to ensure that this colt was petted and cosseted from the day of his birth. Not only was he a full brother to Persimmon and Florizel II, and the embodiment of all the hopes of another royal Derby winner, but as he grew up it was seen that his conformation was quite flawless.

When this pampered product of the royal stud arrived at Egerton he proved a real handful to ride but nothing worse. It was only when he went to Royal Ascot to make his racecourse debut in the Coventry Stakes that the defects in his temperament became fully apparent. At the start he kicked and bucked and plunged and reared, leaving those who had made him 6-5 favourite certain that they had lost their money even before the field was under way. When he reappeared in the July Stakes at Newmarket, the familiar surroundings of the Heath made Diamond Jubilee no more tractable. If anything he behaved worse than he had done at Ascot. To begin with, he unseated Jack Watts and ran loose for some time. When he was eventually caught and the jockey reinstated, Diamond Jubilee made it quite plain he was not going to race that day and finished last of six to Captain Kettle.

The taming of Diamond Jubilee left Dick Marsh with a problem that seemed insoluble at first. Friends of the Prince, and other people whose business it was not, advised that all the colt needed was a good thrashing to teach him his manners, but Marsh knew far too much

Persimmon was trained by Dick Marsh to win the Derby for the Prince of Wales in 1896

about thoroughbreds to consider this silly suggestion for a minute. He was fully aware that if he adopted that course of action he would more than likely break the horse's spirit and make him as useless for racing as he appeared to be already.

One thing that did seem apparent was that Diamond Jubilee loathed the sight of Jack Watts, who reciprocated the sentiment in full, so it was decided to let Morny Cannon try to strike up a partnership with the colt. At first it looked as though his new rider would be able to make him settle down and in the autumn it was with Cannon up that he obtained the first success in the Boscawen Stakes at Newmarket.

In 1900 Jack Watts finally retired from riding and Dick Marsh took a second claim on Morny Cannon, who was expected to have the mount on Diamond Jubilee in the classics. Jack Watts was having greater trouble than ever with his weight during the last few seasons that he was riding and excessive wasting must have done much to undermine his health. As a result his training career was a sadly short one. On Saturday, 19 July 1902, he was taken ill at Sandown Park. So serious was his condition that it was impossible to move him from Esher and on 29 July one of the greatest of all horsemen in the history of British racing died.

Jack Watts was twice married, firstly in 1885 to Miss Annie Lancaster and secondly to Miss L. A. Hammond, daughter of Francis Hammond of Portland House, Newmarket. One of his sons was John Evelyn Watts, who trained Call Boy to win The Derby in 1927. John Evelyn Watts's son was Jack Watts who trained at Machell Place until his retirement in 1973, after being elsewhere earlier in his career.

The first Jack Watts invested a sizeable proportion of his earnings in acquiring or building housing in Newmarket. If you look at those two lodges situated on Hamilton Road on the top of the Racecourse Side of the Heath, for instance, you will see that the left-hand one bears the initials 'J.W.' and that on the right the date 1896. This is one example of his building. On his death at the early age of 41 it was found he was intestate. As the law then stood his eldest son John Evelyn Watts became entitled to all the bricks and mortar owned by his father, while the large amount of cash left by a man who had been at the very top of his profession was shared amongst the younger sons, of whom Harry rode successfully for a while after being apprenticed to Jack Hallick at Lambourn.

Reverting to the story of Diamond Jubilee, by the spring of 1900 his early promise of willingness to co-operate with Morny Cannon had come to vanishing point. In fact he seemed to have brought himself to hate the new stable jockey as much as he had his predecessor. On the other hand, he generally proved himself quite amenable to the handling of Bertie Jones, the 19-year-old lad who rode him in his routine work.

A short time before The 2,000 Guineas, Morny Cannon came to Newmarket to ride Diamond Jubilee in a gallop. After the work was over he jumped off to lead the colt the rest of the way home, whereupon Diamond Jubilee seized him in his teeth and rolled him on to the ground intent on savaging, if not even killing, him. Shortly afterwards Morny Cannon ventured the opinion that it might be possible to find a rider who could hit it off with the horse better than he could.

This left Dick Marsh in a dreadful dilemma. With The Guineas only days away, most of the top jockeys were booked. Even if one could have been found at that late hour the chances of his being able to control Diamond Jubilee were far from good.

As Dick Marsh mulled the matter over in his mind he must have regretted that the only rider for whom Diamond Jubilee would do anything was a young lad with very little experience of riding in public. As he considered that fact he began to see the answer to the problem. On the face of it it seemed a fantastic idea to put up such a rider against the likes of Morny Cannon, Sammy Loates, Fred Rickaby and the rest in a classic, but then Diamond Jubilee was a law unto himself. Both the Prince of Wales and Lord Marcus Beresford saw the soundness of the trainer's reasoning and the little stable lad was told that he was to replace the champion jockey on the Prince's horse.

Herbert Jones was the son of Jack Jones, who had trained jumpers for the Prince and Lord Marcus at Epsom more than 20 years before the world heard of Diamond Jubilee. He began his career with Tom Jennings junior at Phantom Cottage and was still only ten when his indentures were transferred to Dick Marsh. After that he had to wait five years until he rode his first winner on Mr Somerville Tattersall's Good News at the Newmarket Craven Meeting in 1896. Although he could ride, and ride well, there were few opportunities for young Bertie Jones in a stable that retained Jack Watts with Otto Madden riding the lightweights. When Diamond Jubilee gave him the break he badly needed he took the chance with both hands and won not only The 2,000 Guineas, but The Derby and The St Leger as well on that most unreliable of horses.

To the disappointment of very many people besides those intimately concerned, the royal stable entered upon a lean patch after King Edward came to the throne in 1901. The occasions when the crowd could give vent to their favourite cry of "Good old Teddy" became fewer for a time. Dick Marsh must have been very depressed at various periods in the first ten years of the new century, little knowing that the decade was to end with his bringing about the most glittering of all royal triumphs.

Alf Hayhoe, who had taken over the Palace House stable on the death of his father in 1881, was still training the Rothschild horses there when the new reign began. Five years earlier he had won The 2,000 Guineas with St Frusquin and then seen the colt beaten into second place by Persimmon in The Derby. In 1904 he and Mr Leopold de Rothschild received compensation for St Frusquin's defeat in The Derby when that horse's son St Amant won them the race by making all the running to beat John O'Gaunt by three lengths.

Although The Derby has rarely been run in worse weather than it was that year, and everybody was soaked to the skin, St Amant received a particularly enthusiastic reception. There were few owners more popular with the general public than Leopold de Rothschild. Everyone knew they would get a good run for their money from his horses, which he raced on the highest lines, and the generosity with which he contributed to charity from his winnings on The Turf was widely appreciated. This sporting owner died in 1917 when the world that he had known and loved was crumbling about him in the horror of the First World War.

At the end of the season of 1905 Alf Hayhoe left Palace House to live in retirement for another quarter of a century, until he died at the age of 78 at Newmarket in 1930. His daughter Nellie married the Meynell House trainer, Tom Waugh.

Alf Hayhoe's successor at Palace House was John Watson, who had been training some of the other Rothschild horses at Exeter House. The other important owner for whom John Watson trained at Palace House was Leopold de Rothschild's friend Mr Augustus Belmont, a New York banker. The son of a financier and diplomat, he had begun his own career in the Frankfurt branch of the Rothschild banking empire and maintained a close business connection with the family thereafter. Important races that John Watson won for Augustus Belmont included The 2,000 Guineas of 1908 with Norman III and The St Leger with Tracery in 1912. Augustus Belmont died at the age of 72 in 1924 and John Watson ten years later in 1934 when he was still training at Palace House.

The other financier to enjoy the friendship of King Edward was Sir Ernest Cassel. He had been born the son of a small banker at Cologne in 1852. On coming to England he started work as a clerk in Liverpool at £2 a week. In due course he proved himself a financial wizard with a gift for seeing opportunities for making money to which his rivals were completely blind, and his career prospered when his ability came to the notice of Baron Hirsch who entrusted him with a number of complicated assignments. By the time he registered his racing colours in 1895 Ernest Cassel controlled business assets worth several million pounds.

At the turn of the century Cassel's horses were trained at Lowther House, which was soon to be demolished to provide the site of the present King Edward VII Memorial Hall. Evidence that a stable once stood on the spot is still visible. On the wall along the western side of the gardens behind the hall are to be seen the rings to which the horses were tethered by rack-chains when it was the inside wall of a range of boxes in the Lowther House yard. Training for Sir Ernest Cassel in that stable was F. W. Day, father of the former Terrace House trainer, Reg Day and grandfather of the eminent Newmarket veterinary surgeon Fred Day, now retired.

'Bushranger' Day, as his nickname suggests, had trained for a time in Australia. On returning to this country he practised as a veterinary surgeon in his native Cheltenham and later followed the same profession at Newmarket. Turning to training again, he won the Cambridgeshire with the Australian-bred Georgic as well as The Oaks with Airs and Graces in 1898. The most notable success that he obtained during the time he trained for Sir Ernest at Lowther House was with a horse called Handicapper in The 2,000 Guineas of 1901.

By 1903 Sir Ernest Cassel had removed his string to Moulton Paddocks, where he also founded a stud, with George Lambton's brother Francis as his trainer. Two years later the stable was taken over by Bill Leader, brother of the Wroughton House trainer, Tom Leader senior, Francis Lambton continuing his association with it as manager.

Although Sir Ernest Cassel spent huge sums on his horses and the mares for his stud, and equipped his stables lavishly, such success as he did obtain was by no means commensurate with his expenditure. Indeed it is ironical that Handicapper, his only classic winner, cost a mere £300, a paltry sum for a man of his means even in those days. Sir Ernest died in 1921, when 34-year-old Cecil Boyd-Rochfort was acting as his racing manager at Moulton Paddocks.

Among the men who came to the fore at Newmarket during the first decade of the present century was Felix Leach. Right to the end of his life the highly polished leggings and the curly-brimmed bowler that usually contributed to his quite immaculate turn-out made him everybody's idea of what the typical Edwardian looked like.

Like so many of the leading figures at Newmarket during the reigns of Queen Victoria and her son, Felix Leach came from the north, having been born at Wigan in 1867. Some years later his elder brother Ted went to Newmarket to practise as a veterinary surgeon. It was while he was spending a holiday with his brother in 1884 that Felix Leach made the acquaintance of Mat Dawson as he was watching the strings work on the Heath one morning. On discovering the boy's love of horses Mat asked, "Would you like to come to live with me?" Felix explained that he was only on a holiday and he very much doubted whether his parents would entertain the idea. "Never mind", said Mat, "You go back and tell your brother that you are going to live with me".

Quite bewildered by the turn of the conversation, Felix replied, "I don't know your name, sir", to which the old man retorted, "Tell your brother that you are not going home tomorrow, but you are going to live with Mr Mathew Dawson at Heath House".

In due course Felix Leach's father and mother became reconciled to the fact that he had set his heart on spending his life with horses and agreed to his joining Mat Dawson's stable, but for fear of a parental change of mind he was never indentured. In the autumn of the year after their first meeting Mat left Heath House for semi-retirement at Melton House, Exning. For a couple of years Felix remained at Heath House under Mat's nephew and successor, George Dawson, and then he rejoined Mat in the capacity of head lad at Melton House. During the closing years of his life, Mat only had a handful of horses so Felix Leach eventually left him to take over what was then the much more responsible position of head lad to Richard Marsh at Egerton House. The several good horses of whom he gained experience during his time at Egerton included the 1896 Derby winner, Persimmon.

Leaving Egerton House just after the turn of the century, Felix Leach began training with a string of 18 horses at Graham Place in 1903. One of the most notable of his early successes was with Magic who beat the 20-1 on chance Bayardo by a neck in a sensational three-horse race for the Goodwood Cup in 1910. The following year he returned to Goodwood to land the Stewards Cup with Sir Thomas Dewar's Braxted, who was ridden by the stable apprentice, Fred Winter.

Just after the end of the First World War Felix Leach had the best horse ever to come into his stable. This was Orpheus, who won the Champion Stakes of 1920 after having finished third in The Derby earlier in the year. A few years later he had a top-class handicap sprinter in Nothing Venture, who began his career by winning the Brocklesby Stakes at Lincoln in 1925. His subsequent successes included the Wokingham Stakes in 1927 and the Ayr Gold Cup the following season.

As well as training, Felix Leach bred horses at the Meddler Stud, where he stood the stallion Flag of Truce after having bought that horse for 3,000 guineas in 1938.

Outside racing Felix Leach's principal interests lay in the breeding of game fowl and wire-haired fox terriers. The most notable dog with whom he was ever associated was Champion Newmarket Cackler, who was successful both in the show ring and at stud.

As became a man who had been closely associated with the Prince of Wales's great horse, Persimmon, Felix Walmough Leach remained an Edwardian dandy until he died at the age of 84 on 30 August 1952. His three sons were Felix Leach junior, John Edward 'Jack' Leach, and Henry Beresford 'Chubb' Leach. The younger Felix died at the early age of 31 in 1930 shortly after he had begun training. During the three or four years in which he had controlled the Queensberry Lodge stable he had won more than his share of races. The year before that in which he met his unexpected death had been a particularly good one for he had landed the Queen's Prize with Glenhazel and the Ayr Gold Cup with Tommy Atkins. Both were ridden by his younger brother 'Chubb', who took over Queensberry Lodge in 1931. 'Chubb' Leach continued to train until a few years after the end of the Second World War. He then handed in his licence and concentrated on the management of the Meddler Stud, which had been built up so effectively by his father, until he died in March 1970.

Jack Leach enjoyed a highly successful career as a jockey, the big races that he won including The 2,000 Guineas of 1927 on Adam's Apple. Later he took over Graham Place on the retirement of his father.

As has already been noted, the link between the Leach family and Newmarket was first forged by Ted Leach the vet, whose younger brother Felix visited him for that memorable summer holiday in 1884. Ted Leach died in September 1926 after having been a cripple for a number of years as a result of a motoring accident. Like his brother he was deeply involved in breeding and had Lemberg and other notable stallions in his charge at the Hamilton Stud.

Ted Leach built the Chestnuts on the corner of The Severals, where he lived for many years. As his elder son, Captain R. E. Leach, had been killed in the First World War, his lucrative practice was taken over by his second son, Harold Leach, who continued to enjoy the confidence of many of the leading trainers in the town until he died at the comparatively early age of 53 in 1943.

The outstanding horse that Bob Sherwood trained at St Gatien during King Edward's reign was Land League, who won 33 of his 57 races after having cost only 45 guineas as a yearling. His successes included the Chesterfield Cup of 1910 and the Cambridgeshire of 1907. Land League might well have won the Cambridgeshire for a second time the following season had he not been deliberately maimed a few days before the race. Although all the evidence indicated that the crime had been committed by someone employed in the stable, the culprit was never identified.

What may have been a sequel to the cruel nobbling of Land League occurred while Bob Sherwood was on holiday in India during the winter of 1910. Extensive alterations were being made to the stabling at St Gatien, in the course of which a rusty razor was discovered care fully concealed in the ivy running up the boxes.

Land League carried the colours of Sherwood's principal patron, Captain J. G. R. Homfray. When indifferent health obliged the Captain to give up racing in 1929, Bob Sherwood retired, handing over the St Gatien stable to his former head lead, Harry Beadle, whose daughter married Dick Perryman.

Bob Sherwood never married. At times he gave the impression of a gruff man who was hard in his ways, yet this was only a façade, for he was essentially kind and considerate. There were two military hospitals in Newmarket during the First World War, and old Bob used to make a regular habit of lining up the wounded servicemen outside St Gatien so that he could make them small gifts of money.

Charlie Peck, son of Barcaldine's owner Robert Peck, was private trainer to the diamond magnate Solly Joel at Sefton Lodge during the Edwardian decade, while Dawson Waugh acted in a similar capacity for Walter Raphael, a financier of great resources, at Somerville Lodge. Dawson Waugh, who had received an exceptionally thorough grounding in his profession from John Porter at Kingsclere, was, as has already been mentioned, one of the many sons of Jimmy Waugh and a godson of Mat Dawson, after whom he was named. In 1912 he won The Derby with the grey filly Tagalie and the following season The 2,000 Guineas with Louvois. Lord Annandale, who was bought to lead the latter in his work, proved capable of accomplishing far more than the purpose for which he was recruited to the stable. He won the Stewards Cup at Goodwood in 1913 and dead-heated for the same event the following season.

Shortly after Dawson Waugh's brother Willie left Newmarket to take over Kingsclere from John Porter at the end of 1905, he leased his Balaton Lodge stable to the American, Andrew Joyner, who trained the horses of his compatriot, H. P. Whitney. Born in 1860 or 1861, Andrew Jackson Joyner was brought up in North Carolina. At the age of about 18 he joined the stable of W. P. Burch to whom he later became head lad and in 1890 he set up training on his own account. His stable soon prospered and in 1908 he was leading trainer with no fewer than 171 winners to his credit. That same year America introduced puritanical legislation that was bound to have an adverse effect on racing. Hence his decision to move his stable to England. During the few years that he was in Newmarket Andrew Joyner enjoyed considerable popularity and proved himself a most capable trainer although no notable successes came his way. With the outbreak of war in 1914 he returned to his own country, then neutral, and picked up the threads of a successful career. Andrew Joyner was over 80 when he died in 1944.

After Jimmy Ryan began to reduce his interests with increasing age just after the turn of the century, he let some of the boxes at Green Lodge to Albert Gilbert, who lived at Queensberry Cottage on the other side of the town. Albert Gilbert came from an old-established training family and had been apprenticed to his uncle William Gilbert who won The Derby with Cremorne for Henry Savile in 1872. A first-class stableman, who had the misfortune to be very deaf, Gilbert was private trainer for John and Herbert Musker. For these owners he won many races with the horses at Green Lodge, but none of great importance. Albert Gilbert was 64 when he died in a Norwich hospital in 1921.

When George Blackwell moved into Lagrange in 1903, Sammy Loates, who was acting as private trainer to the brothers Jack and Solly Joel, followed him into Beverley House. Until a few years previously Sammy Loates had been in the top flight of jockeys. Like his brothers Tommy and Ben, also successful riders, he was short in the leg and very powerfully built. He had a dark complexion, rather hooded eyes and a bulbous nose, so that his face was a lot more homely than handsome.

As a jockey Sammy had won each of the classics at least once and he was champion in 1899, during which year he won the Gold Cup on Cyllene for Bill Jarvis. In 1895 he brought off the Epsom double on Sir Visto in The Derby and La Sagesse in The Oaks and three years later he performed a similar feat at Newmarket on Disraeli in The 2,000 Guineas and Nun Nicer in The 1,000 Guineas.

The success that Sammy Loates enjoyed as a trainer was in no way comparable to that which had come his way as a jockey. Perhaps his most notable success was obtained with Solly Joel's Blue Danube in the Manchester Cup in 1917. As a result of a fall that had put an end to his career in the saddle, Sammy was left with one leg shorter than the other and throughout the last 30-odd years of his life he walked with a pronounced limp. On his retirement, Sammy Loates went to live at Middleton Cottage. When he died in 1933 he was still quite comfortably off, his will being proved at £9,886.

In 1904 middle-aged Joe Butters began training in the Kremlin House stables with a small string of about eight horses, all of which belonged to a Miss Clinton. Joe Butters had been born on Lord Derby's Knowsley estate in 1847. He was apprenticed to Lord Derby's trainer John Scott at Malton and later came to Newmarket where he was employed in Mat Dawson's stable. There he had the youthful Fred Archer in his charge and it was he who made Archer open that bank account that was eventually to swell to such enormous proportions. On Archer receiving his very first present from a winning owner, which took the form of a cheque for £100, Joe Butters, who was ten years his senior, insisted, "You are not going to spend it; come along with me to Hammond's bank and open an account".

As opportunities for riding in England were scarce, Joe Butters accepted an offer to go to Austria to ride for the Emperor Franz Josef in about 1874. In Austria he met up with Jimmy Waugh, whom he would already have known, and married one of his daughters, Janet. The family that Joe and Janet Butters brought up in Austria included Frank and Fred, both of whom were to train Derby winners, and Isabel, who married King George V's trainer, Willie Jarvis.

After 30 years of riding and training in Austria, Joe Butters returned to England to set up his stable at Kremlin. During the 22 years that he was there he never had anything of the calibre of Bahram, Mahmoud and Dastur that his son Frank was to train, but year after year he turned out his winners, some of whom were rare bargains. With Mushroom, who cost a mere 30 guineas, he won the City and Suburban in 1911, and other particularly smart customers that he had through his hands included Senseless and Nassovian.

Senseless acquired his name when the trainer told his wife that he had bought the horse and she replied, "Oh! Joe what a senseless thing to do". It was not. Senseless went on to win six nice handicaps.

Nassovian came near to winning a war-time substitute Derby in 1916 when he was beaten a neck and a head by Fiffinella and Kwang-Su. Joe Butters wanted the stable jockey, Spear, to ride, but the owner, Mr J. Sanford, insisted on going to the expense of sending for the fashionable Franco-American jockey, Frank O'Neill, from New York. Possibly unfortunately, O'Neill made it just in time for the ride, arriving at Newmarket on the morning of the race.

Joe Butters retired in 1926. After finishing training he remained one of the most popular inhabitants of Newmarket and a familiar figure in the High Street with a cheerful word for everybody. He was 86 when he died in December 1933.

To George Chaloner went the honour of training Osbech, the first horse to win the Coronation Cup, which the Epsom executive inaugurated to commemorate the crowning of King Edward VII in 1902. Born in 1869, George was one of the six sons of Tom Chaloner, who won the historic Derby of 1863 on Macaroni, and Nellie, the sister of the great north-country jockey, Johnny Osborne.

After having followed the somewhat exceptional course of being apprenticed to his widowed mother, George Chaloner made the grade as a jockey and was associated with Captain Machell's Bedford Cottage stable, riding the great Isinglass in all his races as a two-year-old in 1892. He also rode Reminder to be third in The Derby of 1894 and Curzon to be second the following year. Both horses were geldings, who were not barred from The Derby until 1904.

At the end of his riding career George Chaloner set up as a trainer at Machell Place. Other big races besides that first Coronation Cup of which George Chaloner trained the winner, included the Lincolnshire with Kaffir King in 1908, the Chesterfield Cup with Lady Help in 1905, the Royal Hunt Cup with Stealaway in 1901 and the Liverpool Autumn Cup with Fabulist in 1900.

At the early age of 41 George Chaloner retired from training to buy a farm in Bedfordshire in 1910. He had been bedridden for many years when he died at Bedford in 1935.

In the Edwardian era Captain R. H. Dewhurst was training at Bedford Lodge and Charlie Beatty was still next door at Bedford Cottage. Captain Dewhurst, who served in the 4th Hussars, was an extremely successful amateur rider over the sticks in Ireland, one of his most notable successes being obtained on his wife's horse, Abbot, in the Conyngham Cup at Punchestown in 1893. Coming to Bedford Lodge in about 1904, he ran the stable in conjunction with the one

Sammy Loates (1865-1932)

that he already controlled at Greenmount, Clonsilla, in County Dublin. It was not until 1912 that he concentrated excusively upon the string at Bedford Lodge, handing over the Clonsilla yard to his partner, Maxwell Arnott. One of the best horses Captain Dewhurst trained was Ebor, who won the Kempton Park Jubilee Handicap in 1909. He was also responsible for Succour who gave the subsequent Cambridgeshire winner Christmas Daisy 21lb and a beating in the Prince Edward Handicap at Manchester.

At Bedford Cottage Charlie Beatty was private trainer to Lord Howard de Walden, who had bought much of the bloodstock of the stable's previous patron, Colonel Harry McCalmont, upon the death of the latter. Among the horses that Lord Howard de Walden acquired in this way was Zinfandel, who won the Ascot Gold Cup in 1905 following his success in the Coronation Cup the previous year.

When King Edward ascended the throne all the land on the left of the Bury Road on the far side of Bedford Cottage was paddock and had probably altered little since Joe Dawson had laid it out some 40 years previously. Soon after the turn of the century the scene changed radically. Where mares had grazed in the paddocks, horses in training stood in their boxes. This transformation was brought about with the building of what became four of the most famous stables in the town, namely Stanley House, Freemason Lodge, Carlburg and Clarehaven.

As has already been said, when Lord Derby began to build up his racing interests in 1893 he purchased the Sefton Stud from the Duke of Montrose. On what had been the stud of the old Duchess of Montrose, Lord Derby built Stanley House, the stable yard and the trainer's house, which comprise one of the most beautifully laid out racing establishments in the world. Building was completed by 1903 when George Lambton moved Lord Derby's string in from nearby Bedford Lodge.

The first classic success for an inmate of Stanley House came when Keystone II landed The Oaks in 1906, though in a way she was lucky to have been alive to take part in the race. Only a few weeks before the Epsom meeting there had occurred at Stanley House one of those events of which all trainers are constantly in dread. On arriving at Newmarket Station after having been to see the Jubilee Handicap at Kempton Park, George Lambton was informed that his stables were on fire.

Fortunately it had been possible to let all the horses out of their boxes and let them loose on the circular exercise track behind the yard. Around this the terrified animals galloped until they were nearly exhausted after which they were taken to boxes on the adjoining Stanley Stud or any other temporary accommodation available in the vicinity.

Like Keystone II the other horses soon got over the ordeal through which they had gone on the night of the fire. In fact the string recovered so well that by the end of the season George Lambton was leading trainer, having saddled 22 winners of 46 races worth £34,068 Thus the Stanley House stable was soon on the map, but it was no

The hon. George Lambton (1860-1945) laid the foundations of the greatness of Stanley House stable

until the next reign that it was to have its first taste of real greatness.

Like quite a lot of the other property along the Bury Road, Freemason Lodge was built by a Mr A. Stedall, who seems better remembered for his prodigious port drinking than for his horses or his houses. Most of Stedall's horses were given their names by George Everett, a prominent Freemason who was closely associated with the establishing of racing at Kempton Park. The Freemason after whom the Bury Road stable was named was bred by Lady Stamford in 1886. By Barcaldine out of the Oaks winner Geheimniss, Freemason won three races as a three-year-old and five as a four-year-old. On retirement from the course he stood at the Graham Place Stud, which belonged to Alf Saddler senior.

The building of Freemason Lodge was finished by 1901 when Alf Saddler junior commenced training with a string of 23 horses belonging to Stedall and H. E. (later Sir Henry) Randall. From first to last of the 20-odd years that he was in the yard, Alf Saddler was turning out good winners. In 1902 he landed the City and Suburban with First Principal and the following season both the Ascot Stakes and the Goodwood Stakes with Genius. In 1909 he won the Lincoln with Duke of Sparta, then after the First World War he won a substitute Jubilee Handicap at Hurst Park with Arion, who provided a young apprentice called Tommy Weston with his first important success.

Two years later in 1921 Alf Saddler junior sent out Royal Lancer to win The St Leger, in which the colt was ridden by his own apprentice Bobby Jones. Before long Bobby Jones was firmly established as a leading jockey, which he remained until his retirement at the end of the Second World War.

During his final season at Freemason Lodge, that of 1922, Alf Saddler junior won the Newmarket St Leger with Diligence. Subsequently Diligence became the sire of Clarence, the dam of Sun Chariot.

In 1917 old Martin Gurry finally gave up training and sold Abington Place to Alf Saddler junior, with the stipulation that he should continue to occupy the house for the remainder of his life. Following the death of Gurry in 1923, Alf Saddler moved his horses across the Bury Road to Abington Place and Freemason Lodge was bought by Captain Cecil Boyd-Rochfort.

Next door to Freemason Lodge stands Carlburg. This stable was built by Charlie Waugh, who named it after the place on the borders of Poland and Hungary where he spent much of his childhood in the stable of his father Jimmy Waugh.

Born at Russley Park in 1870 while Jimmy Waugh was training for James Merry, Charlie Waugh learned his profession from his father, to whom he acted as assistant at Middleton Cottage on the family's return to England. After coming of age in 1891 he went out to Germany to take over the Imperial stable at Graditz during the illness of his eldest brother, Richard. Soon after returning to Newmarket he had a spell as private trainer to Prince Soltykoff at Kremlin House and then he spent a few seasons at Park Lodge before building Carlburg in 1900.

It was not long before Charlie Waugh was enjoying considerable success in the more important handicaps. He landed the Lincolnshire first with Over Norton in 1903, and then with Sansovino (not to be confused with the 1924 Derby winner) in 1905, the Cambridgeshire with Marcovil in 1908, the Great Metropolitan with Kilbroney in 1911 and the Chesterfield Cup with Kiltoi in 1914.

During the First World War the name of the stable with its obvious Germanic origin aroused great resentment in the town. As a result, Charlie Waugh became the centre of more than one demonstration inspired by completely misplaced patriotism.

No race of outstanding importance fell to Carlburg after things got back to something like normal in 1919, but the winners came out of the yard all right. In the period between the wars Charlie Waugh made a name for himself as being particularly dangerous at Yarmouth, Newmarket's local seaside meeting.

With the outbreak of war in September 1939 Charlie Waugh retired from training. In 1948 he sold Carlburg to Joe Lawson and the following year he died at the age of 79, one of the last links between the drab post-war world and the halcyon days of the latter Victorian era. Right up to 1939 he had continued to wear clothes that had gone out of fashion many years before, and with his broad-bottomed gaiters his was an easily recognisable figure on the Heath. His son, Alf Waugh, enjoyed a successful career as a racing journalist and was for a time resident Newmarket correspondent of the *Sporting Chronicle*, writing under the *nom de plume* of 'Old Rowley'.

In 1900, the last full year of Queen Victoria's reign, a four-year-old filly called Clarehaven carried 7 st 13 lb to win the Cesarewitch. In so doing she landed some hefty bets for Peter Purcell Gilpin, who trained her at Pimperne near Blandford in Dorset.

With his winnings Gilpin built Clarehaven, the last of the stables on the left-hand side of the Bury Road as you leave the town and a mere stone's throw from the Limekilns. This is one of the few yards in the town named after a filly, and it is most appropriate that it should be, for although Gilpin trained some cracking good colts, it is for his achievements with fillies, and one above all, that he will be best remembered. In 1903, the first year in which its boxes were filled, Clarehaven housed a two-year-old called Pretty Polly, one of the greatest racehorses of all time.

Peter Valentine Purcell was born at Pau in 1858, the son of Captain Purcell of the 13th Light Dragoons. In 1886 he followed his father into the army, becoming a subaltern in the 5th Irish Lancers. Later he married a Miss Meux-Smith, and assumed the name of Gilpin in compliance with the will after she had inherited a fortune from her uncle, Sir Ralph Gilpin. On leaving the army, Gilpin, a tall soldierly man with a walrus moustache, trained successively near the Curragh and then at Langton House, Pimperne, arriving at the latter establishment in 1898.

Pretty Polly, the first and greatest of the classic winners to be trained at Clarehaven, was a dark chestnut filly with a star on her fore-

Pretty Polly, owned by Major Eustace Loder and trained by Peter Purcell Gilpin in the Clarehaven stable to win 22 of her 24 races

head by Gallinule out of Admiration by Saraband out of Gaze by Thuringian Prince. She had a wonderfully equable temperament, but in order to keep her completely happy a cob with a docked tail, called Little Missus, would accompany her to the meetings to precede her round the parade ring.

Owned by Major Eustace Loder, Pretty Polly had her first race in the British Dominion Stakes at Sandown Park on 27 June 1903 when she was fourth choice in the market with 6-1 laid against her. This was the only occasion on which she started anything other than clear favourite. To emphasise the extent to which layers and backers had underestimated her talents, she proceeded to beat Vergia by ten lengths. Such was the start of the brilliant career by the end of which she had won 22 of her 24 races and been runner-up in her other two, the first prize money that she earned amounting to £37,295.

The most important races she won as a two-year-old were the National Breeders Produce Stakes, the Champagne Stakes, the Cheveley Park Stakes and the Middle Park Stakes. She also won races at Manchester and Liverpool and two more at Newmarket's Houghton Meeting as a juvenile.

Pretty Polly started her second season by winning The 1,000 Guineas at 4-1 on and then she landed the still longer odds of 100-8 laid on her in The Oaks. At Royal Ascot she won the Coronation Stakes and at Goodwood the Nassau Stakes, while at Doncaster she proved her stoutness by completing the double in The St Leger and the Park Hill Stakes.

In October Pretty Polly went over to France for the Prix de Conseil Municipal at Longchamp, only to meet the first of her two defeats. The French horse Presto II jumped off in front, slipped his field and beat her by two lengths. Many excuses were put forward for her defeat. One was that she had travelled badly. Another was that as Danny Maher was riding her for the first time he did not know enough about her to be able to counter the enterprising tactics employed by the French jockey, Ransch, on the winner. Her regular rider, Billy Lane, who had been champion in 1902, had recently met with a serious accident while riding Blosselsky at Lingfield. He never recovered and was only 37 when he died in 1920.

Pretty Polly soon showed that she was none the worse for her defeat in France. Making her final appearance of 1904 in the Free Handicap, run at the back-end in those days, she won in a canter.

First time out in 1905, Pretty Polly went to Epsom to win the Coronation Cup in record time. Shortly afterwards she strained some muscles in her quarters. This necessitated her missing the Gold Cup and being put on the easy list for six weeks. Returning to action in the autumn, she won the Champion Stakes and the Jockey Club Cup as well as a match for the Limekiln Stakes at the curious odds of 55-1 on.

Kept in training for a fourth season in 1906, Pretty Polly won the March Stakes and a second Coronation Cup before making her farewell appearance in the Gold Cup at Royal Ascot. Coming to the distance, Achilles, the leader, hung to the left as he weakened under pressure and in doing so he carried out Pretty Polly. Despite the ground that cost her, she was soon in the lead with Bachelor's Button chasing her hard, and those who had laid 11-4 on her were shocked to see it was going to be a race. With 100 yards to go, Bachelor's Button struck the front, and though Pretty Polly showed that she was as true a racehorse in defeat as ever she had been in victory by giving of everything she had, she was beaten by a length.

At first it was hoped that Pretty Polly would be able to disprove the Ascot form by going out with a blaze of glory in the Doncaster Cup. The ground remained very firm throughout the late summer of 1906 and Pretty Polly jarred her off fore in her final gallop for the Doncaster Cup with the result that she was unable to run. Leaving Newmarket on 31 October she returned to Major Loder's Eyrefield Lodge Stud where she had been reared. None of her ten offspring were anything like as good as herself, but nevertheless she transmitted her excellence through a flourishing female line. The Newmarket-trained Derby winners St Paddy and Psidium both traced back to her in tail female line as also did Brigadier Gerard who beat Mill Reef in The 2,000 Guineas.

Despite the disappointments occasioned by the defeat of Pretty Polly at Ascot and the setback that caused her to be taken out of training slightly prematurely, the season of 1906 was a good one for Clarehaven. Gilpin had another high class filly in Flair owned by Sir Daniel Cooper, whose monument dominates the western end of the High Street. Sir Daniel, an Australian, lived at Warren Towers and was a great benefactor to the town. His father, the first baronet, had been Speaker of the New South Wales Legislative Assembly. On being asked by his brother William to buy one or two broodmares, Sir Daniel had purchased Footlight and Satire, but because they were so cheap William Cooper declined to have them. Sir Daniel, who died in 1909, was to have no cause to regret keeping them himself. Footlight was the mother of a good racemare in Glare, who became the dam of Flair.

Having won the Middle Park Plate and two of her other three races as a two-year-old, Flair, who was by St Frusquin, beat Lischana by three lengths in The 1,000 Guineas. On the strength of that impressive performance it was decided to train Flair for The Derby and keep a more backward colt belonging to Major Loder called Spearmint for the Grand Prix de Paris. That plan had to be revised as a result of Flair breaking down so badly that she could not run again, and Spearmint was brought on more quickly than had been intended to have him ready for The Derby. When the Newmarket touts, with whom Gilpin maintained a long running feud, learned of the day on which Spearmint was to be tried, they waited outside the gates of Clarehaven from early morning so as to see where the string would go. The meagre reward of what proved a long vigil was the sight of the horses returning to the yard, Gilpin having had his lads tear up some railings so that Spearmint, Pretty Polly and the other two horses in the trial, Hammerkop and Waterchute, could make their way through Lord Derby's private grounds to the Limekilns. Although Pretty Polly, who was two years his senior and giving him 22 lb, won the trial, Spearmint went quite well enough to convince Gilpin he would win The Derby. As soon as they were back at Clarehaven the jockeys who had ridden in the trial were put under lock and key until Gilpin's commissioner had put the stable money on. Ridden by Danny Maher, Spearmint, an elegant bay with a white face and a long sock on his near fore, duly won The Derby and then completed a notable double in the Grand Prix de Paris.

Despite the elaborate precautions that Gilpin had taken to ensure that the trial of Spearmint for The Derby took place in secret it was watched by one of the touts from a long way off. That witness to the way the colt shaped against Pretty Polly was the Yorkshireman Archie Falcon, who won enough money over Spearmint to be able to give up touting and become a successful professional backer. On the death of Martin Gurry he bought the Bungalow Stud at Wood Ditton, which he subsequently sold to Sir Victor Sassoon. Unfortunately he proved a lot less adept as a breeder than he had done as a backer, largely through his misplaced faith in his favourite horse Tremola as a stallion, and was quite poor when he died at Harrogate at the age of 60 in 1932.

Spearmint was by no means the only classic winner over whom Peter Purcell Gilpin outwitted the touts that he detested so thoroughly. When he took St Louis to the Racecourse Side to be tried for The 2,000 Guineas in 1922 the colt and his workmates walked behind the stands and on towards the end of the running rails as though they were going to cross the course at the usual point and gallop Across the Flat. Before they reached the end of the running rails Gilpin suddenly wheeled round on his hack, told his trial jockeys to wait until he had reached the top of the town and then try the horses the reverse way of the Southfields canter. Unfortunately he kept the owner as much in the dark as he did the touts on that occasion. The first that Lord Queenborough knew of his horse having a chance in The 2,000 Guineas was when he saw that St Louis was nearly favourite. St Louis won The Guineas by three lengths from Pondoland but Lord Queenborough's patronage of the Clarehaven stable ended abruptly at the end of that season.

Major Loder's Hammerkop, who was used as trial tackle for Spearmint, was one of the best staying mares trained by Gilpin at Clarehaven, and had given him his second success in the Cesarewitch the previous year. To a mating with Spearmint she bred Spion Kop, who emulated his sire by winning The Derby in 1920. By that time Peter Purcell Gilpin was 62 and Major Eustace Loder dead, so it was the latter's nephew Colonel Giles Loder whose colours were carried by Spion Kop.

Yet again Clarehaven brought off the double in The Derby and the Grand Prix, though this time it was not the Derby winner who landed the second leg. Spion Kop went to the post as England's main hope for the Longchamp race, but it was his stablemate, Comrade, who won. Comrade, who cost a mere 25 guineas as a yearling, soon consolidated his claims to being one of the greatest bargains of all time by landing the Prix de l'Arc de Triomphe as well.

Other important successes obtained by Peter Gilpin while he was at Clarehaven may be summarised briefly. He won The 1,000 Guineas with Electra in 1909 and Cresta Run in 1927, as well as a wartime Oaks with Snow Marten in 1915, another Cesarewitch with Verney in 1910 and his other notable triumphs in handicaps were with Corn Sack (1928) in the City and Suburban, Sandboy (1903) in the Chester Cup, Paragon (1921) in the Kempton Park Jubilee, and Baltinglass (1907) and King John (1919) in the Manchester November Handicap. Another good horse that he had was Llangibby, whom he sent out to win the Eclipse Stakes in 1906. Although he won two Derbies, the only time that Peter Gilpin was leading trainer was in 1904 when Pretty Polly was a three-year-old.

Towards the end of the twenties, Gilpin's health began to fail. He was 70 when he died at his Dollanstown Stud, County Kildare, in his native Ireland in November 1928.

One of the strangest characters in Edwardian Newmarket was the

Chevalier Ginistrelli, the little Italian who trained a few horses of his own breeding at Oaks Lodge. The racing community regarded the Chevalier as an amusing and amiable eccentric, while for his part he found the English quite impossible to understand. Why, for instance, could he not stick his own marking posts into the Heath without provoking the almost unassuageable wrath of the Jockey Club Agent, Mr Marriott?

For all his unconventional methods, the Chevalier obtained some notable results such as winning of the Middle Park Stakes with Signorina in 1889. Retired to stud, Signorina proved a bitter disappointment by being barren in each of her first ten seasons. In 1903 she produced a fair sort of colt in Signorino, who was to be third to Cicero in The Derby. Signorina was to have been covered by that great stallion Cyllene in 1904, but the arrangement fell through. Thereupon the Chevalier decided that his mare should be sent to the much inferior Chaleureux for the perfectly extraordinary reason that he was sure that the pair of them were in love. He had noticed that whenever Chaleureux was led past Signorina's paddock in the course of his exercise he always whinnied and she replied in similar vein. The offspring of this extremely unscientific mating was a filly called Signorinetta.

Neither the form she showed as a two-year-old nor her performances during the first part of 1908 suggested that Signorinetta was

Chevalier Odorado Ginistrelli (1833-1920), on the left, at the December Sales in 1911

anything out of the ordinary. Yet the Chevalier entertained the quaint idea that she was going to win The Derby. To this end he gave her as searching a preparation as the moderate trial tackle that he could muster would allow in a series of strong mile-and-a-half gallops. All these proved was that Signorinetta could at least stay the distance. In 1908 this was the crucial factor, as there was nothing else in the Derby field with any pretensions to getting the trip, so Signorinetta, with Billy Bullock up, landed the odds of 100-1.

The usually vociferous Derby crowd was almost speechless with astonishment. Then after a minute or two men in traditional top hats and morning coats and fashionably dressed women broke into cheers for the funny little man in his short alpaca coat and straw hat, as he led in the filly whom he looked upon as more of a pet than a racehorse.

Two days later, Signorinetta, ridden by Billy Bullock again, won The Oaks. After that second classic success, the Chevalier was sent for by King Edward. Taking him by the elbow, the King ushered him to the front of the royal box so that he could receive fresh applause from

Newmarket High Street in the Edwardian era. The Carlton Hotel (left with tower), where the jockeys of those days took their Turkish Baths, was recently demolished

the crowd, who showed typically English pleasure at the triumph of a little stable.

The Chevalier must have been in a seventh heaven after that memorable Epsom meeting, but he took good care not to betray the fact to his jockey. All that Billy Bullock received for riding the winners of The Derby and The Oaks was his statutory fee of £10 — and a glass of sherry. The entire credit for training Signorinetta to win two classics has all too often been given to her owner whereas the real responsibility for her preparation and well-being was borne by his head lad Lawrence McClean. Always known in stables as 'Manch' McClean, by reason of his being a native of Manchester, he had served his apprenticeship with Mat Dawson at Heath House. Subsequently he left Newmarket for Ayr to join the stable of Tommy Burns, for whom he rode a few winners. In 1893 he returned to Newmarket and spent some time with Fred Webb at Ethelreda House before taking charge of the Oaks Lodge stable. Although not so meagrely rewarded as Billy Bullock for the triumphs of Signorinetta, 'Manch' McClean can hardly have been overwhelmed by the present of £100 that he received from the Chevalier Ginistrelli.

At the outset of King Edward's reign George Blackwell was training at Beverley House. An East Anglian man, he had been born in Cambridge in 1861. After having been apprenticed to A. Gilbert at Newmarket he became travelling head lad to Mat Dawson. Later he was one of Mat's head lads, having charge of St Albans when it was an overspill yard for Heath House. To begin with, George Blackwell had the Australian brothers Daniel and William Cooper as his patrons. Soon other owners joined the stable. Slim and dark in appearance, Blackwell was an excellent stableman, and the sort of trainer who never orders a lad to do anything he cannot do himself. For example, when Signorettina's sire Chaleureux came to Beverley House to lead the Gold Cup hope, Newhaven, in his work, he was so savage that it was impossible to find a lad willing to do him, so Blackwell took off his coat and did the horse himself. Under the personal handling of his new trainer Chaleureux graduated from being a lead horse to a top-class handicapper. In 1898 he won the Chesterfield Cup, the Cesarewitch and the Manchester November Handicap. The same year Blackwell won the Ebor with Invincible II.

George Blackwell saddled his first classic winner when Aida landed The 1,000 Guineas in 1901. Two years later he headed the list of winning trainers after Rock Sand, an exquisitely moulded little brown colt belonging to Sir James Miller, had won the Triple Crown. That Rock Sand stood training for three seasons reflected great credit on Blackwell. Because the colt had bad joints it was no easy job to keep him sound, let alone to get him racing fit. Shortly after the successes of Rock Sand in the classics, Blackwell moved his string into the larger premises at Lagrange.

George Blackwell had practically retired when he trained the 13-year-old Sergeant Murphy to become the oldest horse ever to win the Grand National in 1923. Not long afterwards he closed down his stable completely and lived on in Newmarket until he died at the age of 81 in 1942.

After the death of Sir Blundell Maple in 1903, Willie Waugh left Falmouth Lodge and bought Zetland Lodge, which is almost next door to it on the Fordham Road. One of the first things he did was to change the name of his new stable to Balaton Lodge, thus calling it after the largest lake in Hungary, where he had spent his childhood while his father was training in that country. Willie Waugh did not have much immediate use for the yard as he soon afterwards accepted the offer to take over the Kingsclere stable from John Porter, who was going to retire at the end of the 1905 season.

Throughout his reign King Edward maintained his association with Dick Marsh, who carried on in his capacity of royal trainer for much of the time that George V was on the throne. At the end of the 1924 season he finally gave up training and handed Egerton House over to Willie Jarvis. Retiring to Shelford, near Cambridge, he lived on to well beyond his 80th birthday.

Right to the end of his long life, Dick Marsh must have cherished the vivid memories not only of how he had won The Derby with Persimmon and Diamond Jubilee when their owner was Prince of Wales but of how he provided one of the climaxes of the reign of Edward VII by sending Minoru out to win The Derby of 1909, the last of the King's lifetime.

Minoru is still the only horse to have won The Derby for a reigning monarch, and the crowd went almost delirious as they acclaimed him after one of the closest finishes in the history of the race. As soon as Tattenham Corner had been rounded it was clear that the issue already lay between Minoru, ridden by Bertie Jones, and Dawson Waugh's candidate, Louviers, with George Stern up. All the way up the straight these two were at it hammer and tongs, first one and then the other gaining a slight advantage. At the post it was Minoru who was a short head in front.

A little less than a year after his greatest racing triumph King Edward VII was dead. Almost his last words were to express pleasure that his filly, Witch of the Air, had won at Kempton Park.

Nowhere was the King more deeply mourned than at Newmarket, whence he had derived so much of his pleasure during the latter years of his life. As a tangible expression of the esteem in which everybody in the town held him, the Edward VII Memorial Hall was erected opposite the spot where the Avenue meets the High Street.

22 Newmarket in the Reign of George V

The genius of the Hon George Lambton, who was 50 at the accession of George V, reaped its harvest during the quarter century of the King's reign. For all except the last couple of years he was either training at Lord Derby's Stanley House stable or managing it.

A few months after the King came to the throne George Lambton won The St Leger of 1910 with Swynford, and when war broke out four years later he carried on in austerity conditions, bringing off a hat-trick in the 1,000 Guineas with Canyon in 1916, Diadem in 1917 and Ferry in 1918. In the closing months of the First World War the Stanley House stable jockey, Fred Rickaby, was killed on active service with the Tank Corps. He had had the opportunity to return home a short time previously, but had declined it, preferring to see the war through to the end.

In 1923, Tommy Weston, then only 20 years of age, became first jockey at Stanley House. A tough and fearless rider with wonderfully good hands, Tommy Weston landed The Derby on Sansovino in 1924, and in 1933 he won Lord Derby and George Lambton their second Derby with the brilliant little Hyperion.

At the end of 1926 George Lambton surrendered his licence to train to become manager of the Stanley House stable, the new trainer being Frank Butters. It was Frank Butters who saddled Fairway to win The St Leger in 1928, the Oaks winners Beam in 1927 and Toboggan in 1928, and the 1,000 Guineas winner Fair Isle in 1930.

While Britain was feeling the full effects of the depression in 1930 Lord Derby found he could no longer afford both a manager and a trainer. As a result Frank Butters left and George Lambton resumed training. Three years later Lord Derby decided to make still greater changes at Stanley House and he severed his connection with George Lambton and a year later replaced Tommy Weston by Dick Perryman.

Although past 70 years of age by this time, George Lambton was still at the top of his profession, and on leaving Stanley House he set up a public stable at Kremlin House in 1934. Owners like Major Dermot McCalmont, Sir Abe Bailey, the Duke of Portland and the French textile magnate Marcel Boussac soon sent him horses, and he continued to train important winners. In 1935 alone he won the Victoria Cup with Precious Pearl, the Chester Cup with his own horse Damascus and the Queen's Prize with Apple Peel, who provided Bill Rickaby, son of Fred Rickaby, with his first important winner.

Bill Rickaby comes from one of the oldest and most respected of England's racing families. As long ago as 1855 his great-great-grandfather, Fred Rickaby, trained Wild Dayrell to win The Derby. He

Tommy Weston (1903-1981) won the Derby on Sansovino (1924) and Hyperion (1933) in the heyday of Stanley House

Fred Rickaby (1867-1941) wins the Oaks of 1896 on Canterbury Pilgrim, one of the foundation mares of the Stanley House Stud

was assisted by his sons Sam and John and had his stables in Lord Craven's Ashdown Park at Lambourn.

Fred Rickaby's grandson, also Fred, was born at Hungerford on 20 September 1867. He was apprenticed to Alf Saddler in a stable near Winchester. In 1891 Fred Rickaby won The 1,000 Guineas and The Oaks on Mimi and was shortly afterwards appointed first jockey to Lord Derby. The most important success that he obtained for Lord Derby was on that great mare Canterbury Pilgrim in The Oaks of 1896.

Not long after that Fred Rickaby retired from riding, and his son, yet another Fred, became first jockey to Lord Derby in 1912. George Lambton regarded Fred Rickaby the third as an even better jockey than his father and gave the opinion that he had only reached the peak of his prowess at the outbreak of the First World War in 1914. In the previous year he had won The 1,000 Guineas and Oaks on Mr S. B. Joel's Jest.

The first house that the second Fred Rickaby lived in on his arrival at Newmarket towards the end of the last century was Exeter Villa, opposite the Exeter House training establishement. In due course the former jockey Walter Griggs took over that stable. Fred Rickaby the third married Griggs's sister.

Fred Rickaby the third was survived by two children, Fred and Bill. Bill was only just a year old at his father's death. Fred Rickaby the fourth rode on the flat and over the sticks in this country until a few years after the Second World War. Subsequently he went to South Africa to train with conspicuous success in Durban.

Wally and Billy Griggs, the brothers-in-law of Fred Rickaby the third, were the sons of a butcher in the Canterbury area of Kent. As a sideline their father made a book, and in this way they gained an interest in racing. On leaving school, the Griggs brothers were apprenticed to Bob Sherwood at St Gatien.

Sherwood was an irascible old man, and one day he and Wally Griggs had a frightful row when he accused the boy of knocking a horse about on the Limekilns. The upshot was that Wally quit St Gatien after the morning's work was over and made his way to Hurst Park with the avowed intention of making his living from backing horses and being quit of Sherwood for ever.

On arrival he met the Epsom trainer, Willie Nightingall (father of the late Walter Nightingall), who was looking for a lightweight for three runners. Wally Griggs came in for the spare rides and won on all of them. Abandoning the idea of becoming a professional backer, he returned to St Gatien that evening to be greeted by Bob Sherwood with the words, "Oh, it seems you are a jockey after all".

Before he had finished with being a jockey, Wally Griggs had won The 1,000 Guineas on Cinna in 1920, the Ascot Stakes on Turbine in 1908 and Declare in 1910, the Goodwood Cup on Red Robe in 1905, and a lot of other important races.

For many years Wally Griggs rode for Charlie Morton, who was private trainer to Mr Jack Joel at Wantage. For that stable he won The St Leger on Your Majesty in 1908 and Black Jester in 1914, the City and Suburban on Maiden Erlegh in 1914, as well as the Coronation Cup, the Liverpool Spring Cup and the Chesterfield Cup on that grand old horse, Dean Swift, who has a race named after him at Epsom today. His successes for other trainers included The Oaks on Peter Gilpin's Snow Marten in 1916 and the Goodwood Cup on Charlie Waugh's Kilbroney in 1911.

When he commenced training he had a number of horses in partnership with a Mr Shaw, and one way or another he had shares in most of the 30-odd inmates of his Exeter House yard. This gave him a greater say in the way the stable's not infrequent betting coups were pulled off.

Like his predecessors at Exeter House, Wally Griggs made full use of the covered ride in February and March with the result that his horses were all fit by the first day of the season at Lincoln. There were not many years that he went short of winners early on. For instance in

1926 he won with Mistley at Lincoln on the Monday, with the same horse again on the Tuesday, with Jibtopsail on Wednesday, the third and final day of the meeting, with Loch Sen at Liverpool on the Friday, while the following afternoon he took another race with Jibtopsail. That brought his score up to five winners in the first week of racing and all of them started favourite.

Both Fred and Bill Rickaby were apprenticed to their uncle at Exeter House. When Wally Griggs died in 1935, Bill's indentures were transferred to George Lambton, with whom both his grandfather and father had been so closely associated in their riding days.

Like Fred Rickaby, the Hon Francis Lambton, George Lambton's brother, was amongst the Newmarket men to be killed in the First World War. Before its outbreak he had trained with fair success at Park Lodge. Following his death, the stable was run by Green, his head lad, until Jack Jarvis took the yard on an annual lease from the widow of George Barrett who had ridden Common to win the Triple Crown in 1891.

Jack Jarvis, the son of Cyllene's trainer Bill Jarvis, had come to the end of a successful career as a jockey, when he had become private trainer to Mr A. E. Barton just before the outbreak of the First World War. During his riding days he had won the Cambridgeshire on the heavily-backed Hackler's Pride in 1903. He was also successful on Kilglass in the Ayr Gold Cup, and after increased weight had turned his attention to hurdling he rode the winner of the Liverpool Hurdle.

After a short spell with Mr Barton he became a public trainer, though when he took over Park Lodge, where soldiers were still billeted in the boxes, his string consisted of three horses.

It was not long before his string grew. Sir George Bullough sent his horses to Park Lodge and shortly afterwards the former Prime Minister, Lord Rosebery, did the same. Jack Jarvis enjoyed the first of several brilliant seasons in 1922. At Royal Ascot he sent out Sir George Bullough's Golden Myth to win the Gold Vase and then the Gold Cup two days later, both races in record time. Then to complete a splendid feat, Golden Myth reverted to ten furlongs at Sandown Park the following month and landed the Eclipse Stakes.

In the next season, that of 1923, Jack Jarvis won his first classic with Lord Rosebery's Ellangowan in The 2,000 Guineas. Like Golden Myth, Ellangowan was ridden by the stable apprentice, Charlie Elliott. Born and bred in Newmarket, Elliott was one of the greatest jockeys of all time, a superb stylist with an uncanny sense of timing. He tied with Steve Donoghue for the championship in 1923 and he was still indentured to Jack Jarvis when he became outright champion in 1924.

Jack Jarvis's two brothers were also on the crest of the wave in the early twenties. Basil, who had followed their uncle by marriage, Jimmy Ryan, at Green Lodge, won The Derby with Papyrus in 1923, while Willie succeeded the veteran Dick Marsh as trainer to the King at Egerton House at the end of the following season. In 1928 Willie Jarvis became responsible for the only royal classic winner of the reign when Scuttle took The 1,000 Guineas.

Like Lord Derby and the Aga Khan, Lord Glanely had a large private stable at Newmarket between the wars. In the first year of peace, 1919, Frank Barling trained for him at Falmouth House, winning The Derby of that season with Grand Parade.

Shortly afterwards the Glanely horses went to Lagrange. Lord Glanely, a Cardiff ship-owner, had an intense pride in his country and particularly in the Devon in which he had been born. This pride was reflected in his colours of a red, white and blue sash on a black jacket and in the names of his horses, like Rose of England and Glorious Devon. Needless to say, when he took over Lagrange he anglicised its name to The Grange.

Frank Barling's poor health obliged him to give up training not long after he had won The Derby, and Dick Marsh's son, Charlie Marsh, and then Fred Archer, son of yet another old Newmarket trainer, Charlie Archer, were at The Grange for short periods, before Captain Tommy Hogg trained for a decade for Lord Glanely. Captain Hogg won The Oaks with Rose of England and The St Leger with Singapore in 1930, in 1933 The 2,000 Guineas with Colombo and in 1937 another St Leger with Chulmleigh. At the end of the following season Captain Hogg retired, and was succeeded by Basil Jarvis, who brought the horses he trained for other owners to The Grange. Lord Glanely was killed in an air raid in 1942 when he was 75.

After having served as a captain in the Scots Guards during the war, Cecil Boyd-Rochfort began training in 1921 and bought Freemason Lodge off A. E. Stedall. With owners such as Lady Zia Wernher, Sir Humphrey de Trafford, and a number of wealthy Americans like Mr William Woodward, he soon built up a stable of high-class horses, leaving no one in any doubt that he knew how to get the best out of them.

In 1928 Captain Boyd-Rochfort won the Ebor Handicap with Cinq-à-Sept and the following season the Eclipse Stakes with Royal Minstrel and the Cambridgeshire with Double Life, whom he had bought for a mere 600 guineas on behalf of Lady Zia Wernher. Even at the height of summer the chestnut Double Life always looked a bit rough in her coat, but this did not prevent her from proving one of the greatest bargains in history. Not only did she win the Cambridgeshire, but she became foundation mare of Lady Zia's stud and the great-grand dam of her triple classic winner, Meld.

Looking at some of the other men who trained at Newmarket between the wars, we find Billy Walters at Albert House, whence he sent out his high-class sprinter Sir Cosmo to win the July Cup in 1930. Willie Waugh, who left Kingsclere after the syndicate of owners that had run the stable dissolved in 1919, trained at Balaton Lodge until he died in 1927.

The outstanding horse Willie Waugh trained at Balaton was the filly Verdict. In a dramatic finish to the Cambridgeshire of 1923 she bested Epinard, who had been almost backed off the board by his French connections, by a neck.

Captain Sir Cecil Boyd-Rochfort (1887-1983) trained for H M The Queen and many other important owners at Freemason Lodge

In those inter-war years Phantom Lodge was run by Major Vandy Beatty, to whom the present Royston trainer, Willie Stephenson, was indentured. Born in Ireland in 1875, Major Beatty had served in both the Boer War and the First World War. He was one of those men who never believed in letting the right hand know what the left is doing. When he tried his horses it was generally before the sun, let alone the touts, was up. He trained that brilliant sprinter and influential sire, Gold Bridge, to win two King's Stand Stakes in 1933 and 1934 and the Nunthorpe Stakes in 1934.

Harvey Leader was already making a big name for himself between the wars. He was only 27 when he won The St Leger with Caligula in 1920 and five years later he saddled the Grand National winner, Jack Horner. With Diomedes he won 17 of the 19 races that fast horse contested, and with Shalfleet he won 16 races including the Portland Handicap in 1935 and 1936. It was in honour of the latter that he renamed the Bedford Lodge stables Shalfleet.

Harvey Leader's three elder brothers were also trainers at Newmarket at this time.

Tom Leader had followed their father at Wroughton House, where he trained any number of good jumpers. He won the Grand National twice — with Sprig in 1927 and Gregalach in 1929. Sprig represented a real family triumph as he was ridden by his trainer's son, Ted.

Colledge Leader was at Machell Place. There he trained Cantilever to win the Cambridgeshire in 1913. Although he had been at great pains to nurse the horse back to form after recent disappointments, he had discarded the idea of running him in the Cambridgeshire until the lad who did him, Bert Southey, pleaded for him to be allowed to take his chance. Coll Leader relented, adding, "You'll have to ride him yourself, I can't get a jockey now". Unbacked and unfashionably ridden, Cantilever won by a head.

After wartime service in France, Coll Leader returned to Machell Place and won another Cambridgeshire with Re-Echo in 1922. In 1934 he left Machell Place to succeed George Lambton as private trainer to Lord Derby at Stanley House. In his second season there he won The Oaks with Verdict's daughter, Quashed, and the next year, 1936, he trained the same filly to win the Gold Cup as well as Tideway to land The 1,000 Guineas.

Towards the end of 1938, Coll Leader was taken seriously ill and was only 55 when he died in a London nursing home on 9 December. George Frederick Leader owed his christian names to the horse with which his father had won The Derby in 1874. Fred Leader trained at Warren House and then at Primrose Cottage, where he prepared First Flight to win the Chester Cup in 1929. Four years later he was killed in a road accident returning to Newmarket from Ascot.

Ted Leader was acclaimed by those who saw him ride over fences in the twenties and early thirties as one of the most stylish steeplechase jockeys of all time. In 1925/6 he was champion. As well as the Grand National on Sprig, he won the Cheltenham Gold Cup on Ballinode in 1925 and Golden Miller in 1932. On retiring from the saddle he followed his uncle, Colledge Leader, into Machell Place with immediate success. In 1934, his first season, he won both the Cambridgeshire and the Champion Stakes with Wychwood Abbot and the following year he took a second Champion Stakes with the same horse.

Reg Day became famous as a trainer of stayers. One of the first and best that he had was Son-in-Law, who had to do much of his racing during the First World War before he retired to be an outstanding success at stud. In 1914 he won the Goodwood Cup and the Jockey Club Cup and in 1915 he won the Cesarewitch and the Jockey Club Cup again.

Another fine stayer that Reg Day had at Terrace House was Solario with whom he won The St Leger in 1925 and the Gold Cup in 1926. In 1927 he won the Gold Cup for the second year in succession when he saddled Foxlaw.

Following the example of George Lambton, another peer's son, Lord George Dundas, came to train at Newmarket. He had the horses belonging to his father, the Marquess of Zetland, at Beaufort House, which is near the White Hart in the centre of the town.

After the death of Lord Zetland in 1929, Lord George carried on as trainer to his elder brother, who had inherited the title. Lord George's principal successes were obtained with Pomme de Terre in the Manchester November Handicap (1920), Yutoi in the Cesarewitch (1921), Moneymaker in the Dewhurst Stakes (1926) and High Art in the Ascot Gold Vase (1926). Lord George Dundas gave up training at the outbreak of war in 1939 and lived on until 1968.

Three other trainers responsible for notable winners during this period were Jack Watts, Tom Waugh and Fred Archer.

Jack Watts, son of Persimmon's jockey of the same name, was at Primrose Cottage when he trained Call Boy to win The Derby for the theatrical magnate Frank Curzon in 1927. Although Curzon led the winner in he already knew that he had only a short time to live and he was dead by early July. He had purchased Primrose Cottage in 1919. As a result of his death, Jack Watts was obliged to move to Lansdowne House on the other side of the town. This yard is now known as Holland House.

Tom Waugh, the youngest of Jimmy Waugh's sons, trained a lot of winners for Sir Robert Jardine at Meynell House (now Hurworth House). For that owner he won The 1,000 Guineas and Royal Ascot's Coronation Stakes with Cinna in 1920, and he obtained another notable success at the Royal Meeting with Covenden in the Gold Vase of 1929.

Fred Archer, nephew and namesake of the great jockey, had had stables at Malton until 1925. Moving to Newmarket in the spring of that year, he trained his hack Double Chance to win the Grand National.

In October 1928 Fred Archer was killed when his car crashed into a stationary bus at Woodford. He must have had a premonition of his death, as he left a sealed envelope for his great friend, Jack Colling, bequeathing him Double Chance on condition that he should be hacked or hunted until 1931.

Jack Colling's father, Robert Weston 'Bob' Colling, had come to Newmarket from Middleham in 1917. At first he was at Waterwitch and then at Bedford Lodge. He trained many winners of all sorts of races and it was to him that that great jockey, Harry Wragg, was apprenticed. One of the last of the good horses that Bob Colling had was Esquire, who won the Cambridgeshire in 1945.

When he retired at the end of the 1962 season, Jack Colling had been at Hodcott House at West Ilsley in Berkshire for some years, but before the war he was at Ellesmere House, Newmarket. During those early years of his career he trained Cat O'Nine Tails to win the Ebor Handicap in 1932 and Bellicose to win the July Cup in 1935 and 1936 as well as the Nunthorpe Stakes in 1936.

Jack Watts, the grandson of Persimmon's jockey, who trained the 1964 St Leger winner Indiana at Machell Place

23 Newmarket in the Reign of George VI

The first Derby winner to come from Newmarket in the reign of King George VI was Blue Peter, owned by Lord Rosebery, trained by Jack Jarvis at Park Lodge and ridden by Eph Smith in 1939. Without doubt he was one of the very best Derby winners.

First time out as a three-year-old he won the Blue Riband Trial Stakes at Epsom, then, carrying all before him, Blue Peter took The 2,000 Guineas, The Derby and the Eclipse Stakes. As a result of the outbreak of war on 3 September 1939, The St Leger was cancelled, so Blue Peter did not become the 15th winner of the Triple Crown.

Would Blue Peter have won The St Leger in face of the challenge from France's champion Pharis? If you had asked Sir Jack Jarvis, he would have shown you a picture of Flyon coming home an easy winner of the 1939 Ascot Gold Cup and told you that that was the way Blue Peter used to beat the older Flyon on the gallops.

In these months before the war St Albans was being used as a racing stable for the last time. After John Dawson had retired in 1933 the yard was empty. The last trainer to have his string in the yard was Hugh Sidebottom. The best horse that he had there was a black colt called Buxton, who won the Houghton Stakes as a two-year-old in 1938 and then finished fifth to Blue Peter in The Derby the following year.

After Hugh Sidebottom had volunteered for the army, the St Albans boxes were left empty and never filled again. The property has now been converted into flats and is entirely devoted to residential purposes.

When Newmarket began to get on its feet again after the end of the war in 1945, there were a lot of new faces in the ranks of the trainers and a lot of old and familiar ones were missing.

Dawson Waugh had retired in 1943. He went to live in Bournemouth, where he died in 1955, and handed his string over to his nephew, Jack Waugh, who had been invalided out of the army after the raid on Dieppe.

During the war Willie Jarvis had been taken very ill. As a result the King's horses were transferred from Egerton House to Captain Boyd-Rochfort at Freemason Lodge. Shortly afterwards Willie Jarvis died at the age of 57 on 27 January 1943. The last good horse that he trained was Godiva. This filly was rather difficult to handle and it was found that the apprentice Douglas Marks got on with her a lot better than any of the senior jockeys available. Here history was repeating itself, for at the beginning of the century the previous Egerton House trainer, Dick Marsh, had been faced with the same problem when the brilliant Diamond Jubilee had refused to go for the crack jockeys yet had responded to the handling of the apprentice, Bertie Jones.

The hon. George Lambton with his wife, and son Teddy, the future Kremlin House trainer, watching work on the Heath in 1933

Thus, just as Jones made his name on Diamond Jubilee, Doug Marks had his first taste of the limelight through his riding of Godiva, on whom he won The 1,000 Guineas and Oaks in 1940.

A year or two later Doug Marks had become too heavy for the flat and he finished his career in the saddle by riding over the sticks between 1946 and 1951. He took out a licence to train in 1949 and in recent years has been at the Lethornes stable at Lambourn. The best horse he has had was Golden Fire, who won the Cesarewitch, Chester Cup and two Goodwood Stakes.

Willie Jarvis's son Ryan Jarvis had just begun to train at Marlborough House before he left Newmarket for service with the first battalion of the Grenadier Guards for the duration of the war. On returning he took a five-year lease on Clarehaven between 1946 and 1950, before moving to Phantom House in 1951, in which year he obtained the first of his most important successes with Constantia in the National Breeders Produce Stakes at Sandown Park.

Geoffrey Barling, son of Grand Parade's trainer, was another whose career had been interrupted by the war. After beginning training in 1932, he had won the Ascot Stakes with Frawn in 1938 and 1939 so he was just beginning to come to the fore at the outset of hostilities. Picking up the threads again he soon had a useful string at Primrose Cottage, and in 1952 he had another good stayer in Le Tellier, who won the Chester Cup.

The Hon George Lambton never retired, so it was not until he died at the great age of 85 in 1945 that his phenomenal career came to its close. He was a kind and charming man, who owed many of his countless successes to nothing less than pure genius, though that must on no account be taken to mean that he was any stranger to all the hard work that it takes to run a big stable.

On his death the Kremlin House yard was taken over by his son, Teddy Lambton. In 1946 Teddy Lambton won the Lincolnshire with Langton Abbot, who was ridden by his father's old jockey, Tommy Weston. It was more than appropriate that the first big race of the first post-war season should have been won by Tommy Weston. During the war he had served with distinction in the Royal Navy, at one time being adrift in the Atlantic for three days following the sinking of the *Empress of Canada*.

Another good horse that Teddy Lambton had in his care during his early days in charge at Kremlin was Golden Cloud. That brilliant sprinter won the Nunthorpe Stakes in 1945 and then two races at Manchester in 1946 before retiring to stud at the end of that season.

Harry Wragg, who comes from Sheffield, had wound up his riding career by winning the Manchester November Handicap on Las Vegas as well as the two previous races at Castle Irwell on 16 November 1946. It was not long before he was winning big races in his new capacity as a trainer, for he landed the Chester Cup with Billet in 1948.

Also amongst the new trainers at Newmarket at the end of the war was Sam Armstrong. After having been at Middleham for many years, he came to Warren Place, the magnificent modern stable on the Moulton Road at the top of Warren Hill. There he had the Maharajah of Baroda as his principal patron. It was for the Maharajah that he won The St Leger in 1947 with Sayajirao, who had cost the then record sum of 28,000 guineas as a yearling, and The 2,000 Guineas in 1948 with My Babu.

When the horses of the Maharajah of Baroda left Newmarket, Sam Armstrong moved down the hill from Warren Place to St Gatien where he won a number of important handicaps such as the Cesarewitch in 1955 and the Chester Cup in 1957 with Curry, the Royal Hunt Cup in 1955 with Nicholas Nickleby, the Stewards Cup in 1950, 1951 and 1953 with First Consul, Sugar Bowl and Palpitate, the Ebor in 1954 with By Thunder! and the Lincoln in 1966 with Riot Act.

Sam Armstrong was also responsible for giving a start to a lot of successful jockeys. Josh Gifford, the National Hunt champion, Bill Snaith, Paul Tulk, Jack Egan, Wally Swinburn and 'Kipper' Lynch were all apprenticed to him.

In the first full season of peacetime, 1946, the Newmarket trainers made a clean sweep of the classics. Dick Perryman, who had been a top-class jockey until he retired during the war years, trained the grey Airborne to win The Derby and St Leger from the Beaufort House stable. In both races the colt was beautifully ridden by Tommy Lowrey, who had already been at the top of the tree before the war. Another ex-jockey, Henri Jellis, whose quarters were at Beverley House, was responsible for the success of Happy Knight in The 2,000

Guineas. Captain Boyd-Rochfort sent out Hypericum to win The 1,000 Guineas for the King, and Frank Butters trained Sir Alfred Butt's Steady Aim to win The Oaks.

Following the death of Coll Leader just before the war, Walter Earl succeeded him as trainer to Lord Derby at Stanley House. Born in Bohemia, the son of an English jockey with a retainer in Austria-Hungary, Earl had ridden with some success after being apprenticed to Willie Waugh at Kingsclere. In 1924 he was appointed private trainer to Mr Solly Joel at Moulton Paddocks; then in 1931 he became a public trainer.

Had they not been war years, those between 1940 and 1945 would have been vintage ones for Stanley House. As it was, the stable emerged with a wonderful record in the substitute classics. Watling Street won The Derby in 1942, Herringbone The 1,000 Guineas and The St Leger in 1943, the filly Garden Path The 2,000 Guineas in 1944 and Sun Stream The Oaks in 1945 — six classics in four seasons.

To the sorrow of the whole racing world, particularly that part of it in his native Lancashire, and to people in many walks of public life, the seventeenth Earl of Derby, owner of Sansovino, Hyperion and Fairway, died on 4 February 1948. At the time of his death, he had yet another champion at Stanley House — Alycidon. After having been second to Black Tarquin in The St Leger of 1948, Alycidon reversed the form with that horse in the Gold Cup at Royal Ascot the following season and then went on to win the coveted stayers' Triple Crown by landing the Goodwood and Doncaster Cups.

Dour, brave and brilliant, the liver chestnut Alycidon was nevertheless bone idle, and had to race in blinkers. In order to make sure that he really put his back into his work in the Gold Cup, Lord Derby and Walter Earl gave him two pacemakers. Stockbridge, with Percy Evans up, did the donkey work for the first mile, then Benny Lynch, ridden by Tommy Lowrey, cut out the pace for the next, Doug Smith sending Alycidon to the front as they came to the final bend. At the post he had beaten Black Tarquin by five lengths. Retired to stud, Alycidon assured himself perpetual influence on the breed by siring Meld, Alcide and a lot more high-class performers besides.

The other good horse at Newmarket in 1949 was Nimbus, trained by George Colling at Hurworth House (formerly known as Meynell House). Thanks to no small extent to the superlative riding of Charlie Elliott, who was hardly off his back at home, this colt won The 2,000 Guineas and The Derby. In The Guineas he beat Abernant by a short head and in The Derby Amour Drake by a head with Swallow Tail another head away third.

In the case of Nimbus there were just enough inches of his nose the right side of the post. The following year the luckless Prince Simon, trained by Captain Boyd-Rochfort, had the very opposite experience in the same two classics. For The 2,000 Guineas he was beaten by a short head by Palestine and for The Derby by a head by Galcador; so he lost those races by the very margins by which Nimbus had won them.

24 Frank Butters, Marcus Marsh and the Aga Khan at Fitzroy House

On both sides of his family Frank Butters was closely related to Newmarket trainers, and few men have done more to contribute to the town's fame as a training centre, yet he was neither born there nor established there until he was well into middle age.

His father was Joe Butters, the Kremlin House trainer who had been friend and mentor to Fred Archer in his youth, and his mother Janet was one of the several daughters of Jimmy Waugh of Meynell House. It was while his father was training in Austria that Frank was born in Vienna in 1878.

His early years were passed amongst the horses in his father's stable near the Imperial City. When it was time for him to begin his formal education he came to England to attend Framlingham College in Suffolk, spending his school holidays with his Waugh relatives at Newmarket. Among his contemporaries at Framlingham was Sir Alfred Munnings, who was to become the most accomplished horse painter of his generation and President of the Royal Academy. They were to be associated when both were at the top of their professions some 40 years later and Sir Alfred's painting of Mahmoud being saddled for The Derby of 1936 with Frank Butters in the background is one of the artist's best-known works.

On leaving Framlingham, Frank Butters rejoined his father in Austria and soon began training on his own account in that country, thus following a tradition that was maintained on both sides of his family.

At the outbreak of war in 1914, Frank Butters and his younger brother Fred were interned along with the rest of the English community, but as the American Embassy stood surety for their behaviour their detention was no more than nominal. When the armistice was signed four years later, Butters had come to the end of his savings and as a result of political upheaval and military defeat the economic situation in Austria left him with no prospects of resuming training in that country. Accordingly he left for Italy and there he started a stable which was soon as successful as the one that he had had in Austria.

While Frank Butters was in Italy, George Lambton trained Sansovino to win The Derby of 1924 for Lord Derby. At the end of the following season, at the age of 65, Lambton decided it was time to retire from training the Stanley House string and devote himself to the management of Lord Derby's racing interests.

Although Butters had spent all but his schooldays abroad, appreciation of his ability extended far beyond Austria and Italy, so to anyone conversant with the international racing scene it came as no surprise that Lord Derby should invite him to succeed Lambton. At the age of 48 Butters accepted an offer which brought him limitless opportunities and came to Stanley House with a four-year contract. In a way it was an association that had its roots in the past, for Frank Butters's father had been born on Lord Derby's estate at Knowsley near Liverpool in Lancashire 80 years previously.

Relatives who had not seen him for donkey's years, the other people at Newmarket, and the racing world in general, soon got to know Frank Butters. Almost without exception, they liked him.

As straight as a die, he was absolutely devoted to the welfare of his horses and the interests of their owners. For his success he relied upon knowledge derived from experience and dogged hard work rather than those flashes of inspiration that were characteristic of George Lambton. Betting was something that was of no interest to him. Like the old school of Newmarket trainers from which he sprang, he believed in giving his horses plenty of work to get them fit and make them tough. He did all he knew how to ensure that his horses were completely ready to give of their best in their engagements but was loathe to be drawn into giving an assessment of their chances, so he was not the trainer for a gambling owner. All that concerned him was winning the classics and the other great races with the cream of the blood that was sent to him. Handicaps were very much of secondary interest. No doubt he was lucky to be able to insist on this order of priorities, yet it cannot be gainsaid that he was just the trainer for the many great horses that were under his care during the 32 years that he had a yard at Newmarket.

In his first year at Stanley House he made a flying start on the English Turf by winning The Oaks with Lord Durham's Beam, and by the end of the season he was leading trainer, having won 54 races worth £57,468. It was a great beginning by a newcomer, even with the vast resources of Stanley House behind him, but as if it was not enough to have become champion trainer at the first time of trying, he consolidated his reputation by heading the list the following season too.

By the end of 1928 he had £67,539 to the credit of his owners, and had more luck been on the side of the stable that sum would have been considerably greater.

As a result of his convincing success in the Newmarket Stakes, Fairway became a hot favourite for The Derby at 3-1. Such was the acclamation that the Epsom crowd accorded to a strongly fancied runner carrying Lord Derby's popular black jacket and white cap, that his most enthusiastic admirers even went as far as pulling hairs out of his tail as Tommy Weston took him down to the start. The sort of mobbing that would be more agreeable to a pop star than a highly-strung thoroughbred completely ruined Fairway's chance so that it was impossible to hold it against him that he finished unplaced to Felstead. In The St Leger it was a completely different story and Fairway showed his true quality by beating Palais Royal II a convincing length and a half. That was the second classic success of the season for Lord Derby and Frank Butters, as Toboggan had already taken The Oaks.

In 1930, Frank Butters added to his laurels by landing The 1,000 Guineas with Fair Isle, and Stanley House still seemed to thrive. But all was far from well. The Wall Street Crash had come in October 1929 and by the following year its impact was being felt on this side of the Atlantic. England was soon to be faced with mass unemployment and money was becoming shorter. Even Lord Derby was forced to economise and dispense with having both a manager and a trainer. Thus it was that Frank Butters's contract was not renewed at the end of the original term of four years and George Lambton resumed direct control of Stanley House.

For the second time in his life Frank Butters was deprived of his string by the force of world events and left with nothing but his highly tried ability to offer on the open, but depressed, market.

Without so much as a single yearling, or even the promise of a horse, Frank Butters rented Fitzroy House in December 1930. The previous trainer in that yard had been J. H. Crawford, who had died in 1929. Crawford had moved there from Bishops Canning, Wiltshire, to

Frank Butters with Tommy Weston in the Stanley House yard

be private trainer to Sir Victor Sasson in 1926. After Crawford's death Sir Victor sent his horses to Carlburg to be trained by Charlie Waugh.

Two of the first owners to send horses to Fitzroy House were Mr A. W. Gordon and Sir Alfred Butt. It was the latter's horse, Lord Bill, who did much to put the newly formed stable on the map. Lord Bill came to Butters as a maiden four-year-old with the reputation of being an arrant rogue. Yet so thoroughly did he reform under Butters's care that he won races at Doncaster and Yarmouth in the spring of 1931 and in the summer he did a six-break beginning with a minor success at Birmingham and winding it up by landing the important Chesterfield Cup at Goodwood at the end of July.

Some six weeks after Lord Bill had won the Chesterfield Cup an event took place which was to ensure that Frank Butters would never have to look for a string for a third time. The racing world was amazed to hear that the fabulously successful association between the Aga Khan and the Whatcombe, Berkshire, trainer Dick Dawson (no relation of Mat and others mentioned above) had come to an end.

The Aga Khan was not only the religious leader of a large Islamic sect but one of the richest men in the world. At the age of 21 he saw Jeddah win The Derby in 1898. Six years later in 1904 his interest in racing was further kindled while he was a guest at Colonel Hall Walker's stud at Tully in Ireland. In the course of that visit he began to entertain the idea of owning and breeding on a large scale, but because his time was fully occupied with his political commitments the Aga Khan had to wait 17 years until 1921 before he began to lay the foundations of what was to be one of the greatest studs in the history of racing.

On entering racing the Aga asked George Lambton to train for him. Lambton had to decline as it was impossible to make the necessary arrangements at Stanley House, but he did agree to undertake the purchase of yearlings on the Aga's behalf. Lambton's brief was to concentrate on buying fillies from the best lines in *The Stud Book* but not to the complete exclusion of colts.

The first batch of yearlings that the Aga sent to Dawson at Whatcombe included Cos and Teresina and the second batch had in it Friar's Daughter, Mumtaz Mahal, Diophon and Salmon Trout.

Cos and Teresina were complete contrasts. In his first season as an owner the Aga won the Queen Mary Stakes at Royal Ascot and five other races with Cos, while his other good filly, Teresina, trained on to establish herself as one of the best stayers of her generation by winning the Goodwood Cup.

Amongst the second lot of yearlings George Lambton bought for the Aga were two of the 1924 classic winners, namely Diophon (2,000 Guineas) and Salmon Trout (St Leger), but neither of these made the same impression on the public as did their stablemate, Mumtaz Mahal, in her two-year-old days in 1923. Such was the speed of this grey filly, who cost 9,100 guineas, that she seemed the reincarnation of The Tetrarch in female form. In her first season she won the Queen Mary Stakes, the National Breeders Produce Stakes, the Molecomb

Stakes, the Champagne Stakes and the Imperial Produce Stakes. As a three-year-old 'Mumty' failed to stay the mile and was beaten into second place in The 1,000 Guineas, but on reverting to sprinting she showed that she was as fast as ever by winning the Nunthorpe Stakes and Goodwood's King George Stakes.

The only race that Friar's Daughter ever won was a five-furlong event worth £168 at Alexandra Park as a two-year-old in 1923, but though she was completely outshone by those mentioned above during her days in training she did more than hold her own with them on her retirement to stud.

At the end of the year 1924, only the second in which his colours were carried, the Aga Khan was leading owner. Throughout the rest of the decade the trend continued. In 1929 he was leading owner for a second time and for a third in 1930, when he won his first Derby with

Mumtaz Mahal – "The Flying Mumty" – winner of the Queen Mary Stakes by 10 lengths

Blenheim. Despite these almost fabulous triumphs that they shared, the Aga Khan and Dick Dawson began to have serious disagreements and matters came to a head in the sharp words that were exchanged between them at Newbury races in September 1931. A few days later the Aga's priceless string left Whatcombe.

Like Lord Derby, the Aga Khan had a sound knowledge of continental racing, so he was well acquainted with the enormous success that Frank Butters had achieved on the continent as well as that earned in the comparatively short time that he had been in England. Consequently, it was quite natural that he should have chosen Butters to succeed Dick Dawson as his trainer, and the association continued until Butters was compelled to retire some 20 years later.

Among the horses that the Aga sent to Fitzroy House in the autumn of 1931 were the two-year-olds Dastur, Udaipur and Firdaussi. The Aga was very keen on giving his horses Persian names, as many of his religious followers lived in Persia. The following season Udaipur won The Oaks and Firdaussi The St Leger, while luckless Dastur, whose dam was Friar's Daughter, had to be content with second place in The 2,000 Guineas, The Derby and The St Leger, though he gained a measure of compensation by winning the Irish Derby.

The St Leger of 1932 was almost a supreme triumph for Fitzroy House. Not only was Firdaussi the winner and Dastur second, but the other two horses that Frank Butters saddled for the Aga Khan, Udaipur and Taj Kasra, were fourth and fifth respectively. By the end of the season, Frank Butters was leading trainer for a third time, having won 62 races worth £72,436.

Thus the first full season in which Frank Butters had charge of the Aga's horses had been one of almost unrelieved triumph and the owner-trainer partnership lost none of its momentum during the following season. Dastur won the Coronation Cup and dead-heated for the Champion Stakes in 1933 and the next season Felicitation defeated Hyperion in the Gold Cup. Though Felicitation was a stayer of the highest class, the star of Fitzroy House in 1934 was the two-year-old colt Bahram, a beautifully-moulded dark bay with an elongated star on his forehead. Foaled on 13 April 1932, he was by Blandford out of Friar's Daughter by Friar Marcus, and half-brother to Dastur.

He made his debut in Sandown Park's National Breeders Produce Stakes, which the Aga was expected to win with Theft, though Duke John was favourite. At half-way Gordon Richards had Theft in front and it looked as though he would win, but Bahram came through with such a run that he passed the post a neck in front of his stablemate without being anything like extended. It was now evident that Bahram had been playing games with Frank Butters and everyone else in his work at home, for though he had been shaping promisingly no one supposed that he was as good as Theft. There had been no fluke about his success and he went on to consolidate his reputation by winning the Gimcrack Stakes, the Middle Park Stakes and two other races before retiring to winter quarters undefeated.

The Aga Khan's Bahram, winner of the Triple Crown in 1935

Besides the Gold Cup and those important juvenile races with Bahram, Frank Butters also won The Oaks with Lord Durham's Light Brocade in 1934 and at the end of the season he was leading trainer for a fourth time.

As a three-year-old Bahram swept all before him and became the 14th horse in the history of racing, to win the Triple Crown by landing The 2,000 Guineas, The Derby and St Leger. The only other race he contested in 1935 was the St James's Palace Stakes at Royal Ascot and, needless to say, he won that too. At the end of the season Bahram retired to stud. He had not let anyone know how good he was before he beat Theft at Sandown Park and he kept the secret to himself right to the end of his brilliant career. Because of his innate idleness his jockeys were obliged to shake him up from time to time but he was never extended. It has been argued that his contemporaries were a very moderate lot. Even if that was the case it constitutes no reflection on the excellence of Bahram. Few men have had more experience of top-class horses than Frank Butters acquired, and he always regarded Bahram as the very best he ever had.

While Bahram was being lionised by the sporting public, Frank Butters was busy bringing on another champion in the grey Mahmoud, whose dam, Mah Mahal, was a daughter of the flying Mumtaz Mahal. The great speed that he showed as a two-year-old enabled Mahmoud to win the Champagne Stakes at Doncaster.

As Mahmoud had shown that he had inherited so many of the characteristics of Mumtaz Mahal it seemed as though The 2,000 Guineas was the most likely classic for him to win. Yet in The 2,000 Guineas he was held up for a late run like a non-stayer by Steve Donoghue and beaten by a short head by Pay Up, whereas in The Derby Charlie Smirke accepted the dictates of circumstances when he sent Mahmoud to the front two furlongs out and the grey ran on to beat the Aga Khan's other runner, the better-fancied Taj Akbar, by three lengths in two minutes $33\frac{4}{5}$ seconds, a time that still stands as a record for The Derby.

As had been the case with Bahram, Mahmoud was still as sound as a bell by the end of his three-year-old days, but all the same the Aga Khan, who was never one to allow his commercial instincts to be subordinate to his sporting ones, packed him off to stud.

When the Second World War broke out in September 1939, the Aga Khan had been owning horses for 17 years and controlled a racing empire of unprecedented strength spread over England, France and Ireland. His three Derby winners were making big names for themselves at stud, Bahram and Mahmoud at Newmarket's Egerton Stud, and Blenheim in France. His enormous collection of the choicest bred mares, many tracing back to his foundation matrons, Mumtaz Mahal, Cos and Teresina, were producing an unending stream of high-class winners that made up the long string he had in training with Frank Butters at Fitzroy House.

With England fighting for her existence and France under enemy occupation, the bottom fell out of the racing and bloodstock market.

One choice before the Aga was to reduce his stud and string for the duration and pick up the threads when peace should come. Provided the war was not too long, the best of his stallions, with the exception of Blenheim, would still be at their peak, and he would have ample young mares stocking his studs.

Yet if a bomb should hit Fitzroy House or one of his breeding establishments the Aga would suffer incalculable loss. Rather than take the risk of losing any of the cream of his stud through enemy action, the Aga Khan staggered the racing world by selling his three Derby winners to America, Blenheim for £45,000, Bahram for £40,000 and Mahmoud for £20,000. Breeders were furious and British bloodstock suffered a loss, the effects of which it feels to this day.

Fortunately Newmarket did not suffer as much from bombing as the pessimistic Aga had feared and its studs and stables were unscathed though the town was hit. The White Hart, one of its most historic hotels, was partially destroyed and closed until its restoration was completed in 1956.

Meanwhile Frank Butters, who was already turned 60, carried on with a much depleted string. In the heyday of his stable in the thirties, he had not only had horses in his own yard at Fitzroy House but he had rented more boxes at Stockbridge House and Queensberry Lodge for the overspill. Things were very different by 1941 when his string numbered a mere eleven.

To make his personal contribution to the drastic economies that were being demanded from the civilian population, Frank Butters gave up his car and went out to watch work on a bicycle every morning. The most notable successes that he obtained in the wartime substitute big races were with Turkham in The St Leger at Thirsk in 1940, Winterhalter in the Coronation Cup at Newbury in 1941, Umiddad in the Gold Cup at Newmarket in 1944 and Tehran in The St Leger at Newmarket in the same year.

When racing started to get back on its feet again after the end of the war in 1945, Fitzroy House became as big a power in the land as ever it had been. Frank Butters won the first post-war Oaks at Epsom with Sir Alfred Butt's Steady Aim in 1946, the Eclipse Stakes with the Aga's Migoli, who had been second in The Derby in 1947, and with Sir Alfred's Petition in 1948, and The Oaks with the Aga's Masaka in 1948. In the latter year he sent the grey Migoli over to France to win the Prix de l'Arc de Triomphe.

By the beginning of the 1949 season Migoli, Petition and the other established stars of Fitzroy House had retired to stud, but such was the promise of the two-year-olds that it looked as though Frank Butters and the Aga Khan were on the threshold of an era of success that would surpass anything that even they had experienced hitherto.

In Palestine Frank Butters had the top two-year-old colt and in Diableretta the champion filly of the same age, while the other juveniles in the yard made up a supporting cast that was very much more than adequate. These included the Imperial Produce Stakes winner Kisaki, Tambara, But Beautiful and Bagamoya.

The grey Palestine showed simply brilliant speed when winning the Coventry Stakes at Royal Ascot, the National Breeders Produce Stakes at Sandown Park, the Gimcrack Stakes at York, Doncaster's Champagne Stakes and two other races. It looked as though he might never be beaten.

Diableretta was yet another of that female line that the Aga Khan had developed so successfully. A chestnut filly, she was by Dante out of Dodoma out of Mumtaz Begum by Blenheim out of the great Mumtaz Mahal. After being third to Baroda at Newmarket first time out when she collided with another runner and finished with her rider out of his irons, Diableretta won the Queen Mary Stakes at Royal Ascot, the Molecomb Stakes at Goodwood and five other races.

When Palestine had won six races off the reel and Diableretta seven, Frank Butters decided that each had done enough for one season and let it be known that they would be put away for their respective Guineas in 1950. Critics have said that Frank Butters was somewhat severe in his training methods, particularly upon the fillies, but whether or not this was the case he certainly knew better than to take the pitcher to the well too often.

On the Sunday before Newmarket's Second October Meeting, Press Association reporter Norman Fairchild made a routine telephone call to Frank Butters to ask for the Fitzroy House runners for the coming week. To his amazement he was told that Palestine would go for the Middle Park Stakes on Tuesday and Diableretta the Cheveley Park Stakes on the Friday. What had happened was that the Aga Khan's elder son, Prince Aly Khan, had beome mesmerised with the idea of the Aga becoming the first owner ever to win £100,000 in England in one season. Accordingly he had persuaded his father that Palestine, Diableretta and others should fulfil back-end engagements that they would not otherwise have done.

Frank Butters was absolutely horrified at being asked to do something that was completely contrary to the instincts of a lifetime's experience and all against his professional principles. His worst fears were realised to the full. Both two-year-olds had gone over the top. As a result, Palestine was beaten by a length and a half by Masked Light and Diableretta by a head by the French filly Corejada.

Any chance that there had been of topping the magical £100,000 mark before Palestine and Diableretta ran had completely disappeared after their defeats. At the end of the season the Aga Khan was leading owner but with only £68,916 to his credit while Frank Butters headed the trainers' list for the eighth time with £71,721 accumulated.

The life of Prince Aly Khan, a bon viveur with a talent for diplomacy, was full of irony. One small part of it was that he himself was to be the first owner to win £100,000 in an English racing season. But he had to wait another ten years before he had £100,668 to his credit, largely thanks to his marvellous grey filly, Petite Etoile. Incidentally, like Diableretta, Petite Etoile traced back to Mumtaz Mahal in tail female line, while in tail male line she was a grand-daughter of Palestine's sire, Fair Trial.

The extent to which the disastrous defeats of Palestine and Diableretta affected Frank Butters cannot be calculated. He was already turned 70 and it is arguable that they preyed on his mind to such an extent that they were partially responsible for the far worse disaster that was to follow a few weeks later. Riding through Newmarket on that bicycle, which was a legacy of wartime economy, Frank Butters was run down by a lorry. Although the Aga Khan sent the best specialists in Europe to operate on him, the injuries to his brain were so severe that he was never to train again. In his retirement he lived on in the town until his death on the last day of 1957 at the age of 79.

A kindly man of absolute integrity, whose hobbies were keeping budgerigars and gardening, Frank Butters was one of the greatest trainers of all time.

Left without a trainer, the Aga Khan asked Marcus Marsh if he would leave Egerton House to come across the Racecourse Side of the Heath to Fitzroy House. The son of Dick Marsh, who had trained Diamond Jubilee, Persimmon and Minoru for King Edward at Egerton, Marcus Marsh had run a successful stable at Lambourn during pre-war days, winning The Derby and St Leger of 1934 with Windsor Lad ridden by Charlie Smirke. His friendship and association with Smirke, who became the Aga Khan's jockey, lasted over the years and it was Smirke who recommended him as Frank Butters's successor at Fitzroy House.

After having served as a rear-gunner in Bomber Command, being shot down and spending four years as a prisoner-of-war, Marcus Marsh resumed his career in his father's old yard at Egerton House on demobilisation. The most important of his immediate post-war successes were obtained with The Bug, the unbeaten winner of seven races including the Wokingham Stakes, the July Cup and the Nunthorpe Stakes as a three-year-old in 1946, and Valognes, who took the Chester Vase in 1948.

Coming to Fitzroy House with a contract to train the Aga Khan's horses for three years, Marsh hit the headlines straight away by winning The 2,000 Guines with Palestine, who beat the luckless Prince Simon by a short head. The end of the story of Diableretta was far less happy, for she finished unplaced in The 1,000 Guineas and never ran again.

There was no outstanding two-year-old at Fitzroy House in 1951 though a rather lazy brown colt was found willing to do more on the course than he was at home. This was Tulyar, who paid his way though only by winning such minor events as the Buggins Farm Nursery at Haydock Park and the Kineton Nursery at Birmingham.

The outlook for the Aga's horses in 1952 seemed somewhat bleak unless Tulyar made appreciable improvement. Until the colt got back on to the racecourse it was impossible to tell how much he had come on during the close season, for, like Bahram, the Fitzroy House champion of two decades previously, he simply would not do a stroke at home. When at last he did resume racing this indolent individual showed that he had come on to an almost unbelievable extent and the upshot of it all was that Tulyar went throught the season the unbeaten winner of The Derby, The St Leger, the King George VI and Queen Elizabeth Stakes and the Eclipse Stakes giving his rider, the ever ebullient Smirke, the opportunity to make his pun by crying out delightedly, "What did I Tull'yer?" after their triumph at Epsom.

That far less was expected from Tullyar will be gathered from the fact that at the beginning of the season Aly Khan, who was managing the affairs of his ageing father to an increasing extent, had decided that Marcus Marsh's contract should not be renewed at the end of the year. By the time the Aga heard of what was happening and Marcus Marsh was training Tulyar to make him leading owner on the British Turf for the 13th time it was too late to alter arrangements.

In 1953 the Aga Khan and his son had their English-trained horses with Noel Murless and the following year the Aga Khan consolidated all his interests in France, doubtless attracted by the higher prize money in that country, while Aly Khan continued to keep horses with Murless.

Like the Aga Khan's other Derby winners, Tulyar was retired at the end of his three-year-old career after he had set up a new record of prize money won by a single horse in England with £76,417. 10s. 0d. to his credit. In 1955 he was sold to the Irish National Stud for a reported quarter of a million pounds. The following year he was resold to an American syndicate.

Marcus Marsh stayed at Fitzroy House with some horses that were useful without being outstanding until March 1962, when he moved his string to Somerville Lodge. Two years later he retired.

As for the Aga Khan, he died a few months before Frank Butters in 1957.

25 Newmarket in the Early Years of the Present Reign

Rather appropriately, the start of the new reign saw an almost immediate change in the fortunes of the royal trainer, Captain Cecil Boyd-Rochfort. In the following years he was to have ample compensation for the narrow defeats of Prince Simon in The Guineas and The Derby.

If at first the Captain thought that his luck had taken no turn for the better it is hardly surprising, for Aureole, whom he trained for the Queen, was beaten into second place behind Pinza in The Derby of the Coronation year in 1953.

Pinza, who provided Sir Gordon Richards with his only riding success in The Derby, was trained at Newmarket by Norman Bertie in the Bedford Cottage stable managed by Jack Clayton. Like Sir Gordon, Norman Bertie had been closely associated with Pinza's breeder, the Beckhampton trainer Fred Darling, for whom he was travelling head lad for many years, during which Sir Gordon was retained as jockey. Next time out after The Derby, Pinza confirmed Epsom form by beating Aurole in the King George VI and the Queen Elizabeth Stakes at Ascot.

Pinza never ran again, and although Aureole was not the one to benefit from his absence in The St Leger, that race marked the turn in the road for Freemason Lodge. The Captain won that Leger with Brigadier W. P. Wyatt's Premonition. Aureole, who did not stay, finished third.

It was as a four-year-old the following season that Aureole really came into his own. Largely through his success in the King George VI and the Queen Elizabeth Stakes, the Queen was the leading owner that season, and Captain Boyd-Rochfort headed the list of winning trainers for the third time in his career.

At the end of the following year, 1955, Captain Boyd-Rochfort was the leading trainer again, having won the fillies' Triple Crown, The 1,000 Guineas, The Oaks and The St Leger with the wonderful Meld. Late that summer the Newmarket stables were badly affected by the coughing epidemic, the Heath being almost deserted during working hours in late August and early September. It was touch and go whether Meld would go to the post for The Leger despite all the strict precautions that the Captain took to isolate her. All went well until she coughed twice on the morning of the race. In the afternoon a combination of class and courage enabled her to carry the colours of Lady Zia Wernher to a three-quarters of a length victory over Nucleus whose rider, Lester Piggott, lodged an unsuccessful objection.

In 1957 the Captain won the Gold Cup with Zarathustra and after h had landed The 2,000 Guineas with the Queen's Pall Mall in 1958 it looked as if he, at last, had The Derby at his mercy, for the merits of his colt Alcide were outstanding. As well as ability, Alcide had character and this was manifested in his constant bucking and kicking and the pleasure he took in dislodging his rider, though he was without a trace of vice.

One morning shortly before The Derby Pall Mall got loose while the Freemason Lodge string was on Side Hill and Alcide lashed out at him. As Alcide seemed a little off colour at evening stables it seemed as though he might have strained a muscle or done himself some other minor injury in that incident, but when he showed no signs of recovery during the next day or so, more serious implications had to be considered. A thorough veterinary examination revealed a broken rib, and it became evident that the favourite for The Derby had been nobbled, in all probability by someone inside the stable. There was no question of Alcide being able to run at Epsom but he recovered well enough to be able to obtain an impressive success in The St Leger.

The Captain and Alcide's owner, Sir Humphrey de Trafford, were soon compensated for that Derby having eluded them. The following year, 1959, they won the race with Parthia, a close relative of Alcide, whom Sir Humphrey had also bred at the Newsells Park Stud that he had founded near Royston in 1926. Alcide was by Alycidon out of Chenille, while Parthia was by Persian Gulf out of Chenille's daughter Lightning.

During those seasons in the fifties when his stable was on the crest of the wave, Captain Boyd-Rochfort had a staff of outstanding ability at Freemason Lodge. The value of team work in racing has rarely been better exemplified.

Harry Carr, who had developed into a brilliant race rider since coming from the north to be first jockey for the Captain in 1947, was still retained. As assistant trainer the Captain had that fine horseman Bruce Hobbs, now running his own stable so successfully at Palace House, while Tommy Lowrey, a man of mature judgement and great experience of high-class horses, was on hand to ride the most important work along with a succession of good lightweights like Tony Shrive, Eddie Hide, Jack Egan and Derek Morris. The Captain's own apprentices, such as Harry Fox, Alcide's regular partner, played important parts too.

When Harry Carr retired in 1964 he was succeeded as stable jockey at Freemason Lodge by Stan Clayton, who rode the Queen's Canisbay to win the Eclipse Stakes in 1965. That race was worth £29,451 and was the most valuable ever won by a member of the royal family up to that time.

In 1968 Captain Boyd-Rochfort's services to the royal family were rewarded with a knighthood and at the end of that season he gave up training, handing his string over to his stepson, Henry Cecil, who is married to Sir Noel Murless's daughter, Julia. As he planned to spend his retirement in Ireland, Sir Cecil, as he had become, put Freemason Lodge on the market while leasing it to Henry Cecil for his first season, which turned out to be a highly satisfactory one. With Wolver Hollow he won the Eclipse Stakes and two months later he landed Doncaster's Observer Gold Cup with Sir Humphrey de Trafford's Approval.

Towards the end of the first year of the new reign, Noel Murless came to Newmarket, installing a powerful string at Warren Place on the top of Warren Hill. That very modern stable, built by Sam Darling only a few years before the war had recently been vacated by Sam Armstrong. The arrival of Noel Murless saw the start of a success story for which there are few parallels in the history of the town.

Born in 1910, the son of a Cheshire farmer, Noel Murless had ridden over the sticks before spending five years as assistant trainer to Hubert Hartigan. On taking out a licence in 1935 he had a mixed string at Hambleton above Thirsk in Yorkshire. Then in 1947 he succeeded Fred Darling, the brother of the builder of Warren Place, at Beckhampton. In his first season there he was leading trainer and by the time he came to Newmarket had already won two classics, The 1,000 Guineas with Queenpot in 1948 and The St Leger with Ridgewood in 1949.

Sir Gordon Richards, who continued to ride for Beckhampton after Murless had succeeded Fred Darling, carried on his association with the stable for a short time after it was transferred to Newmarket. His long career in the saddle came to an unexpected end when Abergeldie, whom Murless trained for the Queen, reared over with him at Sandown Park in July 1954. As a result of injuries received in this accident at the age of 50 he was unable to ride again. His successor as first jockey at Warren Place was 18-year-old Lester Piggott.

Crepello, ridden by Lester Piggott, being led in his work on the Heath in 1957

Tom Loates, apprenticed to Joe Cannon at Newmarket won the Derby on Donovan (1889) and Isinglass (1893)

Sir John Astley, founder of the Stableman's Institute, now the New Astley Club

T *Gimcrack, the smallest and gamest of the early racehorses, won his last race at Newmarket in April 1771*

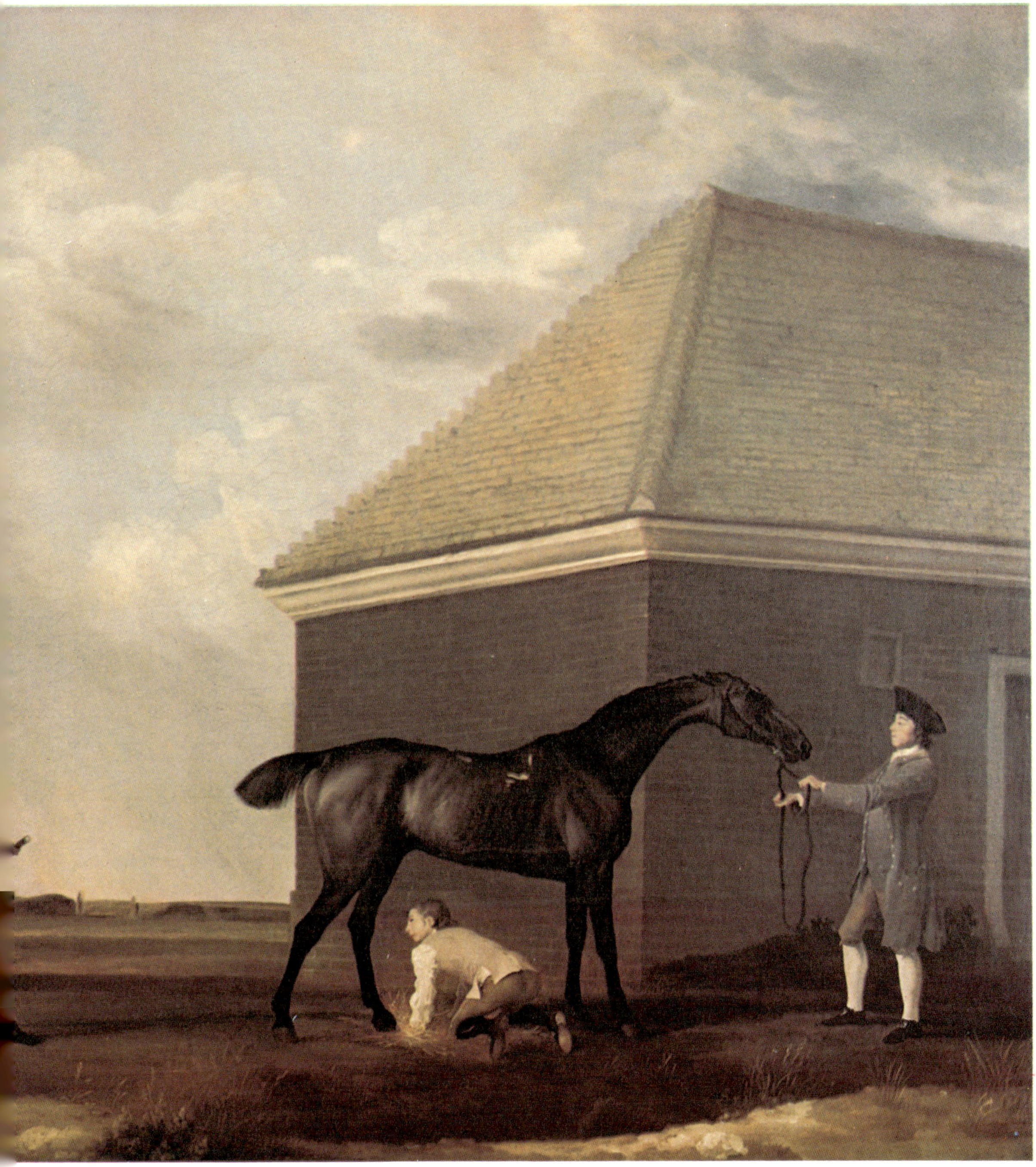

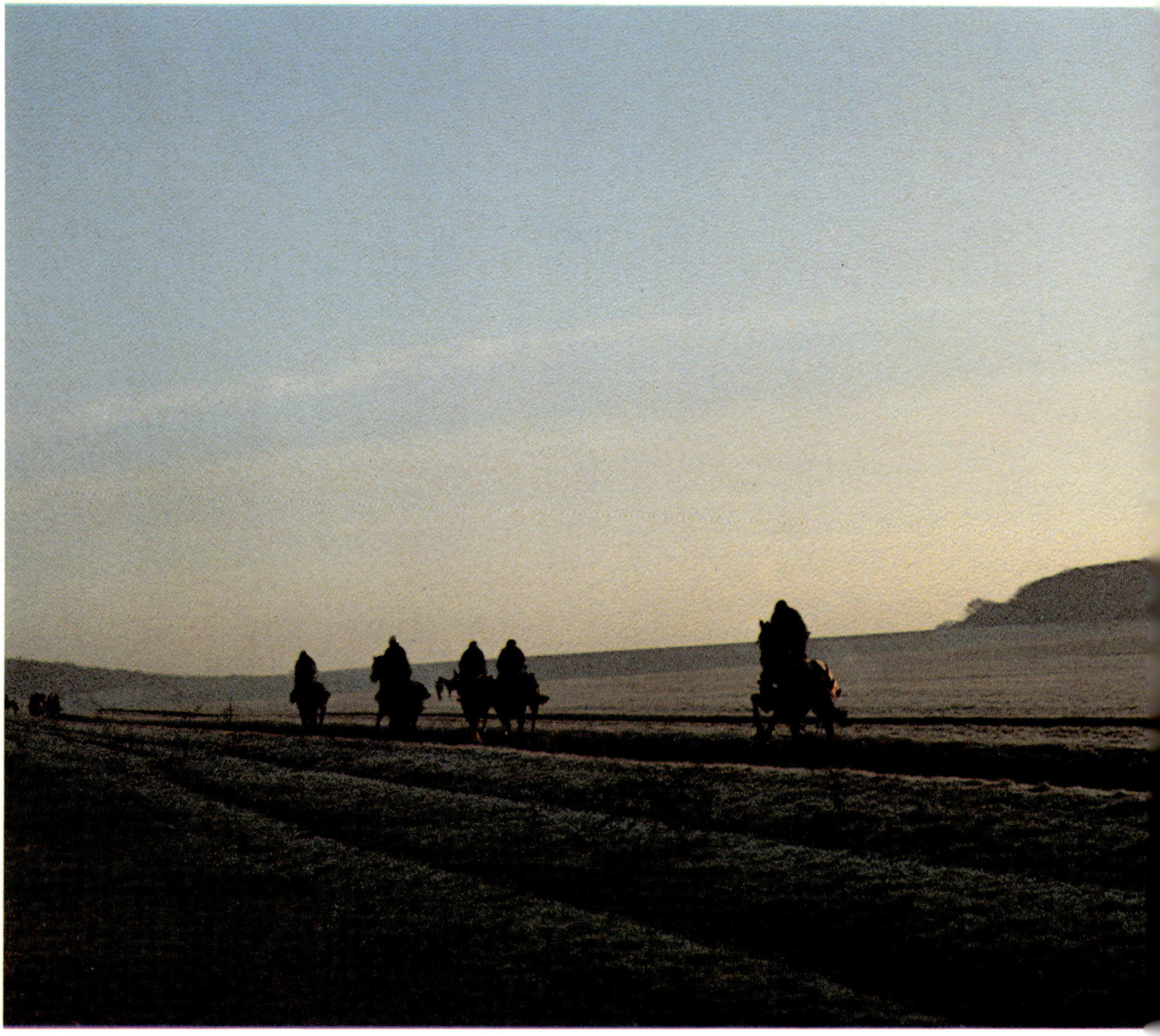

It was in the third year of the partnership between Murless and Piggott that Warren Place burst into the limelight. Crepello won The 2,000 Guineas and The Derby and then Lester Piggott got the Queen's Carrozza home by a short head in The Oaks to complete the Epsom classic double. By the end of the season Noel Murless had become the first man to pass the £100,000 prize money barrier in a year and headed the list of winning trainers with a new record of £116,898.

That record only stood two years until 1959 when Murless himself broke it with earnings of £145,727, thanks largely to that wonderful grey filly, Petite Etoile, who was successful in The 1,000 Guineas, The Oaks, the Sussex Stakes, the Yorkshire Oaks and the Champion Stakes. Remaining in training for two more seasons, her later successes included the Coronation Cup in 1960 and 1961.

In 1960 Murless and Piggott won The Derby and The St Leger with St Paddy. The following year they won another St Leger with Aurelius, who must be unique amongst classic winners in as much as he graduated to steeplechasing after having proved a failure at stud.

Half-way through the 1966 season, Lester Piggott made the momentous decision to end his attachment to Warren Place. Moreover, as he held no retainer, he was able to do so immediately and thus ride the Irish filly Valoris in The Oaks. Valoris justified Piggott's judgement by beating Berkley Springs by two and a half lengths with Murless's candidate Varinia, Stan Clayton up, three lengths away third.

With the departure of Piggott, Murless engaged the Australian George Moore to ride for him in 1967, which was to be his third record-breaking season. The young Scottish lightweight Sandy Barclay was also given a retainer.

Moore made a brilliant start to his association with Warren Place by bringing off the Newmarket classic double, winning The 2,000 Guineas on Royal Palace and The 1,000 Guineas on Fleet. Mr H. J. Joel's Royal Palace went on to win The Derby, and with the former Irish four-year-old Busted, Murless won the Eclipse Stakes and the King George VI and the Queen Elizabeth Stakes. In the former, Busted was ridden by Bill Rickaby, and in the latter by Moore.

By the end of the season Murless had shattered all previous records, having trained the winners of 60 races worth £256,699. It was only a matter of years previously that Captain Boyd-Rochfort had become the first trainer to win a million pounds for his patrons. Now a trainer had won a quarter of a million in just one season. It was a great achievement.

Despite all the successes that he had obtained on Royal Palace and the other horses that he rode for Murless, George Moore did not return to England in 1968 and Sandy Barclay succeeded him as first jockey at Warren Place. The change of rider brought no check to the stable's run in the classics, for Barclay straight away won The 1,000 Guineas on Caergwrle, owned and bred by the trainer's wife.

The new reign was not very old before Harry Wragg obtained his first training success in an English classic through Sir Percy Lor-

Harry Wragg, and his late son-in-law Manny Mercer, with his string on the Heath

raine's Darius in The 2,000 Guineas of 1954. Seven years later he won The Derby though it was not with the much fancied Sovrango, whom George Moore rode into fourth place after flying from the other side of the world for the mount, but the 66-1 outsider Psidium, ridden by Roger Poincelet. The following year, 1962, Harry Wragg won The 1,000 Guineas with Mr R. More O'Farrell's Abermaid.

In the Irish classics Harrry Wragg enjoyed even greater success during that era. As well as the Irish 2,000 Guineas with Lucero in 1956 he won the Irish 1,000 Guineas with Lacqueur in 1967, the Irish Derby with Frais du Bois II in 1951, Talgo in 1956 and Fidalgo in 1959, and the Irish Oaks with Garden State in 1956, Discorea in 1959 and Ambergris in 1961.

At the same period of his career Harry Wragg also had an impressive record in the more valuable handicaps, particularly Redcar's Vaux Gold Tankard. In the course of six years he saddled four winners of that event in Monterrico in 1962, Espresso in 1963, Atilla in 1965 and Salvo in 1966 and provided the runner-up twice — Espresso in 1964 and Chicago in 1967. He also won the Cambridgeshire with Violetta III, who dead-heated in 1961 and Lacqueur in 1967, the Ebor with Hyperion Kid in 1955 and a second Chester Cup with Golovine in 1956.

His frequent forays abroad were rewarded by the success of Nagami in the Gran Premio de Jockey Club at Milan in 1958 as well as by Atilla in the same race in 1965. On the other side of the Alps he did wonderfully well in Germany's Grosser Preis von Baden, winning that event with Espresso in 1963 and 1964, Atilla in 1966 and Salvo in 1967.

As well as training big winners at home and abroad, Harry Wragg also set several of the lads that had been apprenticed to him on the path to riding fame. The late Peter Robinson, who rode so well before taking over Teddy Lambton's stable, Peter Boothman, who won the Royal Hunt Cup on Amos and many other races in this country prior to continuing his career so successfully in Ireland, and Graham Sexton all served their time with Harry Wragg at Abington Place.

In 1961, the year that Psidium caused such an upset in The Derby, Harry Wragg went close to completing the Epsom double, for his filly Ambergris was beaten by only a length and a half by Sweet Solera in The Oaks.

Another of the most important stables at Newmarket during the first 15 years of the present reign was Lagrange, where the private string of the late Major Lionel Holliday, the Yorkshire dye-stuffs manufacturer, thrived under a succession of trainers. The Major was a hard man to please, but unlike so many owners of that ilk had a profound knowledge of racing and breeding.

For many years Major Holliday had had horses with Bob Colling at Bedford Lodge, but it was not until Geoffrey Brooke was installed as the first of his private trainers that he obtained his initial classic success with Neasham Belle in The Oaks of 1951. Soon afterwards Geoffrey Brooke, who had acted as assistant to his brother-in-law, Atty Persse, for many years, set up a public stable at Clarehaven and was succeeded at Lagrange by Humphrey Cottrill, son of the former Lambourn trainer, Harry Cottrill. Amongst the big races that Humphrey Cottrill won for the Major were the Coronation Cup and Champion Stakes with Narrator, two Manchester Cups and a Kempton Park Jubilee with Chatsworth, the Queen Mary Stakes with Bride Elect and Pharsalia and the Nunthorpe Stakes with Gratitude.

Humphrey Cottrill left Lagrange at the end of 1957 and was followed by Major Dick Hern. In common with his predecessors, Geoffrey Brooke and Humphrey Cottrill, Dick Hern had never held a trainer's licence before coming to Lagrange. He soon proved he had ability of an outstanding order. He won The St Leger with Hethersett, the Cesarewitch with Avon's Pride, York's Magnet Cup with Proud Chieftain and Nortia, the Ribblesdale Stakes and the Yorkshire Oaks with None Nicer and the City and Suburban with Setting Star.

Hethersett was the outstanding three-year-old of 1962, and although he credited Dick Hern with his greatest success during his five years at Lagrange, through no fault of his own the colt also caused him his greatest disappointment. Starting favourite for The Derby, Hethersett was one of the seven horses to be brought down six furlongs from home.

On leaving Lagrange, Dick Hern took over the horses of Mr J. J.

Astor and the other owners at the West Ilsley stables on the retirement of Jack Colling. Since he has been at West Ilsley he has won The Derby with Troy in 1979 and Henbit in 1980 as well as almost every other important race in the calendar.

Following Dick Hern, Captain Jimmy James trained for Major Holliday, but was obliged to relinquish the post half-way through the year. Jim Meaney, head lad at Lagrange for many years, took out a temporary licence until the end of the 1963 season.

Abandoning his policy of finding his trainers amongst men who had never previously controlled a stable, Major Holliday looked in the opposite direction for his final trainer, appointing Walter Wharton, who had been turning out winners in Yorkshire since 1951. To Walter Wharton went the credit of preparing the Major's third classic winner, Night Off, who took The 1,000 Guineas of 1965.

At the end of that year Major Holliday died at the age of 75. While his affairs were being wound up Walter Wharton stayed on at Lagrange. He left after the 1967 season, when the Major's son, Mr L. Brook Holliday, decided to break up the stable. Drastically reducing the Holliday racing interests, the Major's executors sent a large batch to Tattersalls' December sales, and of the horses that Mr Holliday retained, some went to France and others to Dick Hern at West Ilsley. Walter Wharton went back north to resume his career as a public trainer and the Lagrange stable was leased to Atty Corbett, the former leading amateur steeplechase jockey, who brought his string from Compton, Berkshire, for the start of the 1968 season. Thus after having housed the horses of the Comte de la Grange in the last century, and those of Lord Glanely before the war, Lagrange had come to the end of its third era of fame as a private stable.

The last of the big winners to carry the Holliday colours of white, maroon hoop and cap trained at Lagrange was Vaguely Noble, who stormed home to win the Observer Gold Cup by seven lengths at Doncaster in 1967. He held no classic engagements and despite his outstanding claims to being the best of his generation, plans to send him to the December sales remained unaltered. When he was knocked down for 136,000 guineas a new record price for a horse bought at public acution was set up.

After leaving Lagrange to train at Clarehaven, Geoffrey Brooke turned out a large number of winners each season until he retired to go to live in Ireland in 1967. He had quickly gained a reputation for handling precocious two-year-olds and won the Coventry Stakes with Xerxes and Crocket, the Queen Mary Stakes with My Dream and Shot Silk, the National Stakes with Rustam, the Cheveley Park Stakes with My Goodness Me and the Middle Park Stakes with Our Babu, Crocket and Masham. In the classic field Geoffrey Brooke won The 2,000 Guineas with Our Babu.

Whereas George Blackwell had left Beverley House to train at Lagrange about half a century previously, Humphrey Cottrill reversed the process and on parting with Major Holliday established a public stable at Beverley House in the centre of the town, Mr Stanhope

Joel being amongst his principal patrons. Good horses that he had in that yard included the Irish Derby winner, Your Highness, that fine sprinter, Bleep-Bleep, who won the Nunthorpe Sweepstakes, a really game and consistent handicapper in Aberdeen and the luckless St Pauli Girl, who had to be content with second place in both The 1,000 Guineas and The Oaks.

When Walter Earl succumbed to his final illness in 1949, Willie Pratt assumed temporary control of Lord Derby's Stanley House stable until George Colling was installed there by the beginning of 1951. As he brought with him those horses that he had had for other owners at Hurworth House, George Colling was not a private trainer but a public one, with Lord Derby as his principal patron. Notable successes that he obtained during his five years at Stanley House were in the Doncaster Cup with Lord Derby's Entente Cordiale, the Yorkshire Oaks and Park Hill Stakes with Mr R. D. Hollingsworth's Ark Royal, who was second to Meld in The Oaks, and, most important of all, with Wilwyn in the first running of the Washington DC International at Laurel Park in 1951.

After the 1955 season, George Colling returned to his old quarters at Hurworth House, and Jack Watts was appointed private trainer to Lord Derby, one or two of Lord Derby's friends like Colonel Bill Stirling also having horses at Stanley House. The grandson of Persimmon's jockey, Jack Watts I, and the son of Call Boy's trainer, Jack Watts II, Jack Watts had held a licence since 1950. While at Wroughton House he had won the Dewhurst Stakes with that great Newmarket course specialist, My Smokey.

Two of the best horses that Jack Watts had during his nine seasons at Stanley House were Alcove and Sing Sing. With Alcove he won the Cesarewitch for Lord Derby and with Sing Sing the National Stakes for Colonel Stirling.

In 1963 Lord Derby decided that Stanley House could no longer continue as a private stable. Accordingly he leased it to his friend the late Bernard van Cutsem, leaving his own horses in the yard.

Bernard van Cutsem was already well-known as a breeder, owner and trainer. He had begun training as a young man in 1939, but within months had had to disperse his string on joining the army. After the war he established the Northmore Stud at his home in Exning, breeding such good horses as Panga and Kalydon. Both of these he had at Graham Place after he resumed training in 1957.

He had his first season at Stanley House in 1964 and wound it up by winning the Manchester Ovaltine Handicap with Osier at Doncaster. The following year he took the Portland Handicap with Lord Derby's Go Shell on the same course.

Two of the outstanding horses trained by Bernard van Cutsem were the Duke of Devonshire's Park Top and Karabas, owned in partnership between the Earl of Iveagh and Mr Frank More O'Farrell. In their different ways both Park Top and Karabas arrived in the top rank after having made comparatively inauspicious starts to their careers.

By Kalydon, the horse that Bernard van Cutsem had owned, bred

The Duke of Devonshire's Park Top was trained by Bernard van Cutsem at Stanley House

and trained himself, out of Nellie Park, Park Top was bred by Mrs L. Scott, whose nephew Peter Scott writes as 'Hotspur' of the *Daily Telegraph*. Although her dam is half-sister to that high-class sprinter Pappa Fourway, when offered for sale Park Top fetched only 500 guineas, an unspectacular price that gave not the slightest hint of what lay in store for her.

A bay filly of great scope and substance, Park Top never ran as a two-year-old and the following season won minor events at Windsor and Newbury before completing her hat-trick and maintaining her unbeaten record in the Ribblesdale Stakes at Royal Ascot. That performance established her as one of the best of her age and sex as she beat St Pauli Girl by half a length without being extended. On her only other two appearances as a three-year-old she won the Brighton Challenge Cup, in which the handicapper had given her a very easy task, and finished unplaced in the Prix Vermeille at Longchamp in the autumn.

As a four-year-old Park Top enjoyed a satisfactory though not spectacular season. Running seven times, she won the Brighton Challenge Cup for a second time and the Prix d'Hedouville on a return visit to

Longchamp. She was also placed in the Ormonde Stakes, the Oxfordshire Stakes and the Cumberland Lodge Stakes.

During her fourth season in training, that of 1969, the 500-guinea bargain Park Top contested nearly all the best weight-for-age races in England and France.

Now that she was a five-year-old Park Top was a big strong mare with a long stride and one burst of speed, the use of which had to be timed with great precision. The way to use her acceleration to best advantage was demonstrated to perfection by Lester Piggott when he won the King George VI and the Queen Elizabeth Stakes on her at Ascot. Beginning to make up ground on the leaders from two furlongs out, Piggott put her into top gear well inside the final furlong and Park Top strode away to beat Crozier by a comfortable length and a half.

First time out as a five-year-old, Park Top went over to France to win the Prix de la Seine over a mile and a half at Longchamp. That success was followed by two much more important ones in the Coronation Cup at Epsom and the Hardwicke Stakes at Royal Ascot. Next time out Park Top was rather surprisingly beaten by Wolver Hollow in the Eclipse Stakes at Sandown Park. After that defeat Park Top landed the King George VI and the Queen Elizabeth Stakes and then she made another successful raid on France to land the Prix Henri Foy at Longchamp.

By the time she had won the Henri Foy, Park Top had established sound claims to being the best middle-distance horse in Europe and the probable winner of the Prix de l'Arc de Triomphe. In the latter race she came through with a terrific run from a long way behind the leaders but failed by three parts of a length to overhaul the Irish stayer, Levmoss. Everyone expected Park Top would obtain compensation for that honourable defeat in the Champion Stakes at Newmarket later in the month, yet once again she had to be content with second place for she never looked like getting to grips with Flossy, who took first run on her and beat her by two lengths.

Karabas was trained in Ireland during his first two seasons. When he came to Bernard van Cutsem after the end of his three-year-old career he seemed nothing more than a pretty useful handicapper, his only successes having been obtained in a maiden race at the Curragh and the Warren Stakes at Goodwood, where he beat the moderate Scipio by two and a half lengths, while on other occasions he was beaten in company that was anything but exalted.

After arrival at Stanley House he made splendid progress and first time out for his new trainer he showed that if he was no more than a handicapper he was very good one indeed by winning the City and Suburban under top weight at Epsom. He then proceeded to pick up the Turn of the Lands Handicap at Newmarket, finish unplaced on going that was much too soft for him in the Mark Lane Jubilee Handicap, and run second in the Zetland Gold Cup at Redcar before being put away for a while.

In an autumn campaign that would seem fantastically ambitious for a horse that had boasted the credentials Karabas had twelve months before, he carried all before him to complete a glittering international nap hand. After winning the Fetcham Handicap at Epsom's Bank Holiday meeting, he took the Scarbrough Stakes at Doncaster, the Coupe de Maisons-Laffitte in France, the Mitre Stakes at Ascot and finally established himself as being in world class by winning the Washington International for Britain at Laurel Park in the United States.

By coincidence, the only other British horse to have won the Washington International, Wilwyn, was also trained at Stanley House.

In 1964 Jack Watts started training for the American owner, Mr Charles Engelhard, Mr Richard Stanley, and other owners, at Machell Place, the stable built by one of the greatest of his grandfather's riding rivals Charlie Wood. In his first season in the yard he won The St Leger with Mr Engelhard's Indiana, who had been second in The Derby and the Oaks Trial Stakes with Mr Stanley's Beaufront, finishing it leading English trainer with £67,236 to the credit of the stable. The following year he won Royal Ascot's Queen Mary Stakes with Mr Edward Benjamin's Visp, and the News of the World Stakes with Mr Cecil Cooper's Super Sam at Goodwood. Other important events won by Jack Watts prior to his retirement in 1973 included the Ebor Handicap in 1967 and the Goodwood Cup in 1968 with Ovaltine and the Kempton Park Jubilee with Pally's Double in 1968.

A member of a fourth generation of the Watts family trained at Newmarket briefly as Jack Watts's son Bill commenced his career at Pegasus House, formerly the yard attached to the Falmouth House establishment built by Fred Archer. Bill Watts won his first flat race and first hurdle race on the same afternoon when Rasping was successful at Catterick Bridge and Prospect Pleases was an easy winner over hurdles at Leicester on 6 April 1968. A few weeks later he won the Oaks Trial Stakes for his landlord Mr Ernie Holt, with Our Ruby. In 1970 he landed the Royal Hunt Cup with Calpurnius and at the end of the season left the town to take over the Hurgill Lodge stable at Richmond in Yorkshire.

Leaving Stanley House in 1955 George Colling returned to Hurworth House for the few remaining years of his life to train for Lord and Lady Irwin, Mr R. D. Hollingsworth, Major-General Sir Randle Feilden and other owners. Having won the Park Hill Stakes with Mr Hollingsworth's Ark Royal in 1955, he completed a treble by winning it again with her half-sisters Kyak in 1956 and Cutter in his last full season in 1958. George Colling had long suffered from indifferent health and died at the early age of 55 on 18 April 1959.

Later the same year a second tragedy struck Hurworth House when stable jockey Manny Mercer was killed at Ascot. As he was taking Priddy Fair down to the post for the Red Deer Stakes on 5 September, he was thrown, and striking his head on the rails, killed instantaneously. A brilliant rider in public, he was one of the most kindhearted of men in his private life, and would be genuinely concerned about such things as whether the sports cars he loved to drive made too much noise for his neighbours in Newmarket's Hamilton Road. A great tribute to Manny's professional ability was that Sir Jack Jarvis put him up on the Park Lodge horses regularly, and he also rode for other important stables. However, nothing would have induced him to accept any other first retainer while he was required by George Colling, with whom he served the most formative years of his apprenticeship.

John Oxley, who had been George Colling's assistant and had run the stable during his final illness, took over Hurworth House at the age of 28 and trained there until obliged to hand in his licence on account of increasing overheads in the poor economic situation at the end of 1975. It was not long before John Oxley proved that he was a worthy successor to even so good a trainer as George Colling. Within about a month of being granted a licence he won the Yorkshire Cup with Cutter. He obtained a classic success with the late Sir Foster Robinson's Homeward Bound in The Oaks of 1964, and continued to do well with the products of Mr Hollingsworth's prolific female line founded by Felucca, the dam of the three Park Hill Stakes winners, Ark Royal, Kyak and Cutter. With Ark Royal's daughter Ocean he won the Coronation Stakes at Royal Ascot, and other high-class winners from this nautically named dynasty were Eagle, Sloop, Hermes, Mariner and Torpid. Most important of the handicaps that John Oxley won were the William Hill Gold Cup in 1967 and the Lincoln in 1968 with Lady Halifax's high-class miler, Frankincense.

A trainer who operated with success under both codes was Basil Foster. He had been apprenticed to Basil Jarvis at about the time of the outbreak of war. After having had his string at Marlborough House when he came back to Newmarket in 1957, Basil Foster bought the Lansdowne House stableyard, renaming it Holland House in honour of a 'chaser called Joe Holland, who had given him his first success after he had started training at Enfield in 1955. Thus an old gelding who finished up in selling 'chases joined Derby winners like Cadland and St Gatien in having a Newmarket stable named after him. The best horses that Basil Foster had while he was at Newmarket were the Fern Hill Stakes winner, Jeanne Michelle, that dashing grey 'chaser, Beau Chevalet, who won the Worcester Royal Porcelain 'chase, Straight Lad, a game and consistent hurdler with more than a bit of class, subsequently a successful sire of jumpers, and Deetease, who won a division of the Gloucestershire Hurdle at Cheltenham's National Hunt meeting. On leaving Newmarket in 1963, Basil Foster went to Lambourn for a few seasons before going to train at Middleham in his native Yorkshire.

Although veteran Reg Day arranged to reduce his Terrace House string by transferring some horses to John Waugh, when his former assistant began training in 1960, he continued to turn out good winners until his retirement at the end of 1968. In 1961 he enjoyed one of the best seasons of his long career, when at the age of 78 he sent out that grand mare, Sweet Solera, to win The 1,000 Guineas and The Oaks.

Sweet Solera was ridden to both her classic victories by Bill

Bill Rickaby rode Sweet Solera to win the 1,000 Guineas and the Oaks for Reg Day's Terrace House stable in 1961

Rickaby. As referred to earlier, this jockey served his apprenticeship with his uncle, Wally Griggs, and finished it with the Hon George Lambton. He obtained his first success on Boldero in October 1933, and was getting plenty of riding from Bill Wightman and other trainers at the outbreak of war. Wartime saw the transformation of Billy Rickaby the jockey to Major Rickaby of the Royal Artillery and he took part in action in the desert. On return to civilian life he found there were precious few mounts to be had, and for time he seriously considered giving up riding. Fortunately he carried on and with the help of Ted Leader and others he gradually re-established himself with the result that his persistence was eventually rewarded with a retainer from Jack Jarvis in 1949. He continued to ride for the Park Lodge stable for eight seasons. Subsequently he was associated with Harry Wragg and Marcus Marsh, and was retained by the McAlpine family. In 1962 Bill Rickaby won The 2,000 Guineas on Privy Councillor for Tom Waugh's stable and in 1966 he nearly won another 2,000 Guineas when he drove Jack Jarvis's second string, Great Nephew, who started at 66-1, to within a short head of Kashmir II. In 1968 Bill Rickaby retired from riding and was appointed assistant stipendiary steward to the Royal Hong Kong Jockey Club, but was seriously injured in a car crash and returned to Newmarket to make a slow recovery.

Members of Newmarket's old training families were as much to the fore as ever during the 1950s and 1960s.

Jack Jarvis's immense services to racing were recognised by the knighthood the Queen conferred upon him in the New Year's Honours List in 1968. For all the success that he enjoyed in his profession he was always as appreciative of other people's problems and difficulties as he must have been of his own when he resumed training with just three horses in his care after the First World War. Whenever he could help anyone he usually did, and the number of people who benefited from his generosity far outnumbered those who felt occasionally the rough side of his tongue.

Sir Jack won The 1,000 Guineas with Happy Laughter in Coronation Year and the following season he landed the Cambridgeshire with Minstrel 51 years after he had ridden the winner of that race as a tiny apprentice. Other important races that Sir Jack won during his latter years included the City and Suburban in 1964 with the Bo'sun, the Victoria Cup in 1961 with Bass Rock, the Chester Cup in 1953 with Eastern Emperor, the Ebor in 1956 with Donald, and the Gimcrack Stakes in 1960 with Test Case.

After the 1965 season, during which he had won both the Dewhurst Stakes and the Observer Gold Cup with Pretendre, Sir Jack decided to reduce his string. Accordingly he relinquished his tenancy of the Palace House yard and concentrated on the 41 horses stabled at Park Lodge. With just a bit of luck his first season with a smaller string might have been the best he ever had. As it was, however, Great Nephew was beaten by a short head in The 2,000 Guineas and Pretendre went down by a neck to Charlottown in The Derby after having won the Blue Riband Trial Stakes.

As Sir Jack trained for such a prominent Scottish peer as Lord Rosebery, the Park Lodge stable was always well represented on the Scottish circuit in the autumn. Three generations of racegoers took the advice to 'Follow Jack Jarvis' at its meetings and profited handsomely by doing so. At Ayr's splendid Western meeting, at Edinburgh, and at Lanark, Sir Jack saddled winners year after year. In Scotland's premier race, the Ayr Gold Cup, he completed a notable though interrupted hat-trick, winning it with Dayton in 1937, Old Reliance in 1938 and again with Royal Charger when racing was resumed at Ayr after the war in 1946. In 1965 the Ayr executive made a public presentation to Sir Jack to mark the 60th anniversary of his riding Kilglass to win the Ayr Gold Cup for the then Lord Howard de Walden and, as was only appropriate, the present Lord Howard performed the ceremony.

Despite the heavy demands that training made upon his time and energy, Sir Jack always had interests in many other sports. During those raids on the Scottish meetings he always managed to fit in some shooting. He was also enthusiastic about coursing and won the Waterloo Cup with Jovial Judge in 1926. Just before the war he decided that he would like to own a Grand National winner, to which end he bought a chaser whom he named after his Waterloo Cup winner. This was trained by his brother-in-law Tom Leader and used to be ridden by 'Fiddler' Goodwill. Unlike his canine namesake, Jovial Judge did not take top honours at Liverpool, but he won the Five Hundred Handicap 'chase at Manchester's Easter meeting in 1938 and other events at Worcester, Lingfield and Kempton Park.

For more than 40 years Sir Jack trained the home-bred horses that Lord Rosebery, and his father before him, sent to Park Lodge from the Mentmore Stud. Over that period the Mentmore stock developed a streak of toughness that became its hallmark. Sir Jack was a firm believer in giving his horses plenty of work and to many people it was a wonder that they stood up to the amount of gallops he gave them. Whereas other Newmarket trainers had two galloping days a week, usually Wednesday and Saturday, Sir Jack had three, Tuesday, Thursday and Saturday, and not only did the horses stand up to that routine, they thrived on it, as was proved by the results achieved year in and year out.

One result of Jack Jarvis's thoroughness in ensuring that his horses were always at peak condition whenever they ran was that they did well in the early weeks of the season, when those from other stables were still short of condition or not ready to run at all. He always said that he believed in getting his horses ready early as there were eight months in the season and it was only sense to make the best of the opportunities offered in all of them. The way in which Sir Jack always insisted on sending his horses to the post trained to the minute also paid rich dividends when heavy going put a premium on fitness and stamina. This was particularly the case with two-year-olds.

As a result of the work he used to give them, Sir Jack's horses invariably stripped light and as they walked round the parade ring they looked for all the world as though the last thing they wanted to do was to race. Yet the raising of the tapes saw a transformation in them, and it was a rare thing for one of them not to run out his race to the death.

Sir Jack Jarvis collapsed and died on the morning of 19 December 1968 just as he was preparing to leave for his annual winter holiday in South Africa. He had been training at Park Lodge for just a few months less than 50 years and in that time he had saddled the winner of almost every big race except The Oaks.

After having had a five-year lease on Clarehaven Sir Jack Jarvis's nephew Ryan Jarvis moved to Phantom House in 1951, winning the Stewards Cup with Smokey Eyes the following year, and in 1966 landing another important handicap when Lomond won the Ebor. In between times he had trained such smart animals as Munch, who won five of her six races as a two-year-old in 1957 and Cardington King, who was fourth in The Derby. Another of his notable successes was with Front Row in the Irish 1,000 Guineas. For many years Ryan Jarvis's horses were ridden by Eric Eldin, who was apprenticed to him. Eric Eldin also had a retainer from Jack Waugh's stable.

Harvey Leader, the youngest of the four trainer sons of Tom Leader senior, was in the old Bedford Lodge yard, which he had renamed Shalfleet, until 1960. In that year he moved his string into newer boxes, some of which he had already been using, on the eastern side of the yard. In this way he formed a completely new establishment for which he retained the name of Shalfleet. The older stable, which he had vacated, then became known as Highfield.

Perhaps the most notable of Harvey Leader's later achievements was the successful gamble that he landed with Hidden Meaning in the Cambridgeshire of 1962. Starting favourite at 7-1, Hidden Meaning beat Hasty Cloud by quite a comfortable couple of lengths in a field of 46. Four years later her trainer won another Cambridgeshire with Dites.

Hidden Meaning was one of several fillies that Harvey Leader trained so brilliantly during their second season in the sixties. Another good one that he had was Fair Astronomer, who won the Rous Memorial Stakes and the Pretty Polly Stakes in 1963, while in 1967 the successes of his three-year-old fillies, Palatch, Resilience II and In Command were one of the features of the season. Palatch won the Musidora Stakes and the Yorkshire Oaks, both at York, Resilience II was successful in the Sandleford Priory Stakes at Newbury, the Falmouth Stakes at Newmarket and the Northern Goldsmiths Handicap at Newcastle, while In Command picked up the Warren Stakes at Goodwood's big meeting, the £11,000 Prix Henry Delamarre over the channel at Longchamp and three minor events at Yarmouth, which was always one of Harvey Leader's favourite courses.

Quite one of the most remarkable, if not one of the best, horses that Harvey Leader has had since the war has been the sprinter, Denikin. Every season from the age of two in 1949 until he was eight in 1955 Denikin was a winner and he subsequently picked up three more races before he ran for the last time at the age of 14. That he went on running so well for so long did much to disprove theories that horses easily become bored by Newmarket. Not only did Denikin thrive on his work on the Heath for a period of a dozen years, but he was also a specialist on his local course. Of the 21 races that he won, nine were on the Rowley Mile. Denikin's final success came in the Summer Stakes at Warwick in 1958, when he was eleven. In that race he was ridden by Brian Taylor claiming the 7 lb allowance. Brian Taylor was then apprenticed to Harvey Leader. Within a few years he had become one of the country's leading riders and was retained as first jockey to the Shalfleet stable.

For part of his apprenticeship Brian Taylor was lent out to Jack Jarvis, who was in need of a good lightweight work rider. After he had made the grade he became regularly associated with the Park Lodge runners, on one of whom, General Gordon, he was probably unlucky not to win The Derby in 1966. In his final gallop General Gordon broke his leg after having gone far better than the stable's other Derby runner, Pretendre, up to the point when the tragedy occurred. As Pretendre was only beaten by a neck at Epsom there must be a strong presumption that General Gordon would have won. Eight years later Brian Taylor had his compensation when winning The Derby on the Lambourn-trained Snow Knight.

At the art of buying yearlings in the bargain basement, Harvey Leader had no equal. As an example of the sort of success that he has had in that sphere one can cite the four yearlings that he bought for 500 guineas or less in 1961. Golden Advisor cost 350 guineas and by the end of the following June he had won three races worth £874. All of a Kind cost 410 guineas. He won the Rous Memorial Stakes at Goodwood and a race at Hurst Park as a two-year-old and the following season he brought his earnings up to more than £2,000 by scoring again at Yarmouth. Aviary and Portrait Attachment both cost 500 guineas. Aviary won at Folkestone and Worcester as a two-year-old and two races at Windsor the next season, earning £1,408 in all, while Portrait Attachment picked up £480 by winning apprentice races at Newmarket and Newbury before being sold for 1,150 guineas at the end of her two-year-old career.

In both the races that she won, Portrait Attachment was ridden by Jeremy Glover. Originally apprenticed to Basil Foster, Jerry Glover obtained the approval of the latter trainer to have his indentures transferred to Harvey Leader in order to obtain more experience on flat racers. As it was he soon became too heavy and made a further move to join Ryan Price's Findon stable from which he emerged a very able jump jockey. Jerry Glover subsequently rode with considerable success for Stan Mellor, Stan Palmer, Desmond McInnes Skinner and other trainers.

Other riders who have served their apprenticeship with Harvey Leader besides Brian Taylor and Jerry Glover include Richard 'Snowy' Fawdon, Peter Pickford, a fearless rider over the sticks, 'Fiddler' Goodwill and Colin Williams. One of Colin Williams's earliest successes was obtained on Peter O'Sullevan's Be Friendly in the first running of the Vernons Sprint Trophy at Haydock Park in 1966.

After John Evelyn Watts retired in 1952, Ted Leader succeeded him as private trainer to Mr H. J. Joel at Sefton Lodge and remained there until that owner's string was split up in 1967. In his first season at

Sefton Lodge Ted Leader won the Nunthorpe Sweepstakes with High Treason, who was then a two-year-old. A few years later he was doing wonderfully well with that grand stayer, Predominate, who became one of the most popular horses of his day and a great character into the bargain. Originally bought as a hurdler, Predominate was sent to Ted Leader for use as a lead horse after it was found that he had little liking for jumping. The older Predominate grew, the better he seemed to be. Between 1958 and 1960 he brought off the hat-trick in the Goodwood Stakes and in 1961 he won the Goodwood Cup. Such was the extent to which this big chestnut gelding with a small star on his forehead captured the public imagination that many of his fans would write to Ted Leader, not for tips, but just to enquire about the old horse's well-being.

In the classics Ted Leader had had a great deal of bad luck. Firm ground in the spring of 1958 brought about the half-length defeat of Major Portion by Pall Mall in The 2,000 Guineas. Rather impercipient observers suggested that Major Portion would have won had he had the benefit of a previous race, without realising that an outing on that hard spring going would have stumped up Major Portion so badly that he would never even have run in The 2,000 Guineas. When Pall Mall and Major Portion met again on good going in the Sussex Stakes at Goodwood, Major Portion had his revenge and won by a length.

In 1962, West Side Story, a rangy chestnut filly by Rockefella, finished third to Abermaid in The 1,000 Guineas after having appeared to be hampered by the winner. Had she been second she might have been awarded the race. In The Oaks the mediocre pace obliged Eph Smith to go to the front at Tattenham Corner and the French filly Monade came through in the closing stages to collar her. To such effect did West Side Story fight back that it looked like a dead heat, but the judge gave it to Monade by a short head, after having taken nearly a quarter of an hour to examine the photograph.

Eph Smith rode for Ted Leader all the time he was at Sefton Lodge, except for the last couple of seasons. One of the very best jockeys of his generation, Eph Smith was apprenticed to Major Sneyd and thereafter had only two first claims upon him during 33 years' riding. Between 1933 and 1948 he rode for Sir Jack Jarvis, winning The Derby on Blue Peter as mentioned above and then in 1949 he accepted a retainer from Mr H. J. Joel.

On many occasions when Eph Smith was at another meeting, Ted Leader would entrust his runners to his trial jockey, Graham Booth, rather than look outside the stable for a fashionable rider. This policy paid ample dividends. From only a handful of mounts in 1957 Booth won on Golden Rocket (10-1) at Leicester and on Out of Sight (33-1) at Birmingham, and finished third on Rugosa (20-1) at Newmarket. In his final season at Sefton, when unable to find a jockey for Photo Flash at Lingfield, Ted Leader put up Ryan Jarvis's trial jockey, Ben Goulden, who had passed the age of 50 without having ridden a winner in England and Photo Flash won.

On leaving Sefton Lodge, Ted Leader started a public stable in his family's old yard at Wroughton House, and won his first race from there when Keep Going beat Pitch by eight lengths at Newmarket in April 1968. He retired in 1971 and died in February 1983.

Two of the sons of Tom Waugh, the old Meynell House trainer who died in 1946, had stables in the town. Jack was at Heath House and Tom at Sefton Lodge.

Like his father, Jack Waugh has a wonderful record at Royal Ascot, having won the Coventry Stakes with Amerigo, the Queen Mary Stakes with Lerida, the Ribblesdale Stakes with French Fern and Ostrya, the Wokingham Stakes with Light Harvest, the Cork and Orrery Stakes with Matador and the Windsor Castle Stakes with Summer Day, who had won her five previous races too. That fine sprinter Matador, now a successful sire, is probably the best horse that Jack Waugh has ever had. Not only did he win the Cork and Orrery Stakes and the July Cup but he carried a record weight for a three-year-old to success in the Stewards Cup at Goodwood.

Two good jockeys to serve their apprenticeship with Jack Waugh were George Duffield, one of the leading riders at Newmarket at the present time, and Eric Apter, who has enjoyed considerable success in the north.

At the end of 1970 Jack Waugh retired from training to manage the Lordship and Egerton Studs for Sir Reginald and Lady Macdonald-Buchanan.

Tom Waugh had been assistant to Frank Butters, Fred Butters and Harvey Leader before beginning to train at Wroughton House in 1956. Six years later he won the Free Handicap and The 2,000 Guineas with Privy Councillor. In 1968 he transferred his string to Sefton Lodge, where he trained Tartar Prince to win the Northumberland Plate and Great Metropolitan as well as Rose Dubarry the Lowther Stakes in 1971 and obtained much other success before retiring in 1980.

Another member of this family to have trained at Newmarket in recent years has been John Waugh, who had the horses of Sir Robin McAlpine at Fitzroy House from 1960 until taking charge of Sir Robin's Wyck Hall Stud on the Dullingham Road in 1971. As well as the Wyck Hall Stud, John Waugh manages the Someries Stud, where Vitiges and Bay Express stand. John is the son of Alec Waugh and the grandson of Richard, who trained for so many years at Graditz in Germany before he died in 1930. Richard was the eldest of Jimmy Waugh's many sons and his grandson John is thus the fourth generation of the family to train at Newmarket. Like his father, Alec trained on the continent for the best part of his career, returning to Newmarket to win the Cambridgeshire with Kelling in 1950 and other races towards the end of his life. He died in 1957.

Geoffrey Barling won the Royal Hunt Cup of 1960 with Small Slam, whom he later used as his hack, but training stayers was always the work that he liked best and no success gave him greater pleasure than that of Piaco in the Northumberland Plate in 1967. Not only was that a long-distance race, but it was the principal one at Newcastle, his

Eph Smith (1915-1972) won the 2,000 Guineas and Derby on Blue Peter for Jack Jarvis's Park Lodge stable in 1939

favourite course. Over the years Barling won many of the other events at Gosforth Park, a large proportion of them with horses owned by the late Major J. L. Priestman of Slaley Hall, Hexham, who always liked to see his colours in evidence at his local meeting.

Other good horses that Geoffrey Barling had at about the same time included Major Priestman's Outcrop, who won the Yorkshire Oaks and the Park Hill Stakes in 1963, and Tower Walk. After having won the National Stakes as a two-year-old in 1968, Tower Walk won the Greenham Stakes and finished second to Right Tack in The 2,000 Guineas. Reverting to sprinting later in 1969, Tower Walk landed the Nunthorpe Sweepstakes.

After Tulyar had won the first Derby of the Queen's reign and Pinza the second, Never Say Die completed a Newmarket hat-trick in 1954. Trained by Joe Lawson at Carlburg for the late American owner, Mr Robert Sterling Clark, he was ridden by the teenage Lester Piggott. Born in County Durham in 1881, Joe Lawson was head lad to Alec Taylor at Manton, eventually taking over that stable on Taylor's retirement in 1927. In only his fourth season, 1931, Lawson set up a new record for a trainer's seasonal winnings with an aggregate of £93,899, his achievement being the more remarkable because of his having no classic success that year. He was also leading trainer in 1936 and 1938. Joe Lawson did not come to Newmarket until 1947, when he bought Carlburg from its builder, Charlie Waugh.

After the retirement of Joe Lawson in 1957, Carlburg was taken over by Captain Fergie Sutherland, who had lost a leg in the Korean War, though that did not prevent him from riding in hunter 'chases. He had gained valuable experience as assistant trainer to Geoffrey Brooke at next-door Clarehaven, and in the few years before he left Carlburg in 1962 made a name for himself by the large number of winners that he saddled at Manchester's now defunct Castle Irwell course.

With the departure of Fergie Sutherland, Carlburg was purchased by Mr David Robinson, who was already established as a leading owner, having won the 2,000 Guineas with Our Babu, and other valuable events. Hitherto his horses had been with Geoffrey Brooke and other public trainers but he now decided to have his own private stable and invited Bruce Hobbs to train for him.

The son of the former Lambourn trainer Reg Hobbs, Bruce Hobbs had been in the top flight of National Hunt jockeys before the war, becoming the youngest to ride a Grand National winner when successful on Battleship at the age of 17 in 1938.

Following service in North Africa during the war, from which he emerged with the rank of captain and the Military Cross, Bruce Hobbs trained jumpers at Wantage before becoming assistant trainer to Captain Boyd-Rochfort at Freemason Lodge. His immense experience soon obtained the results that Mr Robinson expected from his expensive purchases. After having won 19 races with a string dominated by two-year-olds in 1964, he won the Blue Riband Trial Stakes with Cambridge, the Warren Stakes at Goodwood and three other events with Suvretta, and four races including Newbury's Oxfordshire Stakes with Court Gift in 1965.

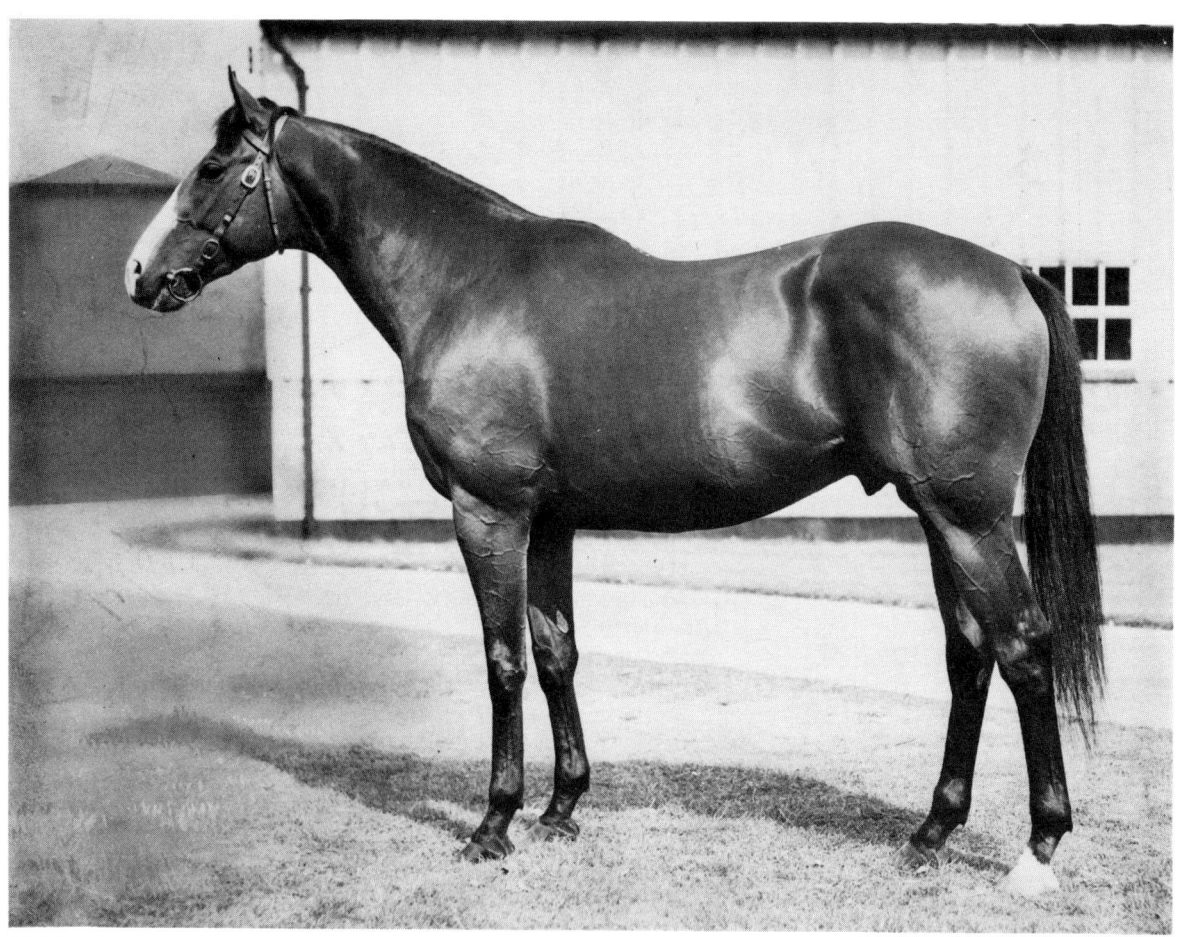

Sir Victor Sassoon's 1953 Derby winner Pinza, trained by Norman Bertie at Bedford House

After Bruce Hobbs, Jimmy Thompson, who had had a successful stable at Beverley, came to Carlburg and stayed for a couple of seasons before returning north in the autumn of 1967. Amongst the races that he won for Mr Robinson was the Victoria Cup of 1966 with Enrico.

By this time Mr Robinson had acquired a string of horses in training which was larger than that of the recently dissolved Holliday empire. And as well as Carlburg he owned Clarehaven, having bought the latter stable from Lord Harrington a few years previously, on the understanding that Geoffrey Brooke should remain there until he finished training. The big house at Clarehaven, which Peter Purcell Gilpin had built and Sir Alfred Butt had lived in later while the Clarehaven trainers had had a smaller house nearer the yard, Mr Robinson demolished, replacing it with a luxurious modern residence, from which he could look out upon both the Carlburg and Clarehaven yards.

With 73 horses to carry his colours at the outset of the 1968 season, Mr Robinson divided them between two private trainers. Michael Jarvis, who followed Jimmy Thompson at Carlburg, had 37 horses, and the other 36 were with Paul Davey at Clarehaven. Both trainers came from racing families. Michael Jarvis, who is no relation to the

Jarvises of Newmarket, is the son of Andy Jarvis, the former National Hunt jockey, who won the Stanley 'chase at Aintree, the Worcester Royal Porcelain 'chase and a lot of other steeplechases on that good horse Shaef just after the war. Paul Davey, who had his first ride on the flat at the age of nine, is the son of the late Ernie Davey, who had Star Cottage stable at Malton for many years. Paul Davey assisted his father for a long time and then trained on his own account at Danby House, Malton.

Both trainers made good starts. On Easter Sunday 1968 Paul Davey performed a wonderful feat when he won five races, Floretti, Little Green Man and Carlburg, a horse named after the stable, being successful at Teeside Park, and London Boy and River Peace at Doncaster.

During the 1969 season Mr David Robinson received substantial returns hor his huge investment in bloodstock and by the end of it he was leading owner with the winners of 96 races worth £91,973. Mrs Robinson also had seven winners, so the combined total for the Clarehaven and Carlburg stables was 103.

The most notable contributor to Mr Robinson's success in 1969 was his brilliant sprinter, Tudor Music, for whom Michael Jarvis was responsible. By winning the Cork and Orrery Stakes at Royal Ascot, the July Cup and the Vernons Sprint Trophy at Haydock Park on the final day of the season, Tudor Music earned £11,796. The best of Mr Robinson's two-year-olds was Yellow God, who collected £13,982 by landing the Imperial Stakes, the Gimcrack Stakes and a minor race at Newmarket, and was the highest stakes winner from either yard. Yellow God was trained by Paul Davey, as also were the other two-year-olds, Fast Track and Lucky Shoes, who made the largest numerical contributions to the amount of races won by chalking up seven successes apiece.

All Fast Track's races were won in Yorkshire — two of them at York and the others at Doncaster, Catterick Bridge, Teeside Park, Thirsk and Pontefract — and they brought in £3,421. The first season efforts of Lucky Shoes yielded £3,677. This Pall Mall colt won two races at Leicester, two more at Hamilton Park and others at Pontefract, Catterick bridge and Nottingham.

The success of Yellow God in the Gimcrack Stakes earned Mr Robinson the right to be guest of honour at the Gimcrack Dinner in December and make the principal speech of the evening. In that speech he pleaded for the introduction of far more business technique into racing.

After leaving Carlburg, Bruce Hobbs opened a public stable at Palace House. Predicatably enough, he had no difficulty in acquiring patrons, such well-known owners as Major the Hon J. P. Philipps, Mr Stanhope Joel and Mr William Hill being amongst those who sent him horses, and sent out his first winner from the yard when Eric the Red carried the colours of actor Peter O'Toole to success in the Blue Mantle Stakes at Ascot in April 1966.

Having started with 35 horses in 1966, Bruce Hobbs's string had grown to 59 two years later, and he was obliged to rent Albert House, where Billy Walters had trained before the war, as an overspill yard.

While expensively bought and expensively bred horses were the stalwarts of stables like Clarehaven and Carlburg, less costly animals were being prepared with equal skill in other yards. At Cadland House the former jump jockey Arthur Goodwill showed much of the discernment of his mentor, Harvey Leader, in the picking up of cheap yearlings. 'Fiddler' Goodwill, as he is called because he had a violin in his luggage when he first came to Newmarket, had a mixed string and won almost every kind of race between January and December.

A small yard that had been nothing more than stabling for spares and hacks or empty for many years was revived as an independent racing establishment when Gerry Blum began training at Bloomsbury Cottage in 1968. Gerry Blum had previously held responsible positions in Harry Wragg's stable at Newmarket and that of the late Captain Charles Elsey at Malton. He obtained his first success with Levee ridden by 'Kipper' Lynch in the first race run at Alexandra Park in 1968.

Paddy O'Gorman, who was training at Graham Place when he died of a heart attack on 2 June 1969, was another expert at winning races with cheap horses. He began his racing career riding in point-to-points in his native Ireland. Coming to England he made a name for himself as a horse-master with a great talent for breaking yearlings and handling difficult horses. Among the trainers who sent him yearlings were Jack Colling, Joe Lawson and Sam Armstrong. At this time he was also managing Jack Colling's Scaltback Stud.

In 1953 Paddy O'Gorman began training in a small way at Exning, and two or three years later the South African owner Jack Gerber sent him some useful horses. For Gerber he won both the Kings Stand Stakes with Drum Beat and the Stewards Cup with Epaulette in 1958, the Northumberland Plate with Utrillo in 1961 and many other races.

On leaving Exning for Newmarket, Paddy O'Gorman had his horses in the older part of the Shalfleet, i.e. the original Bedford Lodge yard, and then moved to Graham Place on the other side of the town. One of his greatest achievements was to win the Gimcrack Stakes with Golden Horus, for whom he had paid 1,500 guineas as a yearling.

After the death of Paddy O'Gorman the Graham Place stable was taken over by his son Bill. Already known to the racing world as a talented amateur rider on the flat, Bill O'Gorman had won the Moet and Chandon Silver Magnum, the Amateur's Derby, on Double Quick at Epsom. He had been in charge of the stable for about two months when he saddled Royal Smoke, a recent recruit to his string, to win the Stewards Cup at Goodwood.

One of the most imposing buildings in Newmarket, and also one of the newest, is Tattersalls Sale Ring which stands on the ground that rises on your left-hand side as you come along the Avenue from the station to the High Street. Nowadays there is no member of the original family in this famous firm of auctioneers, which was founded by Richard Tattersall, a Yorkshire man, in 1766.

Richard Tattersall (1742-1795) founder of the world-famous bloodstock auctioneers whose sales are conducted at Park Paddocks, Newmarket

He began by selling horses under the hammer at Hyde Park Corner in London. By the end of the eighteenth century Tattersalls were also holding their sales outside the Jockey Club rooms in Newmarket High Street. About 1870 these sales were transferred to their present site after land had been purchased from the McCalmont family. Adjoining the property thus acquired was the Park Paddocks stud which was later purchased by the firm. It was at the Park Paddocks stud that the famous stallion, Barcaldine, stood until he died in 1893. His box can still be seen today.

Tattersalls' London sales were transferred from Hyde Park to Knightsbridge Green in 1865, but after the outbreak of the Second World War business in the capital was discontinued. Two of the outstanding features of the Knightsbridge premises had been the famous stone archway and the statue of the fox under a rotunda, which had stood in the sale yard. Both these were transferred to Park Paddocks after the war. The fox stands near the parade area outside the sale ring, while on the other side of the sale ring is the arch.

The new sale ring was built to mark Tattersalls' bicentenary in 1966. With its central heating, 250 loud speakers, office space beneath the ample tiered seating, dining-room and two bars it has become a status symbol for the British bloodstock industry in the eyes of the breeders, owners and trainers who come to Tattersalls' Newmarket sales from all over the world. The sale ring with its landscaped lawns and parades was the final major work of the late Professor Sir Albert Richardson, PPRA.

Further over from the Sale Paddocks and opposite the station are the Coronation stables. Once these were the livery stables in which railway passengers left their carriage horses.

No Newmarket trainer ran a mixed stable for flat racers and jumpers with greater success than Harry Thomson Jones did for nearly 30 years until confining himself to the flat. Having spent four years as assistant trainer to R. Featherstonhaugh in Ireland and another two with Sam Armstrong at St Gatien, Tom Jones began training on his own account at Woodlands at the age of 26 in 1951. One of the most important of his early successes was with Our Betters in the Lowther Stakes at York in 1954. During those first yew years that he was training he had a useful sprinter in Happy Clacton. This gelding was one of those horses without any claim to class who nevertheless won more races than many who have. Happy Clacton, who went on winning until he was eight, had a particular liking for Pontefract and won five of his nine races there.

About the best chaser that Tom Jones had was Frenchman's Cove, with whom he won the Whitbread Gold Cup in 1962 and the King George VI 'chase in 1965. Another good chaser for whose successes he was responsible was Park Ranger, who won the Tom Coulthwaite 'chase at Haydock Park in 1969. Good hurdlers that Tom Jones had include Red Tears and Chorus who won the Gloucester Hurdle at Cheltenham's National Hunt meeting in 1965 and 1966 respectively, and Speedwell, who won the Princess Royal Hurdle at Doncaster in 1961.

Several of the riders who have served their apprenticeship with Tom Jones have made names for themselves both in Britain and abroad. They include Greville Starkey, Bruce Helier, Jock Ferguson, and more recently Richard Hills, one of the twin sons of the successful Lambourn trainer Barry Hills.

A natural horseman, who is in his element riding to hounds in Ireland, as well as brilliant jockey, Greville Starkey has long been amongst the most successful riders in the country. While retained by John Oxley he won The Oaks on Homeward Bound in 1964 and in 1978 he brought off the Epsom classic double by winning The Derby on Shirley Heights and The Oaks on Fair Salinia. In recent years he has been retained by the Sussex trainer Guy Harwood, for whom he has won The 2,000 Guineas on To-Agori-Mou in 1981 and both the Eclipse Stakes and the King George VI the and Queen Elizabeth Stakes on Kalaglow in 1982.

When old Felix Leach was training at Graham Place in the early years of this century, he had amongst his apprentices Fred Winter, who won The Oaks on Cherimoya at the age of 17 in 1911. Later on Fred Winter went to ride for the Kaiser at Graditz. After being interned during the First World War he returned to England to ride for Frank Hartigan and then Solly Joel. Retiring from the saddle in 1930, he trained at Epsom and then at Gravesend in Kent. Meanwhile his elder son, also Fred Winter, had become champion National Hunt jockey, while his younger son John assisted him in running the stable and one of his daughters, Pat, had married the champion flat race jockey, Doug Smith.

In November 1963 Fred Winter returned to Newmarket to train at Bedford Lodge, which he renamed Highfield after the establishment that he had had at Gravesend. Among the horses that he brought with

Greville Starkey, who was apprenticed at H.Thomson Jones at Woodlands, riding To-Agori-Mou

him was Showdown, who had just won the Middle Park Stakes. Two years later Showdown credited him with his last important success by winning the Queen Anne Stakes at Royal Ascot in 1965. A few weeks later Fred Winter died, leaving behind him the memory of a friendly man always ready to extend his hospitality to even complete strangers in need of his help.

On his death, his stable was taken over by John Winter, who in his first full season, won the Northern Goldsmiths Handicap at Newcastle and the Peter Hastings Stakes at Newbury, both worth more than £3,000, with Double-U-Jay. In the following year, 1967, John Winter had the disappointment of seeing Mehari touched off by a short head in the Ascot Gold Cup, but received compensation when the colt won the £11,000 Prix Kergolay at Deauville two months later. The day after Mehari had been so narrowly beaten in the Gold Cup, John Winter won the Wokingham Stakes with Spaniards Mount, who provided his brother-in-law Doug Smith with his last successful mount at the Royal Meeting.

After devoting some ten years to the improvement of his mother's stud, Teddy Lambton resumed training with ten horses in the Kremlin House yard in 1961. It was the two-year-old Compensation, a chestnut colt by Gratitude, who did most to put the stable back into the limelight by winning the Imperial Stakes at Kempton Park and two other good races.

Having shown that he was as fine a trainer as ever, Teddy Lambton found plenty of owners willing to send him horses and the Kremlin boxes were soon full again. For two or three seasons the veteran jockey Stan Smith rode for the stable but when he accepted a retainer from Lord Rosebery he was succeeded by Peter Robinson. The partnership between Teddy Lambton and his new jockey began well with Mighty Gurkha winning the Lincolnshire in 1964 and later the same year Compensation winning the Ayr Gold Cup. Two years later David Jack proved the star of the stable by winning the Scottish and Newcastle Breweries Handicap (£5,578) at Gosforth Park and the Magnet Cup (£4,266) at York and finishing third in The St Leger. By the end of the 1966 season Kremlin had won 38 races worth £30,734.

By contrast with the ten horses with which he had started up the stable again in 1961, Teddy Lambton had 47 in his string six years later in 1967, when the two-year-old filly, Kursaal, distinguished herself by her toughness and consistency. After having been third first time out, she won each of her remaining nine races that year, all in the north, thereby earning £4,391. The following year she trained on to win four races worth another £2,796 while Charicles registered the stable's most important success in 1968 by landing the Wokingham Stakes at Royal Ascot.

When Teddy Lambton retired in 1969 he handed the string over to Peter Robinson, who relinquished his jockey's licence immediately, and the Kremlin House establishment was then put on the market. Among the horses taken over by Peter Robinson was the three-year-old Prince de Galles. This colt became a leading fancy for the Cambridgeshire, for which the stable backed him early on, and after he had shown how well the money was invested by winning the Norwich Handicap over the course and distance by ten lengths in September, the public joined in the gamble wholeheartedly so that he started one of the hottest favourites in the history of the race at 5-2 in a field of 26. Ridden with great confidence by Frankie Durr, Prince de Galles took the lead two furlongs out and proceeded to beat Grandrew by four lengths.

The purchaser of the Kremlin House stable was 25-year-old Jeremy Hindley, who was assistant to Noel Murless and gaining other valuable experience riding the jumpers he had in training with Tom Jones. He was to become one of the young trainers whose success at the outset of their careers was to become such an important part in the story of Newmarket in the following decade.

26 Modern Newmarket

Doug Smith, five times champion jockey before training at Loder House, Newmarket

Just as stabling spread along the Bury Road, to the east of the town during the late Victorian and the Edwardian eras, a series of new yards were built on land, of which the Jockey Club own the freehold, on the Hamilton Road, on the Racecourse Side, in the late 1960s and the first half of the following decade.

The first of these new establishments to be occupied was Loder House, into which former champion jockey Douglas Smith moved the first of the horses to be sent to him in the autumn of 1967. Born in 1917, the son of a Berkshire farmer, Doug Smith had been apprenticed to Major F. B. Sneyd at Wantage, and having ridden his first important winner on Doreen Jane in the Ascot Stakes in 1935 he was retained as lightweight jockey to Frank Butters the following season. By the end of the war he was riding for King George VI and Lord Portal, whose horses were trained by Captain Boyd-Rochfort at Freemason Lodge, and in 1946 won The 1,000 Guineas in the royal colours on Hypericum. The following season he began his long association with Stanley House and was still first jockey to Lord Derby at the time of his retirement 20 years later, the Clarehaven trainer Major Geoffrey Brooke having held second claim on his services during the last twelve years of his riding career.

With the enforced retirement of Sir Gordon Richards in 1954, Smith finished that season as champion jockey. He headed the list again in each of the following two seasons as well as in 1958 and for a fifth time in 1959. A particularly good judge of pace, he excelled in long distance races, and was rarely seen to greater advantage than he was at Newmarket, where he rode six winners of the Cesarewitch, but the greatest stayer with whom he was associated was Lord Derby's Alycidon, on whom he won the Ascot Gold Cup and the Goodwood and Doncaster Cups in 1949.

As Doug Smith was opening his stable at precisely the time that Major Brooke was retiring at the age of 71 in order to return to Ireland it was no more than natural that former patrons of the Clarehaven stable such as Mr Daniel van Clief, Lady Wyfold, Major Dermot McCalmont and Mr Jocelyn Hambro should send him horses, while Lord Derby was also among the owners of the 38 horses with which he embarked upon his new career.

Doug Smith made an immediate impact as a trainer when his first runner, Mr A. G. Samuel's Owen Anthony, was ridden by Tommy Reidy to beat Night Spot in the First Apprentice Handicap at Doncaster, the opening race of the 1968 season. Just under three months later he obtained his first important success when he provided the first and second in the Royal Hunt Cup at Royal Ascot, where Golden Mean won by half a length from Owen Anthony. Not only were these horses stablemates but half-brothers as well.

Following the death of Sir Jack Jarvis in December 1968 Doug Smith extended his responsibilities by taking over the Park Lodge establishment and running it as a private stable for Lord Rosebery, while continuing to train for his other owners at Loder House. In his first season in charge of Park Lodge he was responsible for Lord Rosebery's grey filly Sleeping Partner being successful in The Oaks, ironically the only classic that Sir Jack Jarvis never won. Despite that auspicious beginning the association between owner and trainer was not completely harmonious and at the end of 1971 Lord Rosebery arranged for Bruce Hobbs to assume control of Park Lodge and run it in conjunction with the Palace House stable.

In 1970 Doug Smith brought off the important sprint handicap double in the Wokingham Stakes at Royal Ascot and Doncaster's Portland Stakes with Virginia Boy. The following season he won a second Wokingham Stakes with Whistling Fool while amongst the 42 races that he won in 1972 were the Fred Darling Stakes with Miss Paris at Newbury and the City and Suburban with Owen Anthony, then an eight-year-old.

The next of the Hamilton Road yards to be occupied was the Marriott stables, named after Cecil Wynn Marriott whose word had been law on the Heath while he was Agent to the Jockey Club during the 50 years from 1895 until 1945. Although sometimes accused of being more than a little high handed, and even dictatorial, Mr Marriott earned the gratitude as well as the respect of the trainers. When presenting him with a silver salver on behalf of the Newmarket Trainers' Federation, to mark his retirement, Sir Jack Jarvis, then president, declared that he "devoted himself to the Heath, constantly improved it, and gave us gallops to train on such as there are nowhere else in the world". To his intense sadness his son Captain C. D. W. Marriott was killed at the fall of Singapore, thus his once high hopes of being succeeded by him as Jockey Club Agent were never fulfilled. Cecil Marriott died in Newmarket's Rous Memorial Hospital at the age of 77 in 1947.

The first man to train in the Marriott stables was Henry Cecil, who embarked upon his first season there in 1970. Having been assistant to his step-father Captain Boyd-Rochfort since 1964 he had taken over the string on the retirement of the Captain at the end of 1968 and had the use of the Freemason Lodge yard for his first season, during which he obtained his first notable successes with Mrs C. O. Iselin's Wolver Hollow in the Eclipse Stakes and with Sir Humphrey de Trafford's Approval in the Observer Gold Cup. At the end of the season he was eighth in the list of winning trainers with 27 races worth £60,461 to his credit.

These satisfactory results in his first year with a licence earned Henry Cecil the recognition from the younger owners of which he was so much in need as most of those who had left their horses with him

Henry Cecil, the Warren Place trainer obtained his first English classic success with Bolkonski in the 2,000 Guineas in 1975

after the retirement of the Captain were elderly and unlikely to continue racing for long. Consequently he began his first season at Marriott with a string of 62 horses, half as many again as he had had twelve months earlier. As well as bringing off the stayers' double with Parthenon in the Goodwood Cup and Pride of Alcide in the Goodwood Stakes he won 33 other races and in 1971 increased his tally to 53 including the Cesarewitch with Mr Charles St George's Orosio.

By the time that his string had grown to 76 in 1973 he sent out the first classic winner from Hamilton Road when Cloonagh, owned by his brother Arthur Boyd-Rochfort and ridden by Greville Starkey, was successful in the Irish 1,000 Guineas. Two years later Henry Cecil won his first English classic when Signor Carlo d'Alessio's Bolkonski beat the subsequent Derby winner Grundy in The 2,000 Guineas and put the finishing touches to the making of his reputation by providing that season's leading two-year-old, Wollow, also owned by Signor d'Alessio. As well as the Dewhurst Stakes and the Champagne Stakes Wollow won both his other races as a juvenile while other events won by the Marriott stable that season included the Coronation Stakes and the Nassau Stakes with Mr Nicholas Phillips's Roussalka and a second Observer Gold Cup with Signor d'Alessio's Take Your Place. At the end of 1975 Henry Cecil was second in the list of winning trainers, having sent out 43 horses to win 82 races worth £205,387.

Henry Cecil became leading trainer for the first time in 1976, during which he was responsible for winning 52 races worth £261,301. Completely fulfilling the promise of his first season Wollow won The 2,000 Guineas, the Eclipse Stakes, the Sussex Stakes and the Benson and Hedges Gold Cup at York. A tall bay colt by Wolver Hollow out of Wichuraiana, Wollow was bred by Arthur Boyd-Rochfort at the Tally Ho Stud while it was situated near Mullingar in County Westmeath. Early in 1980 Mr Boyd-Rochfort moved the stud to the well laid out paddocks at Chevington, some 15 miles from Newmarket.

Other notable successes obtained by Henry Cecil in 1976 included the Ribblesdale Stakes with Catalpa and the Queen's Vase with General Ironside at Royal Ascot and the PTS Laurels with Fool's Mate and a second Nassau Stakes with Roussalka at Goodwood.

General Ironside, Roussalka and many of the other winners saddled by Henry Cecil in 1976 were ridden by Lester Piggott, who built the Eve Lodge stable, further down Hamilton Road from the Loder and Marriott stables, against the time that he would retire from riding and turn to training. In giving his stable that name Lester Piggott paid a compliment to the late Sir Victor Sassoon, for whom he won The Derby on Crepello and St Paddy. Before extending his interests to England Sir Victor had raced in India under the *nom-de-course* of 'Mr Eve', a composite of the initial of his forenames Ellice Victor.

Having no use for his newly constructed stable during the immediate future Lester Piggott leased Eve Lodge to former fighter pilot Bill Marshall, who commenced training there in 1976 after having won the City and Suburban and Magnet Cup with My Swanee, the Free Handicap with Panama Canal and a lot of other races while based in

Wiltshire. Among the 30 races that he won during his first season at Eve Lodge was the Northumberland Plate with Philominsky ridden by his son Richard.

Following the retirement of Doug Smith at the end of 1979 the Loder stables were divided into two. Eric Eldin, who had given up riding after the season of 1980, commenced training a string of 43 in 1981 in the half that retained its original name while Bill Marshall moved up the road into the other section that was given the name of Southfields stables. Notable amongst the horses that Eric Eldin trained during his first season was Mr S. Liem's Prowess Prince who won the £11,000 Molecombe Stakes at Goodwood and another race at Doncaster.

Following the departure of Bill Marshall from Eve Lodge, the 40-year-old Jordanian trainer Michael Albina became Lester Piggott's tenant there. After riding 96 winners as an amateur in the Middle East between 1959 and 1964 Michael Albina began training in the Lebanon. In the winter of 1969/70 he took a dozen horses to Egypt but after winning 23 races from 30 runners on the courses at Cairo and Alexandra acceded to the request of the Egyptian sportsmen to depart from their midst by returning to the Lebanon where he continued to train until the political situation obliged him to resume his career in his native Jordan in 1975. Five years later he realised his ambition to run a stable in Europe when his application to train for owner-breeder Mr Mahmoud Foustok was successful.

Although he had only 15 two-year-olds and the four-year-old Mawal in the yard in 1981 Albina made it perfectly clear that he could achieve results in conditions that were greatly dissimilar to those in which he obtained his earlier experience. King Naskra became his first winner in England when beating Olympic Carnival at Yarmouth in July and at the next meeting at Newmarket's local seaside meeting he won with Mr Foustok's American-bred Silver Hawk, a bay colt by the 1972 Derby winner Roberto. Subsequently Silver Hawk confirmed impressions that he had the potential to reach the top class by beating Montekin five lengths in the Intercraft Solario Stakes, transferred to Kempton Park during the re-cambering of Sandown, and finishing a good second to Norwick in the Royal Lodge Stakes at Ascot later in the autumn. With his string increased to 33 in 1982, and Tony Murray retained as stable jockey, Michael Albina made an excellent start to his second season at Eve Lodge by winning the Craven Stakes with Silver Hawk, who was to finish third in The Derby.

The other four yards built on Hamilton Road in the early 1970s were Saffron House, the quarters of David Ringer, the Diomed stables, where Ben Hanbury trains, Calder Park, where Michael Hinchcliffe arrived with a string of 17 from Lambourn in January 1983 after Derek Weeden had had his horses in the yard earlier on, and Neville Callaghan's Rathmoy stables. Among the many races won by Neville Callaghan since he began training with just 18 horses in 1972 has been the Gimrack Stakes with Stanford in 1978. Three years later, in 1981, he had a string of 45 and won 29 races worth £60,899.

The stables at the top of Hamilton Road bore the brunt of the whirlwind that hit the eastern side of Newmarket on the morning of Tuesday 3 January 1978. Roofs were ripped off the barns and tack shed at Loder, and minor damage was caused at Marriott. Continuing on its course the whirlwind swept down to Tattersalls' Sales complex, badly damaging a stable block, and then sent a chimney crashing through the roof of the Coronation Hotel, which had to be closed while repairs were effected.

The development of the stabling along the Hamilton Road took place within a period of ten years that constituted a watershed in the history of Newmarket in as much as in the course of it a large number of the most respected and successful trainers in the town came to the end of their careers. As already mentioned Geoffrey Brooke retired in 1967 then the following year Sir Cecil Boyd-Rochfort, the recipient of a knighthood in the New Year's Honours List, as well as the doyen of the Newmarket trainers Reg Day, who was to die at the age of 88 in 1972, also retired and Sir Jack Jarvis died. The death of Paddy O'Gorman occurred in 1969 and the same year Teddy Lambton relinquished his licence.

This trend continued at the outset of the new decade with Jack Waugh selling the Heath House stable to Sir Mark Prescott in order to assume the management of the Lordship and Egerton Studs for Sir Reginald and Lady Macdonald-Buchanan in 1970. Both Harvey Leader and his nephew Ted Leader relinquished their licences to train at the end of 1971. Harvey Leader, who handed over control of the Shalfleet stable to his former assistant Gavin Pritchard-Gordon, survived retirement only a few weeks, dying on 30 January 1972. Sam Armstrong was succeeded by Robert at St Gatien in 1973, thereafter living in retirement at Newmarket until his death at the age of 78 in December 1982. Geoffrey Barling and Jack Watts also gave up training in 1973. Humphrey Cottrill left Beverley House to pursue a successful new career as a bloodstock agent in the interests of middle-eastern and other clients in 1974. The following year both Bernard van Cutsem and Jack Clayton died while John Oxley closed the Hurworth House stable on account of rising costs in the adverse economic situation. Finally the ten years in question closed with Noel Murless reaching the conclusion of a career in 1976 that had been in many respects unprecedently brilliant, and Atty Corbett was killed a few days after the end of the 1976 season. While walking with his string on Saturday 27 November Atty Corbett was involved in an accident with a car at a road junction and died in Newmarket General Hospital the same evening.

At the outset of the 10 year period during which so many stables in the town were to change hands, important alterations were made to the Rowley Mile Stands and the weighing room while the paddock was re-sited. It was in 1968 that the paddock was moved from the western side of the stands to the rear of them, so that it became as accessible to racegoers in Tattersalls, hiterto obliged to reach it by a long alleyway behind the Members, as it was to the Members. At the same time the weighing room was in effect turned back to front, so that the new entrance, and winner's enclosure in front of it, were facing the paddock, and extensive terracing was constructed at the back of the Member's Stand and Tattersalls to provide a view of the parade ring without a visit to the paddock being necessitated.

The late Duke of Norfolk was largely responsible for the design of this new lay-out, which had the effect of making the Rowley Mile Stands very much more welcoming and comfortable than had formerly been the case. The cost of effecting these major changes was no more than £614,000, a very reasonable sum even by the standards of those days.

With so many leading personalities receding into the background or disappearing from the scene altogether, opportunities for the emergence of new talent became abundant, and as the new stables along Hamilton Road sprang up, some of the older establishments came down or were subject to change of use. The retirement of Geoffrey Barling had been necessitated by the council's decision to demolish the historic Primrose House stable, in which Billy Walters had trained the 1898 Eclipse Stakes winner Velasquez, in order to construct Fred Archer Way. That thoroughfare sweeps down from the Fordham Road to The Rookeries, the modern shopping precinct that

The new parade ring on the Rowley Mile

was built in the middle of the town in the seventies. Following the retirement of Geoffrey Barling his former assistant Hugh Collingridge commenced training and has his string in the Beverley House yard at the time of writing. Horses with whom he has been notably successful include Buzzard's Bay, who won at the Goodwood July meeting and the Ayr Western meeting as well as three times elsewhere in 1981 before his success in the Royal Hunt Cup in 1982.

Sir Mark Prescott, who was once known as a quite fearless amateur rider over hurdles and fences in the West Country, spent the formative part of his career with Sid Kernick in Devonshire before becoming assistant to Jack Waugh. Sir Mark's skill in placing moderate horses to best advantage has enabled him to make regularly successful forays to the North. In 1980 he did well to win 13 races with the two-year-old Spindrifter, a chestnut colt by Sandford Lad, who was also runner-up in three of his other four races at that age. With Heave To Sir Mark won the Victoria Cup for Lord Fairhaven at Ascot in 1972 and on the same course both the Brown Jack Stakes with Carnoch in his first season as a trainer and the Bovis Stakes with Marching On in 1979 for Lady Macdonald-Buchanan.

Gavin Pritchard-Gordon rapidly justified the confidence that Harvey Leader had had in him after taking over the Shalfleet yard, enjoying a particularly good season in 1975. That year he brought off a double with Record Run in the Prince of Wales Stakes and Ardoon in the Royal Hunt Cup at Royal Ascot and won the Hungerford Stakes at Newbury with Court Chad. Following the death of Bernard van Cutsem Gavin Pritchard-Gordon purchased the Stanley House yard from Lord Derby in 1976. The next year he won the Derby Trial Stakes with Caporello and in 1978 the Goodwood Stakes with the same horse.

On Gavin Pritchard-Gordon acquiring Stanley House, Shalfleet became the quarters of the former steeplechase jockey Paul Kelleway who had begun his career as an apprentice to Harry Wragg at Abington Place. Amongst his many achievements in the saddle had been the winning of the Cheltenham Gold Cup on What a Myth in 1969, and the Champion Hurdle on Bula in 1971 and 1972. In only his second season with a trainer's licence Paul Kelleway won the champion Stakes with Mr Max Fine's Swiss Maid, and in 1981 was responsible for Mr G. Kaye's Madam Gay finishing second in The Oaks and winning the French Oaks. Good sprinters to have been trained by Paul Kelleway include African Rhythm who made all the running over the five furlongs of the King's Stand Stakes at Royal Ascot in 1980, and Sparkling Boy, winner of the Ayr Gold Cup the same season.

Mick Ryan, who had been assistant to Bernard van Cutsem, began training in the season after the death of his former employer. He has several Dutch patrons and has achieved considerable success at Duindigt, the principal racecourse in Holland, having won the Dutch Grand Prix with Mr G. J. Kroes's Pink Tank, ridden by Greville Starkey in 1979 and many other events there during recent years. He commenced the season of 1982 with a string of 41 in the Cadland House stable.

More good horses have been trained at St Gatien since Robert Armstrong succeeded his father in that yard, with Moorestyle the outstanding horse that he has trained there in the early years of his career. As brilliant over five furlongs as over seven Moorestyle won the Tote Free Handicap, the William Hill July Cup, the Vernons Sprint Cup, the Prix de L'Abbaye de Longchamp and three other races as a three-year-old in 1980, then before retiring to the National Stud at the end of 1980 enhanced his reputation with further successes that included the Diadem Stakes at Ascot and the Prix de Maurice de Gheest, his trainer's brother-in-law Lester Piggott having been his regular rider. Robert Armstrong's first important success was obtained in the Lockinge Stakes of 1973 with Sparkler, sire of the 1,000 Guineas winner Enstone Spark. Most prestigious of all the two-year-old races won by Robert Armstrong has been the Middle Park Stakes with Mattaboy, bred at the Cheveley Park Stud and bought by Newmarket bloodstock agent 'Tote' Cherry-Downes for 15,000 guineas as a yearling.

Chevalier Odorado Ginistrelli, who brought off the Epsom classic double with Signorinetta in 1908, was the first Italian to make an impact on Newmarket. Luca Cumani became the second when he began training at Bedford House at the age of 26 in 1976, the year after the death of Jack Clayton. The son of an Italian trainer, he had already acquired an international reputation as an amateur jockey on the flat by riding the winners of 83 races including the Moet and Chandon Silver Magnum at Epsom. In his first season as a trainer he won the Duke of York Stakes with Three Legs, the former champion sprinter of Italy, and at the Newmarket Craven Meeting of 1977 brought off a double with Vaguely Deb in the Wood Ditton Stakes and Freeze the Secret in the Nell Gwyn Stakes. A few weeks later Freeze the Secret and Vaguely Deb were second and third respectively in The Oaks.

The dissolution of Mr David Robinson's huge racing empire in the course of the 1970s on account of its owner's declining health inevitably led to significant changes. In the autumn of 1974 he sold Carlburg to the Greek shipping magnate Captain Marcos Lemos while retaining Michael Jarvis as his private trainer at Clarehaven for one more season, during which he won the Northumberland Plate with Grey God and 56 other races. The following season, that of 1976, Michael Jarvis remained at Clarehaven as a public trainer his string of 55 including horses belonging to Lady Beaverbrook, Lord Harrington, Mr S. Vanian and other owners besides Mr Robinson. By 1977 Michael Jarvis had moved to Pegasus House, which had been greatly enlarged since the days when Fred Archer kept his hacks there, but spent only two seasons in that yard before taking his string into Kremlin House, whence Jeremy Hindley moved to Clarehaven on purchasing that establishment from Mr Robinson who had ceased to own any horses at all. Thus, in effect, Michael Jarvis and Jeremy Hindley swapped stables.

The best horse that Michael Jarvis has trained since leaving Clarehaven has been Mr A. Kelly's Beldale Flutter, who beat Shergar in the William Hill Futurity at Doncaster in 1980. Having been successful in the Mecca-Dante Stakes at York the following May Beldale Flutter became a leading fancy for The Derby until getting loose on the Heath shortly before the race, colliding with Moorestyle and finally coming down on a road, cutting his off-fore knee and bruising his ribs so badly that he had to be kept in his box for almost a month. Fortunately both Moorestyle and Beldale Flutter recovered from the effects of their violent encounter. By August Michael Jarvis had brought Beldale Flutter back to peak form and was able to send him to York to win the Benson and Hedges by three parts of a length from Kirtling with Master Willie, runner-up in the previous year's Derby, the same distance away third. Having been syndicated for £60,000 a share Beldale Flutter was retired to Newmarket's Banstead Manor Stud, which was founded by Mr H. E. Morris to stand the 1925 Derby winner Manna.

Another good horse trained by Michael Jarvis in recent years has been Lady Beaverbrook's Totowah, with whom he won the Ebor Handicap in 1978 and the Northumberland Plate in 1979.

The most important of the races that Jeremy Hindley won during his final seasons at Kremlin House was the Cambridgeshire with Lady Brigid Ness's Sin Timon in 1977. Since moving to Clarehaven, where he had 71 horses in 1982, his achievements have included developing the potential of Protection Racket who won the Ebor Handicap in 1981 then being stepped up in class and beating Erin's Isle by three lengths in the Irish St Leger.

On purchasing Carlburg from Mr David Robinson Captain Marcos Lemos installed Clive Brittain as trainer in that yard and at the outset of the season of 1975 Brittain had charge of some 80 horses of which about 30 belonged to Captain Lemos and the remainder to other owners including Colonel and Mrs Roger Hue-Williams, Mr Rabi Khan, Mr A. J. Richards and Mr C. M. Elliot. After serving his apprenticeship with Sir Noel Murless, Clive Brittain remained on the staff at Warren Place until commencing to train with a string of 37 at Pegasus House in 1972. Since taking up his quarters at Carlburg he has obtained his first classic success with Captain Lemos's Julio Mariner in The St Leger of 1978. The following season he won the Stewards Cup with Mr Richards's Standaan, ridden by his apprentice Paul Bradwell, and in 1981 the Cambridgeshire with Mr Bill Gredley's outsider Braughing, ridden by the American jockey Steve Cauthen.

As well as having a large number of horses in training with Clive Brittain at Carlburg and being the owner of that yard, Captain Lemos has other substantial interests at Newmarket. In 1968, the year after he had won the Gimcrack Stakes with Petingo, he founded the Warren Hill Stud and in 1974 acquired the adjoining Ashley Heath Stud where he stands Julio Mariner. These two establishments, combined run to 300 acres. In 1982 Captain Lemos increased his investment in Newmarket by purchasing the Fitzroy House stable through Captain Christopher Stephenson, an amateur rider during his soldiering days now an estate agent specialising in racing properties and responsible for a number of important sales in the town during recent years.

It was at Fitzroy House that Peter Robinson was training at the time of his premature death at the age of 42 in 1978 when he collapsed while driving home from Salisbury races. Having made that auspicious start to his training career by winning the Cambridgeshire with Prince de Galles in 1969 he won the race again with the same horse in 1970, and obtained another of his important successes with Sovereign Bill in the Lincoln in 1972.

Happily Peter Robinson was spared long enough to see his son Philip embarked upon a successful career as jockey, though not to ee him become champion apprentice in 1979 and 1980. Philip Robinson rode his first winner on Busting at Yarmouth on 14 June 1978 shortly before the death of his father.

At the end of the year during which Peter Robinson died Frank Durr retired from riding at the age of 52 and commenced training at Fitzroy House the following season, during which he won the William Hill Sprint Championship with Mr Essa Alkhalifa's Ahonnoora at York. The following year he won the Portland Handicap with Swelter ridden by Philip Robinson whose indentures had been transferred to him.

While Frank Durr, Clive Brittain and so many of the other men who have taken out licences in the last dozen years or so have been quick to flourish in their new ventures the senior Newmarket trainers like Harry Wragg, Thomson Jones and Bruce Hobbs have continued to turn out high class horses. Within just six weeks of his 80th birthday Harry Wragg sent out his sixth winner of an English classic as a trainer when Sir Philip Oppenheimer's bay filly On The House won The 1,000 Guineas in the hands of John Reid. Other notable successes enjoyed by Harry Wragg in recent years have been in the Cesarewitch with Mr Roderic More O'Farrell's Shantallah in 1975 and in the Benson and Hedges at York with Moulton in 1973. Moulton was one of the many good horses trained by Harry Wragg for the late Mr R. B. 'Budgie' Moller and his brother Mr Eric Moller, who were partners in the White Lodge Stud at Cheveley. Other winners they bred there included Full Dress II (1,000 Guineas), Lacquer (Irish 1,000 Guineas and Cambridgeshire) and Sovereign and Amaranda, both of whom were successful in the Queen Mary Stakes at Royal Ascot. Like Moulton many of the other colts and fillies bred at the White Lodge Stud recently, such as Cherry Hinton, Abington, Barrow, Dalham and Six Mile Bottom were named after villages in the Newmarket area. In January 1983 Harry Wragg announced his retirement and at the end of the month handed over the Abington Place string to his son Geoffrey who had been his assistant for a number of years.

Having run the most successful mixed stable in the town for many years, Thomson Jones won his first English classic with the late Mrs John Rogerson's Athens Wood who landed The St Leger in 1971. The same year he brought off a notable double with Fleet Wahine in the Ribblesdale Stakes at Royal Ascot and the Yorkshire Oaks and was sixth in the list of winning trainers. Seven years later he trained Devon Ditty to become the leading two-year-old filly of the season by winning York's Lowther Stakes and the Cheveley Park Stakes together with five other races. Thomson Jones also won the Lowther Stakes with Icena in 1976 as well as the Queen Alexandra Stakes at Royal Ascot with John Cherry in 1977 and 1979 and the Princess of Wales Stakes with Pollerton in 1978, then in 1982 he won a second St Leger with Maktoum al Maktoum's Touching Wood, ridden by stable jockey Paul Cook.

Shortly after the retirement of John Oxley, Thomson Jones acquired Hurworth House as his second yard, and concentrated on flat racing to the exclusion of hurdling and steeplechasing.

Four of the best horses trained by Bruce Hobbs at Palace House of late were bred by the late Mr George Cambanis from his fast mare Stilvi over a period of five years. They were the colts Tachypous (1974 by Hotfoot), Tromos (1976 by Busted), and Tyrnavos (1977 by Blakeney) and their half-sister Tolmi (1978 by Great Nephew). While in training with Bruce Hobbs Stilvi won the National Stakes from Sallust at Sandown Park and two of her other three races as a two-year-old in 1971 and the Duke of York Stakes and the King George Stakes at Goodwood the following season. On retiring she went to Mr Pat McCalmont's Gazeley Stud, where her son Tyrnavos has recently taken up stallion duties alongside her first mate Hotfoot.

After winning at Ascot and being second in the Dewhurst Stakes as a two-year-old Tyrnavos established himself as a top class performer by international standards by making all the running to beat Prince Bee a comfortable length and a half in the Irish Sweeps Derby. Tachypous, the first foal of Stilvi, won the Middle Park Stakes in 1976 and finished second in The 2,000 Guineas. Tromos emerged as one of the best two-year-olds of 1978.. He was third at Doncaster's St Leger meeting in the first of his three races of his first season and then won by ten lengths at Ascot before leading all the way to win the Dewhurst Stakes. Tolmi won at Newmarket and Ascot in July 1980 the only times that she ran as a two-year-old. The highlights of her second season came when she ran Fairy Footsteps to a neck in The 1,000 Guineas and won the Coronation Stakes at Royal Ascot.

Hotfoot, sire of Tachypous, is one of several good horses that Bruce Hobbs has trained for Mr Tony Villar who farms near Bury St Edmunds. A brown horse by Firestreak, Hotfoot proved particularly effective as a four-year-old in 1970, beating the previous year's Derby runner-up Shoemaker in the Coronation Stakes at Sandown Park and winning five other races including the Players-Wills Stakes at the Curragh and the PTS Laurels at Goodwood. Take a Reef, whom Bruce Hobbs also trained for Mr Villar, was officially rated the best three-year-old to have raced over distances from a mile to a mile and a quarter in 1974 after beating the older Superior Sam in the John Smith's Magnet Cup at York and defying top weight in the Extel Handicap at Goodwood on his only subsequent appearance. More recently Bruce Hobbs has won both the William Hill Futurity and the Blue Riband Trial Stakes for Mr Villar with Count Pahlen, another son of Hotfoot.

Another of Bruce Hobbs's patrons living near Newmarket is Mr Tom Blackwell, a member of the Jockey Club, who has bred a lot of winners at the stud that he runs at his Langham Hall home near Bury St Edmunds. Important races that he has won since sending his horses to Palace House following the death of Sir Jack Jarvis have included the Chester Vase with Jupiter Pluvius in 1974, the Cheshire Oaks with Princess Eboli in 1978, the Nassau Stakes with Vielle in 1980, the Goodwood Cup with Richmond Fair in 1969 and the New Ham Stakes with Mrs Tiggywinkle, who was third in The 1,000 Guineas, a place that another of his high class fillies Catherine Wheel occupied in the same classic in 1971. Bruce Hobbs has also won the Cheveley Park Stakes of 1972 and Royal Ascot's Coronation Stakes with Lady Butt's Jacinth and a second Cheveley Park Stakes with Miss P. Johnston's Cry of Truth in 1974. The best of the races that he won for Lord Rosebery during the short time he had charge of his horses before the death of the veteran owner at the age of 92 in 1974 was the Northumberland Plate with Tom Cribb in 1973.

Ryan Jarvis accomplished more characteristically fine feats of training before retiring at the end of 1979. In 1969 he obtained yet another big handicap success with Mr S. Terry's Even Say in the Northumberland Plate and in 1972 won the Horris Hill Stakes at Newbury and two other races with Long Row, whose dam Front Row had won the Irish 1,000 Guineas for the Phantom House stable. Four years later in 1976 Ryan Jarvis placed Mrs F. Allen's five-year-old handicapper Royal Match to win no fewer than seven races, including the Kempton Park Jubilee, the Bessborough Stakes at Royal Ascot and the Liverpool Spring Cup, then the following year he deployed similar skill to enable Dred Scott to win the same number of times after the horse had failed in eleven attempts while in another stable the previous season.

The last good horse trained by Ryan Jarvis before his retirement at the end of 1979 was Mrs C. Alington's grey sprinter Absalom. He won the Cornwallis Stakes at Ascot as a two-year-old in 1977, the Vernons Sprint Cup at Haydock Park the following season and returned to Ascot for a success in the Diadem Stakes in the autumn of 1979. Finally Lester Piggott rode him to win the £10,000 Premio Chiusura over seven furlongs on very heavy ground at Milan in early November.

Ryan Jarvis's son William was only 16 when riding his first winner on Chance Belle, his first mount in public, in an amateurs' race at Redcar in June 1977. He is now assistant to Henry Cecil and the Phantom House yard occupied by former successful point-to-point rider Willie Musson. Commencing to train there at the outset of 1981 after a spell at Bramley near Guildford, Willie Musson sent out Hurricane Hill to be third in the Lincoln and won the £7,000 Holsten Diat Pils Handicap over six furlongs on the Rowley Mile Course with Sharp Venetia a few weeks later.

The former jump jockey Eric Campbell, who was head lad to Ryan Jarvis, joined Robert Williams in the same capacity. After six years as assistant to Barry Hills at Lambourn Robert Williams began the season of 1981 with a string of 26 in the Sackville House stable and Mr Richard Swift, who owned the yard, as his principal patron. It was for

Mr Swift that he obtained his first success when Great Light made all the running at Nottingham in early April. Robert Williams won eleven more races in his first season, his winners including Diamond Cutter, who beat Bronowski at Newmarket on 2,000 Guineas day and Myra's Pet, successful twice at Yarmouth and once at Chepstow.

Two other young trainers to enjoy their first successes in 1981 were James Toller and Chuck Spares. James Toller, son of Captain Charles Toller, Clerk of the Course at Newbury, Bath and Chester, produced a useful two-year-old filly in Mosso to win the Kingsclere Stakes at Newbury and another event. Chuck Spares, whose father the late Charlie Spares rode Arctic Prince to win The Derby in 1951, had been travelling head lad to Michael Stoute before taking a string of 29 into the Savile House yard, formerly the quarters of John Powney. He obtained his initial success with Singing Sailor, who had cost only 1,300 guineas as a yearling, at Salisbury in May and won with him again at Beverley and Pontefract.

Mark Tomkins, assistant to Ryan Jarvis for the three years until the end of 1979, quickly turned out his first winner, as it was in January 1980 that Timmatemma beat Misty Bay eight lengths in a division of the Sleaford Novices Hurdle at Market Rasen. Later that year he won four races on the flat with the horses that he trained at the Raynes Lane stable, into which he had followed Peter Poston, and in 1981 showed improvement on these first results by saddling nine winners.

For the first time for more than 100 years there were no members of Newmarket's Jarvis or Waugh families training in the town in 1981, though Willie Jarvis was waiting in the wings to revive a long tradition. At the end of 1980 Tom Waugh had retired. Most important of his later successes as mentioned earlier were achieved through the medium of Mr J. D. Parker's Tartar Prince in the Great Metropolitan and the Northumberland Plate in 1971 and Mr H. J. Joel's Rose Dubarry in the Lowther Sweepstakes at York later that year.

In the same season that Rose Dubarry established herself among the best of the two-year-old fillies, colts trained by Bernard van Cutsem at Stanley House dominated the important juvenile races in the autumn. Mr Frank Mahon's Crowned Prince, who had cost the then world record price for a yearling of 510,000 dollars, won both the Champagne Stakes at Doncaster and the Dewhurst Stakes, Sir Jules Thorn's High Top won Doncaster's Observer Gold Cup (now the William Hill Futurity) and Sharpen Up, owned by his trainer's wife, was successful in the Middle Park Stakes. The following spring High Top gave Bernard van Cutsem the only English classic success of his all too short career by making all the running to beat the subsequent Derby winner Roberto by half a length in The 2,000 Guineas. At the back-end of that season Bernard van Cutsem obtained further success in the more valuable two-year-old races when Mr Nelson Bunker Hunt's Noble Decree beat his stablemate Ksar in the Observer Gold Cup and Otha, also owned by Mr Hunt, won the Champagne Stakes. Bernard van Cutsem finally lost his long battle against cancer, which he had fought with a calm courage at the age of 59 on 9 December

The Stanley House trainer Bernard van Cutsem (1916-1975)

1975. The last of his big winners had been Old Lucky with which he had brought off one of those old-fashioned gambles that he relished so greatly in the Royal Hunt Cup in 1974. A tall man with an impassive, almost disdainful, dignity about him, Bernard van Cutsem could convey the impression of being aloof but the lads, who worked for him, and admired his sheer professionalism, and those who kept his company in his Newmarket Club, the Subscription Rooms, were able to appreciate the essential warmth of his personality and his enormous sense of humour.

When Noel Murless was champion trainer for the eighth time in 1970 he won The Oaks with Mrs Stanhope Joel's Lupe, the Coronation Cup with Caliban and the Eclipse Stakes with Connaught as well as the Champion Stakes in which Lorenzaccio became the only horse ever to beat Nijinski in England or Ireland. In 1971 he completed the double in The 1,000 Guineas and The Oaks with Altesse Royale and completed the same classic double with Mr George Pope junior's Mysterious in 1973, in which season he headed the list for a ninth time.

Maintaining a long ingrained habit to the end, Noel Murless brought his great career to a conclusion by producing one last champion in the American-bred brown colt J. O. Tobin, who was acclaimed best of the two-year-olds of 1976. A winner at Newmarket's July Meeting on the first of his four appearances, J. O. Tobin won both the Richmond Stakes at Goodwood and the Champagne Stakes at Doncaster in impressive fashion and then finished third to Blushing Groom in the Grand Criterium.

In his last season as a trainer, Noel Murless happily renewed his association with Lester Piggott, who had caused a major sensation by relinquishing his position as stable jockey at Warren Place ten years earlier. As well as riding J. O. Tobin on each of his four appearances, Lester Piggott won the Royal Hunt Cup on Jumping Hill and 19 other races for Noel Murless in 1976. The last of all the 1,431 races won by Noel Murless was the Ticehurst Stakes, in which Tinsley Green ridden by Lester Piggott, held Careless Princess by a neck at Lingfield on 2 November.

Sir Noel Murless received his knighthood in the Queen's Silver Jubilee Honours List in June 1977 and was elected to the Jockey Club the following month. Since retiring he has managed the Woodditton Stud, where Connaught, Welsh Pageant and Owen Dudley stand as stallions.

At about the time of the death of Bernard van Cutsem and the retirement of Noel Murless several commentators professed to discern signs of the decline in the importance of Newmarket as a training centre. In the six seasons from 1972 to 1977 inclusive just four English classic winners were trained on the Heath — High Top, Mysterious, Bolkonski and Wollow. On the other hand the Berkshire horses Morston in 1973, Snow Knight in 1974 and Grundy in 1975 completed a hat-trick in The Derby and four other horses trained in that county — Highclere, Polygamy, Bustino and Dunfermline won classics during the period. Superficially, at least, it did seem that history was repeating itself with Newmarket falling out of favour as the horses trained on the South Downs came into the ascendancy as they had done after the decline of the fortunes of the Chifneys during the middle of the previous century. Had the observers of the scene in 1975 and 1976 been able to foresee the state of play by the end of the decade they might have been yet more anxious about the effects of that rapid turnover in the control of stables in the ten years between 1967 and 1976. No winner of The Derby was trained on the Heath in the 1970s, during which the town's tally in the classics amounted to just twelve (24%) as opposed to the 19 (38%) that had been won in the 1960s and 23 (46%) in the 1950s.

At that time when the Newmarket stables were going through a decidedly lean period relations between the trainers and the lads, normally harmonious, not to say happy, broke down. The lads, many of whom were members of the Transport and General Workers' Union, demanded an increase of £1.47 in their wages in the spring of 1975. The Newmarket Trainers' Federation, fearful that the consequent raising of their fees would lead to a loss of horses, refused to meet the claim. In consequence some 600 lads came out on strike, with various degrees of enthusiam, after the efforts of Sam Horncastle, district organiser of the TGWU, had failed to obtain an acceptable settlement, and trainers were obliged to rely upon the assistance of members of their families, friends and owners, together with those lads who had no wish to withdraw their labour, in order to feed and exercise their horses, and travel them to the meetings.

On Thursday 1 May, the opening day of the Guineas meeting, an element of violence was introduced into the dispute when an ugly scene took place on the Rowley Mile. A group of strikers and sympathisers assembled on the course as the runners were going to the start for the second race, and focusing their anger on the luckless Willie Carson rider of Pericet, dragged him from the saddle and subjected him to further violence. The unprovoked attack on a popular jockey enraged racegoers in the nearby Silver Ring who flooded onto the course to prevent any further harm befalling the riders or their horses and fighting broke out for long enough to delay the start of the race by 24 minutes.

In the early hours of Saturday morning the strikers and their allies tried to prevent the running of The 2,000 Guineas that afternoon by using a bulldozer to sink more than a dozen craters in the Rowley Mile. Captain Nick Lees, who had been appointed Clerk of the Course at the age of 34 the previous year, was able to make good the damage in time for racing to start on schedule, though under the threat of further trouble which duly materialised. Just as the runners for The 2,000 Guineas were going into the stalls strikers sat down in front of them so that the horses had to be taken out again while mounted police cleared the course. As soon as this had been achieved Major Michael Eveleigh lined the field up in front of the stalls, rather than go through the longer process of reloading them, and used the flag to start the race, which Bolkonski won by half a length from Grundy.

A stable lads' picket on Racecourse Side in 1975

Thereafter the dispute dragged on for another three months. Racing disappeared from the television screens as a result of the cameramen coming out in sympathy with the lads, though Lord Wigg used his influence to ensure the showing of The Derby, and members of the Newmarket Stable Staff Liaison Committee distributed leaflets stating their case to racegoers at Royal Ascot. Eventually, though, the Advisory, Conciliation and Arbitration Service produced a formula whereby the lads received a minimum wage of £37 a week from 1 August, which was worth more than twice as much as it is at the present time.

Those people who foresaw Newmarket receding into eclipse again as a result of the death and retirement of so many of its most experienced trainers in so short a time had greatly underestimated the energy and talent of the younger men. These were spear-headed by Henry Cecil and Michael Stoute, the first two members of the town's new generation of trainers to head the list.

Michael Stoute was born in Barbados, where his father was Commissioner of Police. The family home was close to the island's only racecourse at the Garrison Savannah and the early interest that he took in the activities on it intensified on his making the acquaintance of one of the trainers, Freddie Thirkell, who had served his apprenticeship with Matt Peacock at Middleham. Thus having been increasingly fascinated by racehorses since beginning to ride out in early boyhood Michael Stoute determined to find a job in the racing industry, preferably in England, where he arrived with an introduction to Malton trainer Pat Rohan at the age of 20 in 1965.

After gaining invaluable experience by working in Pat Rohan's stable in varying capacities for three years Michael Stoute went south to be assistant to Doug Smith, having charge of the Park Lodge stable in which Lord Rosebery's horses were trained. While responsible for the running of that yard he had his first opportunity to obtain first-hand knowledge of a high class horse, as it was there that Doug Smith trained Lord Rosebery's grey filly Sleeping Partner to win The Oaks in 1969. The following week Michael Stoute married Miss Pat Baker, one of the most experienced racereaders on the staff of *Raceform*.

The season after Sleeping Partner had won The Oaks Michael Stoute became assistant to Tom Jones in the Woodlands yard, where he was able to increase his experience of handling classic material as he was involved in preparing Athens Wood to win The St Leger in 1971.

Sometime before the success of Athens Wood in the Doncaster classic he had begun to implement his decision to set up on his own by acquiring orders to buy yearlings at the autumn sales and securing a lease of the Cadland stables, in which he began the 1972 season with a string of just 15 — a dozen two-year-olds, a couple of three-year-olds and the five-year-old Sandal. It was Sandal who was to provide him with his initial success as a trainer when Lester Piggott rode him to beat Sir Lark by a neck in the Turn of the Lands Handicap at Newmarket on 28 April. Ironically the runner-up was trained by Pat Rohan.

Of the twelve yearlings with which Michael Stoute began, all had been bought at modest prices with the exception of Blue Cashmere, who necessarily represented the brightest hope of the new stable. Acting on behalf of Mr R. Clifford Turner, Stoute had paid 9,000 guineas for that horse, a brown colt by the 2,000 Guineas winner, Kashmir II. As well as with Blue Cashmere at Yarmouth on the second of his two appearances as a juvenile, Michael Stoute won twelve other races with his string of 15 in his first season, at the end of which he moved into the Beech Hurst stable at the top of the Bury Road.

While occupied by Percy Allden until his retirement at the end of 1970 that stable had been known as Gondola, the former jockey having a propensity for calling any yard in which he trained by that name. Having obtained his most important riding success on Mr Jimmy de Rothschild's Broadwood in the Ascot Stakes in 1914, Allden trained at Epsom from 1921 until going to France for a four year stint as private trainer to Mr R. B. Strassburger at Chantilly from 1927 until 1931, arriving at Newmarket in 1935. Thirty-three years later he achieved his most notable feat as a trainer by winning the Cambridgeshire of 1968 with Emilio. After Michael Stoute had taken over the stable recently vacated by Percy Allden he reverted to the use of the name by which it had been known when the one-time champion jockey Otto Madden trained Chapeau to win the 1925 Ebor Handicap there.

Coming up to the high expectations held of him Blue Cashmere made a large contribution to enabling Michael Stoute to establish himself by winning the Ayr Gold Cup as a three-year-old in 1973. Somewhat earlier in his second season Stoute had also won the Stewards Cup at Goodwood with Mrs J. Mountfield's Alphadamus, who had cost a modest 1,200 guineas as a yearling.

Five years later, in 1978, Michael Stoute was training a string of 67, the Beech Hurst stable having been modernised and greatly enlarged. By that time his owners included Mrs Dana Brudenell-Bruce, the Duke of Devonshire, Mr Edmund Loder, whose great-uncle owned and bred Pretty Polly, Captain John Macdonald-Buchanan, Major the Hon J. P. Philipps, Sir Gordon White and the bookmaking firm of William Hill. That season he won his first classic when Greville Starkey drove Fair Salinia up in the last stride to beat Dancing Maid a short head in The Oaks. A few weeks later Fair Salinia was awarded the Irish Oaks on the disqualification of Sorbus before completing a valuable hat-trick in the Yorkshire Oaks. Also among the 80 races he won that year were the Gold Cup with Shangamuzzo and a second Ayr Gold Cup with Vaigly Great. At the end of the season he was third in the list of winning trainers with prize money of £284,541 to the credit of his owners. By 1979 his string had grown to 92 and the stabling at Freemason Lodge, which had not been pulled down along with the house, acquired as a second yard. Two years later he appointed as his stable jockey 19-year-old Walter Swinburn, whose father and namesake had won the Ebor on By Thunder! while apprenticed to Sam Armstrong at St Gatien in 1954.

The outstanding horse at Beech Hurst when Michael Stoute became champion trainer in 1981 was, the Aga Khan's Shergar, a robust bay with well-sprung ribs, a broad blaze and four socks. As well as The Derby in which Swinburn brought him home ten lengths clear of Glint of Gold, Shergar won the Irish Sweeps Derby, the King George VI and the Queen Elizabeth Stakes, the Guardian Newspaper Classic Trial at Sandown Park and the Chester Vase but was only fourth in The St Leger the only other time he ran as a three-year-old. Other good horses that Michael Stoute trained in the season of his championship were Mr Loder's fast three-year-old filly Marwell, the Snailwell Stud's Circus Ring, officially rated the best of the two-year-old fillies, and the useful staying handicapper Dawn Johnny. Marwell won the King's Stand Stakes at Royal Ascot, the William Hill July Cup, the Prix de L'Abbaye de Longchamp and two other races, Circus Ring the Lowther Sweepstakes at York and Dawn Johnny, who carried the colours of Sir George White, the Northumberland Plate. In 1981 Newmarket trainers were first and second in the list for the first time since Major Dick Hern, then in charge of Major Holliday's horses at Lagrange, and Harry Wragg occupied those positions 19 years earlier. Michael Stoute had won 95 races worth £723,786 and Henry Cecil 107 worth £588,356.

On the retirement of Sir Noel Murless at the end of 1976 control of the Warren Place stable passed to his 33-year-old son-in-law Henry Cecil who had married Julia Murless, probably the best horsewoman

The 1981 Derby winner, Shergar, with Walter Swinburn, and Michael Stoute (right)

at Newmarket, in 1966, and Sir Noel's former assistant William Hastings-Bass began training in the Marriott stable with a string of 28 in 1977. The son of Captain Peter Hastings-Bass, who trained so successfully at Kingsclere until his premature death in 1964, William Hastings-Bass wound up his first season by winning the William Hill November Handicap with Sailcloth, who carried the colours of the Queen's racing manager Lord Porchester, after obtaining 25 earlier successes. In his second season he trained two two-year-old fillies for the Queen, Contralto and Manushi, and saddled his first royal winner on the Saturday after the Royal Meeting when Contralto beat Wind of Change a length in the Fenwolf Stakes at Ascot. Earlier in the week he had won the Queen Mary Stakes with Greenland Park owned by the limited company of that name. William Hastings-Bass began 1982 with 72 horses in the Marriott stables and Sir Noel Murless's former work rider John Gibson as his head lad. 'Spider' Gibson had ridden Crepello, Royal Palace and very many other high class horses in their work during his years at Warren Place. At the end of 1982 William Hastings-Bass left Newmarket to open a stable in Australia.

Henry Cecil had 113 horses in his string in his first season at Warren Place in 1977 with Joe Mercer, who had terminated his long association with West Ilsley the previous year, as stable jockey. Among the 72 races worth £120,263 that he won that year were the Park Hill Stakes with Royal Hive, the Prince of Wales Stakes with Lucky Wednesday at Royal Ascot and Redcar's William Hill Gold Cup with Aliante. Still more impressive results were obtained in 1978 when Henry Cecil was leading trainer for a second time as a result of the Warren Place horses having won 109 races worth £382,301. The best of these races were the Eclipse Stakes and the Prince of Wales Stakes won by Gunner B, the Champagne Stakes by R. B. Chesne, the Doncaster Cup and Jockey Club Cup by Buckskin, a stayer of the most delightful temperament imaginable, and the July Stakes by Main Reef.

When champion trainer for a third time in 1979 Henry Cecil set a new record for stake money won by a single stable during one season by amassing £683,971 after turning out the winners of 128 races.

After Helena Springfield Ltd's One in a Million had become the first company-owned horse to win a classic by beating Abbeydale in The 1,000 Guineas the Warren Place stable came close to bringing off the same double as it had done with Royal Palace and Fleet in 1967 when Lord Howard de Walden's Kris was second to Tap on Wood in The 2,000 Guineas. Subsequently Kris established himself as a truly top class miler by winning the St James's Palace Stakes, the Sussex Stakes and the Queen Elizabeth II Stakes. The other outstanding horses at Warren Place in 1979 were that high class stayer Le Moss, Lyphard's Wish, the three-year-old filly Connaught Bridge and the two-year-old colt Hello Gorgeous, one of the 33 horses that Henry Cecil was training for Paris art dealer Mr Daniel Wildenstein. Le Moss, who carried the colours of Wollow's owner Mr Carlo d'Alessio, completed the Cup treble by winning the Gold Cup at Ascot and then the Doncaster and

Le Moss (centre) is ridden by Joe Mercer to win Goodwood's March Stakes for the Warren Place stable in 1978

Goodwood Cups. Lyphard's Wish, also owned by Mr d'Alessio, made a good start to the season by winning the Craven Stakes and York's Mecca-Dante Stakes and when Mr P. Harris's Connaught Bridge came to her best in the summer she won the Nassau Stakes at Goodwood and the Yorkshire Oaks while Hello Gorgeous brought off the double in two of the most valuable races for staying two-year-olds by winning the Royal Lodge Stakes at Ascot and the William Hill Futurity at Doncaster in the autumn.

Hello Gorgeous trained on to win the Mecca-Dante Stakes but more substantial contributors to the £461,036 that enabled Henry Cecil to finish second in the trainers' list in 1980 were Le Moss, Kris and Light Cavalry. Le Moss justified the decision to keep him in training as a five-year-old by winning the Gold Cup as well as the Goodwood and Doncaster Cups again, though only after considerable difficulties arising from his temperament had been overcome. Early in the season he developed an aversion to going onto the gallops and it was very largely due to the skill of his regular rider, 46-year-old Alan Welborne, who hacked him all over the Heath while the string was in routine work, that he was coaxed into a great deal more co-operative frame of mind. Alan Welborne, who served his apprenticeship with Joe Lawson at Carlburg, received the Derby Award after the Horserace Writers' and Reporters' Association voted him the Stable Lad of the Year.

Kris enhanced his prestige by winning the £24,000 Tote Lockinge Stakes as well as other events at Goodwood and Haydock Park before retiring to the Thornton Stud in Yorkshire. Light Cavalry, a big strong bay by Brigadier Gerard, belonging to Mr Jim Joel, improved steadily

Champion miler Kris (Joe Mercer) in full flight

throughout the season until winning The St Leger and his half-sister Fairy Footsteps (by Mill Reef) held out hope of being top class by winning the seven furlong Waterford Candelabra Stakes at Goodwood in August. The 134 horses that Henry Cecil trained in 1980 constituted the biggest string ever assembled at Newmarket.

After four extraordinarily successful seasons, during which he had been champion jockey for the first time at the age of 45 in 1979, Joe Mercer left Warren Place at the end of 1980. Having ridden a classic winner before any of his colleagues in the weighing room he had reached that stage of his career when continual travelling had lost any charm it might ever have had, and he accepted the retainer offered by Peter Walwyn, whose Lambourn stable is only a few miles from his Berkshire home. Thus Lester Piggott was retained as first jockey to Henry Cecil in 1981 and renewed an association with Warren Place that had begun more than a quarter century earlier in 1955.

Hardly had the season of 1981 got under way than Lester Piggott was subjected to a terrifying experience that could have unnerved a man of half his age when he was dragged under the firmly closed door of a starting stall by the petrified Windsor Boy at Epsom. But though badly cut and bruised, and needing 31 stitches in an ear almost wrenched from his head, he was able to ride Fairy Footsteps to make all the running in The 1,000 Guineas a week later. Thereafter the Warren Place horses continued to win big races throughout the season. The five-year-old Ardross justified his being bought from Ireland as a replacement for Le Moss by winning both the Gold Cup and the

Goodwood Cup, Belmont Bay established himself as a top class miler with successes in the Tote Lockinge Stakes, Royal Ascot's Queen Anne Stakes and three other races, Strigida won the Ribblesdale Stakes, Light Cavalry trained on to win the Princess of Wales Stakes and Cajun took his place among the best of the two-year-olds by landing both the Chesham Stakes at the Royal Meeting and the Middle Park Stakes.

The large majority of the 107 winners trained by Henry Cecil in 1981 were ridden by Lester Piggott, but the Warren Place apprentice Nigel Day made the best of his opportunities, winning 35 races in all, and Julie Cecil was successful on two of her three mounts.

In the autumn of 1982 Geoffrey Huffer completed the purchase of the Lagrange stable in association with a partner with a view to using that yard and the neighbouring one at Somerville Lodge to accommodate his greatly increased string in 1983. Geoff Huffer was apprenticed to Willie Stephenson at Royston, and had acted as assistant to Dickie Westbrooke at Newmarket as well as to J. D. Bingham in Yorkshire before commencing to train in the Cheveley Park stable at the back-end of 1978. His first season was made memorable by his winning the Cesarewitch with Sir Michael together with 22 other events that brought the stable's earnings to £58,008. Two years later in 1981 he achieved the not inconsiderable feat of saddling the first and second in the Ayr Gold Cup, First Movement, ridden by Michael Miller, getting up in the last few strides to beat Tina's Pet, the mount of Bryn Crossley, by a head.

Robert Williams also announced a change of quarters toward the end of 1982. After a highly satisfactory second season with a licence, he left Sackville House to take over the more spacious Marriott stables on the departure of William Hastings-Bass for Australia.

Earlier in 1982 the Cadland House trainer Mick Ryan had added substantially to his successes in Holland by making a clean sweep of the Dutch Classics. He was also responsible for Royal Heroine winning the Princess Margaret Stakes at Ascot and another six furlong race at Newmarket before she was sold to the season's leading owner Mr Robert Sangster and transferred to Michael Stoute. Mick Ryan is one of the relatively few trainers to have been born in Newmarket, where his late father and namesake was Lord Derby's much respected stud groom for many years.

Another of the younger trainers who had laid the foundations of his reputation by the end of 1982 was Patrick Haslam. Having been assistant to George Todd, Alec Kerr and Gordon Smyth he set up on his own in 1972 with a yard at Lambourn, where his great-uncle Ted Gwilt had trained Free Fare, winner of the Manchester November Handicap and the Champion Hurdle, and other useful horses in the Saxon House stable between the wars. Ted Gwilt, who died at the age of 72 in 1946, was the son of a Suffolk clergyman.

Patrick Haslam had his first full season in the Pegasus stables in 1979, during which year he sent out the winners of 25 races, a tally that rose to 35 in 1981. The best horse that he trained during the seasons immediately after his arrival at Newmarket was the sprinter Pencil Point, a chestnut colt by Sharpen Up. As well as the William Hill Handicap at Ascot, Pencil Point won three other races and was placed in both the Portland handicap and the Ayr Gold Cup as a three-year-old in 1981.

By late 1982 plans for the re-opening of the Moulton Paddocks stable, where Eddie de Mestre and then Walter Earl had been private trainers to Mr Solly Joel in the 1920s, were far advanced as Alex Stewart had secured a lease on that establishment in order to commence training in 1983. After gaining experience in the United States, Alex Stewart had spent four years as assistant to Thomson Jones. It was for his father, Colonel Robert Stewart of Kinrosshire, that Tom Jones trained Arndean to win four races, including the Strathclyde Stakes at Ayr, as a two-year-old in 1980.

While Palace House, the oldest racing stable in the world, continues to flourish with a history of more than 200 years behind it, the successful traditions of other long established yards like Phantom House, Kremlin, Fitzroy and Heath House are as well maintained as ever. At the same time the construction of Marriott stables, Eve Lodge, Loder and other yards of recent date have compensated for the disappearance of the likes of Freemason Lodge, Primrose Cottage and Ellesmere House, and the change of use of Terrace House, St Albans and Oaks Lodge. Then again, yards like Beech Hurst have come out into the limelight after periods of varying degrees of obscurity as others such as Osborne House, long the quarters of the Chaloners recede into the background as overspill yards.

Although the stables, together with the horses, the trainers and the jockeys associated with them, and the racecourses are responsible for Newmarket being a continual focus of public attention the 50-odd studs that are scattered amidst the Suffolk and Cambridgeshire countryside in the immediate vicinity of the town also make a substantial contribution to the international reputation it enjoys. Notable breeding establishments, besides those already mentioned elsewhere include the Banstead Manor Stud, where Ile de Bourbon stands, the Beech House Stud, where the great Nearco was located until his death in 1957, Dalham Hall, whose home-bred stallion is Great Nephew, sire of the Derby winners Grundy and Shergar, Dunchurch Lodge, the Hamilton Stud, founded in 1905 to accommodate the Triple Crown winner Rock Sand, Lanwades Stud, once the property of the Duchess of Montrose, the Snailwell Stud, formerly the quarters of the champion stallion Chamossaire and now those of Busted, and the Stetchworth Stud, founded by a member of the Egerton family as long ago as 1833.

The importance of Newmarket as a breeding centre became greater than ever when the National Stud was transferred to purpose-built accommodation on 500 acres to the west of the town, that had been taken on a long lease from the Jockey Club, in 1967. The National Stud had come into being when the government accepted the offer of all the bloodstock of Colonel William Hall Walker, subsequently Lord

Wavertree, as a gift, on the condition that it purchased his stud at Tully in County Kildare in 1916 when the First World War was at its height and stock was needed from which to breed light horses for the cavalry. On the National Stud becoming the property of the government the Ministry of Agriculture was given the responsibility for its administration, and Captain Harry Greer, who had made the inspired purchase of Gallinule from George Alexander Baird 27 years earlier, was appointed its first director. On the need for cavalry horses becoming minimal in the years after the end of the war in 1918 the Stud concentrated on the accumulation of a collection of high class mares, most of whose stock was sold. Those few colts and fillies that were retained were leased for the duration of their racing careers firstly to Lord Lonsdale then to King George VI and, in the last few years that that policy was pursued, to Her Majesty the Queen. Carrozza, whom Sir Noel Murless trained to carry the royal colours successfully in the The Oaks in 1957, was bred by the Stud from the mating of Dante with Calash, a full sister to Sun Chariot.

In 1943 the stud at Tully was transferred to the ownership of the Irish Government and new quarters were found for the stock at Gillingham, in Dorest. Twenty years later, in 1963, the National Stud adopted a new role by selling off its mares and devoting its resources to the acquisition of important stallions, many of whom might otherwise have been sold abroad, for the overall benefit of the British bloodstock industry. As the existing premises were not large enough to allow for the implementation of that policy on the scale envisaged,

The National Stud stallion unit

the present stud at Newmarket was laid out under the direction of Mr Peter Burrell in the vicinity of the July Course and opened by Her Majesty in 1967. Accommodation was thus provided for the Stud's stallions, which are four in number at the time of writing, together with the 40-odd mares that are sent to them in the late winter and spring together with whatever foals are born to them in the course of their visits.

The four stallions standing at the National Stud in 1982 were the Derby winners Grundy and Mill Reef together with Moorestyle and Star Appeal. The Stud also owned or had interests in four other stallions, namely Final Straw, who was located at the Egerton House Stud, Homing at the Highclere Stud in Berkshire, the 1967 Derby winner Royal Palace at the Chesters Stud in Northumberland, and Sagaro, three times winner of the Ascot Gold Cup, at Lincolnshire's Limestone Stud.

Mr Peter Burrell, who had been largely responsible for the substantial increase in the National Stud's contribution to the success of British breeders, retired in 1971. He was followed by Lieutenant-Colonel Douglas Gray on whose retirement in 1975 Mr Michael Bramwell became director.

As befits the Headquarters of the British Turf, Newmarket has within its boundaries a number of other establishments of importance to the racing industry and the people whose livelihoods are dependent upon it. The Animal Health Trust, founded in 1942, has its Equine Research Station at Balaton Lodge, the former Zetland Lodge stable, on the Snailwell Road, and its Equine Virology Unit in neighbouring Lanwades Park. All the veterinary research carried out under the direction of Mr W. B. Singleton at Balaton Lodge is on diseases that afflict horses and the other problems to which they are prone. The Animal Health Trust is a registered charity to which the Levy Board increased its contribution from £95,000 to £115,000 in 1981.

Another important institution run by a charitable trust is the Apprentice School, which is to be built on 120 acres adjoining the Snailwell Road. In the summer of 1982 Lord McAlpine of Moffatt, the chairman of the trustees, was able to announce that outline planning permission had been obtained and vacant possession was expected in October. The school was intended to turn out 100 qualified stable employees every year and would comprise a complex including stableyard, outdoor and indoor riding schools, and straight and all-weather gallops together with a residential centre and bungalows for the chief instructor and his or her assistant.

The work of Sir John Astley, who took the first steps towards raising funds to provide leisure facilities for stablelads and stud hands, has been maintained and the scope of it widened considerably. The Astley Club, built as a memorial to one of the truest philanthropists that Newmarket has ever known, was eventually found to be unsuitable for further conversion to meet modern needs. In consequence an appeal was successfully launched for the building of the New Astley Institute, appropriately situated on Fred Archer Way, the road named after one of Sir John's closest friends in racing. As well as for members of the racing community the New Astley Institute is able to provide recreational and refreshment facilities for a sizeable proportion of young people in the town.

Another project sure to have had the enthusiastic support of Sir John Astley would have been the construction of 29 flats for retired stable staff by the Stable Lads Welfare Trust. These were erected on land formerly part of the late Sir Jack Jarvis's Park Lodge stable and generously given to the Trust by his daughter Miss Vivian Jarvis, who unveiled the nameplate on Jack Jarvis Close on 9 July 1980.

Over the years the town has been changing all the time as progress blends with tradition in nice proportions while amenities available to trainers on the Heath are being constantly improved and increased. Very soon after Mr Robert Fellowes had become Jockey Club Agent in 1964 it was apparent that he was going to maintain the standards that Captain Marriott had set himself in endeavouring to ensure that the training grounds surrounding Newmarket are the best in the world.

Since 1964 another 300 acres have been laid down to gallops on Racecourse Side. On Bury Side 100 acres on Waterhall, the working ground furthest from the town on that bearing, have been turned to plough on account of the little use that was made of them, but the very much more central 80 acres of what were Lord Derby's private gallops have been acquired by the Jockey Club.

In 1964 the watered gallop that runs along nine furlongs parallel to the Cambridgeshire course came into use, and four years later the heavily peated Bad Legged Horse Gallop, for the use of which special application has to be made, was opened on Warren Hill for the benefit of trainers of horses with particularly serious problems. The first of the wood chip working strips came into use in 1976 and there are now three of these on the Heath — a six and a half furlong gallop up Warren Hill for putting condition onto horses during the season, a four and a half furlong canter that is open in the same vicinity during the winter and a nine furlong canter parallel to the A11 road on the Racecourse Side. The latter replaced the old tan canter after tan ceased to be available. There is also a sand gallop constructed from crushed sea shells and sand deposited near Ipswich, 40 miles from Newmarket, when that part of East Anglia was covered by the sea some four million years ago.

In order to prevent the ground being spoiled by too much use being made of it the lines of the gallops are being constantly moved. For very many years the gallops open to trainers at any given time were marked out by fir bushes, which had to be obtained from the Forestry Commission and lasted only a fortnight. With a view to saving a great deal of time, as well as a certain amount of money, Robert Fellowes discontinued the use of the natural bushes in 1972 and had the gallops marked out by very much more durable plastic bushes. The marking of the gallops and all the other work that goes towards maintaining the working grounds in top class condition is carried out by a team of 28 heathmen with Vic Taylor foreman on Bury Side and Alan Roberts on Racecourse Side.

As well as to the gallops and canters, attention has to be given to the walking grounds, along which the horses cross the heath. Until long after the end of the Second World War generation after generation of trainers and lads complained about the way these became dusty and flint-ridden in summer then boggy in winter. To improve conditions for all concerned, not least the horses, some £100,000 was spent in laying concrete over the principal walking grounds between 1972 and 1982.

The town has grown and its streetscape changed out of recognition since the courtiers built their stables and houses around the palace of Charles II. By contrast the superb, majestic expanse of the Heath has altered little since the opportunities it afforded for sport first commended themselves to James I in 1605. It remains the principal glory of Newmarket, and one of the greatest glories of England.

Bibliography

Acton, C. R. *Silk and Spur*, Richards, London, 1935.
Allison, William. *Memories of Men and Horse*, Grant Richards, London, 1922.
Astley, Sir John. *Fifty Years of My Life*, Hurst and Blackett, London, 1895.
Bird, T. H. *Admiral Rous and The English Turf*, Putnam, London 1939.
Black, Robert. *Horse-Racing in France*, Sampson Low, Marston, Searle and Rivington, London, 1886.
Black, Robert. *The Jockey Club and its Founders*, Smith, Elder, London, 1891.
Brock, D.W.E. *The Racing Man's Week-end Book*, Seeley Service, London, 1950.
Butler, Ewan. *The Cecils*, Frederick Muller, London, 1964.
Carr, Harry. *Queen's Jockey*, Stanley Paul, London, 1966.
Cawthorne, George James, and Herod, Richard S. *Royal Ascot*, A. Treherne, London, 1902.
Chalmers, Patrick R. *Racing England*, Batsford, London, 1939.
Chetwynd, Sir George. *Racing Reminiscences*, Longmans, Green, London, 1891.
Curling, Bill. *The Captain*, Barrie and Jenkins, London, 1970.
Custance, Harry. *Riding Recollections*, Edward Arnold, London, 1894.
Day, William. *Reminiscences of The Turf*, Richard Bentley, London, 1891.
Dixon, H. Sydenham. *From Gladiateur to Persimmon*, Grant Richards, London, 1901.
'Druid, The', (Henry Hall Dixon). *Post and Paddock*, Vinton, London, 1895, (first published 1856).
'Druid, The'. *Silk and Scarlet*, Vinton, London, 1895, (first published 1859).
Fairfax-Blakeborough, J. *Hambleton and Richmond*, J. A. Allen, London, 1948.
Fairfax-Blakeborough, J. *Malton Memories and L'Anson Triumphs*, Truslove and Bray, London, 1925.
Fairfax-Blakeborough, J. *Paddock Personalities*, Hutchinson, 1938.
Fairfax-Blakeborough, J. *York and Doncaster Races*, J. A. Allen, London, 1950.
Falk, Bernard. *The Royal Fitzroys*, Hutchinson, London, 1950.
Felstead, S. Theodore. *Racing Romance*, Werner Laurie, London, 1949.

Fletcher, J. J. *The History of The St Leger Stakes*, Hutchinson, London, 1926.
Galtrey, Sidney. *Memories of a Racing Journalist*, Hutchinson, London, 1934.
Good, Meyrick. *Good Days*, Hutchinson, London, 1941.
Good, Meyrick. *The Lure of The Turf*, Odhams, London, 1957.
Harewood, Lord and others. *Flat Racing*, (Lonsdale Library), Seeley Service, London, 1948.
Hislop, John. *The Turf*, Collins, London, 1948.
Hodgman, George. *Sixty Years on The Turf*, Grant Richard, London, 1901.
Humphris, Edith M. *The Life of Fred Archer*, Hutchinson, London, 1923.
Humphris, Edith M. *The Life of Mathew Dawson*, Witherby, London, 1928.
Jarvis, Sir Jack. *They're Off*, Michael Joseph, London, 1969.
Kent, John. *Racing Life of Lord George Cavendish Bentinck*, William Blackwood, Edinburgh and London, 1892.
Lambton, The Hon George. *Men and Horses I Have Known*, Thornton Butterworth, London, 1924.
Leach, Jack. *Sods I Have Cut on The Turf*, Victor Gollancz, London, 1961.
Lechmere, Jocelyne. *Pretty Polly*, The Bodley Head, London, 1907.
Londonderry, The Marchioness of. *Henry Chaplin*, MacMillan, London, 1926.
Lyle, R. C. *The Aga Khan's Horses*, Putnam, London, 1938.
Lyle, R. C. *Royal Newmarket*, Putnam, London, 1945.
Marsh, Marcus. *Racing with The Gods*, Pelham, London, 1968.
Marsh, Richard. *A Trainer to Two Kings*, Cassell, London, 1925.
May, Peter. *Newmarket Medieval and Tudor*, published privately, 1982.
Mortimer, Roger. *The History of The Derby Stakes*, Michael Joseph, London, 1973.
Mortimer, Roger. *The Jockey Club*, Cassell, London, 1958.
Mortimer, Roger, Onslow, Richard and Willett, Peter. *Biographical Encyclopaedia of British Flat Racing*, MacDonald and Jane, London, 1978.
Morton, Charles. *My Sixty Years on The Turf*, Hutchinson, London, n.d.
Morton, Frederic. *The Rothschilds*, Secker and Warburg, London, 1963.
Muir, J. B. *Raciana*, published privately, London 1890.
Nevill, Ralph. *The Gay Victorians*, Eveleigh, Nash and Grayson. London, 1930.
Nevill, Ralph. *The Sport of Kings*, Methuen, London, 1926.
'Nimrod', (Charles James Apperley). *The Chace, The Road and The Turf*, The Bodley Head, London, 1927 reprint.
Orchard, Vincent. *Tattersalls*, Hutchinson, London, 1953.
Osbaldeston, George. *His Autobiography*, ed. E. D. Cuming, The Bodley Head, London, 1926.

Porter, John. *John Porter of Kingsclere*, Grant Richards, London, 1919.

Radcliffe, John Ashgill. *The Life and Times of John Osbourne*, Sands, London, 1900.

Richards, Sir Gordon. *My Story*, Hodder and Stoughton, London, 1955.

Rickaby, Bill. *First to Finish*, Souvenir Press, London, 1969.

Rickman, Eric, *On and off the Racecourse*, George Routledge and Sons, London, 1937.

Rodrigo, R. *The Racing Game*, Phoenix Sports Books, London, 1958.

Rossmore, Lord. *Things I Can Tell*, Eveleigh Nash, London, 1912.

Russell, Campbell. *Triumphs and Tragedies of the Turf*, John Long, London, n.d.

Sarl, Arthur J. *Gamblers of The Turf*, Hutchinson, London, 1938.

Scott, Alexander. *Turf Memories of Sixty Years*, Hutchinson, London, 1925.

Seth-Smith, Michael. *Bred for the Purple*, Leslie Frewin, London, 1969.

Siltzer, Frank. *Newmarket*, Cassell, London, 1923.

Smith, Doug, (with Peter Willett). *Five Times Champion*, Pelham, London, 1968.

Smith, Eph. *Riding to Win*, Stanley Paul, London, 1968.

Suffolk, Earl of and others. *Racing and Steeplechasing*, Longmans, Green, London, 1887.

Sutherland, Douglas. *The Yellow Earl*, Cassell, London, 1965.

'Sylvanus'. *The Bye-Lanes and Downs of England*, Richard Bentley, London, 1859.

'Thormanby', (W. W. Dixon). *Famous Racing Men*, James Hogg, London, 1882.

'Thormanby'. *Kings of The Turf*, Hutchinson, London, n.d.

Voigt, Charles Adolph. *Famous Gentlemen Riders*, Hutchinson, London, 1925.

Watson, Alfred E. T. *A Sporting and Dramatic Career*, MacMillan, London, 1918.

Welcome, John. *Fred Archer*, Faber and Faber, London, 1967.

Weston, Tommy. *My Racing Life*, Hutchinson, London, 1952.

Whyte, James Christie. *A History of The British Turf*, Henry Colburn, London, 1840.

Wilkinson, Dyke. *A Wasted Life*, Grant Richards, London, 1902.

Willett, Peter. *An Introduction to The Thoroughbred*, Stanley Paul, London, 1975.

Willett, Peter. *The Thoroughbred*, Weidenfeld and Nicolson, London, 1970.

Periodicals, including annual publications.
The British Racehorse
Cope's Racegoers Encyclopaedia
The Directory of The Turf
The General Stud Book
Horses in Training
Racehorses of 19--
The Racing Calendar
Racing Illustrated, 1894-6
Racing-up-to-date
Ruff's Guide to The Turf
The Sporting Chronicle
The Sporting Life
Stud and Stable
Tote Investors' Who's Who in Racing
The Tote Racing Annual

Illustrations

1 Photo. *Geoff Hayes*
4 Engraving. *BBC Hulton Picture Library*
13 Engraving. *The British Turf, Jockey Club*
15 Engraving after John Wootton. *British Flat Racing, The Jockey Club*
16 Engraving after Tillemans. *The Jockey Club*
20 Engraving. *BBC Hulton Picture Library*
21 Engraving. *The British Turf, The Jockey Club*
22 Engraving. *The British Turf, The Jockey Club*
25 Engraving after Gilpin. *British Flat Racing, The Jockey Club*
27 Cartoon. *BBC Hulton Picture Library*
29 Engraving. *BBC Hulton Picture Library*
30 Cartoon by Rowlandson. *The Jockey Club*
35 Sketch. *The British Turf, The Jockey Club*
37 Engraving. *BBC Hulton Picture Library*
38 Engraving by C. Turner. *BBC Hulton Picture Library*
40 Sketch. *The British Turf, The Jockey Club*
42 Engraving. *The British Turf, The Jockey Club*
47 Photo. *European Racehorse*
48 Engraving after Herring. *European Racehorse*
50 Photo. *Central Press Photos Ltd.*
53 Photo by Jack Esten. *The Observer*
59 Painting by Emil Adam. *The Jockey Club*
61 Photo. *Sport and General*
63 Painting by Emil Adam. *The Jockey Club*
68 Painting. *The Jockey Club*
71 Engraving. *BBC Hulton Picture Library*
75 Engraving after Lambert Marshall. *The Sporting Magazine*
73 Engraving after Herring. *European Racehorse*
79 Painting by Harry Hall. *European Racehorse*
95 Engraving. *A History of The English Turf*
97 Photo. *BBC Hulton Picture Library*
98 Photo by Griggs. *European Racehorse*
100 Sketch by Finch Mason. *The Life of a Great Sportsman (author's collection)*
103 Engraving. *The British Turf, The Jockey Club*
112 Photo. *Racing Illustrated*
115 Photo. *Racing Illustrated*
118 Painting by Linwood Palmer. *The Jockey Club*
122 Painting. *European Racehorse*
132 Photo. *Racing Illustrated*
139 Engraving. *BBC Hulton Picture Library*
141 Cartoon by Lib. *(author's collection)*
149 Photo. *Racing Illustrated*
153 Photo. *Racing Illustrated*
154 Photo. *Racing Illustrated*
156 Photo. *Racing Illustrated*
158 Photo. *Racing Illustrated*
163 Cartoon by Lib. *(author's collection)*
173 Photo. *Racing Illustrated*
183 Cartoon by Spy. *BBC Hulton Picture Library*
184 Painting by G. D. Giles. *BBC Hulton Picture Library*
186 Painting by Isaac Cullin. *The Jockey Club*
189 Photo. *Racing Illustrated*
193 Painting. *H.M. The Queen*
195 Photo. *European Racehorse*
199 Photo. *Racing Illustrated*
201 Photo. *W. W. Rouch and Co.*
209 Cartoon by Lib. *(author's collection)*
210 Photo. *European Racehorse*
213 Engraving after Percy Earl. *BBC Hulton Picture Library*
217 Photo. *BBC Hulton Picture Library*
218 Photo. *BBC Hulton Picture Library*
221 Photo. *European Racehorse*
222 Photo. *Racing Illustrated*
225 Photo. *European Racehorse*
228 Photo. *The Thomson Organization Ltd.*
230 Photo. *BBC Hulton Picture Library*
235 Photo. *European Racehorse*
237 Photo by W. A. Rouch. *British Flat Racing, The Jockey Club*
239 Sketch by Lionel Edwards. *European Racehorse*
246 Photo. *Evening Standard*
248 Photo. *BBC Hulton Picture Library*
252 Photo. *R. Anscomb*
256 Photo. *Press Association*
261 Photo. *P.A. Reuter Photos Ltd.*
263 Photo. *R. Anscomb, European Racehorse*
265 Painting by Thomas Beach. *European Racehorse*
267 Photo. *Selwyn Photos*
270 Photo. *Press Association*
272 Photo. *Provincial Press Agency*
275 Photo. *Racing Information Bureau*
283 Photo. *The Thomson Organization Ltd.*
285 Photo. *The Press Association*
287 Photo. *The Press Association*
289 Photo. *Sport and General*
290 Photo. *Selwyn Photos*
293 Photo. *John Slater Photography Ltd.*

Colour plates
A Coloured engraving. *Jockey Club*
B Photo. *Geoff Hayes*
C Panel of Jockeys painting. *Jockey Club*
D Painting. *Jockey Club*
E View of the Round Course, Tillemans. *Mellon Collection*
F Eclipse by Sartorius. *Jockey Club*
G Admiral Rous portrait. *Jockey Club*
H Flying Childers portrait. *Jockey Club*
I Diomed portrait. *Jockey Club*
J Photo. *Geoff Hayes*
K Photo. *Geoff Hayes*
L Photo. *Geoff Hayes*
M Cartoon by Lib. *Jockey Club*
N Sam portrait. *Jockey Club*
O Persimmon by Emil Adam. *Jockey Club*
P Coloured engraving. *BBC Hulton Picture Library*
Q View of Warren Hill. *Jockey Club*
R Cartoon by Spy. *Author's collection*
S Cartoon by Spy. *BBC Hulton Picture Library*
T Gimcrack portrait. *Jockey Club*
U Photo. *Geoff Hayes*

General Index

Abingdon, Earl of, 23
Abington Place stable, 171, 211, 249, 276
Aga Khan, 19, 61, 225, 236-43, 287
Ailesbury, Marquess of and Lady P., 167-8
Albermarle, Lord, 75
Albert House, 190, 225, 265
Albina, Michael, 273
Alessio, Signor Carlo d', 272, 288-9
Alexandra, Queen, 63
Alexander II of Russia, Emperor, 55-6
Alington, Lord, 107
Alington, Mrs C., 281
Alington, William, 3
Alix, Mr, 35
Alkhalifa, Mr Essa, 279
Allden, Percy, 286
Allen, Mrs F., 281
All Saints Church, 15, 79, 81, 135
Allsop, Frederick, 175
Aly Khan, 241, 243
Ancaster, Duchess of, 31
Anglesey, Marquess of, 101
Anne, Queen, 13-15
Apprentice School, 294
Apsley, Sir Allen, 6
Apter, Eric, 261
Archer, Charles, 183-4, 188, 225
Archer, Emma, 133
Archer, Frederick (jockey), 53, 80, 104-6, 109, 113, 115-6, 118-20, 126-8, 133-39, 157, 166, 179, 208
Archer, Frederick (trainer), 194, 225, 227, 233, 254, 277
Archer, Nellie (see Dawson, Nellie)
Archer, William, 133
Archer, William (son of William), 133
Argentine, John d', 3
Argentine, Richard d', 2-3
Arlington, Earl of, Henry Bennet I, 9
Armstrong, Robert, 164
Armstrong, Robert (son of Samuel), 274, 277
Armstrong, Samuel, 231, 246, 265-6, 274, 287
Arnott, Maxwell, 210
Arnull, John, 70
Arnull, Samuel, 70-1
Arnull, William, 70
Arthur, Sir George, 142
Ashby, George, 187
Ashdown Park, Lambourn, 222
Ashley Heath Stud, 278
Astley Club, 294
Astley Institute for Stablemen, 128-9
Astley, Sir John Dugdale 'The Mate' 52, 123-30, 141, 148, 294-5
Astor, Lord, 57
Astor, Mr J. J., 249

Bailey, Sir Abe, 57, 221
Baird, Alexander, 161
Baird, Sir David, 154
Baird, George Alexander 'Mr Abington', 117, 161-73, 293
Baker, Miss Patricia, 286
Balaton Lodge (see also Zetland Lodge), 187, 207, 220, 225, 294
Baltazzi, Alexander, 60, 98, 103
Baltazzi, Hector, 98, 103, 194

Barbee, George, 92
Barclay, Mr H. T. 'Buck', 53
Barclay, Sandy, 247
Barker, Mr, 52
Barling, Frank, 225
Barling, Geoffrey, 230, 261-2, 274-5
Baroda, Maharajah of, 231
Barrett, Frederick, 11
Barrett, George, 224
Barrymore, Richard, Earl of, 28,30,32
Barry, Mr, 23-4
Barton, Mr A. E., 224
Bass, Mr Hamar, 187
Batthyanny, Prince, 100, 117, 152-3
Beadle, Harry, 207
Beatty, Major Charles, 175-7, 209-10
Beatty, David, 175
Beatty, Captain D. L., 175
Beatty, Major Vandy, 175, 226
Beauclerk, Charles, Duke of St Albans, 9
Beaufort House, 227, 231
Beaverbrook, Lady, 64, 277-8
Bedford Cottage stable, 99-100, 102-4, 106-8, 172, 175-6, 209, 244
Bedford, Duke of, 61, 68-9, 73, 77, 79
Bedford Lodge (see also Shalfleet and Highfield) 84-8, 115, 125-7, 141-2, 159, 161, 164-70, 172, 187, 191, 194, 210, 226, 228, 249, 258, 265, 267, 277
Beech House Stud, 292
Beech Hurst stable, 286-7
Behan, Philip, 182
Bellingham Mr, 11
Belmont, Mr Augustus, 180, 203-4
Benjamin, Mr Edward, 284
Bennet, Henry, Earl of Arlington, 9
Bennet, Isabella, 9
Benstead, John, 54
Bentinck, Lord George, 35, 49, 78-9
Bentinck, Lord Henry, 35
Benzon, Ernest, the 'Jubilee Plunger', 142
Beresford, Lord Marcus, 194, 196, 198, 203
Beresford, Lord William, 60, 181, 183
Berners, Lord, 75-6
Bertie, Norman, 244
Beverley House stable, 148, 208, 219, 231, 250, 263, 274, 276
Bingham, J. D., 291
Birdcage, The, 45
Bishop, Cecil, 33
Bisquit Cognac, 65
Blackwell, George, 120, 208, 219, 250
Blackwell, Thomas, 280
Bland, Messrs, 33
Blanton, Charles 'Nigger', 94, 186-7
Blenkiron, William, 58, 85, 92
Bloomsbury Cottage Yard, 265
Bloss, Alfred, 101
Bloss, Charles, 100, 102, 190
Bloss, George, 100, 102, 190
Blum, Gerald, 150, 265
Boadicea, 1-2
Bolingbroke, Lord, 25
Bolton, Duke of, 15
Booth, Graham, 260
Booth, J. B., 165
Booth, Sir W., 56
Boothman, Peter, 249

Boswell, Sir J., 154
Boussac, Marcel, 221
Bowes, Mr John, 48
Bowles, Dr, 33
Boyce, Frank, 76
Boyce, Richard, 70
Boyd-Rochfort, Arthur, 272
Boyd-Rochfort, Captain Cecil, 204, 211, 225, 229, 232, 244-5, 247, 262, 271-2, 274
Bradwell, Paul, 278
Bramwell, Mr Michael, 294
Brett, Mr Reginald, 191
Brewer, Charles, 186
Brittain, Clive, 278-9
Brooke, Major Geoffrey, 57, 177, 249-50, 262, 270, 274
Brown, Mr, 179
Bruckshaw, Thomas, 103
Brudenell Bruce, Mrs Dana, 286
Buckingham, 2nd Duke of, George Villiers, 7
Buckle, Frank (senior), 71-2, 76-8, 80
Buckle, Frank (junior), 39
Bullock, Mary Ann, 28
Bullock, William, 218-9
Bullough, Sir George, 224
Bunbury, Sir Charles, 19, 25, 31-5. 61, 69
Bungalow Stud, 215
Burch, W. P., 207
Burghley, Lord, 43
Burghley House, 43
Burleigh Stud, 77
Burns, Thomas, 219
Burrell, Mr Peter, 294
Bury Hill, 1
Butler, Frank, 73, 77
Butler, Mr, 69
Butler, William, 85
Butt, Sir Alfred, 232, 236, 240, 263
Butt, Lady, 281
Butt, Sir Kenneth, 66
Butters, Frank, 61, 69, 208-9, 221, 232-43, 261, 270
Butters, Frederick, 208, 233, 261
Butters, Isabel, 208
Butters, Joseph, 208-9, 233

Cabaret Club, 42
Cadland House stable, 187, 265, 276, 286, 291
Calder Park, 273
Callaghan, Neville, 273
Calthorpe, Lord, 100-1
Cambanis, Mr George, 280
Cambridge Hill, 15
Campbell, Eric, 281
Cannon, J. H. S. 'Boxer', 172, 190
Cannon, Joseph, 53, 103-4, 109, 170-2, 190
Cannon, Kempton, 171
Cannon, Mornington, 110, 176, 181, 190, 199, 201-2
Cannon, Thomas, 66, 80, 104, 162, 166, 186, 190, 200
Carlburg, 85, 210-12, 235, 262-5, 277-8, 289
Carlisle, Lord, 12
Carr, Harry, 245
Carr, Sir Robert, 11
Carson, William, 284

302

Carter, James, 186
Carter, Thomas, 90
Carter, William, 95
Cartwright, Mr W. S., 186
Cassel, Sir Ernest, 192, 204
Castlemaine, Countess of, 10
Cauthen, Stephen, 278
Cave, Stanley, 175
Cecil, Brownlow, 2nd Marquess of Exeter, 43-4
Cecil, Henry, 64, 245, 271-2, 281, 287-91
Cecil, Julie, 291
Chaloner, George, 83, 107-8, 110, 174, 209
Chaloner, Harry, 83
Chaloner, Nellie, 83, 209
Chaloner, Philip, 83
Chaloner, Richard, 83
Chaloner, Thomas (junior), 82-3, 150
Chaloner, Thomas (senior), 81-3, 209
Chamberlain, Mr John, 92
Chaplin, Henry 'Harry', 101-2, 193
Charettie, Colonel, 40
Charles I, King, 5-7
Charles II, King, 6-12, 35, 196
Charlotte, Queen, 31
Cherry-Downes, Anthony, 277
Chesterfield, Lord, 73-4
Chesters Stud, 294
Chestnuts, The, 206
Chetwynd, Sir George, 140-6
Chetwynd House stable (see also Machell Place), 108, 140, 142, 143, 189
Cheveley Park, 3, 21, 172, 175, 277, 291
Chevington, 272
Chifney, Mary, 39, 152
Chifney, Samuel (junior), 39-41, 44, 72-3
Chifney, Samuel (senior),18, 29-31, 37, 39, 67-73, 77
Chifney, William (junior), 43
Chifney, William (senior), 37, 39-44, 73, 77, 152
Childers, Leonard, 15
Churchill, Lord Randolph, 189
Clarehaven, 57, 85, 177, 210, 212, 215-6, 230, 249-50, 258, 262-5, 277-8
Clarendon, Lord, 5
Clark, Mr Robert Sterling, 262
Clarke, John, F., 42, 156
Clarke, Mary Ann, 34
Clarke, Mr E. R., 55
Clarke, Vauxhall, 39
Clayton, Jack, 244, 274, 277
Clayton, Stanley, 245, 247
Clermont, Lord, 25, 28, 30, 61
Cleveland, Duke of, 39-41
Cleveland House, 39
Clief, Mr Daniel van, 270
Clifford-Turner, Mr R., 286
Clift, William, 47, 49, 71-2
Clifton, Sir Robert, 102
Clinton, Miss, 208
Clock Tower, 34
Cloete, Broderick, 196
Cockfield Hall, 92, 94
Coffee Room, 19, 34
Colchester, 2
Cole, Paul, 21
Coleman, Mrs, 136-8
Colling, George, 24, 232, 251, 254-5
Colling, Jack, 227-8, 250, 265
Colling, Robert Weston, 228, 249
Collingridge, Hugh, 276
Combe, Mr. R. H., 190
Connolly, Patrick, 74
Constable, Harold, 53
Cook, Paul, 280
Cookson, Mr, 104
Cooper, Arthur, 134
Cooper, Mr Cecil, 254

Cooper, Sir Daniel, 215, 219
Cooper, William, 79, 215, 219
Cooper, William (trainer), 34
Corbett, Atty, 250, 274
Coronation Hotel, 274
Coronation stables, 266
Cottrill, Harry, 249
Cottrill, Humphrey, 249-50, 274
Coventry, Arthur, 150
Cox, Mr A. W. 'Mr Fairie', 32, 256
Craven, Mr, 75
Crawford, J. H., 235-6
Crawfurd, William Stuart Stirling, 55, 78, 103, 108, 142, 158-9
Crockford, William, 44, 78
Croker, Mr Daniel, 23
Crossley, Bryn, 291
Crown, The, 101
Cumani, Luca, 100, 277
Cumberland, Henry, Duke of, 28
Cumberland, William, Duke of, 20, 27, 36
Curzon, Frank, 227
Custance, Harry, 100-1, 128, 136
Cutsem, Bernard van, 251, 253, 274, 276, 282-3

Daley, John, 102
Dalham Hall Stud, 292
Darling, Frederick, 49, 60, 244, 246
Darling, Samuel, 57, 146, 246
Darlington, Lord, 1st Duke of Cleveland, 39, 73
Dashwood, Sir Francis, 16
Davey, Ernest, 264
Davey, Paul, 263-4
Dawson, Daniel, 33, 41
Dawson, George, 84, 113-4, 121, 205
Dawson, Harriet, 88-9
Dawson, John, 84, 152-3, 229
Dawson, John (junior), 120-1, 135, 153, 181, 187-8
Dawson, Joseph, 58, 84-6, 88-9, 115, 125-6, 141, 158, 210
Dawson, Mathew, 14, 84, 93, 113-121, 133-6, 150-1, 154-5, 164, 187-8, 205, 207, 208, 219
Dawson, Nellie, 135-6, 153
Dawson, Richard, 236, 238
Dawson, Thomas, 52,82, 84, 88, 113, 152
Day, Alfred, 79
Day, Frederick, 204
Day, F. W. 'Bushranger', 204
Day, John Barham, 37, 49, 55, 61, 71
Day, John (junior), 61, 71, 188
Day, Nigel, 291
Day, Reginald, 203, 227, 255, 274
Day, Samuel, 40
Day, William, 53, 126, 180, 193
Decies, 2nd Lord, 138
Delamarre, M., 92
Delatre, M., 92
Derby, 12th Earl of, 26, 70
Derby, 16th Earl of, 190-1, 210, 215, 232
Derby, 17th Earl of, 221-2, 225-6, 232-5, 238
Derby, 18th Earl of, 232, 251, 270, 276
Devil's Dyke, 1-2, 17, 23-4, 40, 42, 46, 51-2
Devonshire, 2nd Duke of, 14-15
Devonshire, 8th Duke of, 196
Devonshire, 11th Duke of, 251, 287
Dewar, Mr J. A., 49
Dewar, Sir Thomas, 205
Dewhurst, Captain R. H., 209
Dewhurst Stud, 60
Diomed stables, 273
Docking and Nicking Act, 26
Donoghue, Stephen, 224, 239
Don-Wauchope, Sir John, 114
Dorset, Duke of, 72
Drake, James, 182-4

Drewett, Richard, 123, 187
Drogheda, Lord, 15
Dryden, J., 7, 9
Duffield, George, 261
Dunchurch Lodge, 292
Dundas, Lord George, 227
Dundas, Sir Lawrence, 25
Dunlop, John, 65
Dunn, Mr Salisbury, 35
Dupplin, Lord, 153
Durham, Earl of, 140-6, 190, 234, 238
Durr, Frank, 269, 279
Dutton, Ralph, 31

Earl, Walter, 232, 251, 292
Eaton Stud, 23
Edward VII, King, 63, 192-220
Edward, Prince of Wales (see Edward VII)
Edwards, Arthur, 91
Edwards, Charles, 74
Edwards, Edward, 74-5
Edwards, Frederick, 74
Edwards, George, 74-5
Edwards, Harry, 74-5, 80
Edwards, James 'Tiny', 45, 74
Edwards, William, 74-5
Edwards, William (trainer), 43
Egan, Jack, 231, 245
Egerton, Major, 160, 220
Egerton House Stud, 195-8, 205, 224, 229, 239, 243, 261, 274, 294
Eglington, Earl of, 16, 113
Egremont, Lord, 68, 74
Eldin, Eric, 258, 273
Elizabeth I, Queen, 4, 43
Elizabeth II, HM Queen, 63, 246-7, 256, 293-4
Ellesmere House, 188, 228, 292
Ellesmere, Lord, 188, 195
Elliot, Charles, 224, 232
Elliot, Mr C. M., 278
Elliot, Mr, 11
Elsey, Captain Charles, 265
Elwes, Mr, 23
Ely Cathedral, 2
Engelhard, Mr Charles, 254
Enoch, Joseph, 187
Erratt, Mr, 19
Essex, Earl of, 12
Ethelreda, 2
Ethelreda House, 2, 219
Euston, Earl of, 36-7
Euston Hall, 9, 36
Evans, Percy, 232
Eveleigh, Major Michael, 284
Eve Lodge stable, 272-3, 292
Evelyn, John, 6-7
Everett, George, 211
Exeter, Lord, 43-4
Exeter House (see also Foley House), 43, 48, 96, 109, 188-9, 203, 223-4
Exning, 1-3

Fairchild, Norman, 241
Fairstead House, 42
Faistok, Mr Mahmoud, 273
Falcon, Archibald, 215
Fallon, Jack, 54
Falmouth, Viscount Lord, 60, 93, 105, 109, 113-4, 116-7, 124, 134-5, 137, 162
Falmouth House, 135, 225, 254
Falmouth Lodge Yard, 188, 220
Fanning, William Atmar, 177
Fawcus, Captain Jack, 160
Fawdon, Richard 'Snowy', 259
Featherstonhaugh, Sir Harry, 27-8, 32
Feilden, Major-General Sir Randle, 254
Fellowes, Mr Robert, 295
Fenn, Walter, 196
Fenwick, Noel, 196
Ferguson, Jock, 267
Findon stable, 259
Fine, Mr Max, 276

303

Fitzroy, Augustus Henry, Duke of Grafton, 25, 35
Fitzroy, Reverend Lord Henry, 36
Fitzroy House, 61, 235-6, 238-43, 261, 278-9, 292
Fitzsimmons, Robert, 170
Fitzwilliam, Lord, 72
Five Bells, 33, 108
Flatman, Nathaniel, 79-80
Fobert, John, 88
Foley House (see also Exeter House), 43
Foley, 2nd Lord, 29, 33, 43, 69
Fordham, 4
Fordham Road Paddock, 169
Fordham, Charles, 119
Fordham, George, 56, 80, 98-9, 105, 109
Fordham, Thomas, 187
Forester, Captain Frank, 54
Foster, Basil, 255, 259
Fox, Charles James, 19, 28-9
Fox, Harry, 245
Frampton, William Tregonwell 'Governor Frampton', 13-15, 18, 31
Frederick, Duke of York, 28, 33-4, 73
Freemason Lodge, 85, 210-11, 225, 229, 244, 262, 270, 287, 292
French, Thomas, 115, 134

Gardner, Frank P., 182
Garton, Sir Richard, 190
Gates, William 'Betcha-a-Million', 182-3
Gazeley Stud, 178, 280
Gee, Mr T., 60, 125
Geere, Sir Robert, 11
George I, King, 15
George II, King, 20
George IV, King (see also George, Prince of Wales), 25, 39-40
George V, King, 60, 62, 73, 220, 221-8
George VI, King, 229-282, 270, 293
George, Prince of Wales (see also George IV), 27-34, 39-40, 61, 69-70, 75
Gerard, Lord, 169
Gerard, Mr W., 105
Gerber, Jack, 265
Gibson, John 'Spider', 288
Gifford, Joshua, 231
Gilbert, A. J., 157
Gilbert, Albert, 207-8, 219
Gilbert, William, 87, 142, 207
Giles, Mr, 127
Gilpin, Peter Purcell (see also Valentine), 212, 215-6, 223, 263
Ginistrelli, Chevalier Odorado, 216, 218-9, 277
Gladiateur Paddocks, 187
Glanely, Lord, 225, 250
Glasgow, Earl of, 82
Glover, Jeremy, 258
Godding, James Kealey, 56, 81-2, 96, 185
Godolphin, Earl of, 15
Gogmagog stable, 14
Golding, Mr, 159
Goldings Messrs, 34
Goodisson, Charles, 73
Goodisson, Richard, 18, 27, 69-70, 73
Goodisson, Thomas, 73
Goodwill, A. W. 'Fiddler', 257, 259, 265
Gordon, Mr A. W., 286
Gordon, Lord William, 19
Goulden, Benjamin, 260
Grafton, 1st Duke of, 9-10, 35
Grafton, 3rd Duke of, Augustus Henry Fitzroy, 25, 35-7
Grafton, 4th Duke of, Augustus Henry Fitzroy, 36-7, 47, 49, 61, 71, 74
Graham, Mr, 92
Graham Place stable, 189-90, 205-6, 211, 265, 267

Grainger, Mr, 154
Grange, The (see also Lagrange), 225
Gray, Lieutenant Colonel Douglas, 294
Gray, Mr, 159
Greaves, William, 86
Gredley, Mr William, 278
Green, Mr, 224
Green Lodge, 42, 66, 156, 207-8, 224
Green Man, The, 8
Greer, Captain Henry, 168, 293
Gretton, Mr Frederick, 52
Greville, Mr Charles, 79
Greyhound, The, 42, 164
Griffin, Mr, 11
Griffin, The, 4
Griggs, Walter, 223-4, 256
Griggs, William, 223
Grimshaw, Harry, 92
Grosvenor, Countess, 28
Grosvenor, Earl, 22-3, 28, 30, 61, 68, 71
Grosvenor, General, 39
Gully, John, 40
Gurry, Martin, 187, 148, 150, 164-7, 171, 211, 215
Gwilt, Edward, 291
Gwyn, Nell, 9

Hackness stable, 150
Halifax, Earl of, 65
Halifax, Lady Ruth, 255
Hall, James, 170
Hall Walker, Colonel William (Lord Wavertree), 292
Hallick, Jack, 202
Hambro, Mr Jocelyn, 270
Hamilton, Duke of, 114, 155, 192, 194-7, 200
Hamilton Stud, 206, 272-4, 292
Hammon, T., 187
Hammond, Francis, 202
Hammond, John, 99-111, 134
Hanbury, Benjamin, 273
Hanbury, Mr J. M., 187
Hancock, Mr Malcolm, 42
Hare Park, 24
Harlock, Mr, 48
Harraton Court, Exning, 146, 151
Harrington, Lord, 162, 263, 277
Harris, Mrs F., 54
Harris, Mr P., 289
Hartigan, Frank, 267
Hartigan, Hubert, 246
Harvey, William, 5
Harwood, Guy, 49, 267
Haslam, Patrick, 291
Hastings, The Marchioness of, 141
Hastings, The Marquess of, 62, 88, 101-2, 135, 187
Hastings-Bass, Captain Peter, 288
Hastings-Bass, William, 288, 291
Hawkesworth, Dr John, 13
Hawkins, Mr, 34
Hawley, Sir Joseph, 58, 85
Hayhoe, Alfred, 98, 198, 203
Hayhoe, Joseph, 60, 96-8
Hayhoe, Nellie, 203
Heath House stable, 14, 115-6, 119-20, 134, 162, 181, 183, 205, 219, 274, 292
Heathorns, 65
Heaton, Percy, 195-6
Hednesford, 141
Helena Springfield Ltd, 288
Hell-Fire Club, 16
Hellier, Bruce, 267
Henshel, Count, 155
Hern, Major Richard, 57, 62, 64, 249-50, 287
Herring, John Frederick (senior), 26
Heseltine, Mr, 13
Hibbert, Charles, 108, 169, 171
Hide, Anthony, 124
Hide, Edward, 245
Highclere Stud, 294

Highfield (see also Bedford Lodge and Shalfleet), 258, 267
High Street, 34, 42-4
Hill, Harry, 78
Hill, Mr William, 264
Hills, Barry, 62, 267, 281
Hills, Richard, 267
Hinchcliffe, Michael, 273
Hindley, Jeremy, 269, 277-8
Hindlip, Lord, 188, 196
Hobbs, Bruce, 96, 245, 262-4, 271, 279-81
Hobbs, Reginald, 262
Hodgeman, George, 56
Hogg, Captain Thomas, 225
Holland, Lord, 29
Holland House (see Lansdowne House), 227, 255
Holliday, Major Lionel, 249-50, 287
Holliday, Mr L. Brook, 250
Hollingsworth, Mr R. D., 251, 254
Holstein Distributors, 66
Holt, Mr Ernest, 254
Homfray, J. G. R., 207
Hopper, James, 148
Horncastle, Samuel, 284
Horse Shoe Inn, The, 70
Horton, Anne, 28
Houghton, Fulke Johnson, 64
Houghton Hall, 41,
Houldsworth, Mr J. H., 63, 66, 156
Howard, Mr C. F., 57
Howard, James, 3rd Earl of Suffolk, 9
Huby, John, 119,
Hue-Williams, Colonel and Mrs Roger, 278
Huffer, Geoffrey, 291
Huggins, John, 60, 181-3
Humphreys, Charles, 166
Hurworth House (see also Meynell House), 24, 227, 282, 251, 254-5, 274, 280
Huxtable, Harry, 159

I'Anson, William, 148
Iceni, 1-2
Irwin, Lord and Lady (later Lord and Lady Halifax), 254
Iselin, Mrs C. O., 271
Iveagh, Earl of, 251

James I, King, 1, 4-6, 14, 296
James II, King, 7, 12-3
James, Sir Henry, 140, 145
James, Captain James, 250
Jardine, Sir Robert, 227
Jarvis, Andrew, 52, 264
Jarvis, Basil, 82, 175, 224-5, 255
Jarvis, Sir Jack, 82, 156, 175, 229, 255-60, 271, 274, 281, 295
Jarvis, Michael, 66, 263-4, 277-8
Jarvis, Ryan, 230, 258, 260, 281-2
Jarvis, Miss Vivian, 295
Jarvis, William Arthur 1852-1921, 82, 94, 107, 156, 174-5, 185, 224
Jarvis, William 'Willie' 1885-1943, 82, 175, 197, 208, 220, 224, 229-30, 291
Jarvis, William 1960-, 282
Jarvis's Booth, 45
Jellis, Henri, 171, 231
Jennings, Henry 'Hat', 90
Jennings, John, 90
Jennings, Thomas (junior), 93, 135, 188, 203
Jennings, Thomas (senior), 90-5, 118, 187
Jersey, 5th Earl of, 43, 47, 49
Jewett, James, 104-5, 107, 175
Jockey Club, 18-21, 23, 31-2, 34-5, 37, 42, 55, 57-8, 60, 78, 80, 98, 101-2, 120, 124, 140-141, 144, 146, 149, 152-3, 162, 172, 174, 181, 184, 266, 270-1, 280, 283, 292, 294
Joel, Mr H. J., 63, 65, 247, 259-60, 282

Joel, Mr Jack, 111, 151, 208, 223-4
Joel, Mr James, 289
Joel, Mr S. B. 'Solly', 54, 207-8, 222, 232, 267, 292
Joel, Mr Stanhope, 250, 264
Joel, Mrs Stanhope, 63, 283
Johnson, Samuel, 24
Johnston, Sir Frederick, 189, 193
Johnston, Miss P., 281
Johnstone, Mr Wallace, 153
Jones, Jack, 193-4, 202
Jones, Mr, 87
Jones, Harry Thomson, 24, 66, 156, 266-7, 269, 279-80, 286, 292
Jones, Herbert, 202-3, 220, 229-30
Jones, Robert, 211
Jousiffe, Charles, 53
Joyner, Andrew, 207
Jugg, W., 169
Junius, 35

Kaye, Mr G., 276
Keene, James R., 53, 180, 182
Kelly, Mr A., 277
Kennett schooling ground, 104, 107
Kentford, 167, 169, 171
Kent, John, 33, 41
Kenyon, Samuel, 52
Kernick, Sidney, 276
Kerr, Alec, 291
Kerr, Colonel Robert, 6
Khan, Mr Rabi, 278
Killigrew, Thomas, 6
King Edward VII Memorial Hall, 220
King's Chair, 11
Kremlin House, 177, 187, 208, 211, 221, 231, 233, 268-9, 277-8, 292
Kroes, Mr G. J., 276

Ladbrokes, 64-5
Lade, Sir John, 28
Lagrange (see also Grange, The), 93, 208, 219, 225, 249-50, 287, 291
Lagrange, Comte Frederic de, 90-3, 250
Lake, Mr Warwick, 34
Lambton, Edward 'Teddy', 231, 249, 268, 274
Lambton, The Hon Francis, 224
Lambton, The Hon George, 98, 140, 150-1, 177, 184, 190, 210, 221-2, 224, 226-7, 231, 253-6, 256
Lancaster, Miss Annie, 202
Landsdowne House, 227, 255
Lane, William, 214
Langtry, Lily, 2, 57, 168, 170-1, 177
Lanwades Stud, 292
Lascelles, Lord, 121
Lawson, Joseph, 212, 262, 265, 289
Leach, Edward, 205-6
Leach, Felix (junior), 206
Leach, Felix (senior), 120, 204-5, 267
Leach, Harold, 206
Leach, Henry Beresford 'Chubb', 27, 171, 206
Leach, John Edward 'Jack', 206
Leach, Captain R. E., 206
Leach, Mr W. B., 171
Leader, Colledge, 187, 226-7, 232
Leader, George Frederick, 187, 226
Leader, Harvey, 187, 226, 258-9, 261, 265, 274, 276
Leader, Thomas Edward 'Ted', 187, 226, 256, 259-60, 274
Leader, Thomas (junior), 187, 226, 257
Leader, Thomas (senior), 186-7, 204, 258
Lees, Captain Nicholas, 62-3, 284
Lefèvre, J., 159
Leigh, Colonel, 39
Lemos, Marcus, 277-8
Lennox, 6th Duke of, Charles Stuart, 10
Lennox, Lady Sarah, 19

Lewis, Joseph, 129
Lewis, Samuel, 126, 142
Lewis, Thomas, 54
Lichfield, Lord, 71
Liem, Mr S., 273
Limekilns, The, 1, 85, 126, 162, 212, 215, 223
Links, The, 1, 44
'Little Peter', 70
L'Isle, Cassandra de, 2
L'Isle, Robert de, 2
Loates, Benjamin, 208
Loates, Jack, 58
Loates, Samuel, 105, 165, 208
Loates, Thomas, 208
Loder, Mr Edmund, 62, 287
Loder, Major Eustace, 213-6
Loder, Colonel Giles, 216
Loder stables, 270-4, 292
Londonderry, Lord, 121, 136
Long Hill, 1
Lonsdale, 3rd Earl of, 100, 102-4
Lonsdale, 4th Earl of, St George Lowther, 50, 104
Lonsdale, 5th Earl of, 104, 293
Lordship Farm stable, 171, 190, 195-6, 200, 261, 274
Lorillard, Mr Pierre, 179, 181-2
Lorraine, Sir Percy, 247
Low, George, 148-9
Lower Hare Park, 23, 195
Lowrey, Thomas, 281-2, 245
Lowther House, 204
Lowther, James, 140
Luke, Harry, 53
Lupin, M, 92
Lurgan, Lord, 140, 142
Lynch, John 'Kipper', 231, 265

Macdonald-Buchanan, Sir Reginald and Lady, 171, 261, 274, 176
Macdonald-Buchanan, Captain John, 287
Machell, Captain James Octavius, 99-111, 126, 138, 141, 164, 169, 172-6, 193-4
Machell Place (see also Chetwynd House stable), 108, 123, 187, 202, 209, 226-7, 254
Madden, Otto, 203, 286
Maher, Daniel, 213, 215
Mahon, Mr Frank, 282
Maidment, Charles, 52, 60, 97
Maktoum, Maktoum al, 66, 280
Manser, W. H., 187
Mainwaring, Reginald, 160
Maple, Sir John Blundell, 188, 220
March, Earl of, William Douglas, 16-18, 24
March, Lord, 140
Marks, Douglas, 229
Marlborough, Duchess of, 181
Marlborough House, 230, 255
Marriott, Cecil, 217, 271, 295
Marriott stable, 271-2, 274, 288, 291-2
Marsh, Charles, 225
Marsh, Marcus, 242-3, 255
Marsh, Richard, 157, 160, 190, 194-203, 205, 220, 224-5, 229, 242
Marshall, Benjamin, 25
Marshall, Richard, 273
Marshall, William, 272-3
McAlpine, Sir Robin, 261
McAlpine of Moffat, Lord, 294
McCalmont, Ann Hyacinth, 176
McCalmont, Major Dermot, 177, 221, 270
McCalmont, Colonel Harry, 59, 107-8, 110, 172-8, 210
McCalmont, Hugh, 177-8
McCalmont, Hugh Barklie, 172
McCalmont, Patrick, 177-8, 280
McCalmont, Robert, 172
McCalmont, Winifred, 177
McClean, Lawrence 'Manch', 219
McGeorge, Thomas, 150

Meaney, James, 250
Mecklenburg, Duke and Duchess of, 155
Meddler Stud, 171
Melgund, Lord, 103
Melton House, Exning, 120, 205
Mercer, Joseph, 57, 288, 290
Mercer, Emmanuel, 254-5
Merry, Mr James, 114-5, 148, 155, 211
Mestre, Eddie de, 292
Meux-Smith, Miss, 212
Meynell, Hugo, 23-4
Meynell House (see also Hurworth House), 24, 110, 155, 227, 232-3
Middleton Cottage stables, 208, 211
Mill Hill, 29, 33
Miller, Sir James, 171, 219
Miller, Michael, 291
Milltown, Lord, 55
Milner, Henry, 160
Milsom, Squadron Leader Alan, 66
Ministry of Agriculture, 293
Mitchell, Charles, 164, 168, 170-1
Moller, Mr Eric, 279
Moller, R. B. 'Budgie', 279
Monmouth, Duke of, 9, 11
Montrose, Duchess of 'Mr Manton', 108, 116, 135-6, 142, 158-60, 191, 210, 292
Montrose, Duke of, 158, 172, 210
Moore, George, 247-8
Morbey, Charles, 169
Mordan, Samuel, 56
Morgan, Mr T. V., 88
Morris, Derek, 245
Morris, Mr H. E., 278
Morris, John, 153
Morris, Tubby, 56
Mortimer, Mr Roger, 18
Morton, Charles, 111, 167-70, 189, 220
Moulton Paddocks, 169, 204, 232, 292
Mountfield, Mrs J., 287
Mumford, W., 190
Munnings, Sir Alfred, 233
Murless, Julia, 245, 287
Murless, Sir Noel, 62, 64, 243, 245-7, 269, 274, 278, 283, 287-8, 293
Murray, Anthony, 273
Musker, Herbert, 208
Musker, John, 157, 208
Musson, William, 281

Napier, The Hon George, 19
National Stud, 292-4
Naylor, Mr Richard, 56, 81-3
Neale, Frank, 28-9, 70
Ness, Lady Brigid, 278
New Astley Institute, 294-5
Newcastle, Duke of, 10, 16, 114
Newmarket, Thomas, Bishop of Carlisle, 3
Newmarket Stable Staff Liaison Committee, 285
Newmarket Trainers Federation, 284
Newnes, Sir George, 175
Newsells Park Stud, 245
Nightingall, Walter, 223
Nightingall, William, 223
Niviers, Baron, 90, 92
Noble, William, 52
North, Colonel John Thomas, 170, 189
Northmore Stud, Exning, 251
Nun, Mr, 52
Nunnery stables, 142

Oaks Lodge, 218, 292
Oates, William, 164
O'Brien, M. V., 49, 61-2
O'Farrell, Mr Frank More, 251
O'Farrell, Mr R. More, 248, 279
O'Gorman, Patrick, 265, 274
O'Gorman, William, 65, 265
O'Kelly, Colonel, 70

305

Old Station Road, 39, 44
Oliver, Thomas, 186
O'Neill, Frank, 209
Oppenheimer, Sir Philip, 279
Orford, Lord, 41
Orleans, Duke of, 75-6
Osbaldeston, George, 40-1
Osbourne, John, 82-3, 209
Osbourne, Nellie, 83
Osborne House, 83
Osborne House stable, 292
Osborne, Thomas, 63
O'Sullevan, Peter, 259
O'Toole, Peter, 264
Owens Group, 66
Oxcroft Farm, Balsham
Oxley, John, 255, 267, 274, 280

Padwick, Henry 'Mr Howard', 49
Paget, Lady Florence, 101
Palace House, 7, 60, 81, 96, 98, 192, 203-4, 245, 256, 271, 180-1, 191
Palmer, Mr Roger, 10
Palmerston, Lord, 55
Panton, Mr Thomas, 25, 27, 31, 44
Park Lodge, 44, 137, 148, 150, 156, 211, 224, 256-9, 271, 286, 295
Park Paddocks, 50, 149, 266
Parker, Mr J. D., 282
Parr, Thomas, 56, 167
Parsons, Nancy, 36
Pasha, Ismail, 187
Pavis, Arthur, 75-6
Pavis, Edward, 76
Payne, Mr George, 79
Peace, Mr, 159
Peacock, Matthew, 285
Pearson, Colonel, 58
Peck, Charles, 151, 207
Peck, Percy, 114, 146, 151, 188, 190
Peck, Robert, 75, 105, 148-151, 164, 191, 207
Peel, General Jonathan, 75-6, 79, 125
Pegasus House,188, 254, 277-8, 291
Pelham, Miss Frances, 16
Pemberton Mr, 35
Pennington, Alec, 175
Perram, Mr John, 25
Perryman, Richard, 207, 221, 281
Persse, Atty, 177, 249
Phantom House, 90-3, 188, 230, 258, 281, 292
Philip Cornes and Co, 66
Philips, Major the Hon J. P., 178, 264, 287
Phillips, Mr Nicholas, 272
Pickford, Peter, 259
Piggott, Lester, 21, 62, 76-7, 190, 244, 246-7, 253, 262, 272, 277, 281, 283, 286, 290-1
Pincus, Jacob, 179-80, 182
Poincelet, Roger, 248
Pond, John, 19, 24
Poole, Sir Ferdinand, 37
Pope, Mr George (junior), 283
Porchester, Lord, 288
Portal, Lord, 270
Portarlington, Lord, 40
Porter, John, 52, 58, 85, 121, 135, 150, 193-4, 207, 220
Portland, Dukes of, 34
Portland, 4th Duke of, 34-5, 72
Portland, 5th Duke of, 35
Portland, 6th Duke of, 35, 63, 113, 116-7, 119-21, 221
Portland Stand, 34
Portsmouth, Duchess of, Louise de Querouaille, 9
Poston, Peter, 282
Powell, Miss, 76
Powney, John, 282
Pratt, William, 251
Prescott, Sir Mark, 14, 83-4, 114, 119, 121, 274, 276
Price, Peter, 169, 187

Price, Captain Ryan, 65, 259
Priestman, Major J. L., 262
Prime, Captain, 104
Primrose Cottage, 190, 226-7, 230, 275, 292
Prince, Richard, 29, 32-33, 41, 45, 69
Pritchard, Professor,
Pritchard-Gordon, Gavin, 274, 276
Probyn, Sir Dighton, 194
Pryor, Mr T., 58, 101
Purcell, Peter Valentine (see also Gilpin), 213
Purefoy, Captain William, 54, 212

Queenborough, Lord, 216
Queensberry, 3rd Duke of, 24
Queensberry, 4th Duke of 'Old Q', 24-7, 67, 70, 73
Queensberry House, 27
Queensberry Lodge, 27, 119, 187, 206-7, 240
Querouaille, Louise de, Duchess of Portsmouth, 9
Quince, Samuel, 97

Racecourse Side, 1
Racing Kalendar, 24
Railway Land, 1
Ram, The, 41
Ramsay, Mr, 52
Randall, H. E., 211
Ransch, Mr, 214
Raphael, Walter, 207
Rathmoy stables, 273
Raynes Lane stable, 282
Reach, 2
Red Lion, The, 19
Reid, John, 279
Reidy, Thomas, 270
Reiff, John, 183-4
Reiff, Lester, 183-4
Richard II, King, 3
Richards, Mr A. J., 278
Richards, Sir Gordon, 46, 238, 244, 246, 270
Richardson, Sir Albert PPRA, 266
Richardson, John Maunsell 'Cat', 103
Richmond, Duchess of, Frances Teresa Stuart, 9-10
Richmond, 2nd Duke of, 19
Richmond, 5th Duke of, 76
Rickaby, Frederick I, 221
Rickaby, Frederick II, 181, 189, 222-3
Rickaby, Frederick III, 221-4
Rickaby, Frederick IV, 223
Rickaby, John, 222
Rickaby, Samuel, 222
Rickaby, William, 221, 223-4, 247, 255-6
Rickman, Major Eric, 95
Rickman, John, 95
Riley, William, 164
Ringer, David, 273
Roberts, Alan, 295
Robinson, C. A., 42
Robinson, Charles Edward, 42
Robinson, Mr David, 262-4, 277-8
Robinson, Sir Foster, 255
Robinson, James, 37, 44, 76-7, 80, 123, 141
Robinson, John, 108
Robinson, Mrs, 264
Robinson, Peter, 249, 268, 278-9
Robinson, Philip, 279
Robinson, Mr W. T. 'Jack', 106
Robinson, Wybrow, 154
Robson, Robert, 37, 39, 45, 71, 76, 113
Rochester, Earl of, John Wilmot, 8
Rockingham, Marquess of, 72
Rodney, The 7th Lord, 106
Roe, Mr, 11
Roettiers, John, 10
Rogers, Joseph, 78

Rogers, Samuel, 44, 78, 80
Rogerson, Mrs John, 279
Rohan, Patrick, 286
Rosbrook, George, 108
Rose, Sir Charles Day, 174, 185
Rosebery, 5th Earl of, 98, 104, 109, 120, 146, 151, 169, 190, 224, 229
Rosebery, 6th Earl of, 39, 98, 257, 268, 271, 281, 286
Rossmore, Lord, 76, 82, 106, 117, 180
Rothschild, Mr Evelyn de, 96
Rothschild, Hannah, 97-8
Rothschild, Mr James de, 286
Rothschild, Leopold de 'Mr Acton', 98, 146, 192, 198, 203
Rothschild, Baron Meyer de, 56, 96-8
Rothschild family, 96
Rous, Admiral, 79-80
Rouse, Brian, 54, 66
Rowlands, Fothergill 'Fog', 194
Rowley Mile, 1, 6, 44-6, 55
Rubens, Peter Paul, 5
Rudolf, Crown Prince, 60
Russell, Sir Charles, 140, 143-4
Russel, Lord William, 12
Rutland, Dukes of, 3, 13, 77, 172
Rutland Arms, 3, 6, 40-1, 50-1, 82, 135
Ryan, James, 66, 156-7, 207, 224
Ryan, Michael, (junior), 276, 291
Ryan, Michael (senior), 291
Ryan, Rosa, 156

Sackville House stable, 281, 291
Saddler, Alfred, 171, 211, 222
Saddler, Alfred Brettle, 189, 211
Saddler, Isaac, 190
Saffron House, 273
St Agnes Church, 171
St Albans, Duke of, 188
St Albans stable, 119, 188, 292
St Gatien stable, 189, 271, 287
St George, Richard Sir Charles, 272
St Mary's Square, 33
Salisbury, Lord, 4-5
Samuel, Mr, 7
Samuel, Mr A. G., 270
Sandford, Mr M.H., 179
Sanford, Mr J., 209
Sangster, Mr Robert, 291
Sassoon, Sir Ellice Victor, 61, 215, 286, 272
Saunderson, William, 141
Savile, Henry, 142, 207
Savile House, 282
Scaltback Stud, 110, 265
Schickler, Baron, 92
Scott, General John, 34
Scott, John, 74, 77-8, 96, 114-5, 208
Scott, Mrs L., 252
Scott, Peter 'Hotspur', 252
Scott's stables, Newmarket, 74
Sefton Lodge, 159, 172, 187, 207, 259-61
Sefton Stud, 191, 210
Severals, The, 33, 42, 135, 156, 206
Sexton, Graham, 249
Shafto, Captain Jenison, 24
Shalfleet, (see also Bedford Lodge and Highfield), 187, 226, 258-9, 265, 274, 276
Shaw, Mr, 223
Shelburne, Lord, 35
Shelley, Sir John, 75
Sherborne, Lord, 31
Sherrard, Richard 'Buck', 89, 126, 140, 142, 146, 158, 180
Sherwood, Robert, 109-10, 188-9, 206-7, 223
Sherwood, Robert Louis Vodoz, 189
Shrewsbury, Countess, 7-8
Shrive, Anthony, 245
Side Hill, 1
Sidebottom, Hugh, 229

306

Sievier, Robert, 50-1, 200
Simpson, Mr, 44
Sims, Mr, 181
Singleton, Mr W. B., 294
Sitwell, Sir Sitwell, 33
Six Mile Bottom, 8, 15
Six Mile House, 23
Sloan, James 'Tod', 60, 67, 181-3
Smallman, Frank, 69
Smirke, Charles, 46, 239, 242-3
Smith, Douglas, 232, 267-8, 270-1, 273, 286
Smith, Eph, 229, 260
Smith, James, 53
Smith, Sidney, 53
Smith, Stanley, 268
Smith, 'Stiffy', 162
Smyth, Gordon, 291
Snailwell Stud, 292
Snaith, William, 231
Sneyd, Major F. B., 260, 270
Snowden, James, 54
Soltykoff, Prince Dimitri, 94, 140, 187, 211
Someries Stud, 49, 261
Somerset, Duke of, 12, 14-15
Somerville Lodge stable, 169, 187, 207, 243, 291
Southey, Herbert, 226
Southfield stables, 278
Spares, Charles, 282
Spares, Charles 'Chuck', 282
Spear, Mr, 209
Sporting Kalendar, 19
Stag, 55
Stamford, Earl of, 84, 88, 148
Stamford, Lady, 149, 211
Stanley, The Hon Richard, 254
Stanley, Lord, 55, 78, 191
Stanley House, 61, 85-6, 104, 160, 187, 210, 221, 226, 232-6, 251, 253-4, 276, 282
Starkey, Greville, 267, 272, 276, 287
Stedall, Mr A. E., 211, 225
Steel, Mr, 183
Stephenson, Mr Christopher, 278
Stephenson, William, 226, 291
Stern, George, 220
Stetchworth Stud, 292
Stevens, Thomas (junior), 166
Stevens, William, 164, 166
Stewart, Alexander, 292
Stewart, Colonel Robert, 292
Stirling, Colonel William, 251
Stirling Stuart, Major R., 160
Stockbridge House, 189-90, 240
Stoute, Michael, 66, 282, 285-7, 291
Strassburger, Mr R. B., 286
Strickland, Sir William, 13
Stuart, Frances Teresa, 'La Belle Stuart', Duchess of Richmond, 9-10
Stubbs, George, 67
Suffolk House, 141, 185
Sunderland, Lord, 12
Sutherland, Captain Fergus, 262
Sutton, Mr Richard, 52
Swan, The, Bottisham, 90, 175
Swift, Mr Richard, 281-2
Swinburn, Walter, 231, 287

Taafe, Theobald, 17
Tally Ho Stud, 272
Tankesley, 56
Tattersalls, 44, 50-1, 65, 150, 266, 274-5
Tattersall, Mr Edmund, 116, 149, 162
Tattersall, Richard, 18, 265
Tattersall, Mr Somerville, 50-2, 203
Taylor, Alec, 61, 158, 262
Taylor, Brian, 65, 259
Taylor, Victor, 295
Ten Broek, Mr Richard, 56, 179, 182
Terrace House, 204, 227, 255, 292
Terry, Mr S., 281
TGWU, 284

Tharp, Mrs Montague, 162
Thetford, 4
Thirkell, Frederick, 285
Thomond, Lord, 6
Thompson, James, 263
Thompson, John, 182
Thorn, Sir Jules, 282
Thornhill, Mr Thomas, 39, 73
Thynne, Thomas, 11
Tillbrook, Mrs, 33
Todd, George, 291
Toller, Captain Charles, 282
Toller, James, 282
Tolly Cobbold, 66
Tomkins, Mark, 282
Tomlinson, Mr, 100
Tote, The, 64-5
Townsend, Lord, 10
Trafford, Sir Humphrey de, 225, 245-6, 271
Tulk, Paul, 231
Tupgill Yard, 82, 88

Udny, John, 77

Vanian, Mr S., 277
Vernon, The Hon Richard, 71
Vernon, Sir Robert, 4
Villar, Mr Anthony, 280
Villiers, Barbara, Duchess of Cleveland, 9-10, 35
Villiers, George, 2nd Duke of Buckingham, 7
Vyner, Mr H. C., 116
Vyner, Mr R. C., 150

Wagon and Horses, 135
Walden, Lord Howard de, 66, 177, 210, 257, 288
Walker, Edmund, 194
Walker, Colonel Hall, 236, 292
Wallace, Edgar, 172
Wallace, Lady, 129
Wallis, Rev Colville, 159
Wallis, Laurence, 66
Walpole, Horace, 20, 23
Walters, William, 120, 190, 225, 265, 275
Walton, Mr, 142
Walwyn, Peter, 57, 178, 290
Ward, Mr, 52, 194
Ward Hill, 66
Warne, William, 110
Warren Hill, 1-2, 6, 11, 14, 83, 162
Warren Hill Stud, 278
Warren House, 39, 42, 134, 151, 153, 187, 226
Warren Place stable, 231, 245-7, 278, 283, 287-8, 290-1
Warren Towers, 93-4
Waterhall, 1
Waterwitch House, 107, 228
Watson, Alfred, 176
Watson, John, 189, 203-4
Watts, Harry, 202
Watts, Jack I, 164, 167, 181, 199-203, 251
Watts, Jack II, 227, 251
Watts, Jack III, 202, 251, 254, 274
Watts, John Evelyn, 202, 259
Watts, William, 254
Waugh, Alec, 261
Waugh, Alfred, 212
Waugh, Charles, 187, 211-12, 223, 236, 262
Waugh, Dawson, 155, 207, 220, 229
Waugh, Grace, 155
Waugh, Isabella, 155
Waugh, Jack, 229, 258, 261, 274, 276
Waugh, James, 24, 110, 114-5, 153-55, 188, 207-8, 211, 227, 233, 261
Waugh, Janet, 155, 208
Waugh, John, 255, 261
Waugh, Richard, 120, 155, 211, 261
Waugh, Thomas (junior), 256, 261, 282

Waugh, Thomas (senior), 24, 155, 203, 227, 261
Waugh, William, 155, 188, 207, 220, 225, 232
Weatherby, Edward, 119, 150
Weatherby, Mr, 33, 69
Webb, Frederick, 2, 56, 105, 109, 157, 166, 219
Weeden, Derek, 273
Welbourne, Alan, 289
Wentworth, Mr, 21
Wernher, Lady Zia, 49, 225, 244
Westbrooke, Richard, 291
Westminster, Duke of, 50, 148, 150-1
Weston, Thomas, 211, 221, 231, 284
Wharncliffe, Lord, 34
Wharton, Marquess of, 12
Wharton, Walter, 250
White, Sir Gordon, 287
White Hart, The, 44, 76
White Lodge Stud, Cheveley, 279
Whitney, Mr W. C., 183
Wigg, Lord, 285
Wightman, William, 256
Wildenstein, Mr Daniel, 288
William, Prince of Orange (William III), 12
William Hill Organisation, 62, 64-5, 287
Williams, Colin, 259
Williams, General Owen, 142, 148, 150-1
Williams, Robert, 291
Williams, Robert, 281-2
Willoughby, Sir John, 105,
Wilmot, John, Earl of Rochester, 8
Wilson, Mr Christopher, 47, 49, 61, 72-3
Winter, Frederick, 267-8
Winter, John, 85, 267-8
Winter, Patricia, 267
Wishard, Enoch, 183
Wood, Charles, 83, 104-5, 118, 126-7, 138, 140-2, 143-6, 181, 185, 254
Wood, James, 146
Woodcock, John, 24
Woodlands, 156, 266, 286
Woodward, Mr William, 225
Woolcott, Harry, 141
Wragg, Geoffrey, 279
Wragg, Harry, 171, 228, 231, 247-9, 256, 265, 276, 279, 287
Wraughton House, 186-7, 204, 226, 259, 261
Wright, (Long Acre coachmaker), 17
Wyatt, Brigadier W. P., 244
Wyck Hall Stud, 261
Wyfold, Lady, 270
Wyndham, Mr, 44, 48

Yarmouth, Lady, 27
York, Duke and Duchess of, 198
York Buildings, 34

Zetland, The Marquess of, 129, 187, 227
Zetland Lodge (see also Balaton Lodge), 187, 220, 294

Index of Horses

Abbeydale, 288
Abbott, 209
Abelia, 62
Abermaid, 248, 260
Abernant, 63-4, 232
Abington, 279
Abjer, 77
Absalom, 281
Achievement, 58, 62, 83
Achilles, 214
Achmet, 48
Adam Bede, 171
Adam's Apple, 206
Admiral, The, 46
Admiration, 213
African Rhythm, 276
Ahonoora, 279
Aida, 219
Airborne, 63, 231
Air Raid, 57
Airs and Graces, 204
Alarm, 79
Albert Victor, 58, 97
Alcide, 232, 245
Alcove, 251
Aldegonde, 176
Aldritch, 169
Alice, 170
All of a Kind, 259
Almedar, 74
Alphadamus, 287
Altesse Royale, 283
Alycidon, 63, 191, 232, 245, 270
Amaranda, 279
Amato, 188
Ambergris, 248-9
Amerigo, 261
Amos, 249
Amour Drake, 232
Amphora, 174
Amurath, 189
Antar, 75
Antinous, 36
Apollo, 79
Apology, 50
Apple Peel, 221
Apple Sammy, 62
Approval, 246, 271
Archibald, 76
Archiduc, 109
Arctic Prince, 200, 282
Ard Patrick, 63
Ardross, 290
Ardrossan, 77
Arion, 211
Aristocrat, 200
Ark Royal, 251, 254-5
Arndean, 292
Artless, 56
Asmet, 75
Athens Wood, 279, 286
Athol Daisy, 183
Atilla, 248-9
Atlantic, 116, 134
Auction Ring, 62
Aurelius, 29, 247
Aureole, 244
Autoscope, 146
Aviary, 259
Avon's Pride, 249
Ayrshire, 121
Azor, 37, 77

Bacchus, 99-100
Bachelor's Button, 151, 214
Bagamoya, 240
Bahram, 209, 238-40, 242
Bailidar, 171
Bala Hissar, 61
Baldur, 182
Ballinode, 226
Balloon, 29
Balsamo, 198
Baltinglass, 216
Barcaldine, 148, 207, 211, 266
Barcarolle, 75
Bard, The, 150-1
Barefoot, 73
Baroda, 241
Baron, The, 79
Baronet, 54
Barrow, 279
Bass Rock, 256
Battleship, 262
Bayardo, 61, 205
Bay Express, 261
Bay Middleton, 48, 76
Bayuda, 60
Beam, 146, 221, 234
Beau Chevalet, 255
Beaufront, 254
Be Cannie, 174
Be Friendly, 259
Beggarman, 75
Beldale Flutter, 277-8
Bellacose, 63
Belle of All, 60
Bellicose, 228
Belmont Bay, 62, 291
Bendigo, 53-4, 57, 106
Bend Or, 66, 148, 186
Bennington, 73
Benny Lynch, 232
Berkeley Springs, 247
Berrill, 182
Billet, 231
Bismarck, 167
Black Jester, 223
Black Tarquin, 232
Blair Athol, 48
Blakeney, 36, 280
Blanchard, 137
Blandford, 63, 72, 238
Blank, 36
Bleep-Bleep, 251
Blenheim, 239-41
Bloomsbury, 55
Blosselsky, 214
Blue Cashmere, 171, 286-7
Blue Danube, 208
Blue Gown, 56
Blue Peter, 229, 260
Blunderbuss, 25
Blushing Groom, 283
Boldboy, 64
Boldero, 256
Bolkonski, 272, 283-4
Bonavista, 185
Bo'sun, 256
Boswell, 188
Braughing, 278
Braxted, 205
Brewer, The, 56
Briar Root, 156
Bride Elect, 249

Bridget, 70
Brigadier Gerard, 49, 59, 66, 214, 289
Broadwood, 286
Bronze, 75
Brown Betty, 60
Brownie, The, 40
Bucco Bay, 66
Bucephalus, 21
Buckskin, 288
Bug, The, 242
Bullfinch, 61
Bullingdon, 63 Burford, 194
Burgundy, 26
Busted, 247, 280, 292
Busting, 279, 283
Bustino, 21, 72
Busybody, 59, 117, 162, 170
But Beautiful, 240
Buxton, 229
Buzzard's Bay, 276
By Thunder!, 231, 287

Cabin Boy, 187
Cadland, 255
Caergwrle, 247
Cajun, 291
Calash, 293
Caliban, 283
Caligula, 226
Call Boy, 202, 227, 251
Caller Ou, 83
Calpurnius, 254
Camballo, 116
Cambridge, 262
Cambusmore, 136
Campanjo, 107
Canisbay, 245
Cannobie, 114
Canterbury Pilgrim, 104, 191, 222
Cantilever, 226
Canyon, 221
Caporello, 276
Captain Kettle, 200
Captain Plume, 29
Cara, 75
Caractacus, 123
Caravan, 76
Cardinal of York, 23
Cardington King, 258
Careless, 12
Careless Princess, 283
Carlburg, 264
Carlton Grange, 188
Caroline, 74
Carrozza, 247, 293
Castle Keep, 64
Catalpa, 272
Catastrophe, 129
Catherine Hayes, 114, 116
Catherine Wheel, 281
Catmint, 188
Cat O'Nine Tails, 228
Cecilia, 116
Cedric, 76
Cellini, 61
Ceves, 68
Chaleureux, 217, 219
Chalon, 64
Chamant, 59-60
Chamossaire, 292
Champion, 49, 72
Chance Belle, 281

Chandos, 104-5
Chanter, 15
Chanticleer, 30
Chapeau, 286
Charibert, 116
Charicles, 268
Charlotte, 49, 72
Charlottown, 200
Chatsworth, 249
Chaucer, 104
Chelandry, 190
Chenille, 245
Chéri, 56
Cherimoya, 267
Cherry Hinton, 279
Chicago, 248
Chilblain, 194
Chorus, 266
Christmas Daisy, 54, 210
Chulmleigh, 225
Chypre, 141
Cicero, 151, 217
Cider with Rosie, 46
Cinna, 223, 227
Cinq-à-Sept, 225
Circus King, 287
Clarhaven, 212
Claremont, 153
Clarence, 211
Claret, 99
Claribelle, 110
Clarion, 55
Clementina, 79
Cloonagh, 272
Cobweb, 76
Codoman, 182
Coelebs, 33
Colleen Bawn, 168
Colombo, 225
Coltness, 156
Comfrey, 181
Common, 224
Commotion, 103
Compensation, 268
Comrade, 216
Connaught, 283
Connaught Bridge, 288-9
Constantia, 230
Contralto, 288
Cool Customer, 160
Corejada, 241
Coriander, 30
Corisande, 97
Corn Sack, 216
Coronet, 157
Corrie Roy, 158-9
Corunna, 190
Cos, 236, 289
Count Pahlen, 178, 280
Country Boy, 166
Court Chad, 276
Court Gift, 262
Courtier, 199
Covenden, 227
Craig Millar, 83
Crann Tair, 63
Cremorne, 86-7, 97, 142, 207
Crepello, 49, 61, 247, 272, 288
Cresta Run, 216
Crocket, 250
Crowned Prince, 282
Crozier, 253
Crucifix, 49, 51, 61
Cruiskeen, 55
Cry of Truth, 281
Csardas, 171
Cub, 73
Curry, 231
Cur, The, 55, 78
Curzon, 209
Cutter, 254-5
Cyllene, 22, 185, 208, 217, 224
Cymbeline, 61
Cypria, 94

Dacia, 55
Daedalus, 23
Dalham, 279
Dalmane, 66
Dalmatian, 172, 190
Damascus, 221
Dancing Maid, 287
Dandy, The, 33
Dangerous, 190
Dante, 241, 293
Dapper, 25
Darius, 62, 248
Darley Arabian, 15, 36
Dash, 26
Dastur, 209, 238
David Jack, 268
Dawn Johnny, 287
Dayton, 257
Dead Lock, 107
Dean Swift, 223
Declare 223
Deetease, 255
Defence, 103
Denikin, 258-9
Dervise, 37, 47, 71
Devon Ditty, 279
Diabletta, 240-2
Diadem, 63, 221
Diamond Cutter, 282
Diamond Jubilee, 63, 200-3, 220, 242
Diligence, 211
Diomed, 29, 32, 70
Diomedes, 226
Diophantus, 84
Diophion, 62, 236
Discorea, 248
Disraeli, 153, 208
Disturbance, 103
Dites, 258
Ditto, 72
Dodoma, 241
Dog Rose, 185
Donald, 256
Doncaster, 48, 148
Don John, 73-4
Donovan, 59, 61, 121
Doreen Jane, 270
Double Chance, 227
Double Life, 49, 225
Double Quick, 265
Double-U-Jay, 268
Dragon, 13
Drake, 102
Dred Scott, 281
Drizzle, 146
Drum Beat, 265
Drumour, 61
Duke John, 238
Duke of Sparta, 211
Dumplin, 20, 22
Durante, 177
Dutch Oven, 60, 109, 116, 118, 134

Eager, 85, 156
Eagle, 255
Earl, The, 104
Eastern Emperor, 256
Ebor, 210
Echanson, 63
Eclipse, 21.23, 28
Eleanor, 32
Electra, 216
El Hakim, 56
Elizabeth, 88, 141
Ellangowen, 224
Ellerdale, 55-6
Ellington, 56, 88
Eltham, 155
Elzevir, 105
Emilio, 286
Emilius, 37, 40
Emita, 170
Empery, 72
Emsworth, 174
Enamel, 44

End of the Line, 62
Enigma, 109
Enrico, 263
Enstone Spark, 277
Entente Cordial, 251
Enterprise, 156
Enthusiast, 156
Epaulette, 265
Epirus, 74
Epigram, 57
Epinard, 225
Epsom Lad, 63
Era, The, 114
Eric the Red, 264
Erin's Isle, 279
Escape, 30-2, 39, 43, 69
Espresso, 248-9
Esquire, 228
Eurasian, 110
Even Say, 281
Evenus, 79
Everitt, 167
Evita, 64
Extempore, 73

Fabulist, 209
Fair Astronomer, 258
Fair Castle, 189
Fair Isle, 221, 235
Fair Salinia, 267, 287
Fair Trial, 241
Fairway, 54, 62-3, 221, 232, 234
Fairy Footsteps, 64, 280, 290
Faith, 70
Fast Track, 264
Favonius, 52, 97-8
Fazzoletto, 79
Felicitation, 238
Felstead, 234
Felucca, 255
Feramorz, 77
Fernandez, 126
Ferry, 221
Feu de Joie, 81, 83
Feve, 103
Fichu, 148
Fidalgo, 248
Fiffinella, 209
Figaro, 34
Filbert, 176
Fille de l'Air, 91-2
Final Straw, 294
Firdaussi, 61, 238
Firebrand, 79
Firestreak, 280
First Consul, 231
First Flight, 226
First Movement, 291
First Principal, 211
Fisherman, 167
Flag of Truce, 205
Flair, 215
Flatfoot, 11
Fleet, 60, 247, 288
Fleet Wahine, 279
Florence, 53-4, 109, 188
Floretti, 264
Florizel II, 197, 200
Flossy, 253
Flying Childers, 15
Flying Duchess, 152
Flying Duchman, 61, 88
Flying Water, 64
Flyon, 229
Fool's Mate, 272
Footlight, 215
Formosa, 50, 58, 83
Four Course, 62
Fox, 15
Foxhall, 53, 56, 126, 180
Foxlaw, 57, 227
Frais du Bois, 248
Frankincense, 255
Frawn, 230
Free Fare, 291

Freemason, 211
Free State, 178
Freeze The Secret, 277
French Fern, 261
Frenchman's Cave, 266
Friar Marcus, 238
Friars Daughter, 236-8
Frivolity, 58, 86
Front Row, 258, 281
Full Dress, 279
Fullerton, 143
Fulmen, 117, 149
Furley, 103

Galata, 44, 70
Galcador, 232
Galliard, 116-7, 153
Gallinule, 167-8, 213, 293
Galopin, 117, 152-3
Galtee More, 59
Gang Forward, 83
Garden Path, 232
Garden State, 248
Gardevisure, 52
Gaspard, 56
Gay Lothair, 189
Gaze, 213
Geheimniss, 109, 211
General Ironside, 272
General Peel, 179
Genius, 211
Gentilhombre, 62
George Frederick, 101, 187
Georgic, 204
Gervas, 107
Gimcrack, 22-3
Gladiateur, 52, 91-4, 155
Glare, 215
Glass Jug, 176
Glencoe, 48
Glenhazel, 206
Gloriation, 83
Glorious Devon, 225
Godiva, 229-30
Gold, 187
Gold Bridge, 226
Golden Advisor, 259
Golden Cloud, 231
Golden Fire, 230
Golden Horus, 265
Golden Mean, 271
Golden Miller, 226
Golden Myth, 224
Golden Pippin, 79
Golden Rocket, 260
Golovine, 248
Gondolette, 50
Gondolic, 152
Good News, 203
Go Shell, 251
Grand Composer, 166
Grand Parade, 225
Grandew, 269
Gratitude, 155, 249, 268
Great Light, 282
Great Nephew, 256, 292
Grecian, 61
Greenland Park, 288
Green Sleeve, 58
Gregalach, 226
Grey Diomed, 29
Grey God, 277
Grey of Falloden, 57
Grey Robin, 22
Grisi, 99
Grundy, 21, 272, 283-4, 292, 294
Gulnare, 76
Gunner B, 288
Gustavus, 61, 185
Gypsy Dancer, 65

Habena, 79
Hackler's Pride, 54, 224
Hackness, 150
Halsbury, 57

Hammerkop, 62, 168, 215
Hampton, 72, 195
Handicapper, 204
Hannah, 50, 52, 58, 62, 97
Happy Clacton, 266
Happy Knight, 231
Happy Laughter, 256
Harvester, 105, 108, 117, 141
Hasty Cloud, 258
Hautesse, 176
Hawthornden, 88
Heave To, 276
Hello Gorgeous, 288-9
Henbit, 250
Hermes, 255
Herminius, 110
Hermione, 70
Hermit, 27, 88, 101-3, 107, 141, 174, 194
Hernandez, 79
Herod, 36
Herringbone, 282
Hesper, 123
Hethersett, 249
Hettie Sorrell, 191
Hidden Meaning, 258
High Art, 227
Highclere, 283
Highflyer, 36
Highland Chief, 116
High Top, 282-3
High Treason, 260
Hippolyta, 69
Hobbie Noble, 114
Hollington, 190
Homebrewed, 48
Homeward Bound, 255, 267
Homing, 294
Honoria, 133
Hopbloom, 53
Hopeful Venture, 63
Hotfoot, 178, 280
Hot Grove, 178
House of Lords, 107
Hulcot, 189
Humble Duty, 60
Humewood, 106
Hungarian, 166
Huntercombe, 54
Hurricane Hill, 281
Hydaspes, 24
Hypericum, 232, 270
Hyperion, 60, 72, 221, 232, 238
Hyperion Kid, 248

Ibraham, 48
Icena, 280
Idas, 79
Ikey Solomons, 40
Ile de Bourbon, 65, 292
Iliona, 55
Imperieuse, 79
Inca, 29
In Command, 258
Indiana, 254
Industry, 73
Invincible II, 219
Ion, 55
Iroquois, 53, 179-81
Isidore, 136
Isinglass, 59, 63, 72, 107, 172, 174, 176, 209
Isonomy, 52, 107

Jacinth, 281
Jack Horner, 226
Jacob, 83
Janette, 66, 104, 116
Jeanne Michelle, 255
Jeddah, 50, 185, 236
Jest, 189, 222
Jibtopsail, 223
Joe Holland, 255
John Bull, 23, 71
John Cherry, 280

John Davis, 56
John O'Gaunt, 203
J. O. Tobin, 283
Jovial Judge, 257
Juggler, 167, 169
Julia, 36
Julio Mariner, 36, 278
Julius, 114
Julius Caesar, 88
Jumping Hill, 283
Jupiter Pluvius, 281

Kaffir Chief, 54
Kaffir King, 209
Kalaglow, 267
Kalydon, 251
Karabas, 251, 253
Kashmir II, 256, 286
Keep Going, 261
Kelling, 261
Kennymore, 61
Kestrel, 176
Keystone II, 210
Kilbroney, 212, 223
Kilglass, 224, 257
Kilmeny, 114
Kilsallaghan, 107
Kiltoi, 212
Kilwarlin, 106
Kind of Hush, 64
Kingcraft, 56, 115, 117
King John, 216
King Lud, 102-3
King Naskra, 273
King of Diamonds, 167, 169-70
King of the Forest, 97
Kingsclare, 52-3
King Tom, 56, 102
Kirtling, 278
Kisaki, 240
Kisber, 60, 97-8, 153
Knight of the Thistle, 175, 181
Known Fact, 59
Kris, 66, 288-9
Ksar, 282
Kursaal, 268
Kwang-Su, 209
Kyak, 254-5

L'Abbé, 29
L'Abbesse de Jouarre, 189
La Bohème, 11, 171
Laburnam, 86
Lacqueur, 248, 279
Ladas, 59, 63, 120
Lady Audley, 104
Lady Augusta, 88
Lady Elizabeth, 61
Lady Help, 209
La Flèche, 50, 52, 66, 171
Land League, 206-7
Lanercost, 52
Langton Abbot, 231
Lapel, 177
La Sagesse, 171, 208
Las Vegas, 231
Laureate, 110
Legerdemain, 55
Le Moss, 288-9
Lemberg, 61, 63, 206
Lerida, 261
Le Tellier, 230
Levee, 265
Levmoss, 253
Lexicon, 171, 190
Lianga, 63
Light Brocade, 60, 289
Light Cavalry, 63, 289, 291
Light Harvest, 261
Lightning, 245
Limasol, 188
Lischana, 215
Little Charlie, 133
Little Green Man, 264
Little Missus, 213

Little Nelly, 99
Llangibby, 216
Loch Sen, 223
Lomond, 258
London Boy, 264
Long Row, 281
Lord Bill, 286
Lord Lyon, 48
Lorenzaccio, 62, 283
Louviers, 220
Louvois, 207
Loved One, 50
Lowland Chief, 188
Lucasland, 63
Lucero, 248
Lucetta, 186
Lucky Shoes, 264
Lupe, 63, 285
Lutetia, 60
Lyphard's Wish, 288-9

Macaroni, 81, 83, 209
Maccabeus 'Running Rein', 78-9
Madam Gay, 276
Magic, 205
Magic Court, 57
Mah Mahal, 239
Mahmoud, 209, 233, 239-40
Maid of the Oaks, 68
Maid of Trent, 133
Maiden Erlegh, 223
Main Reef, 288
Mandarin, The, 104
Manna, 278
Manrico, 194
Manushi, 288
Marching On, 276
Marco, 83, 150
Marcovil, 212
Marie Stuart, 103, 148
Mariner, 255
Marinsky, 62
Marksman, 102
Marquis, The, 83, 123
Marske, 20
Martini, 158
Marvellous, 107
Marwell, 62, 287
Masaka, 62, 240
Masham, 250
Masked Light, 241
Master Richard, 99
Master Willie, 278
Matador, 261
Matilda, 76
Mattaboy, 277
Mawal, 273
May-Day, 76
McGregor, 155
Meddler, 170-2
Mehari, 268
Meld, 51, 225, 232, 244, 251
Melton, 59, 63, 119-21, 136
Memoir, 63
Mercutio, 171
Merman, 2, 57, 182
Merry Gal, 63
Merry Hampton, 106, 167, 169
Mid-Day Sun, 65
Mighty Gurkha, 268
Migoli, 61, 240
Milford, 168, 170
Mill Reef, 21, 49, 290, 294
Millstream, 151
Mimi, 120, 222
Minoru, 220, 242
Minstrel, 256
Minstrel, The, 61, 76
Minthe, 62
Minting, 120, 136, 150-1
Minuet, 61, 73
Mirska, 188
Miss Jummy, 195
Miss Paris, 271
Mistley, 224

Misty Bay, 282
Molly Bawn, 194
Molly Desmond, 60
Monade, 260
Monarch, 91
Moneymaker, 227
Montekin, 273
Monterrico, 248
Monteverdi, 61
Moorestyle, 62, 66, 277-8, 294
Morston, 283
Moses, 34, 73
Moslem, 83
Mosso, 282
Moulton, 279
Mr Jinks, 62
Mr Sykes, 56
Mrs McArdy, 65
Mrs Rustom, 61
Mrs Tiggywinkle, 281
Mulberry, 26
Mumtaz Begum, 241
Mumtaz Mahal, 236-7, 239, 241
Munch, 258
Muscovite, 79
Mushroom, 209
Music, 73
My Babu, 231
My Dear, 61
My Dream, 250
My Goodness Me, 250
My Lover, 66
Myrobella, 63
My Smokey, 251
My Swanee, 272
Mysterious, 283

Nagami, 249
Narrator, 249
Nassovian, 209
Nativa, 90
Nearco, 54, 72, 292
Nearula, 59
Neasham Belle, 249
Nellie Park, 252
Never Say Die, 262
Newhaven, 219
Newminster, 101
Nicholas Nickleby, 231
Night Hawk, 196
Night Off, 60, 250
Nightshade, 76
Night Spot, 270
Nijinsky, 21, 49, 61, 283
Nimbus, 62, 232
Noble Decree, 282
Noirio, 21
Norman III, 204
Northern Dancer, 21, 72
Nortia, 249
Nothing Venture, 205
Nucleus, 244
Nuneham, 86
Nun Nicer, 188, 208, 249

Ocean, 255
Old England, 61
Old Joe, 157
Old Lucky, 283
Old Merlin, 13
Old Reliance, 257
Old Rowley, 6
Olive, 48
Omladina, 198
On The House, 279
One in a Million, 64, 288
Optimist, 179
Orlando, 79
Ormonde, 61, 66, 117, 150-1
Orosio, 272
Orpheus, 205
Osbech, 146, 209
Osier, 251
Ossian, 195
Ostregor, 128

Ostrya, 261
Our Babu, 59, 250, 262
Our Betters, 266
Our Ruby, 254
Outcrop, 262
Out of Sight, 260
Ovaltine, 254
Ovaszar, 155
Over Norton, 212
Owen Anthony, 270-1
Owen Dudley, 283

Palais Royal, 234
Palatch, 258
Palestine, 46, 232, 240-2
Pall Mall, 245, 260, 264
Pally's Double, 254
Palmer, The, 104
Palpitate, 231
Panama Canal 272
Panga, 252
Paperweight, 61
Pappa Fairway, 252
Papyrus, 224
Paragon, 216
Paris, 179
Park Ranger, 266
Park Top, 251-3
Parole, 179
Parthenon, 272
Parthia, 245
Pastille, 47, 74
Pathfinder, 113
Patron, 76
Pay Up, 65, 239
Pecker, 73
Pelisse, 36
Pencil Point, 292
Penelope, 36
Peppermint, 109
Perdita II, 194, 200
Peregrine, 29, 279
Pericet, 284
Pero Gomez, 58
Persian Gulf, 245
Persimmon, 63, 177, 197-200, 203,
    205-6, 220, 227, 242, 251
Peter, 58, 86, 125-8
Petingo, 278
Petite Etoile, 51, 241, 247
Petition, 240
Petrarch, 59, 110, 153
Peut-Etre, 87
Phalaris, 54
Pharis, 54, 229
Pharsalia, 249
Philominsky, 273
Phoebus Apollo, 155
Phosphorus, 75-6
Photo Flash, 260
Piaco, 261
Piety, 155
Pilgrimage, 50, 60, 104
Pindarrie, 47
Pink Tank, 276
Pinza, 61, 244, 262
Pioneer, 167
Pipator, 30
Pirouette, 33
Pitcher, 187
Plaisanterie, 53, 174
Planet, 172, 190
Playfair, 106
Plenipotentiary, 41
Poetess, 91
Poison, 77
Polemic, 56, 109
Pollerton, 280
Polygamy, 283
Poylmelus, 54
Pomme de Terre, 227
Pommern, 151
Pondoland, 216
Pope, 36, 73
Portnellan, 145

311

Portrait Attachment, 239
Pot-8-O's, 23
Precious Pearl, 221
Predominate, 260
Premonition, 150
Preserve, 79
Presto II, 214
Pretender, 83, 88
Pretendre, 256, 259
Pretty Polly, 50-1, 60, 66, 168, 212-6, 287
Priam, 40-1, 43
Priddy Fair, 254
Pride of Alcide, 272
Primera, 63
Prince, 4, 203
Prince Bee, 280
Prince Charlie, 58, 86-7, 152
Prince de Galles, 268-9, 279
Prince Leopold, 34
Prince Palatine, 200
Prince Simon, 46, 232, 242, 244
Princely Gift, 62
Princess Eboli, 281
Prior of St Margaret, 52
Priory Park, 151
Privy Councillor, 256, 261
Problem, 37, 71
Proclamation, 181, 188
Promise, 36
Prospect Pleases, 254
Protection Racket, 278
Proud Chieftain, 249
Prowess Prince, 273
Prunella, 36-7
Pryoress, 55, 179
Psidium, 214, 248-9

Quashed, 226
Queen Adelaide, 105
Queen Bee, 105
Queen Bertha, 114
Queen Bess, 56
Queenpot, 246

R. B. Chesne, 288
Raconteur, 174
Radical, 176
Raeburn, 170
Raffaello, 169
Ragotsky, 185
Rake, The, 58, 86, 88, 101-2
Rama, 101
Rasping, 254
Rathbeal, 110
Ratan, 44, 78
Ravensbury, 107, 185
Ravensdale, 185
Record Run, 276
Red Robe, 223
Re-Echo, 226
Refractor, 155
Regal, 104
Regalia, 92
Reginald, 47
Remainder Man, 65
Reminder, 209
Resilience II, 258
Reugny, 103
Rêve D'Or, 61
Reveller, 33
Rhadamanthus, 23
Richmond Fair, 281
Riddlesworth, 47
Ridgewood, 246
Rifle, 93
Right Boy, 63
Right Tack, 59, 262
Ringlet, 106
Riot Act, 231
Rising Glass, 176
River Peace, 264
Riversdale, 151
Roberto, 21, 76, 273, 282
Robert the Devil, 66, 186

Rockefella, 260
Rocket (1778), 24
Rocket (1859), 56
Rock Sand, 63, 156, 177, 219, 292
Rosalba, 25
Rosebery, 53
Rose Bowl, 64
Rose Dubarry, 261, 282
Rose of England, 225
Rotherhill, 105
Roussalka, 272
Rover, The, 105, 109
Royal Flush, 183
Royal George, 103
Royal Heroine, 291
Royal Hive, 288
Royal Lancer, 211
Royal Match, 281
Royal Minstrel, 225
Royal Palace, 49, 247, 288, 294
Royal Smoke, 265
Rugosa, 260
Runnymede, 62
Rush, The, 155
Ruskie, 124
Rustam, 250

Sacrilege, 21
Safety Pin, 198
Sagaro, 294
Sagitta, 49
Sailcloth, 288
Sailor, 39, 43, 73, 137
Sainfoin, 156
St Amant, 203
St Angela, 117
St Blaise, 102, 116, 141
Saint-Cloud, 181
St Frusquin, 59, 61, 63, 98, 198-9, 203, 215
St Gatien, 53, 56, 105, 108-9, 141, 170, 188, 255
St Louis, 216
St Maclou, 176
St Medard, 105
St Mirin, 136-8, 151
St Paddy, 214, 247, 272
St Pauli Girl, 251-2
St Simon, 14, 35, 116-20, 174, 200
Sallust, 280
Salmon Trout, 236
Salvanos, 134
Salvator, 88
Salvo, 248-9
Sam, 39, 43, 73
Sandal, 286
Sandboy, 216
Sandford Lad, 276
Sansovino (1901), 212
Sansovino (1921), 221, 232-3
Santa Claus, 150
Santoi, 171
Saraband, 168, 213
Satire, 215
Saucebox, 167
Sayajirao, 231
Sceptre, 50-1, 62, 66, 176, 200
Scintillant, 185
Scipio, 253
Scud, 39
Scullion, 146
Scuttle, 60, 225
Seclusion, 101
Sefton, 56, 158-9
Selene, 60
Senseless, 209
Sergeant, 70
Sergeant Murphy, 219
Setting Star, 249
Shaef, 264
Shalfleet, 226
Shangamuzzo, 287
Shantallah, 279
Shareef Dancer, 66
Sharpen Up, 282, 292

Sharp Venetia, 281
Sheen, 94, 187
Sherburn, 146
Shergar, 277, 287, 292
Shilelagh, 41, 42
Shirley Heights, 65, 267
Shoemaker, 280
Shotover, 162
Shot Silk, 250
Showdown, 268
Sibola, 181
Signorina, 217
Signorinetta, 217-9, 277
Signorino, 217
Silver Hawk, 273
Silvio, 116, 156
Singapore, 225
Singing Sailor, 282
Sing Sing, 251
Sin Timon, 278
Sir Bevys, 98
Sir Cosmo, 190, 225
Sir Ivor, 49
Sir Joseph, 104
Sir Lark, 286
Sir Michael, 291
Sir Peter Teazle, 26, 70
Sir Thomas, 29
Sir Visto, 120, 150, 208
Sister to Pharamond, 85
Six Mile Bottom, 279
Skylark, 30, 53
Skyscraper, 68, 85, 189
Sleeping Partner, 271, 286
Slieve Gallion, 108
Slim, 25,
Sloop, 255
Small Slam, 261
Smoker, 17
Smokey Eyes, 258
Smolensko, 32, 73
Snap, 36
Snaplock, 167
Snow Knight, 259, 283
Snow Marten, 216, 223
Solario, 63, 227
Solinus, 62
Son-in-Law, 227
Son of Shaka, 65
Sorbus, 287
Sovereign, 279
Sovereign Bill, 279
Sovrango, 248
Spaniard, 33
Spaniard's Mount, 268
Sparkler, 277
Sparkling Boy, 276
Spearmint, 215-6
Speedwell, 15, 178, 266
Spiletta, 21
Spinaway, 116-7
Spindle, 61
Spindrifter, 276
Spion Kop, 62, 168, 216
Spot, 12
Sprig, 226
Springfield, 63, 66, 156
Springy Jack, 77
Squirrel, 25
Stafaralla, 60
Standaan, 278
Star Appeal, 294
Starke, 179
Steady Aim, 232, 240
Stealaway, 209
Sterling, 105
Stiff Dick, 12
Stilvi, 178, 280
Stockbridge, 232
Stockwell, 44, 48, 56, 72
Storm Bird, 61
Stray Shot, 152
Strigida, 291
Suburban, 100
Succour, 210

Sugar Bowl, 231
Sugar Cane, 200
Sultan Mahomed, 61
Summer Day, 261
Sunbeam, 114
Sun Chariot, 211, 293
Sundridge, 63
Sun Stream, 232
Superior Sam, 280
Super Sam, 254
Surplice, 41, 55-6, 77
Surprise, 27
Survivor, 92
Suspender, 107, 174
Suvretta, 262
Swallow Tail, 282
Sweetheart, 61
Sweet Solera, 249
Swelter, 279
Swiss Maid, 276
Swynford, 63, 104, 221

Tachypous, 178, 280
Tag, 68
Tagalie, 207
Taj Akbar, 239
Taj Kasra, 238
Take a Reef, 280
Take Your Place, 272
Talgo, 248
Tambara, 240
Tap on Wood, 288
Tartar Prince, 261, 282
Teetotum, 70
Tehran, 60, 240
Teresina, 286, 239
Test Case, 256
Tetrarch, The, 177, 236
Tetratema, 63
Thebais, 135, 158
Theft, 238-9
Thormanby, 114
Three Legs, 277
Thuringian Prince, 88, 213
Tideway, 226
Tiffin, 60
Timmatemma, 282
Timothy, 174
Tina's Pet, 291
Tinsley Green, 283
Tiresias, 34, 72
To-Agori-Mou, 49, 64, 267
Toboggan, 61, 221, 235
Tolmi, 280
Tom Cribb, 281
Tommy Atkins, 206
Tommy Tittlemouse, 137
Tontine, 49
Torpid, 255
Totowah, 278
Touching Wood, 66, 280
Touchstone, 72
Tower Walk, 262
Tracery, 204
Tranby, 40
Trappist, 104
Traveller, 11
Tremola, 215
Trimdon, 57
Tristan, 94, 118, 149
Tromos, 280
Troy, 250
Trumpator, 36
Try My Best, 61
Tudor Minstrel, 49
Tudor Music, 264
Tulyar, 174, 242-3, 262
Turbine, 223
Turcoman, 47
Turk, 12
Turkham, 240
Tyrant, 36
Tyrnavos, 178, 280

Ubedizzy, 66

Udiapur, 238
Ugly Buck, The, 71
Umiddad, 61, 240
Union Jack, 171
Utrillo, 265

Vaguely Deb, 277
Vaguely Noble, 21,72, 250
Vaigly Great, 65, 287
Valet, 171, 190
Valognes, 242
Valoris, 247
Valour, 126
Van Diemansland, 169
Variation, 74
Varinia, 247
Vedette, 60, 152
Velasquez, 190, 275
Verdict, 225-6
Vergia, 213
Verneuil, 94
Verney, 216
Vicissitude, 77
Vielle, 281
Violetta III, 248
Virago, 49
Virginia Boy, 271
Visp, 254
Vitiges, 261
Volodyovski, 183
Volunteer, 82
Vulcan, 79

Wallenstein, 188
Waterchute, 215
Waterloo, 60
Watling Street, 232
Waxy, 37, 72
Welsh Pageant, 65, 283
West Australian, 48, 73, 78
West Side Story, 260
Whalebone, 36, 72
Wheatear, 115
Wheel of Fortune, 60, 93, 116
Whipper-in, 17
Whisker, 36-7, 73
Whiskey, 32
Whisperer, 174
Whistling Fool, 271
Wichuraiana, 272
Widow, The, 52
Wild Dayrell, 188, 221
Wildfowler, 146, 168
Willonyx, 57
Wilwyn, 251, 254
Wind and Wuthering 65
Windham, 14
Wind of Change, 288
Windsor, 125
Windsor Boy, 290
Windsor Lad, 242
Wings, 39
Winterhalter, 240
Witch of the Air, 220
Wizard, 47-9
Wizard, The, 48-9, 71
Wollow, 49, 61, 272, 283, 288
Wolver Hollow, 246, 253, 271-2
Woodcock, 11
Woodpecker, 61
Woolsthorpe, 187
Wychwood Abbott, 227

Xerxes, 250

Yellow God, 264
Yentoi, 57
Young Giantess, 32
Your Highness, 251
Your Majesty, 200, 223
Yutoi, 227

Zabara, 60
Zaleucus, 177
Zarathustra, 244
Zinfandel, 177, 210